I0879224

Seeing Stars

Sports Celebrity, Identity, and Body Culture in Modern Japan

Harvard East Asian Monographs 331

Seeing Stars

Sports Celebrity, Identity, and Body Culture in Modern Japan

Dennis J. Frost

Published by the Harvard University Asia Center
and distributed by Harvard University Press
Cambridge (Massachusetts) and London, 2010

© 2010 by The President and Fellows of Harvard College

Printed in the United States of America

The Harvard University Asia Center publishes a monograph series and, in coordination with the Fairbank Center for Chinese Studies, the Korea Institute, the Reischauer Institute of Japanese Studies, and other faculties and institutes, administers research projects designed to further scholarly understanding of China, Japan, Vietnam, Korea, and other Asian countries. The Center also sponsors projects addressing multidisciplinary and regional issues in Asia.

Library of Congress Cataloging-in-Publication Data

Frost, Dennis J.

Seeing stars : sports celebrity, identity, and body culture in modern Japan / Dennis J. Frost.

p. cm. -- (Harvard East Asian monographs ; v. 331)

Includes bibliographical references and index.

ISBN 978-0-674-05610-7 (hardcover : alk. paper)

1. Athletes--Japan--Public opinion. 2. Celebrities--Japan--Public opinion. 3. Sports in popular culture--Japan. 4. Athletes in mass media. 5. Human body--Social aspects--Japan. 6. National characteristics, Japanese. 7. Public opinion--Japan. 8. Japan--Social life and customs. I. Title.

GV655.F76 2010

796.0952--dc22

2010045149

Index by Kelly M. Frost

♾ Printed on acid-free paper

Last figure below indicates year of this printing

20 19 18 17 16 15 14 13 12 11 10

To my sister, Alisha

Acknowledgments

Throughout this project so many people have provided their advice, assistance, and encouragement that I cannot possibly mention all of them here. To those I have omitted, I apologize and wish to offer an all-too-inadequate thank you. I must also express my appreciation for the generous financial support that allowed me to pursue this project, including Columbia University Fellowships, Weatherhead Fellows Training Grants, a Fulbright-Hays DDRA Fellowship, and a Wittenberg University Freeman East Asian Studies Teaching Fellowship.

In Japan, many have assisted me at various stages of my research; several merit particular mention here, including Hosaka Hiroshi of the University of the Ryukyus and both Arima Tetsuo and Thomas Cogan at Waseda University. Kobayashi Norio introduced me to the former world-champion boxer, Gushiken Yōkō, and I am especially grateful to Gushiken himself for taking the time to meet with me for an interview.

In the United States, Gregory Pflugfelder encouraged me to develop my project in challenging and ultimately rewarding ways and offered numerous suggestions on earlier drafts. Carol Gluck and Henry Smith have also contributed to my work in more ways than I can mention. The advice and suggestions of Andrew Gordon, William Kelly, Eugenia Lean, Tomi Suzuki, and an anonymous reviewer have also helped me strengthen this book. I am deeply indebted to Valerie Barske, who took time away from her own work to offer comprehensive feedback on the entire draft, and to James Huffman, who first inspired my interest in Japanese history and has continued to encourage and support me. Though Jim had no obligation to do so, he read every chapter, providing detailed suggestions on each. I am also grateful to the participants of the Midwest Japan Seminar, as well as Samuel Yamashita and Yoshikuni Igarashi, for their constructive feedback on an early draft of the wartime baseball chapter. My work is undoubtedly better for having known and worked with Tobias Barske, Steven Bryan, Paul Droubie, Joy Kim, Ian Miller, Thomas Mullaney, David Obermiller, Lee Pennington, Satoru Saito, Tomoko Sakomura, Mathew Thompson, and many outstanding colleagues at Kalamazoo College, Wittenberg University, and Xavier University. All of them have offered their support and insightful suggestions at various points, but they have also genuinely enriched my life through their friendship. Anne Davies, Doug Hanson, and Nan Moore at Xavier University provided invaluable assistance with the book's images, and I have also benefited immensely from the advice and guidance provided by my editor, William Hammell.

Above all, I would like to thank the librarians in Japan and the United States who helped make this project possible. In particular, Sachie Noguchi at Columbia's Starr East Asian Library, Higuchi Keiko from the International House of Japan, Kusano Eri of the Japan Sumo Association, both Yamane Reiko and Ogawa Akiko from the Baseball Hall of Fame Museum in Tokyo, and Sato Sumiko of the Japan Amateur Athletic Association, all went out of their way to help me find materials related to my research.

Finally, I wish to thank my favorite librarian, my wife Kelly, without whose support, patience, and regular assistance in the form of editing, organizing, and listening, I never could have completed this book. Kelly and my sons Dominick and Xander have helped me remember that there is more to life than writing and research, and I cannot express how much I have appreciated their unwavering love and support throughout this long process.

Contents

List of Figures

Author's Note

Throughout the book, personal names for all Japanese individuals, including authors, are given in standard Japanese form with family name listed first, unless they were written otherwise in a quoted source. Long vowels in Japanese words or names have been marked with macrons, except in cases of well-known geographic names or words that have been adopted in English without the vowel marker. It is also worth noting that the usages of the words "sport" and "sports" in this work diverge from that of many other scholars. I employ the plural "sports" in almost all instances, including references to stars and sports in a generic or general sense. The singular "sport" appears here only when describing a particular sport, such as baseball or sumo wrestling.

Seeing Stars

Sports Celebrity, Identity, and Body Culture in Modern Japan

INTRODUCTION
Sports Celebrity in Japan: A Transnational History

The men of Japan are brought to tears in spite of themselves.
Naturally, the women cry, too.
—Emi Sui'in, "Mourning Dewanoumi"

At 2:10 in the afternoon on 19 June 1922, Japan lost a saint. The sudden death of the retired wrestler Hitachiyama Taniemon initiated what the writer Emi Sui'in and others described as a nationwide wave of grief. A skeptic might suspect hyperbole, especially since Emi's ode to Hitachiyama first appeared in a sumo specialty magazine. Certainly the loss of a national leader might evoke such a reaction—one need only consider the Japanese response to the death of Emperor Meiji ten years earlier—but a retired sumo wrestler?

There is, however, good reason to believe Emi's reference to a national outpouring of emotion on the loss of Hitachiyama. Compared with earlier wrestlers, Hitachiyama's death generated an unprecedented degree of press coverage, which would have made his passing difficult to miss.[1] Numerous articles comment specifically on the popular response, noting that several thousands waited to say a final farewell to Hitachiyama as his body was taken to Ueno train station and then to his hometown of Mito, in Ibaraki prefecture. Papers also reported that the monetary gifts of condolence within days of his death had already reached 18,000 yen.[2] A memorial service held in December attracted thousands of people, including representatives from throughout Japan and a number of Japan's military and political elite.

It was not just Hitachiyama's death that attracted attention. Fifteen years earlier, in 1907, an editorial in the *Yomiuri shinbun* began by noting that Hitachiyama was one of the most recognized individuals in Japan, his fame such that "from the nobles above to the servant boys below, there are none who do not know his name." The editorial also pointed out that Hitachiyama's name had become virtually synonymous with sumo.[3] Hitachiyama figured prominently in various Japanese "Who's Who" books of his day, including several that listed him along with both national and international nobility, military leaders, and intellectuals.[4] Courted as a potential candidate for the National Diet because of his fame at home, he was also known abroad, having toured internationally and met such foreign dignitaries as President Theodore Roosevelt.

Often called the "saint of sumo," Hitachiyama has regularly been credited with having "saved" sumo through his popularity and his influence on the sport after retirement.[5] Hitachiyama was more than just a sumo wrestler, more even than the sumo grand champion that his rank of *yokozuna* denoted. He was a national celebrity, and more importantly from the perspective of this book, he was one of Japan's first modern sports stars, whose passing seized the attention and emotions of Japanese society.[6]

Given his standing as a sports star, the media and popular attention Hitachiyama received are hardly surprising. In the sports-saturated world of the twenty-first century, details about the personal lives, training regimens, and bodily measurements of sports stars appear in the mass media with such regularity that information of this sort is largely taken for granted. It is not hard to imagine that almost anyone could locate a number of specific details about a particular athlete, including age, height, weight, hometown, or marital status. Even without the advantages of an internet search engine, these and other kinds of information are easily accessible in any number of articles and television reports, on the back of collectors' cards, on team rosters, or in pregame introductions at sporting events. A dedicated sports fan might be able to provide these kinds of details from memory. Indeed, the sparing use of adjectives like "media-shy" and "private" to describe celebrities of all sorts suggests that the *absence* of detailed information about stars is more striking than its presence. Yet why do we know so much about these people?

This book challenges the assumed naturalness of knowledge about sports stars by exploring how and why it became acceptable, and almost expected, to have access to intimate details about athletes. Tracing the emergence and evolution of sports celebrity in Japan from the seventeenth through the twenty-first centuries, this study reveals that sports stars are socially constructed phenomena, the products of both particular historical moments and broader, cumulative discourses of celebrity that became transnational in reach. At the same time, this work argues that the largely unquestioned mass of information about sports stars not only reflects, but also shapes society and body culture. By examining how various constituencies, including stars themselves, have molded and deployed the celebrity images of individual athletes, this book exposes the ways in which representations of sports stars mediated Japan's emergence into the putatively universal realm of sports, unsettled orthodox notions of gender, facilitated the wartime mobilization of physically fit men and women, and later, masked lingering inequalities in postwar Japanese society. Despite the prominent role that sports stars have played in Japanese history, most narratives of Japan's past have, intentionally or not, written them out. This book writes them back in.

As the first critical examination of the history of sports celebrity outside a Euro-American context, this work also sheds new light on the transnational forces at play in the social construction and impact of celebrity images. A general lack of attention to historical specificity has fostered powerful misconceptions that sports stars in the non-West are mere imitations of some Western "source." In fact, standard narratives of the history of sports celebrity are based on some grossly oversimplifying and lamentably ethnocentric assumptions. Two stand out in particular: that the emergence of modern sports stars began when William Randolph Hearst created the first newspaper sports section in the *New York Journal* in 1895, and that Hearst's innovation was then imitated in other countries.[7] This book challenges these kinds of assumptions by examining how domestic traditions, practices, and concerns in Japan actively engaged with incoming international trends and ideas to produce forms of sports celebrity that simultaneously influenced sports stardom in the West, which was itself far from coherent when it first arrived in Japan.[8]

Origins: Continuities, Changes, and Cultural Imperialism

As Hitachiyama's fame suggests, sports stars in Japan have been subject to intense public scrutiny since at least the late 1800s, when sumo wrestlers were recruited to represent Japan's newly reinvented "national" sport at home and abroad. Of course, celebrities, including the many sumo wrestlers whose portraits survive in Tokugawa-era (1600–1868) woodblock prints, had been around long before this. Any discussion of sports stardom in Japan must necessarily address the ways in which these earlier examples of sumo celebrity shaped later manifestations, an issue explored in Chapter 1 of this study. It is worth noting in particular that in contrast to stardom in Europe and the United States, Japan's sports culture was centered on individual stars almost from the beginning, a fact that not only belies common stereotypes about Japanese society, but also helps account for the rapid emergence of individual sports stars in team sports such as baseball.[9] Examining such continuities in representations of sumo stars helps to check the all-too-easy assumption that sports stars are simply by-products of Japan's efforts to "Westernize." It also brings the distinctive features of what I describe as "modern" sports celebrity into perspective, for even in the case of sumo stars, a number of factors combined, beginning in the latter half of the nineteenth century, to produce something very different from earlier forms of celebrity.[10]

Among the most crucial developments of this period was the emergence of new kinds of media networks, both in Japan and around the world. From at least the 1890s, sumo coverage was a staple in many Japanese newspapers. By the turn of the century, newspapers and nascent specialty magazines frequently published "day in the life" reports about such sumo stars as Hitachiyama. The new media networks meant that increasing numbers of Japanese could follow the daily exploits of their favorite star—whether that star visited a geisha or a doctor. The advent of new media forms such as magazines, film, radio, television, and now the internet have provided ever more ways for people to learn about sports stars, and have also altered the nature of stardom itself.

Another factor shaping modern forms of sports celebrity in Japan from the late nineteenth century onward was the introduction and diffusion of new, primarily Euro-American, ideas about sports and physical culture. This process led not only to the emergence of Western sports in Japan, but also to the "sportification" of such native forms of physical culture as sumo and the martial arts. The institutionalization of sports organizations and the creation of numerous sports competitions at the local, national, and international levels provided Japanese athletes with multiple forums at home and abroad where they could be seen and demonstrate their abilities. But Japanese athletes were not the only ones being seen.

Beginning in the early 1900s, images and descriptions of Western sports figures appeared with increasing regularity in Japanese media sources, offering an important reminder that the average Japanese reader of a sports page has long been aware of a world outside the archipelago. In light of this simple fact, the histories of sports and modern sports celebrity in Japan cannot be viewed solely in a nationally bounded vacuum; they *must* be addressed as multi-dimensional, transnational phenomena. While domestic traditions and practices played a critical role in the emergence and evolution of sports stardom, these same factors—and increasingly, sports stars themselves—constantly interacted with and were shaped by broader forces, particularly those associated with imperialism.

The early presence of Western stars in the Japanese media points to the need to conceptualize sports and sports stars as products of a highly conspicuous (if often ignored) form of cultural imperialism. The willingness on the part of Japanese society to embrace Western sports should not blind us to the power relations that lie behind them. Western sports were introduced to Japan, and much of the world, as a defining and necessary feature of "civilized" societies. According to the hegemonic imperialist logic of the late nineteenth century, especially in the United States, a lack of sports was a sign of backwardness and underdevelopment in both body and mind.[11] Indigenous forms of physical culture were by and large classified as unscientific, undisciplined, inferior, or simply "barbaric," thus justifying their exclusion from the allegedly universal category of sports. One American writer, for instance, described sumo in 1898 as an "unscienced [*sic*] tug between two big overfed creatures who would rather be sitting over a pipe and cup of saké. They would make but a short stand against a disciple of the catch-as-catch-can or Græco-Roman style of Anglo-Saxon wrestling."[12]

Given remarks such as these, "teaching" sports to the Japanese was as much about Westerners confirming their own superiority as it was about sharing a "love of the game." The Japanese acceptance of, and eventual success in, sports provided further proof, ex post facto, of claims to universality. From a Euro-American perspective, Japanese interest in sports proved that the West had been right about sports all along. But Japanese successes in sports also revealed the tensions inherent in what was, at its very core, a co-constitutional process.[13]

By co-constitution, I refer specifically to the fact that both Japanese and non-Japanese looked to one another to define themselves, a process of mutual self-definition through opposition. In other words, the transnational interactions at the heart of modern sports have helped reinforce and even create distinct national and regional identities on all sides. That is not to say that co-constitutional processes are symmetrical or equal. As the following chapters demonstrate, Westerners have looked to Japanese sports and sports stars to define themselves, but not nearly to the same extent that Japan has looked to the West. Moreover, transnational sporting exchanges have often been premised on mutual assumptions of Euro-American superiority. The co-constitutional nature of such exchanges becomes especially apparent when these assumptions are challenged, as perhaps best exemplified by Japanese and Western media commentaries about a so-called "yellow peril in sports" linked to Japan's international sporting gains in the years before World War II. The peril only emerged when the "student" threatened to outperform the "teacher." Understandably, the co-constitution evident in the introduction and diffusion of sports in Japan also figures centrally in the social production of sports stars.

Frameworks

In order to understand how these transnational and co-constitutional processes have operated in a Japanese context, this study draws from a wide variety of source materials—media coverage, biographical accounts, bureaucratic memoranda, literary works, athletes' memoirs, interviews, and films—to examine sports celebrities from multiple perspectives. In doing so, it employs insights from an equally diverse range of disciplinary and theoretical approaches, including history, anthropology, sociology, sports studies, and media studies, as well as gender, film, and literary theory. Among this deliberately eclectic mix of analytical tools, four concepts and frameworks that inform the following chapters merit particular attention here, beginning with the central role of image and representation for sports stars.

SPORTS-CELEBRITY IMAGES

Because of the seemingly quantified and achievement-based nature of sports celebrity, athletes are sometimes portrayed as more "real" or "authentic" than other types of celebrities.[14] Closer examination, however, reveals that the celebrity status of sports stars is produced and consumed in the form of various representations, or what film scholar Richard Dyer calls "star images."[15] Treating sports stars as products of socially constructed celebrity images does not make them or their accomplishments any less "real" or significant, but rather opens up the potential for "mining the cultural significance of a star by examining the network of ideological discourses from which they emerge."[16]

As subsequent chapters demonstrate, the celebrity images of sports stars are not only real, but also quite powerful and useful, even long after the sports celebrity has died. Such power and usefulness stem in large part from the malleability of star images, which allows people to extract and mobilize the "meanings and feelings, the variations, inflections and contradictions, that work for them."[17] Sports stars themselves often willingly employ their own fame to represent diverse, and at times conflicting, causes. Consequently, both the production and consumption of these sports-celebrity images vary depending on the particular socio-historical contexts. As Daisuke Miyao has pointed out in his study of transnational film star Sessue Hayakawa, geographical space also shapes celebrity images, since a star's image can take on dramatically different meanings depending on the location where it is being produced or consumed.[18]

Moreover, like the movie stars Dyer and Miyao have examined, the images of sports celebrities "are extensive, multimedia, intertextual."[19] Far from a lack of source materials, for most sports stars the issue at hand is an overabundance of sometimes minutely detailed information about seemingly every aspect of their lives. While commentary about athletic performances is central for sports stars, media coverage of various sorts, biographies, illustrations, photographs, fictional works, advertisements, and even what Dyer describes as the "way the star can become part of the coinage of everyday speech," all serve as critical elements of a sports star's image.[20] The result is an inescapable web of representation where some strands (athletic achievements, for instance) may be particularly significant, but are necessarily interwoven with others.

The emerging images of sports stars blend the visual and the written, integrate fact and fiction, and are themselves composites of earlier images. A staged photo became emblematic of Hitachiyama's career-long rivalry with another wrestler. A children's story turned details from Hitachiyama's autopsy into a science and health lesson. Biographies selectively combined all these "facts" to tell why Hitachiyama was the saint of sumo. The point in this study is not so much to determine the accuracy or reality of these images, but rather to dissect them, exploring both the factors involved in their production and their societal influence.

SPORTS-STAR SYSTEMS

If sports-celebrity images share much in common with those of other stars, they are also unique. Although comparisons of actors, singers, and other celebrities are common and certainly contribute to celebrity images, from the very moment of their emergence, sports stars are *necessarily* defined through differentiation with other sports stars, becoming instantly embedded in what I call "star systems." Previous scholars have used this phrase to describe the socio-economic and institutional factors that produce celebrities, especially in the movie and music industries; however, I employ the concept of star systems as a kind of shorthand for describing the process by which sports stars are constructed in relation to, and frequently in opposition to, other stars.[21]

This approach highlights the critical—though often overlooked—role that such comparisons and differentiations play in defining how images of sports celebrities are produced and how these images are understood in a society. In many ways, this differentiation is built into sports in the form of direct competition between athletes. Even team sports are often cast as contests between individual players (pitcher versus hitter, goalkeeper versus kicker, Shaquille O'Neal versus Yao Ming, and so forth). The obsession with records, a defining feature of modern sports, also acts as a kind of star system in which any record-breaking athlete is instantly placed into a comparative framework with all record holders before and after. It is important to note, however, that any given sports celebrity operates simultaneously in multiple systems of differentiation, and that the particular stars being compared or the evaluations of the comparisons depend on the situation and context. It is not hard to imagine that an individual sports star might simultaneously be compared to a contemporary rival, a "great" from an earlier time, a competitor from another country, or a player in a completely different sport. American baseball star Barry Bonds offers a case in point. His highly publicized quest to break the Major League record for career homeruns linked him to Babe Ruth, Hank Aaron, and the still-reigning world-record holder, Oh Sadaharu, a Japanese baseball star. At the same time, Bonds' alleged involvement in a doping scandal linked him to such recent baseball players as Roger Clemens, Mark McGwire, and Alex Rodriguez, as well as several athletes in track and field. In this sense, star systems can transcend time, space, or sport—or even real life.

For example, Gushiken Yōkō, the boxing world champion examined in Chapter 5, was frequently described as "Japan's Rocky" (*Nihon no Rokkī*). This designation referred, of course, to the fictitious boxer portrayed by Sylvester Stallone in a movie that originally appeared around the time that Gushiken became champion. The Japanese weekly magazine *Purēbōi* (Playboy) linked this reference to Gushiken's impoverished childhood, which, the magazine claimed, helped produce the strong punches of "Japan's Rocky."[22] Gushiken himself dismissively pointed out that no *real* boxer would coddle a pet turtle or call out his lover's name at a title match, because if he did, he would obviously lose.[23] Here, the same comparison from different perspectives results in different evaluations, but all of them contribute to the celebrity image of "Gushiken Yōkō." In another case, a biography comparing Gushiken with Japanese baseball great Oh Sadaharu adds another facet to Gushiken's celebrity image, suggesting that Gushiken possessed the same dedication to craft and work ethic that were so often credited for Oh's success.[24] This comparison serves at the same time as an affirmation of Oh's impressiveness, since the baseball player was represented as a great not only within his own sport of baseball, but in the sports world in general.

The particular value of thinking about sports stars within the context of star systems lies in two points. First, star systems highlight the co-constitutional nature of sports celebrity. As in the case of Gushiken and Oh, the respective images of the stars being compared are shaped, in part, through an exchange of what Pierre Bourdieu has called "symbolic capital . . . the acquisition of a reputation for competence and an image of respectability and honourability."[25] Such exchanges need not be positive, nor are they necessarily equal; in most cases the lesser-known figure has more to gain or lose from the comparison. Moreover, even in those cases where the comparisons are specifically based on shared characteristics, they produce an excess of meanings beyond those intended. Readers more familiar with Rocky, for instance, bring to the comparison a particular understanding of what that figure represents: boxer, manliness, hard work, the American Dream, lower-class background, Italian-American ethnicity, to name a few possibilities. These preconceived ideas, in turn, create a parallel (or in a negative contrast, an antithetical) image of Gushiken, whether or not the issues associated with Rocky are actually relevant to Gushiken as a celebrity. The point here is not to question the validity of particular comparisons, but to see these "loaded" comparisons as central in the creation of sports stars. I want to consider how such polysemic star systems reflect and shape the concerns of the societies producing them.

This raises a second point: star systems also draw attention to the construction of sports stars as a situational phenomenon, emphasizing the importance of the particular contexts, social forces, and agendas involved in the production and consumption of sports-celebrity images. Female track star Hitomi Kinue (discussed in Chapter 3), was frequently represented as a national hero and even featured in school textbooks.

Yet she was also an object of profound gender anxieties in society at large. In the context of international competition and world records, Hitomi's Japanese-ness served as the defining aspect of her identity, but when viewed in comparison with male and other female athletes at home, it was Hitomi's femininity—or more accurately, concerns about her lack thereof—that proved most salient. By exposing these kinds of seeming inconsistencies in how sports stars are portrayed or portray themselves, star systems also point to the need to see identities, whether national, racial, gender, ethnic, or class, as themselves situationally defined. This fact is all the more significant given that sports stars are frequently called upon to represent identities of all sorts, often simultaneously. The popular appeal of sports stars stems, in part, from their larger-than-life embodiment of the performative and situational nature of identity, issues that people face daily in their own lives, whether consciously or not.[26]

SPORTS-STAR PARADIGM

In addition to star systems, another key element shaping sports-celebrity images is what I describe as a "sports-star paradigm," a pattern or model shaping how sports stars have been conceptualized, depicted, and interpreted. As argued in Chapter 2, this paradigm began to take shape in Japan in the early 1900s, arising with particular vividness and lasting effect in the narratives surrounding sumo star Hitachiyama, who was cast in the role of an athletic self-made man. Because Hitachiyama was one of Japan's first modern sports stars, the narrative patterns and rhetorical techniques used in crafting his image have had a profound impact on how later athletic celebrities have been portrayed and understood. Just as in Hitachiyama's case, later images of sports stars would rely on depictions of their exceptional skills, bodies, and character to explain their rise to sports stardom. At the same time, these exceptional features were conventionally downplayed to give simultaneous prominence, or even precedence, to the "self-made" nature of their stardom, achieved through hard work and dedication. Devotion—to sports, to nation, and perhaps especially to families—also appears as a central component of the sports-star paradigm from Hitachiyama's time up to the present. Popular imaginings of sports stars regularly portray sporting success as both consequence and proof of the stars' filial piety and their willingness and desire to serve the interests of the nation. Naturally, sports stars after Hitachiyama show considerable variety, stemming from the particulars of their situation, but they also retain, to a surprising degree, many of the central components of the paradigm already apparent in Hitachiyama's celebrity image.

The sports-star paradigm examined in this book shares several similarities with developments occurring outside Japan around the same time, especially in the United States. Charles Ponce de Leon's examination of the role of sports journalism in the construction of American sports celebrities reveals the prominence of what he describes as the "ideal of sport, a set of values that journalists in the early twentieth century crafted to insulate themselves from the ballyhoo that was central to the commercialization of sports."[27] At the center of this ideal was an appreciation of the exceptional skills and bodies of athletes, exemplified by increasing use of techniques and devices aimed at giving readers the "tale of the tape" about various stars, as well as details about their seemingly superhuman exploits. This American ideal of sport placed concomitant emphasis on the self-discipline, motivation, personal sacrifices, and hard work that allowed these stars to excel.[28]

In the face of parallels with developments occurring in the United States during a similar time frame, it is imperative to note that the emergence of a sports-star paradigm in Japan is *not* simply a case of mimicry. As Chapter 2 illustrates, the dominant patterns of representing sports celebrities that arose in connection with Hitachiyama were in no small part the product of domestic societal concerns, coupled with a number of preexisting representational practices and contemporary trends in biographical writing in Japan. That said, the similar methods simultaneously employed to depict sports stars in the United States almost certainly melded with, and reinforced, what was happening in Japan, especially because of transnational star systems, which eventually assumed a defining role in the production and consumption of sports-celebrity images in Japan and beyond.

BODY CULTURE

Aside from athletic achievements, details about bodies and bodily practices are among the most prominent elements of representations and comparisons of athletes. In other contexts, publication of such "personal" details might seem strange or even invasive. For sports stars, however, it is the norm. The examinations of sports stars in this study seek to draw attention to this generally taken-for-granted information, emphasizing the ways in which sports stars both reflect and shape body culture. The concept of body culture, as anthropologist Susan Brownell has observed, is a "broad term that includes daily practices of health, hygiene, fitness, beauty, dress, and decoration, as well as gestures, postures, manners, ways of speaking and eating, and so on. It also includes the way these practices are trained in the body, the way the body is publicly displayed, and the lifestyle that is expressed in that display."[29] In short, body culture serves as a useful umbrella concept for describing the various ways in which people portray, understand, use, and shape bodies in particular socio-historical contexts.

The impact of sports celebrities on body culture comes in both direct and indirect forms. Sports stars often exert direct influences by using their fame to promote a particular sport or sports in general. In many cases, their techniques and training are deployed as models for other athletes, seeking to replicate their success. But sports celebrities also shape body culture in more subtle ways. As the following chapters demonstrate, the abundance of widely publicized, seemingly objective facts about athletes' bodily measurements, habits, and experiences can have profound effects on popular perceptions and awareness of the human body and its expected role in society. In particular, the dominant images of sports stars tend to idealize them as models of the "strenuously disciplined and achieved healthy body."[30] Although such a model is certainly well suited to the needs of a Foucauldian modern state interested in promoting the health and self-discipline of its citizens, sports-celebrity images are open to alternate and far less ideal interpretations.[31] Sports stars are, after all, human and as subject to flaws and failures as any other person might be. They also exemplify what sociologist Henning Eichberg has described as the "historical obstinacy" of sports; as Eichberg points out, sporting bodies not only illustrate values of industrial culture, such as achievement, discipline, and measurement, but can also serve as vehicles for "expressions of obscenity, violence, and laughter, other worlds of sensuality."[32] By giving due consideration to the varying and often contradictory bodily descriptions of sports stars, this book highlights the central and at times contentious role that athletes have played in the ongoing negotiations of body politics in Japanese society.

Positioning

Despite the significance of sports stars in societies worldwide, they have received surprisingly little attention from scholars. Most of the existing scholarship on sports stars dates from the 1990s onward and has been conceptualized, almost exclusively, in terms of European and American contexts.[33] The majority of these works have also focused overwhelmingly on contemporary stars, giving little attention to historical changes or continuities.[34] The history of sports celebrity outside Europe and the United States has remained largely unexplored.[35] Given the current state of the field, a few comments about the particular emphases, limits, and outlines of this book seem especially merited.

This study focuses on the historical emergence and evolution of sports stardom in Japan, but it also insists that the broader history of sports celebrity cannot be fully understood unless the transnational, co-constitutional processes involved in the production of sports-celebrity images are taken into account. The chapters that follow concentrate on developments within Japan, while situating them in international contexts and giving particular attention to star systems that include non-Japanese stars. Although I have sought to explore a variety of comparative international examples, the vast majority of those used here come from Western, and especially American, contexts. This imbalance reflects both historical Euro-American hegemony in the realm of modern sports and the relative lack of secondary works addressing non-Western sports stars. Consequently, this work provides only the most general observations about the use of sports celebrity in efforts to differentiate Japan from its Asian neighbors. The place of sports and sports stars in Japan's own history of imperialism in Asia merits a serious examination in its own right, but in the end, limitations of space and resources, together with the overwhelming presence of European and American sports stars in Japanese source materials, led me to preclude such an examination in this book. Nevertheless, it is my belief and hope that future studies will not only explore these and other aspects of sports celebrity, but also find the concepts and ideas raised here useful in that process.

The emphasis on the transnational nature of sports celebrity in this work shares some similarities with recent scholarly examinations of sports and sports stars as both products and producers of globalization. It bears noting, however, that this project was never conceptualized solely, or even secondarily, in terms of globalization, and the focus on the *history* of sports celebrity distinguishes this work from much of that existing literature.[36] Indeed, my attention to historical continuities and changes in the Japanese case reveals that the conceptual basis of modern sports celebrity and often the individual celebrities themselves were global far earlier than most accounts of globalization suggest. This book also highlights the fact that much of what we see in sports celebrity today draws upon significantly older patterns and practices. That is not to say that sports stardom has not changed. The stars examined here clearly show that it has—perhaps especially in more recent times—but in order to distinguish the new from the old in today's global culture of sports celebrity, the history of that celebrity has to be taken seriously.

This examination of the history of sports celebrity specifically as it relates to Japan covers a period stretching roughly from the 1600s through the 1980s, with five main chapters arranged chronologically. Every chapter addresses a specific theme, and each centers on an individual sports star, whose life, career, and, especially, representations speak to the particular aspects of sports celebrity that the chapter thematically explores. Despite some overlaps, the stars examined here are associated with distinct time periods and come from different sports: sumo, track and field, baseball, and boxing. I focus on these stars precisely because of their fame; in their own times, all were—and in most cases, they still are—seen as representative and meaningful figures in both their particular sports and Japanese society more generally.

These sports stars and others like them are important elements of a much broader celebrity culture in Japan that would include individuals ranging from imperial household members and so-called idols to famous Western visitors and infamous Japanese criminals. Recent scholarship examining such non-sports celebrities suggests a number of significant parallels between sports stars and other celebrities, and in several instances the chapters here explore overlaps between athletes and other stars.[37] Nevertheless, many famous and influential celebrities are necessarily absent from these pages, and a detailed comparative study of the various manifestations of celebrity culture falls beyond the intended focus of this book. I will be pleased, however, if my examinations of sports stars and their largely overlooked history can help provide a more complete picture of Japan's diverse and fascinating celebrity culture.

Given this work's subject, the concentration on individual sports stars would appear to be far from unusual or distinctive. In other ways, it flies in the face of widely held assumptions about Japan's group-oriented culture and the broader historical connections between individualism and sports celebrity. As the book's chapters point out, individualism in sports is not as quintessentially Western as it has sometimes been portrayed.[38] Attention to historical source materials clearly shows that athletes in Japan were being singled out before Western sports were introduced and that individual stars, even in team sports, have long been, and continue to be, at the forefront of media and popular attention. To be sure, self-sacrifice—for the sake of nation, family, team, or otherwise—has served as a key element of these athletes' celebrity images, but to overemphasize that ideal as the sole defining feature of Japanese sports celebrity is both to deny the historical impact of individual stars and to miss an opportunity to draw international comparisons that go beyond simple stereotypes.

Outside Japan, and even within Japan among younger generations, the sports stars examined in the following chapters are relatively unknown, a circumstance that necessitates a certain degree of background information about them and their sports. That said, these chapters do not provide comprehensive histories of the sports in question, nor are they intended as biographies revealing the "true" stories about these athletes. Because of the nature of sports stardom, efforts to uncover the "true" stars behind the web of representations frequently prove frustrating, if not outright impossible. Even seemingly objective facts about stars—details about their bodies, statistics about their athletic achievements, or information about their family or class backgrounds—have been employed selectively to construct particular images of these stars, often in response to the needs of specific, and at times very different, agendas. The goal of this study, then, is not to document the "true" people behind the sports-celebrity images, but rather to examine how these images themselves have been constructed at different times and how they affect the production of future celebrity representations.

In my examinations of celebrity images, I have also sought to give particular attention to the ways in which varying representations both reflect and influence the concerns of those who produce and consume them. I must admit, however, that the production of these images receives greater attention here than their consumption, especially in relation to fans. In many instances, the chapters do address the influence and perceptions of various fans, and I would suggest that the historically widespread availability of personal details about sports stars described in this book offers new insights into the fanatical consumption and production of information associated with the "*otaku* culture" of Japan today.[39] However, a full treatment of the complex and source-rich history of various forms of sports fandom in Japan is left for another study. At the same time, it is important to keep in mind that the process of producing sports-celebrity images itself necessarily involves some form of consumption. Even the earliest representations of sports stars addressing their initial competitions and achievements are inherently intertextual. Any person writing about or otherwise depicting sports stars does so by referencing, explicitly or not, earlier images, ideas, or events. This book explores how and why different people at different times have put these various pieces together in the ways that they did.

I would be remiss, at this point, if I failed to acknowledge my own participation in this interlocking process of consuming and producing sports-celebrity images. My in-depth research of the stars discussed here clearly constitutes a form of consumption that differs from that of the average person, and I am also well aware that my examinations are molding the images of these sports stars in new ways that undoubtedly bear the influence of my own twofold agenda. By raising and exploring the relationships between various sports stars and several key issues and themes in the history of Japan, I have sought to demonstrate that sports and sports stars are worthy of far more scholarly inquiry than they have received to date. As the popular response to Hitachiyama's death suggests, sports stars have meant a great deal to many people in the past, and I would argue that it is time for academic interpretations of that past to recognize the sports stars who have been there all along. But I would also suggest that reintroducing sports stars into historical narratives is not enough; we need to *see* sports stars, both past and present, in new ways, for they are far more complex and meaningful than they often appear. I speak, to some extent, from personal experience. I originally came to this topic out of historical curiosity rather than a love of sports, but as I studied these stars and their images seeking to understand their role in Japanese society, I began to see something that I had largely overlooked: the richness, the appeal, and perhaps most importantly, the power of sports celebrity. In the end, my examination of the history of sports stars in Japan enriched my understandings of the past and simultaneously forced me to rethink my own assumptions about sports and sports stars. I hope this book will do the same for others.

Although the stars examined here constitute only a selective sampling of the many sports heroes who have arisen in Japan, the insights they provide into the multifaceted nature of sports celebrity are relevant, and to a certain extent generalizable, to a much broader spectrum of athletes. Sports-celebrity images are always open to multiple meanings and interpretations, but I have consciously limited the thematic focus of each chapter to allow for greater clarity and attention to detail. For the most part, my selections of central themes were determined by the dominant issues emerging from the sources about each star, but each of these athletes could have been examined in relation to several other issues, which would have produced different, yet no less insightful, observations about sports celebrity. These chapters, then, are perhaps best viewed as historical case studies; taken as a whole, they explain the emergence, operation, and influence of sports stars throughout much of Japan's modern history.

Chapter 1 focuses on the key factors shaping the emergence of modern sports celebrity in Japan during the late nineteenth and early twentieth centuries. It begins, however, by looking back to the 1600s, the period when sumo emerged as a popular spectator sport. After highlighting important continuities with earlier aspects of celebrity, the chapter explores the impact of several changes, including new media forms, transnational star systems, and different understandings of sports and body culture. This liminal period in the history of sports celebrity in Japan is exemplified by the sumo star Hitachiyama, who benefited and capitalized on several of these developments, becoming known as the "saint" who, quite literally, re-presented sumo as Japan's national sport both at home and abroad.

The second chapter concentrates on the central role of representations and narratives in the production and consumption of sports stars. Returning to Hitachiyama, it explains why he, in particular, stood out among his fellow wrestlers to emerge as one of Japan's first modern sports stars. The chapter also interrogates the socio-historical factors that helped mold the story that came to define Hitachiyama's life—a heroic tale of a self-made man. It concludes by considering how Hitachiyama and his image makers established important precedents, putting in place a sports-star paradigm that shaped how later sports stars in Japan have been depicted and interpreted.

Chapter 3 centers on interwar female track star Hitomi Kinue, whose career highlights an often contentious relationship between gender and nationalism. Despite her successes in international competitions, including Japan's first Olympic medal in women's sports, the chapter considers how Hitomi's seemingly unfeminine appearance, her rejection of marriage, rumors about her sexual preferences, and her devotion to the promotion of women's sports in Japan, placed this highly conspicuous athlete at the very center of gender anxieties wracking Japanese society at the time. Examinations of Hitomi's complex sports-celebrity image provide insights into how she has continued to serve as both an idealized pioneer and an unsettling figure long after her death.

The fourth chapter focuses on baseball star Sawamura Eiji, whose celebrity image remains closely linked with such American celebrities as Babe Ruth, Lou Gehrig, and Cy Young. While the chapter discusses the origins of these relationships, it also moves the inquiry forward chronologically into the era of Japanese militarism, arguing that the relationship between baseball and Japan's wartime state was far less antagonistic than most accounts of the sport's history suggest. Drawing comparisons with laudatory wartime accounts of Sawamura's military service, the chapter investigates how Sawamura's story was recast in the postwar period as a tragic narrative of wartime loss, a retelling that obscured, or even willfully forgot, his—and by extension baseball's—complicity in the project of militarism.

The final chapter explores the role of sports celebrity in forging understandings of ethnic difference in Japanese society. It examines popular attention to the ethnic identity of world-champion boxer Gushiken Yōkō in the context of Okinawa's historically ambiguous status within Japan. Analyzing how Gushiken was used to "introduce" the culture and history of Okinawa, the chapter reveals that differences and tensions were often muted by the very circumstances of Gushiken's story. The image of Gushiken that emerged from this story sustained a form of what I call "spectacular difference" that coexisted with, and in ways reinforced, views of Japan as a homogeneous society.

As the subsequent examinations of these athletes demonstrate, paradigmatic models and transnational, co-constitutional star systems have shaped Japanese sports stars, and Japanese society, for more than a century. Analyzing the ways in which the complex images of these sports stars have been constructed and deployed reveals much about the times and people who produced and consumed them. But examining how and why sports stars have been represented and mobilized in the past also provides new insights on sports celebrity in the present. In the early decades of a new millennium, sports stars continue to play a central role both at home and abroad. As societies worldwide have become increasingly interconnected and as access to a previously unimaginable degree of information has become available with little more than a few keystrokes, the influence and reach of sports stars have been noticeably enhanced. Attention to the past renders the present-day global obsession with sports celebrities more understandable. At the same time, it provides us with tools for appreciating—and perhaps questioning—the too-often unacknowledged power of media practices that mold sports stars' stories in ways that make us believe that we "know them," and that, through them, we also know ourselves.

ONE

Saving Sumo: Re-Presenting the National Sport

From the nobles above to the servant boys below, there are none who do not know his name. Over the last decade, his name alone has come to represent the sport of sumo. . . . But the vitality of youth is truly short-lived. . . . The era of Hitachiyama is passing.

—*Yomiuri shinbun*, "A Hero's Fate"

On 7 June 1907, the leading, page-one editorial of the *Yomiuri shinbun* newspaper offered readers "life lessons" about fleeting fame and short-lived youth, especially among male wrestlers and female "beauties." Behind these semi-philosophical musings on the ephemeral nature of life was an issue of more immediate importance: the future of *yokozuna* Hitachiyama Taniemon's sumo career. The spur for the article appears to have been Hitachiyama's public announcement several days earlier that he intended to visit the United States and Europe.[1] While praising the planned trip as "befitting his heroic spirit," the editorial asserted that the trip would "demarcate the boundary between his life as a wrestler and his life as an ordinary person." Repeating its general observations about the inevitable decline of a wrestler's strength, skills, and physique over time, the *Yomiuri* reminded readers that such a transition for Hitachiyama was natural: "The era of Hitachiyama is passing."

Yet all was not lost, the editorial assured. Offering solace to fans, it predicted that Hitachiyama would be spared the fate of other famed wrestlers whose last days were spent as "furious beasts." Hitachiyama's personal dignity would not allow that to happen; his would be a hero's fate. What was more, his legacy would live on in the form of a rising new sumo star, Komagatake, Hitachiyama's "quasi-disciple, drilled for several years now by Hitachiyama himself."

As it turned out, Hitachiyama successfully completed what proved to be a historic trip abroad later in 1907, and his performances in the sumo ring after his return rarely matched those from before his trip. Nevertheless, the *Yomiuri*'s speculation about the end of Hitachiyama's life as a wrestler proved about seven years premature. Hitachiyama remained an active *yokozuna* until his retirement from wrestling in 1914, at which point he assumed a leading role as a sumo stable master, trainer, and organizer until his death in 1922. Hitachiyama, it seems, was not as eager to see the era of Hitachiyama pass as those at the *Yomiuri* surmised.

From the perspective of today's media, with its extensive coverage of sports stars, it might be easy to dismiss the *Yomiuri* editorial as simply another (ultimately incorrect) article speculating about the direction of an athlete's career. However, the circumstances of this editorial—on the front page of a substantial daily newspaper, in Japan, in 1907, seriously analyzing the possible retirement of an individual athlete—offers good reason to pause. Why would those at the *Yomiuri* and their readers be so interested in Hitachiyama? How did it become possible for a sumo wrestler, an athlete, to attract this degree of attention in Japanese society at this point in time?

The *Yomiuri* editorial itself offered several observations on the roots of Hitachiyama's fame. As the opening paragraphs made clear, Hitachiyama's plans in 1907 merited particular attention precisely because Hitachiyama was already known as "one of the greatest figures in our country." Hitachiyama's initial success and media attention had generated what Tyler Cowen calls "snowball effects," resulting in the kind of popular interest reflected in the editorial.[2] Yet, the snowball effect alone does not explain why and how Hitachiyama came to be deemed worthy of attention in the first place. Here, too, the editorial offers clues, highlighting three factors to explain Hitachiyama's fame and reputation: his achievements and skill as a wrestler, his excellent physique and strength, and his dignified character. These same three elements—skill, body, and character—appear repeatedly in a variety of evaluations of Hitachiyama's greatness. (Their centrality to Hitachiyama's celebrity image will be examined more fully in Chapter 2.)

There was another factor that shaped Hitachiyama's fame: what the *Yomiuri* editorial described as the "rich opportunities of the world he arrived in" and Hitachiyama's ability to "seize opportunities shrewdly, whether natural or man-made." Although the editorial failed to explain what such opportunities were, or how Hitachiyama took advantage of them, issues of timing and circumstance were key to his rise. Examining the socio-historical elements that combined to produce Hitachiyama as a celebrity allows us to see how and why he became one of Japan's earliest sports stars.

In a very real sense, Hitachiyama was in the right place at the right time, having arrived in the world of sumo at a pivotal juncture affecting not just the sport, but Japanese society as a whole. It is useful to imagine Hitachiyama's emergence as a sports celebrity as a point where three major historical threads intersect. The first and perhaps most obvious of these threads is sumo. The history of sumo and its early stars had a clear bearing on how Hitachiyama and his performances were evaluated. When Hitachiyama entered professional sumo in 1891, the sport was in a state of flux, still seeking to deal with the ramifications of the rapid political and social changes that swept Japan in the wake of the Meiji Restoration of 1868. Sumo was also struggling to come to terms with a second thread, the arrival and diffusion of Western approaches to sports and body culture. That such Western ideas and practices influenced sumo and Hitachiyama's image is clear, figuring prominently in his reputation for "saving" the sport. A final thread may be seen in the rise of mass media networks and the concomitant evolution of press coverage of sports and athletes. Here, too, Western influences were important, but earlier forms of attention to sumo stars also played a pivotal role in shaping journalistic coverage of stars like Hitachiyama. The end result of these intersecting threads, especially as they were interwoven with the particular celebrity aspects that Hitachiyama brought to sumo, was the production of something very different from what had previously existed, a form of celebrity that would continue to have an impact long after Hitachiyama's death. In this way, Hitachiyama represents a bridging figure connecting the long line of sumo stars before him with the multitude of sports stars appearing in Japan ever since.

Sumo: A Not-So-Ancient History

The particularities and continuities of Hitachiyama's fame become apparent when viewed in the context of sumo's history and the nature of sumo celebrities before him. Considering sumo's long-standing presence in Japanese society, it is not surprising and certainly more than mere happenstance that one of Japan's earliest sports celebrities should have emerged from this sport. Despite popular and even scholarly accounts to the contrary, sumo is not as timeless and ancient as it is sometimes made out to be. To be sure, in Japan, as in many places worldwide, wrestling in one form or another does have a long history. Descriptions of wrestling matches may be found in Japanese written accounts dating from the eighth century, and clay figures depicting what are believed to be wrestlers have been identified from even earlier periods.[3] Yet sumo—the popular, professional sport that Hitachiyama came to represent—owes much more to the seventeenth century than to the seventh. In large part, the rise of this particular form of wrestling is the result of fundamental socio-political changes that shaped Japan beginning in the late sixteenth century. After centuries of internal conflict, a series of three samurai warrior leaders were able to unify much of Japan under their sole control. The last of the three, Tokugawa Ieyasu, claimed the title of shogun in 1603 and upon his retirement succeeded in passing that title to his son, initiating the hereditary rule of the Tokugawa shogunate, which governed Japan until the Meiji Restoration.

A NEW ORDER

Several aspects of the social and political order that developed under Tokugawa Ieyasu and his descendants proved central to the emergence of sumo as a popular and professional sport. One of the most significant factors was the Tokugawa shogunate's overwhelming emphasis on the maintenance of order, a logical concern when considering the political instability and bloody violence preceding this period. In the end, various efforts to preserve order were largely effective, as suggested by nearly three centuries of relatively peaceful Tokugawa rule. To maintain discipline among the ruling samurai elite, the Tokugawa system relied on a series of alliances between the ruling Tokugawa and several hundred lesser hereditary lords, known as daimyo, who controlled domains of varying sizes throughout Japan. In exchange for recognition of Tokugawa authority and loyalty to the shogunate, these daimyo and their descendants were allowed a large degree of autonomy over their own domains as well as the samurai they retained as vassals. Tokugawa leaders also instituted a practice known as alternate attendance (*sankin kōtai*), which required the daimyo to spend alternate years in Edo, the castle town that served as the shogunate's base of power. In addition, family members of the daimyo were required to live in Edo even when the daimyo returned to their home domains, making the family and heirs virtual hostages. Alternate attendance required that the daimyo maintain elaborate residences in Edo as well as their home domains and necessitated time-consuming and expensive trips between the two.[4]

The institutionalization of alternate attendance had important consequences, many of which had a direct impact on sumo. With so many daimyo, their families, and their retainers living in Edo, the city grew rapidly and came to include large numbers of commoners—merchants, artisans, servants, and entertainers—who served both the warrior population and their fellow commoners. Reflecting the Tokugawa-era obsession with social order and especially the maintenance of distinct status groups, the commoner and warrior populations were segregated both officially and unofficially.[5] In addition to Edo and other smaller daimyo castle towns, commercial urban centers emerged, including Osaka, the most prominent example. Alternate attendance, coupled with urbanization, contributed to the development of extensive transport systems, communication networks, and other forms of infrastructure to connect these cities, allowing for the flow of people, goods, and information throughout much of Japan, both within and outside the limits of official regulations.

The growth of major cities with large commoner populations, especially Edo and Osaka, fostered the emergence of a lively urban, popular culture, which arose partly in opposition to more elite forms of culture that were ostensibly reserved for members of the ruling warrior class. Although the boundaries between differing status groups in Tokugawa society could be and frequently were crossed, efforts to maintain distinctions between status groups were common, as evidenced by the frequent, if ineffective, sumptuary laws aimed at non-samurai.[6] Naturally, Tokugawa authorities did not ignore popular culture, seeking instead to regulate it as they did much else. Sumo became a key element of this regulated popular culture scene, sparking modifications of the most basic rules and structures of the sport, as well as transformations of the wrestlers themselves.

As entertainers, sumo wrestlers figured prominently in Japan's urban popular culture. They not only traveled widely, journeying from tournament to tournament, but also provided rich subject matter for the booming Tokugawa-era publishing industry. Together with novels, travel guides, and a variety of other texts, woodblock prints were mass-produced and sold at relatively cheap prices in Edo and other urban centers. But published materials often reached an audience beyond these cities, carried along by and with the flow of samurai, traders, wrestlers, and other travelers.[7] The constant movement of all these people, images, and publications helped create a widespread familiarity with sumo and its stars, especially after the sport itself became more organized during the years of Tokugawa rule.

PROFESSIONALS TAKE TO THE RING

The origins of sumo as an organized, professional, spectator sport lie in the gradual emergence of troupes of wrestlers during the late sixteenth century who traveled the countryside agreeing to accept challenges from all-comers in exchange for a fee. The large urban centers of Edo, Osaka, and Kyoto quickly proved the most profitable venue for wrestlers interested in making a living from their sport. For instance, in Edo, which reached a population of over one million inhabitants by the early eighteenth century (making it one of the largest cities in the world at the time), each day of a ten-day sumo tournament could attract upward of 3,000 paying customers. By 1843, Edo sumo was successful enough to support 226 professional wrestlers.[8]

As the sumo wrestlers and their promoters went about establishing themselves in the cities, and in Edo in particular, they initially met a good deal of official resistance. From an official standpoint, sumo was threatening for a couple of reasons, both related to the maintenance of order. As late as 1711, Tokugawa leaders issued a decree expressing concerns about popular forms of sumo organized by and for commoners. Status distinctions were a primary factor. Wrestling had previously been associated with the military training of warriors, and therefore, many among the warrior elite saw wrestling as a form of entertainment that should be reserved for themselves. Popular forms of sumo making their appearance in the cities challenged both status boundaries and the warriors' claim to a special form of "military" knowledge. By posing such a challenge even inadvertently, popular sumo threatened to undermine social hierarchies that placed warriors at the apex of Tokugawa society in large part because of their monopoly on such knowledge. Perhaps even more threatening, however, was sumo's ability to attract potentially unruly crowds. Anxiety about such crowds motivated many of the earliest efforts to ban or prevent various forms of wrestling in the city, including organized tournaments up through the 1670s. Even after succumbing to what was obviously a losing battle and allowing sumo tournaments to be held in Edo, the Tokugawa shogunate imposed strict regulations on sumo, seeking to keep it "as circumscribed as possible."[9]

These regulatory efforts resulted in significant changes in sumo. Among the most dramatic transformations was a literal circumscription: the creation during the late seventeenth century of the *dohyō*, the raised ring that surrounds the competing wrestlers. Although not explicitly ordered by officials, the development of the ring suggests the efforts of sumo organizers to address potential threats to public order, such as fights or injuries to fans.[10] The new *dohyō* created a clear boundary, separating the wrestlers from the audience. Of course, the sumo ring would hardly prevent someone from crossing; anyone who has seen sumo will know that wrestlers occasionally topple into the audience. Yet when considered in contrast to earlier forms of sumo that encouraged challenges from "all-comers," the ring proved pivotal in sumo's emergence as both a spectator and a professional sport. By separating athletes from nonparticipants, the ring effectively marked those in the ring as professionals, since only those deemed so, including referees, would be allowed to enter it for the contest. Denying others the possibility of entering, unlike earlier forms, effectively turned all those in the audience into spectators—that is, people who came, and paid, to watch, without even the intention of participating in the actual contest.

The use of the ring as a boundary also changed the nature of the contest, since a wrestler could now win not only by taking down or throwing an opponent to the ground, but also by pushing him out of the ring. Considering this change, it is perhaps not surprising that new techniques of pushing began appearing alongside previous throwing techniques in books addressing sumo skills between 1687 and 1735.[11] Like the creation of the *dohyō* ring itself, the change in techniques suggests efforts to limit the potential for trouble, especially in the form of wounds or injuries to the wrestlers, concerns also reflected in increasingly codified sumo rules. The *Sumō densho*, a guide to sumo techniques dating from the early eighteenth century, included an extensive list of forbidden practices: gouging, breaking fingers, grabbing genitals, kicking at the chest or abdomen, striking with a clenched fist, upward thrusts with open palms to the nose, and simultaneous strikes with both hands to the ears. If the rules were not clear enough, before tournament matches wrestlers were also shown diagrams of the human body, which marked prohibited areas.[12]

The emergence of pushing techniques accompanying the creation of the sumo ring also transformed the wrestlers.[13] With the institution of the ring, size and bulk became even more important because they offered advantages over mobility and agility in terms of both pushing one's opponent out of the ring and avoiding being pushed out. In this way, the *dohyō* effectively limited the types of possible participants who could compete successfully, contributing to further professionalization. At the same time, the ring and the new techniques contributed to the emergence of particular body types that the public eventually came to associate with wrestlers. In other words, the extraordinary appearance of wrestlers' bodies that has generated much popular attention and comment stems, in part, from unintended consequences of regulatory efforts.

Other forms of regulation imposed on the sport also proved critical in the limitation of sumo to professionals. In order to hold a tournament, promoters had to receive official permission from the Tokugawa government and had to demonstrate that they would do everything possible to avoid public disruptions. By the eighteenth century promoters' efforts to address such issues led to the emergence of an officially sanctioned hierarchy of sumo *toshiyori*, or elders, in Edo and other cities. In exchange for recognized status and protected privileges, elders, who came almost exclusively from the ranks of retired wrestlers, served as regulators of the sport on behalf of the Tokugawa government.[14] Additionally, in 1751, a group of men who ran the centers where wrestlers lived and trained formed an organization known as the *sumō kaisho* in Edo. After successfully challenging the right of "village 'amateurs'" to charge fees for sumo unless they belonged to "proper groups," in 1772 the *sumō kaisho*, which presumably consisted of, or at least acted in conjunction with, sumo elders, effectively monopolized control over sumo performances in Edo.[15]

Promoters were not the only ones affected by the regulations. From at least 1684, permission to hold tournaments was premised on the fact that only professional wrestlers would be allowed to participate, a requirement once again aimed at limiting potential disorder by making certain that only those who were properly trained and disciplined would be wrestling.[16] Tournaments themselves became regulated and more scheduled, with professional wrestlers traveling to appear in the four regular sumo tournaments held during the year: spring and fall in Edo, summer in Kyoto, and fall in Osaka.[17] Sumo referees also had to be officially licensed, and as a result, several hereditary referee lines emerged during this period.[18] In all these ways, the basic contours of sumo organizations and regulations were put in place by the end of the eighteenth century. Despite a number of significant transformations in later periods, Hitachiyama's active role in managing and promoting sumo following his retirement attests to the important institutional precedents established during this period.

RECEIVING RECOGNITION

The ultimate benefit of this self-regulation and consequent professionalization came in the form of de facto recognition from the samurai elite.

By the eighteenth century, 27 daimyo from throughout the country were providing stipends to the best-known professional wrestlers. Whereas most wrestlers were dependent on income from the various tournaments, some profited from the patronage of daimyo, especially early in the eighteenth century, when one wrestler received a stipend of 40 *koku* from his patron, a salary comparable to a lower-ranking warrior. Patronage also offered symbolic benefits for both the wrestler and the patron, since the wrestlers were given and often wore decoratively embroidered ceremonial aprons known as *keshō-mawashi*, which identified their connection to a particular lordly supporter.[19] While wrestlers' victories could bring vicarious honor to such supporters, patrons' prestige could also influence the rankings of wrestlers and even the results of matches. Powerful benefactors could easily forbid their wrestler from participating in future matches if they were unhappy with the outcomes.[20] In addition to attention from daimyo, sumo gained the shogunate's acknowledgement. In 1791, Shogun Tokugawa Ienari hosted a viewing of the sport in his own castle, providing sumo with unparalleled official recognition.[21] Patronage, albeit in an altered form, continued to be a critical element of professional sumo during and after Hitachiyama's time.

Efforts to gain elite recognition for sumo sparked further, long-lasting changes in the sport. To prepare for the shogun's viewing, sumo promoters turned to Yoshida Zenzaemon, who claimed that referees from his family had long-standing ties to the sport and secret knowledge of ancient sumo rituals. As it turned out, much of what Yoshida initiated in the late eighteenth century was more new than ancient, aimed at solidifying his family's control over sumo rituals and making the sport suitable for a shogunal audience. Offering wonderful examples of invented traditions, Yoshida's innovations were often cloaked in religiosity and linked explicitly, albeit tenuously, to centuries-old practices. Many of the rituals that Yoshida introduced are still seen in sumo today, including the bow-twirling ceremony performed at the end of the day's matches and the ring-purification ceremony.[22] As part of efforts to elevate the status of sumo, Yoshida also instituted ceremonies and procedures associated with the *yokozuna* when he granted licenses to two wrestlers in 1789 authorizing them to perform ring-entering ceremonies while wearing a white rope, or *yokozuna*. Like many of his other ceremonies, Yoshida's invention of the *yokozuna* made links with the distant past, creating a "great deal of spurious history going back to the ninth century."[23]

Although the Yoshida family continued to award licenses after the initial performance before the shogun, the term *yokozuna*, at least officially, designated not a championship or rank, but merely the rope and the right to perform Yoshida's ring-entering ceremony. Over time the relatively infrequent granting of these *yokozuna* rights came to serve as an informal acknowledgment of a wrestler's high standing in the sport. However, the word *yokozuna* did not appear in rankings until 1890, and the Sumo Association did not officially recognize the title as the highest rank in sumo until 1909.[24] Significantly, Hitachiyama's career as an active wrestler (1891–1914) spanned these important years in the evolution of the *yokozuna* distinction.

LAND OF THE RISING STARS

Of course, the shogun and samurai patrons were not the only ones watching and taking notice of sumo during the Tokugawa period. As an emerging professional and spectator sport with regularly scheduled tournaments based in large cities, sumo quickly developed a following among the non-samurai population, especially the increasingly well-to-do merchants and other townspeople. At the center of such attention from both rulers and ruled were the wrestlers themselves, many of whom became well known, even outside the major metropolitan areas where tournaments were held. Popular and official interest in particular wrestlers almost certainly fed off each other, since the most successful and popular wrestlers attracted the most powerful patrons, something that in turn enhanced their own popular appeal. As both cause and consequence of such society-wide attention, the abundant depictions of sumo stars produced by the booming Tokugawa-era publishing industry reveal striking continuities with later sumo celebrities, including Hitachiyama, while also highlighting some of the key differences.

Like other popular celebrities of the Tokugawa period, especially kabuki actors and female entertainers from the pleasure quarters, sumo stars featured prominently in woodblock prints and textual sources, but also gained recognition through printed rankings known as *banzuke*. The earliest *banzuke* dates to 1699 in Kyoto, and consisted of two wooden planks displayed to list all the names of the wrestlers appearing in the competition that day. For each new tournament a new *banzuke* was printed. It would often be posted on the wrestling grounds and at key crossroads, and thus served as a source of advertising for promoters. By 1717 *banzuke* were being printed and distributed as programs for spectators. Along with the wrestling names (*shikona*) of the participants, the *banzuke* ranked them and included details about their home province and the domains of their daimyo patrons (if they had one). The printing and distribution of *banzuke* helped promote the standardization of the ranking system in sumo, although today's highest rank of *yokozuna* did not appear on *banzuke* until 1890. It is important to note that these early rankings were not necessarily based solely on performance within the sumo ring. The views of prominent patrons, together with promoters' need to keep the top wrestlers appearing before the crowds, often influenced not only the rankings, but also the outcomes of the matches themselves.[25] *Banzuke* standings based strictly on achievement in the ring are a more recent phenomenon.

Nevertheless, the lack of objectivity or accuracy in these early *banzuke* proves less significant than their establishment of key precedents. For one thing, *banzuke*, in modified form, continue today to serve as a means of publicizing the rankings of wrestlers before tournaments. Furthermore, *banzuke*, including the earliest versions, offered an instant, visual indicator of a wrestler's status in relation to others—in a sense, each *banzuke* was a kind of star system. Since the top wrestlers' names often appeared larger and included more information (details about patronage, for instance), even a spectator relatively unfamiliar with sumo could make a distinction among the wrestlers. In this way, the use of (literally) big-name stars to attract crowds also worked to alert spectators about which wrestlers were the most important. Viewed over a period of time, *banzuke* also offered the potential for tracking a wrestler's progress, or lack thereof. Finally, *banzuke* themselves quickly gained a hold on the popular imagination, often serving as a means of interpreting other aspects of society. By the late 1700s, *banzuke* using sumo ranks offered evaluations of Confucian scholars, Dutch Learning experts, and Osaka doctors.[26]

In addition to *banzuke*, which clearly acted as a kind of guide to sumo stars and eventually other celebrities as well, other forms of print culture played a central role in promoting images of wrestlers. Among the publications that emerged during the Tokugawa period were guidebooks to *meisho*, or famous places. Like the *banzuke*, many of these guidebooks consisted of rankings and evaluations of the particular sites depicted. These books were aimed at tourists and pilgrims and reflected the emergence of a significant domestic tourist industry in Japan during the Tokugawa shogunate. By the late eighteenth century, guidebooks were available for most popular tourist destinations.[27] Both sumo wrestlers and Ryōgoku, the area of Edo where most of the wrestlers were based, often featured in these *meisho* guides. Tournaments themselves served as important tourist destinations, and sumo-related souvenirs, including prints, playing cards, dolls, and no doubt the *banzuke* and *meisho* guides as well, were marketed to tourists.[28] Through tourism and the widespread availability and transportability of things like souvenirs, wrestlers achieved a degree of recognition and fame far beyond the tournament centers in Edo, Osaka, and Kyoto.

Wrestlers themselves traveled frequently to attend the major tournaments and to participate in provincial sumo tours, contributing further to their broad-based celebrity. Raiden Tame'emon (1767–1825), one of the most famous wrestlers of the Tokugawa period, serves as a case in point. Famed for his strength and size—6 feet 5 inches (196 centimeters) and 372 pounds (169 kilograms)—Raiden spent 16 of his 21 years in sumo at the highest rank of *ōzeki*. As part of his duties as a wrestler retained by the powerful daimyo of Matsue domain in Izumo, he carefully recorded his daily activities in a logbook called *Shokoku sumō hikae-chō* (Journal of Sumo in Various Provinces). His journal reveals extensive travels over the course of his career, including tours to almost every part of the island of Honshu, as well as visits to the islands of Kyushu and Shikoku. The availability of these journals, with their recountings of Raiden's wanderings and exploits throughout Japan, no doubt contributed to his lasting popularity long after his death in 1825.[29]

In addition to travel guides and journals, wrestlers appeared in other forms of popular literature and in the writings of some intellectuals. In particular, Tanikaze Kajinosuke (1750–95), one of the most famous Tokugawa-era wrestlers, appeared as a subject of various literary genres. One popular account offered a humorous tale of Tanikaze's interactions with his disciples and a young mistress in the pleasure quarters. The twist (and presumably the humor) of the story lies in the fact that the mistress, all of seventeen years old, is able to "move" Tanikaze to act when all of his disciples fail to do so, leading the disciples to conclude that the "united strength of this many wrestlers does not even come near that of a young lady."[30] With its overtly sexualized setting and portrayal of Tanikaze as strong enough to fight off a horde of wrestlers, yet soft enough to respond to the desires of a young (and by implication, attractive) woman, this account offers a glimpse of popular perceptions of his masculinity and sexuality. Whether real or fictitious, stories of this sort obviously reflected and contributed to the construction of Tanikaze's celebrity.

Comparative references to wrestlers in the works of several Tokugawa intellectuals attest to the existence of nascent sports star systems that were shaping understandings of sumo celebrities and especially their bodies. The writer Ueda Akinari (1734–1809), for instance, was quite crit-

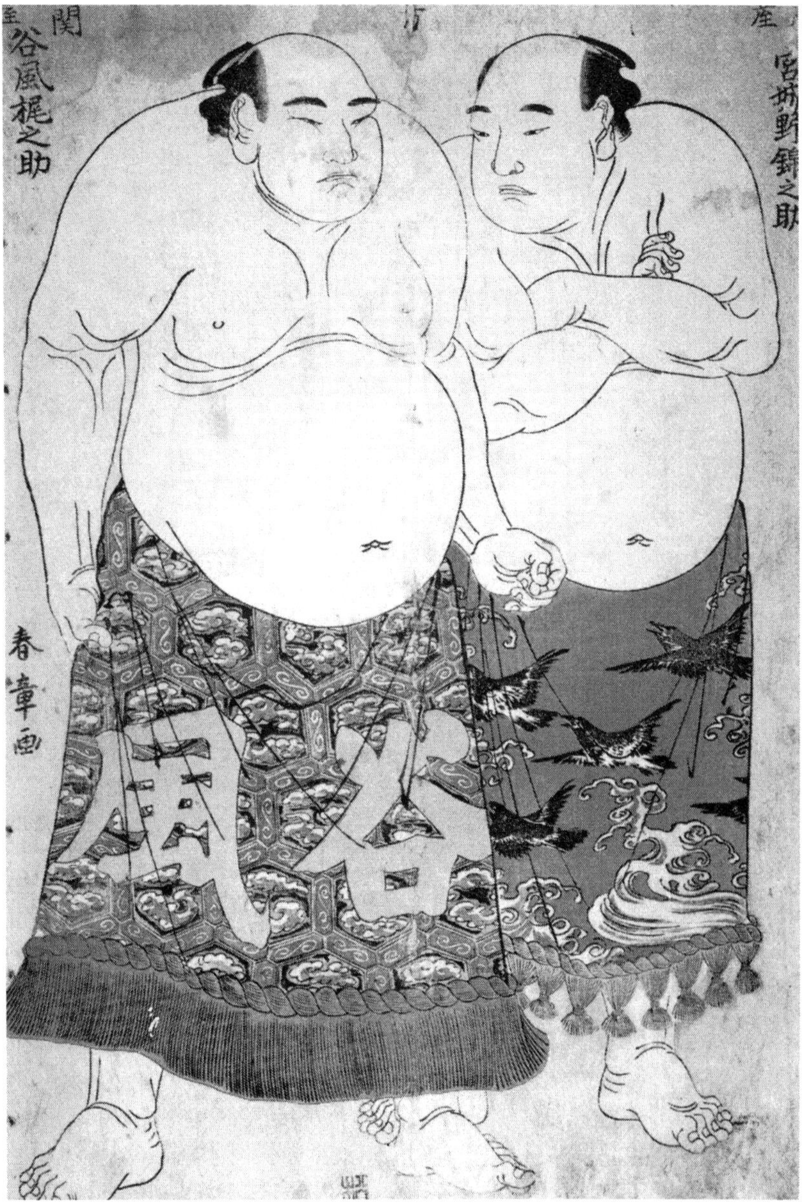

Figure 1.1 Woodblock print of sumo wrestlers Tanikaze (left) and Miyagino (right). One among a larger series of wrestlers' portraits produced by Shunshō from 1783 through 1784. Bickford, *Sumo and the Woodblock Print Masters*, 22. Courtesy of Mr. Takashi Yoshida.

ical of Tanikaze. Ueda's miscellany *Tandai shōshin roku* (Courage and caution, 1808) compared the sumo celebrity to great wrestlers from the 1730s through the 1750s, finding that Tanikaze "had the strength of a child . . . and that is not sumo."[31] The decline of sumo was a common theme among intellectuals and other writers. Like Ueda, Kanzawa Sadamoto (1710–95) complained in his late eighteenth-century essay collection *Okinagusa* (Old man grass) that the wrestlers of the past had been bigger and stronger: "Today's top wrestlers are much inferior to the middle-ranking wrestlers of former days . . . [and] they have grown smaller over the past thirty years."[32] The anonymously written *Shinpan kasen sumō hyōrin* (New poetic critiques of sumo, 1756) offered a status-informed critique of sumo's professionalization and decline in moral standards, complaining about the bad behavior of wrestlers who "ignore old ways and do as they please." Furthermore, it contended, wrestlers had transformed sumo from a "samurai skill, studied so that it might be of use on the battlefield" into "just a way of making a living."[33] With their nostalgic and clearly critical tone, these essays highlight not only a thorough familiarity with a wide variety of wrestlers, but also a seeming need to evaluate them in relation to other wrestlers, even if the individuals being compared had never met in competition.

As the comments of Ueda and Kanzawa suggest, much of the attention toward famous wrestlers focused on their bodies. Another comical account highlighting Tanikaze's unusual bulk appeared in 1800, five years after his death:

> Tanikaze said, somewhat sadly, to his wife: "Oi, old woman. To have been born with a figure like this, I am handicapped. I have never even seen my own navel." His wife said: "Try taking a peek. I can give you a hand." And she began to help him. Tanikaze was embarrassed, but bent over. His wife said: "Bend over some more. It's farther." Saying this, she pushed down on his head, but Tanikaze said: "Oh, it's too embarrassing. Let's give up." His wife only replied: "Bend over a little bit more." And she kept pushing on Tanikaze's head. Tanikaze then bent over a little too far and fell, rolling over onto his back. His wife, lifting her arms wide, said: "Haa! I threw you!"[34]

The humor of this particular account stems, in part, from the unique disadvantages of Tanikaze's large body, especially the inability to do even basic things without some assistance. At the same time, the story juxtaposes two images of Tanikaze. First, there is the well-known wrestler, earliest-documented *yokozuna*, and fierce competitor, who was said to have lost only 14 matches across a span of 44 tournaments.[35] Then

Figure 1.2 Print of the non-wrestling giant Ōzora Buzaemon produced in 1827 by Kuniyasu. The text provides details about Ōzora, including his place of origin, height, weight, and several other measurements. Bickford, *Sumo and the Woodblock Print Masters*, 34. Courtesy of Mr. Takashi Yoshida.

there is the less imposing figure in the story, who nearly gives up on a simple task and ends up being "thrown" by an old woman. The story's comedic effect, then, depends upon certain preexisting popular images of Tanikaze, and the very ridiculousness of the situation serves to reinforce Tanikaze's postmortem reputation for greatness and size.

There is good reason to suspect that even more than the wrestling, it was the wrestlers, and in particular their large bodies, that appealed to many sumo fans of the period. For one thing, we know a great deal about various bodily aspects of many Tokugawa-era wrestlers. Both Raiden and Tanikaze, for instance, were reportedly more than 6 feet (183 centimeters) tall and weighed more than 370 pounds (168 kilograms).[36] In his *Bukō nenpyō* (Chronology of Edo in Musashi province), a chronicle of contemporary urban life, Saitō Gesshin (1804–78) carefully recorded the measurements of several sumo celebrities, including several giants who either never wrestled or fared poorly in the sport. In 1827, the work documented the measurements of one such figure Ōzora Buzaemon (see Figure 1.2), who reportedly weighed over 300 pounds (136 kilograms) and stood 7 feet 5 inches (226 centimeters) with feet measuring 1 foot 3 inches (38 centimeters) and palms of 1 foot 2 inches (36 centimeters). In 1843

Saitō included details about another giant, Mitateyama Kisaku, who allegedly weighed some 260 pounds (118 kilograms).[37] The following year, Saitō reported the arrival of yet another physical prodigy: "A giant called Ikezuki Geitazaemon, from Hirado in Hizen, has come to be a wrestler. . . . [He] is 7 feet 5 inches [226 centimeters] in height, and weighs 314 pounds [142 kilograms]; his hands are 1 foot 8 inches [51 centimeters] long. He is eighteen years old, and is said to have the strength of eighteen men."[38] Famed for his appetite in particular, Ikezuki allegedly consumed more than 6 pints (3 liters) of rice each day. Although Ikezuki and the other giants never achieved success as wrestlers, what is striking here is the amount of detailed information that was already available about them. No doubt exaggerations, such accounts nonetheless reveal a remarkable degree of awareness of and interest in details concerning the bodies of sumo stars.

Popular recognition of sumo wrestlers' bodily uniqueness was created and reinforced visually through woodblock prints as well as wrestlers' handprints. Even today it is not unusual to see an exceptionally large handprint of a sumo wrestler displayed publicly, so that all who are interested can compare their own hands with the print.[39] Such handprints have served as a defining marker of wrestlers since the eighteenth century.[40] Created by the wrestler himself (at least in theory), a handprint is second only to actually meeting and comparing palms with the real wrestler.

That said, woodblock prints did their utmost to give viewers a sense of wrestlers' bulk and strength. In addition to depictions of tournaments and matches, they also featured wrestlers in a variety of settings—in the pleasure quarters, on boats, with children—that drew attention to their great size. An important subgenre of prints pictured famous wrestlers alongside famous geisha or kabuki actors, something perhaps offered as a two-for-one deal for tourists or other souvenir seekers. Another type of print, possibly intended for comedic effect, showed women holding miniature puppets of wrestlers whose names were provided on their *keshō-mawashi* ceremonial aprons. But the wrestlers more often appeared alone.[41] The sheer number of prints focusing solely on individual wrestlers indicates that it was the wrestlers themselves whom artists and consumers saw as important.[42] In other words, wrestlers were celebrities in their own right. Produced as souvenirs for both city residents and tourists, sumo prints often included wrestlers' names and other biographical information.

In his examination of sumo prints, historian Harold Bolitho points out that prints of wrestlers treated their subjects in ways designed to emphasize their size:

> What the wrestler prints display, quite unambiguously, is bulk, and what they suggest, with equal force, is phenomenal strength accompanied in many instances by an indefinable air of menace. These qualities emerge most clearly in portraits of individual wrestlers, in all of which the subject, his rippling muscles and billowing rolls of fat exaggerated to the point of caricature, is placed squarely in the foreground as if threatening to burst out of the borders which confine him.[43]

Print artists sought to present sumo wrestlers as not simply large, but also well muscled, often employing special techniques to depict exaggerated and stylized arm and leg muscles.[44] In their analysis of sumo prints, Matsunami Kenshirō and Araki Yūji contend that despite such exaggeration, the prints necessitated a certain degree of realism in order to appeal to the public. Pointing in particular to images of Tanikaze, they explain, "No matter which print, Tanikaze's face depicts the same person, and his distinctive characteristics are captured masterfully."[45] Depictions of Tanikaze, when viewed over time, also reveal a decline in his physique, despite their stylized exaggeration. The decline is especially apparent in prints that juxtapose him with his younger rival Onogawa Kisaburō (1758–1806), who was awarded the *yokozuna* license at the same time as Tanikaze.[46] Such group images, with their implicit comparisons, offered observers a kind of visual star system that drew particular attention to apparent differences in the wrestlers' bodies.

However, not every wrestler was depicted as faithfully as stars like Tanikaze and Onogawa. Matsunami and Araki describe two nearly identical images, which according to the names included on the prints depict two different wrestlers. In this instance, the print of a popular wrestler may have sold out unexpectedly, and at that point a different (and less popular) wrestler's print was probably altered and then marketed under the name of the sold-out individual.[47] Aside from such instances of perhaps deliberate misrepresentation, Matsunami and Araki's analysis demonstrates that those purchasing and observing prints could see—indeed, expected to see—representations of wrestlers that were recognizable, especially in the case of the most famous wrestlers. Prints, then, were central in the emergence of cults of personality around particular wrestlers, cults that often centered on the individual's extraordinary body, as the prints themselves suggest.

Popular obsession with the size of wrestlers is perhaps most apparent in the prominence of several non-wrestler sumo celebrities. The giants described in Saitō's *Bukō nenpyō* were among this group. Although Mitateyama Kisaku, according to Saitō, was "not good enough" to be a wrestler, he nonetheless appeared regularly in the sumo ring and was even the subject of at least one sumo print by the artist Kunisada.[48] Because such figures attracted the attention of samurai and commoners alike, sumo promoters often had giants appear in the ring dressed as sumo wrestlers, though many of them never competed. Among the most famous of these non-wrestlers was Daidōzan Bungorō, a giant child, who at age 7 reportedly stood 3 feet 10 inches (117 centimeters), but weighed 183 pounds (83 kilograms). Popular from 1794 through 1798, Daidōzan became famous for dressing as a wrestler and performing the ring-entering ceremonies. He appeared in no less than 25 different prints by some of the most eminent woodblock artists. Sumo promoters obviously found such child giants profitable, since several others appeared in the ring after Daidōzan, including Maizuru Komakichi, a 218-pound (99-kilogram), 8-year-old boy, who appeared in a total of 11 tournaments beginning in 1859.[49]

What are we to make of such sumo celebrities who never wrestled? Anthropologist Kenji Tierney has observed that they serve as an important reminder that sumo during this period was a "performance, a spectacle, a site/sight, something to be seen. That is not to say that it was not physical, . . . that there were not tests of strength. The strength and power of many wrestlers is legendary, but they shared the stage with participants . . . exemplified by Daidōzan."[50] Many people reportedly left after the ring-entering rituals and did not even stay to watch the wrestling matches, supporting the idea that sumo was as much about entertaining performances (similar to those of kabuki actors and geisha) as athletic achievements.[51] But what distinguished sumo stars and served as the central aspect of their fame—and provided the common link between the non-wrestling giants and the actual wrestlers—was popular fascination with their unusually large bodies.

Questioning the nature of this interest, Bolitho has cited connections between sumo and "freak shows" that were common during the Tokugawa period. Pointing in particular to the fame of non-wrestling giant children and the obsessive documentation of wrestlers' measurements and size, Bolitho contends: "The wrestlers, whether they were athletes or no . . . were there not so much to wrestle as to gratify that ancient and instinctive impulse, defined by Leslie Fielder as 'quasi-religious awe,' that we all feel in the presence of the abnormal."[52] Expanding on Bolitho's point, I would argue that the power and appeal of wrestlers' bodies stemmed in large part from a recognition that they exemplified the human form at its very limits. The reported measurements of Tokugawa-era wrestlers would have made them dramatically larger than most people. Historian Susan Hanley has estimated that the average height for men at the time would have been about 5 feet 2 inches (157 centimeters) and for women, about 4 feet 10 inches (148 centimeters).[53] In this sense, the awe generated by a wrestler, and by extension any athlete with a "superior" body or abilities, promotes—indeed, depends upon—a recognition, or reaffirmation, of one's own body, its size, its limitations, and its benefits. Unlike Tanikaze in the story, most people can at least claim to have seen their navels. People comparing their palms with a wrestler's handprint become instantly aware of not only the great size of the wrestler, but also their own relative size. Printed and visual references to height, weight, and strength allow for easy comparisons among various wrestlers, but they also set up implicit contrasts between wrestlers and anyone viewing that information.

HITACHIYAMA: ROOTS OF A SPORTS FREAK

As a sumo celebrity, Hitachiyama is clearly indebted to the Tokugawa period in many ways. The particular socio-political and cultural climate of the era not only led to sumo's emergence as a professional and spectator sport, but also produced several of the sport's key institutions: the *dohyō* ring, *banzuke* rankings, various ceremonies, and the *yokozuna*, to cite just a few. This climate also occasioned the rise of sumo celebrities, together with a variety of means for presenting them to an admiring public. In comparing Hitachiyama's image and reputation with celebrities from earlier periods, one of the clearest continuities turns out to be the emphasis on their bodies.

After more than two centuries of close attention to the bodily measurements and features of sumo stars, the popular mindset was already well trained to look out for, even expect, specific details about Hitachiyama's body from the very moment he entered sumo, an issue examined more closely in Chapter 2. The degree to which images, descriptions, and even touring wrestlers themselves had reached significant portions of the Japanese population during the Tokugawa period contributed to the presumed availability of knowledge about wrestlers' bodies. Yet, if Hitachiyama shared characteristics with earlier sumo celebrities, he was also unique. To understand his differences it is necessary to explore the other threads that were interwoven in the creation of his celebrity.

Rising to the Challenge

With such an illustrious history, including both popular and official recognition and a vibrant celebrity culture, one might wonder how Hitachiyama achieved a reputation for having "saved" sumo. What, after all, did he have to save it from? Accounts of the history of sumo reveal that during the years preceding Hitachiyama's rise to fame, sumo did, in fact, face a number of serious threats.[54] Because they figure centrally in the construction of Hitachiyama's image, two specific threats merit particular attention: first, the loss of daimyo patronage, and second, a general decline in the popular support and reputation of sumo tied especially to the arrival of Western sporting practices and conceptions of body culture. Examining these threats, as well as the measures that promoters and wrestlers took to address them, helps to explain why Hitachiyama achieved the level of fame and recognition that he did.

RESPONDING TO ANOTHER NEW ORDER

Just as the emergence of the Tokugawa order shaped sumo, so too, did the collapse of the regime. Although some wrestlers are said to have played a role, albeit a fairly minor one, in the events leading to the toppling of the Tokugawa shogunate and the Meiji Restoration in 1868, changes occurring in the aftermath of this transition had the most direct effect on sumo.[55] Generally speaking, times of political and social turmoil (not to mention civil war) are not conducive to generating the kinds of crowds that had proven critical to sumo's emergence and success during the more stable years of the Tokugawa period. This was especially true in Edo, which lost half of its population in the years leading up to and immediately following the Meiji Restoration, including more than 300,000 people during 1868 alone. The city, renamed Tokyo and designated as the new imperial capital in 1868, did not reach Edo's pre-Restoration population until around 1890, roughly the same time that Hitachiyama joined professional sumo.[56] Given these statistics, there is little wonder that sumo tournaments in the city faced poor attendance, only beginning to recover during the mid-1880s.

One segment of the declining population proved especially significant for sumo: the daimyo. Facing both domestic financial crises and foreign threats, in 1862, the Tokugawa shogunate changed the system of alternate attendance by allowing daimyo family hostages to leave Edo and drastically reducing the time that the lords themselves were required to spend in the city. By the end of 1868 the daimyo population (including family members, retained samurai, and servants) in Edo had dropped by more than 85 percent to an estimated 30,000.[57] Since daimyo had long served as patrons of the top-ranked wrestlers, changes in alternate attendance had clear implications for sumo. If nothing else, one of the prime reasons for maintaining patronage of the top wrestlers—keeping up appearances in Edo—would have lost a great deal of appeal for most regional lords. The declining stipends of even the best retained wrestlers during the late Tokugawa period further suggest that the financial crises of the time made potential symbolic benefits of patronage less worthwhile.

Whatever systems of daimyo patronage managed to survive amidst these population shifts and economic crises were dealt a deathblow by changes instituted by the leaders of the new Meiji state. As part of their effort to remake Japan along the lines of its Western, nation-state rivals, Meiji leaders dismantled the Tokugawa order. In 1871 daimyo domains were abolished and replaced by prefectures with appointed governors. In 1873 the government announced plans to develop a conscript army, undermining the martial monopoly of the samurai elite. And as historian Harry Harootunian has noted, the samurai as a whole were stripped of their privileged status in society so that the "ostensible equalization of classes, the injunctions against sword bearing, the discontinuation of old-style head dress (*chonmage*) and garb, the rulings against vendettas and traditional legal privileges all constitute decisive aspects of this story."[58] With the abolishment of government-paid stipends to samurai in 1876, the members of this hereditary group lost their main source of financial support.

Understandably, such changes effectively spelled the end of daimyo patronage of sumo wrestlers. Since the benefits of retaining sumo wrestlers were largely symbolic from the beginning, patronage of wrestlers was perhaps particularly expendable, especially as the public reputation of sumo itself faced a general decline. Even though many of the daimyo were incorporated into the new system of peerage and a number of key players in the new Meiji government continued to support sumo, the old domain heads no longer had the means to support the wrestlers themselves.

Efforts to address the loss of daimyo patronage affected sumo in several ways. Prior to this point, wrestlers' primary loyalties lay with their daimyo patrons, rather than each other or their sport. Faced with new challenges, wrestlers were forced to organize and work together in ways that had not been necessary before. In 1876, for instance, to prove that they made a valuable contribution to society beyond mere entertainment, wrestlers volunteered to serve as firefighters.[59] In 1885 an article in the *Tōkyō Nichinichi shinbun* newspaper, referring to the great size of wrestlers, announced that several of them had declared their intention to enter into service as a transport corps (*shichōtai*) in the event of a national emergency.[60] Around the same time, the *sumō kaisho*, the sumo-promotion organization based in Edo since 1751, underwent a series of reforms in order to allow for more standardized systems of ranking and salary assessment and to give lower-ranked wrestlers a greater say in the organization.[61]

The loss of official patronage and recognition enjoyed during the Tokugawa period also necessitated the creation of new forms of support. Several high-level figures in the new Meiji establishment, including Saigō Takamori, Itō Hirobumi, Kuroda Kiyotaka, and Itagaki Taisuke, provided various sorts of support for sumo. By taking advantage of such connections, sumo wrestlers were able to perform before the Meiji Emperor in 1868, 1869, and 1870, and then again in 1881 on the estate of Duke (*kōshaku*) Shimazu Tadayoshi, the former daimyo of Satsuma.[62] In 1884 the Meiji Emperor indicated his support of sumo when he called for an imperial tournament, thus officially instituting the practice of sumo performances in the imperial presence, or *tenran-zumō*. Similar to the countless other imperial ceremonies and rituals initiated during the Meiji era, this imperial tournament was meant to connect both the Meiji Emperor and sumo with Japan's ancient imperial past, but ironically, the organizers' plans to recreate ancient sumo rituals had to be abandoned because of a lack of time to prepare and a lack of records explaining such a display. Instead, a form of professional, Tokugawa-era sumo was performed.[63] One should not assume, however, that this failure implied poor planning. Descriptions of this landmark event suggest that every detail received careful attention, from the design of the banners to the promotion of a new *yokozuna*.[64] Such imperial exhibitions of sumo were also carefully documented in woodblock prints and photos and widely reported in the press.[65] *Tenran-zumō* and the popular attention it received contributed significantly to a "sumo boom" in the mid- to late 1880s. By the time Hitachiyama entered the world of professional sumo a few years later, imperial support had already bestowed renewed credibility to the sport, a fact that made Hitachiyama's rise as a popular star and alleged savior of the sport easier than might have been the case otherwise.

In addition to performances before the emperor, sumo wrestlers sought to strengthen their affiliations with the Meiji establishment in other ways, including participation in state Shinto rituals and imperial events such as those celebrating Emperor Meiji's 30th jubilee.[66] They also regularly provided donations of time and money for a variety of causes. When the crown prince married in 1900, wrestlers offered a large monetary gift to the Imperial Wedding Commemoration Association.[67] In response to the Boxer Uprising and its aftermath in China, wrestlers donated funds to the Red Cross, and in 1901, a group of 30 wrestlers from Osaka toured northern China to entertain allied troops based there.[68] Such performances for the military were not exceptional. In 1899, for example, sumo stars from Tokyo held exhibition matches at the elite Rikugun kaikōsha military club, and in 1904, top wrestlers performed at the Red Cross Hospital for the benefit of soldiers injured in the Russo-Japanese War (1904–5).[69] As these examples suggest, sumo wrestlers and promoters made every effort to link themselves and their sport to Japan's broader imperial projects.

Like many of his wrestling contemporaries, Hitachiyama played an active role in fostering these kinds of connections. In the earliest stages of his career he participated in ceremonies to commemorate the return of soldiers from the Sino-Japanese War (1894–95). After achieving fame he continued and even expanded upon such early activities. In addition to high-profile visits to Europe and America, Hitachiyama and a contingent of other top wrestlers visited Korea and parts of Manchuria, just months before Japan formally annexed Korea in 1910. Towards the end of the trip, Hitachiyama is said to have convinced the group to make an unplanned pilgrimage in southern Manchuria to pay homage to Japanese soldiers killed in the recent war.[70]

Over the course of Hitachiyama's career, several members of the imperial family attended sumo tournaments where he wrestled, a fact we know because sumo press coverage highlighted the attendance of the figures associated with the imperial household. However, Hitachiyama never performed before Emperor Meiji himself, even though doing so was, in the words of the sumo specialty newspaper *Sumō sekai*, "Hitachiyama's life-long desire."[71] The paper indicated that Hitachiyama had been delaying retirement in hopes of having an opportunity to perform the ring-entering ceremony of the *yokozuna* before the emperor and that he and his supporters had been actively petitioning the imperial household to stage an exhibition. As the paper noted two months later in an article titled "Hitachiyama's Disappointment," the emperor's death meant that Hitachiyama's longtime desire could not be achieved.[72] Despite the ultimately failed efforts at attaining an imperial audience, by emphasizing Hitachiyama's earnestness, self-sacrifice, and disappointment, these articles accentuated his reverence for and loyalty to the emperor.

HITACHIYAMA AND THE FANS: THE EMERGENCE OF *KŌENKAI*

Although the support of the Meiji Emperor and other elites proved central to sumo in the aftermath of the Restoration, Hitachiyama was more closely associated with another emerging form of patronage, the *kōenkai*, or patronage clubs. The first sumo *kōenkai* was the Banzai-kai, organized in 1900, at the prompting of Kuroiwa Shūroku (Ruikō), a writer, journalist, and founder of the *Yorozu chōhō* newspaper, which by that time was one of Japan's largest dailies. The Hinomoto-kai was established the following year under the leadership of Viscount Akimoto Okitomo, the adopted son of the former daimyo of Tatebayashi domain. In 1904 two other *kōenkai* were organized, the Dōkan-kai and the Hitachiyama-kai.[73]

Like much else in sumo, *kōenkai* have important precursors dating from the Tokugawa period. In addition to the daimyo and warrior patronage that proved critical for the most famous wrestlers, commoners in Edo organized their own groups known as *teuchi renchū* or hand-clapping clubs to support particular wrestlers, as well as kabuki actors. Using color-coded scarves and seat cushions, these clubs demonstrated their loyalty to their favorite stars with cheers and hand-clapping routines, but were also infamous for fighting with rival groups.[74] In the case of kabuki, these groups aided in the production of performances, gave gifts, and arranged ceremonies for welcoming and entertaining actors.[75] It is not clear whether such groups assumed a similarly active role in sumo, though at the very least they could be said to have contributed to the sport by offering moral support, creating a lively atmosphere, and also, no doubt, paying entry fees.

The new Meiji-era *kōenkai* differed from their Tokugawa predecessors in several critical ways. For one thing, *kōenkai* influenced sumo and its wrestlers directly, not only offering rewards and various forms of assistance to wrestlers, but also explicitly seeking to elevate the status of sumo as a whole. Indeed, the early *kōenkai*, by and large, represented an effort to rescue sumo from what these groups portrayed as the debasing influence of commoner support like the *teuchi renchū*.[76] *Kōenkai* descriptions of sumo often omit references to its Tokugawa origins as a form of commoner entertainment. Instead, such accounts highlight sumo's connections to warrior culture and daimyo patronage, suggesting that it was only with the loss of such patronage in the wake of the Meiji Restoration that sumo wrestlers descended to the geisha-like status of "male entertainers" (*hōkan geinin*). These selective retellings of sumo's recent past reflected *kōenkai* efforts to draw distinctions between the "sport-like" (*taiikuteki*) sumo that they envisioned and the performative, freak-show elements that Daidōzan and other non-wrestling "wrestlers" represented.[77] At the same time, negative references to wrestlers perceived as "male entertainers" betrayed organizers' concerns about the need to defend the masculinity and nobility of wrestlers, especially in the face of comparisons with foreign sports. After all, as the Hinomoto-kai charter observed, the state of wrestlers "did not decline because of one wrestler's sins. In truth, it is because of society's treatment of wrestlers that we have come to this point." Wrestlers needed to be "greatly respected and cherished," perhaps especially by those who could become members of the Hinomoto-kai.[78]

The anti-commoner strain in *kōenkai* charters and mission statements no doubt reflected the composition of their members. On one hand, *kōenkai* made it possible for a wider range of people to assume a role supporting sumo than had been the case with earlier (especially daimyo) forms of elite patronage, and it is worth noting that the provisions for choosing leaders of the organizations were remarkably democratic. Press announcements concerning the organization of these clubs also suggest that founders were interested in recruiting widely. Furthermore, although the leaders and most of the members in these groups would have been men, various photos and media references reveal that a number of women, especially geisha, participated in *kōenkai* activities on at least some level. On the other hand, the founding members of these groups often came from Japan's middle and upper classes, and the need to contribute financially to support the clubs and their respective missions would have placed significant restrictions on those who could join. Those who wanted to be regular members of the Dōkan-kai, for instance, had to be able to contribute 10 yen, twice yearly; the fee for "special members" was 20 yen twice a year.[79] The Hinomoto-kai's regulations noted only that those interested in becoming members had to apply to the club headquarters and provide funds to carry out the club's mission "as needed, voluntarily."[80] For the vast majority of Japanese at the time, whose salaries barely covered basic living expenses, such fees and "donations" would have been out of the question.[81] In this sense, these new groups almost certainly assumed a more elite feel than the commoner groups of the Tokugawa period.

The emergence of these early *kōenkai* and their emphasis on elevating sumo's status are inseparable from Hitachiyama's career and reputation. Of the four groups, the Hitachiyama-kai, as its name suggests, was most closely linked with the champion wrestler. Founded in 1904 after he became a *yokozuna*, the club's purpose was threefold: "to reward prizes to all the wrestlers of Hitachiyama's stable based on their results at the January and May tournaments, to aid wrestlers dealing with illness or injury, and to cultivate and support wrestlers who demonstrate the essence of *sumōdō* [the way of sumo]."[82] According to the club's mission statement, Hitachiyama himself was the embodiment of *sumōdō*, his appearance in the sumo world having rescued the sport from its supposedly debased state: "When Hitachiyama arrived, for the first time, wrestlers were seen at their best, their honor was upheld, and characteristics of sumo wrestlers from the distant past reappeared."[83] Similarly, the charter establishing the Hinomoto-kai three years earlier had proclaimed the need to "promote *sumōdō* and protect wrestlers of high character and principle who have not lost the true spirit of *bushidō* [the way of the warrior]."[84] Although he was not mentioned by name in this case, by 1901 Hitachiyama had already emerged as a sumo star, and in light of the widely known fact that he was the first sumo wrestler from a former samurai family, he seems the likely candidate for the model wrestler envisioned by the Hinomoto-kai.

Kuroiwa's Banzai-kai, the first *kōenkai*, also reflects Hitachiyama's influence, in this instance through opposition. The club was initially established to reward the wrestler with the best record at the previous tournament with an elaborate *keshō-mawashi* or ceremonial apron. Because the first apron was awarded to a wrestler who had defeated the rising star Hitachiyama, stories emerged that the club was established to reward anyone who defeated him. Stories and rumors of the Banzai-kai's perceived opposition to Hitachiyama reflected both popular assumptions about his dominant role in the sport and the underdog stance for which Kuroiwa and his paper became famous. As James Huffman has noted, "Kuroiwa used his news columns as levers for pushing the mighty and the rich off their perches, and his readers loved him for it."[85] In keeping with his anti-establishment reputation, Kuroiwa and the Banzai-kai eventually aligned with one of Hitachiyama's rivals. Among those joining Kuroiwa in the new affiliation was Miki Aika, a sumo commentator and one of Hitachiyama's most vocal critics.[86]

Even with the opposition of someone like Kuroiwa, the benefits of all the attention from the new *kōenkai* were clear, and such rewards as *keshō-mawashi* aprons were only the beginning for a star like Hitachiyama. In addition to supporting Hitachiyama and his associated wrestlers financially, the Hitachiyama-kai assumed a central role in Hitachiyama's career in other ways. It was club members, for instance, who had been most active in seeking—ultimately without success—to secure an imperial audience for Hitachiyama in the months before Emperor Meiji's death. Earlier, Hitachiyama first announced his plans to travel abroad at a meeting of the club in 1907, and members responded enthusiastically. Upon the wrestler's retirement, the Hitachiyama-kai also republished his book *Sumō taikan* (1909), a kind of encyclopedia of sumo facts and history, thus assuring that his reputation would extend far beyond his years in the ring.[87] The branch organizations of the Hitachiyama-kai that sprang up in various regions sponsored group trips to see Hitachiyama at tournaments and also served as important support networks when Hitachiyama traveled.[88] *Kōenkai* and their branches throughout Japan continue to play a critical role in sumo today, representing another way in which Hitachiyama's celebrity status intersected with the modern history of the sport.[89]

EXTERNAL THREATS: MAKING SUMO THE NATIONAL SPORT

The emergence of strong patronage networks proved especially important since sumo was facing another threat: the arrival and diffusion of new Western sporting practices and conceptions of body culture following Japan's "opening" and consequent rapid modernization. The new threat was two-fold: first, sumo and its wrestlers were quite literally being re-viewed through the lens of Western-influenced understandings of the body and sports. In this context, the once celebrated bodies of wrestlers came to be seen as an embarrassment, leading many to call for an elimination of sumo altogether.[90]

At the same time, sumo faced increased competition from new forms of popular sports entertainment. Sports such as baseball, rugby, track and field, tennis, and boxing entered Japan in the mid- to late 1800s. Until well after the turn of the century, however, most of these sports lacked both the mass-appeal and institutional structures that had long benefited sumo. Even baseball, which had begun to attract greater popular interest than many of the other new sports by the late 1890s, was primarily an elite game for many years.[91] Although sumo initially remained more popular and better organized than these other sports, the perceived danger for sumo lay in the elite appeal of sports like baseball. It was among the Westernizing elite, the very people initially most aware of and drawn to Western sports, that criticisms of sumo were most trenchant. In response to such challenges, sumo advocates, including Hitachiyama and various *kōenkai*, sought to redefine sumo as a sport and simultaneously to reestablish (and in many ways invent) sumo's traditional status.

Although I have consciously used the word "sport" to refer to sumo throughout the Tokugawa period, it is important to keep in mind that when Westerners first encountered sumo they did not see it as a sport. Rather, it was seen as "athletically suspect" and quickly came to be viewed as a "sign of Japanese racial, social, and evolutionary backwardness."[92] Influenced by Western, Victorian notions of nudity, the nakedness of wrestlers, which had not been a matter of particular concern in the Tokugawa period, now became a point of anxiety for many commentators. Little wonder then that calls for the abolition of sumo and the promotion of Western sports often came side by side. Since sports in the late nineteenth century were deemed an essential element of "civilized societies" and a key to Western dominance, sumo's dismissal meant that filling this void in Japanese society necessitated the introduction of Western sports practices. For sumo to play a role in modern society, it would have to be redefined as a sport, on Western terms. Declarations of sumo's unfitness as a sport and the efforts to redefine it as such reflect the co-constitutional processes at work in the introduction and diffusion of sports culture in Japan. Both Westerners and Japanese commenting on and reshaping sumo were looking to each other to define themselves.

Describing what they term the "modernization" of sumo, Allen Guttmann and Lee Thompson have highlighted several ways in which sumo was transformed during the Meiji period, including rationalized rankings, increased quantification, and the awarding of championships. Beginning in 1890, the title of *yokuzuna* appeared for the first time on the *banzuke*, and in 1909 it officially became the highest rank in sumo. Also in 1909, the construction of the Kokugikan, an indoor sumo stadium, removed the variable of unpredictable weather, which had often interrupted sumo tournaments in the past.[93] Many of these changes occurred during or in the years immediately preceding Hitachiyama's wrestling career. In fact, Hitachiyama is often linked explicitly to the construction of the Kokugikan, with claims that his popularity made possible the construction of this indoor facility—the first in the history of the sport.[94] At the very least, Hitachiyama's years as an active wrestler coincided with a remarkable increase in the profitability of the sport, and his timing again proved fortuitous, since Meiji-era adaptations to sumo helped bolster, if not produce, his celebrity status.[95]

Although the above changes were part of the larger redefinition of sumo in response to challenges from Western sporting practices and ideas, they also built upon preexisting trends. Rankings in the form of *banzuke* and various types of quantification had a long history in sumo. These types of adaptations in sumo, we might also note, are far from unique in the history of sports. Baseball has been altered over the course of its history to make homeruns more likely; American football was modified to allow the forward pass; basketball added a three-point line; and the Olympic Games now allow professional athletes to participate.[96] What such changes have in common is a desire to make the games more appealing for fans. As with other sports, the evolution of professional sumo was as much about the need to attract an audience as it was about specific measures taken to address perceived Western threats. The two are related, of course, but to overemphasize the Western threat alone is to miss important commonalities across national boundaries. That said, explicit measures were taken to change the image of sumo in ways that made it more sport-like in the eyes of both Japanese and Westerners. Arguments in support of sumo, especially in the early 1900s, often sought to link sumo both to the nation and to notions of promoting physical education, and it was only during this period that sumo came to be known as the *kokugi*, or national sport.[97]

Early *kōenkai*, in particular, championed this sportification. The Hinomoto-kai proclaimed sumo an equal of European boxing and bull-fighting, asserting, "Sumo is truly Japan's only national manly art."[98] The Hitachiyama-kai was even more explicit: "*Sumōdō* is one of our national treasures, a sport-like martial art passed down from ancient times."[99] The prominent Meiji statesman and avid sumo supporter Itagaki Taisuke declared sumo ideally suited for viewing by visiting Western dignitaries because "it consists in hard physical exercises, is cosmopolitan in character, and is quite as easily intelligible to foreigners as to Japanese."[100] Not surprisingly, positive comments about sumo from such visitors featured prominently in media coverage of the sport.[101]

Wrestlers joined their more elite patrons in demonstrating connections between sumo and Western-influenced notions of sports and physical fitness. In 1899, for instance, wrestlers donated proceeds from a match to the Japan Physical Training Association, and in 1901, several top wrestlers, including Hitachiyama, participated in a two-day exhibition sponsored by the Japan Athletic Sports Association.[102] According to Hitachiyama's own book, *Sumō hisshō dokugakusho* (Self-study guide to sumo, 1918), sumo was an "embodiment of our nation's martial spirit and collective soundness of character" and the "most masculine, most fair, most heroic, and most stimulating sport," all words commonly associated with Western sporting ideals.[103] Closing his description, he declared, "Sumo is a sport that exhibits the dignity of men; watching and enjoying sumo also displays men's dignity."[104] For Hitachiyama and other promoters, sumo was clearly more than just popular entertainment.

The repeated references in Hitachiyama's text to men or masculinity merit particular attention for two overlapping reasons. First, such references (appearing three times in the first paragraph alone) highlight the relationships between sportification efforts and concerns about Western perceptions of Japanese men. In the views of many Europeans and Americans at the time, a society without sports as defined in the West was one lacking in masculinity. In this context, sumo not only had to be reclassified as a sport, but also had to be clearly identified as a male practice; women could (perhaps even should) appreciate it, but not perform it, which raises a second point. Hitachiyama's description of sumo as a "male sport" effectively denied the validity of "women's sumo" (*onnazumō*). Various types of women's sumo, including touring professionals, had been part of the regulated, Tokugawa-era popular culture, and several forms continued to exist after the Meiji Restoration. The very existence of female wrestlers, both in the past and at the time, belied many of the claims from sumo's advocates and posed further potential of foreign criticism. Little wonder then that Hitachiyama literally wrote women's sumo out and that Tokyo sumo organizers banned women entirely from entering the ring after the Kokugikan opened in 1909. Despite such opposition and even a government ban on *onnazumō* in 1926, women's sumo also offers a reminder that the process of sumo's envisioned transformation was far from orderly and quick. Photographs of female wrestlers appeared in elite sumo specialty magazines into the 1910s, and media references to them can be found as late as 1930.[105]

PROMOTING SUMO AS SPORT: HITACHIYAMA AS SUMO MISSIONARY IN 1907

As Hitachiyama's own writings indicate, he situated himself at the center of efforts to redefine sumo as a sport, a fact exemplified in particular by his trip abroad in 1907. The trip had clear political undertones, coming as it did in the aftermath of Japan's victory in the Russo-Japanese War and in an era of increasing sentiment against Asian immigration in North America. Hitachiyama's trip should also be read as an attempt to re-present sumo to the West as a sport, and it is clear that he was viewed as the most appropriate candidate for this task. Prior to his journey, the wrestler Genjiyama had been denied permission to make a similar trip on the grounds that "Americans would not understand sumo . . . and the performances in America would certainly fail," and in so doing, insult the distinguished history of sumo and thereby embarrass the Japanese nation.[106] Upon learning of Hitachiyama's planned voyage, Genjiyama was furious, arguing that his own planned trip had been sabotaged for the sake of Hitachiyama, a claim that seems not completely unfounded.[107]

Aside from timing, Hitachiyama's visit overseas differed from the one Genjiyama had proposed in several ways. First, Hitachiyama was a higher-ranking wrestler than Genjiyama and also had a unique status as a former samurai, which made him a more acceptable national representative in the minds of Meiji government officials. Second, unlike Genjiyama's planned trip, Hitachiyama's was not classified as a *jungyō* or barnstorming tour with multiple wrestling bouts planned. From the beginning Hitachiyama declared that his expedition abroad was a "sports investigation" (*taiiku shisatsu*).[108]

Over the course of his trip, Hitachiyama and his entourage traveled extensively in the United States, performing at a number of venues, including Yale University and several elite athletic clubs in New York, Kansas City, and other cities.[109] At the time, university and club sports still dominated the athletic scene in the United States, as they did in Europe and Japan, so the selection of these particular sites indicated an effort to promote a specific image of sumo. In addition, Hitachiyama's traveling companions in the United States included not only wrestlers, but also a Kōdōkan judo specialist, Satake Nobushirō. Satake's presence testifies to a direct effort to take advantage of Western interest in judo to bolster the image of sumo as a sport.[110] Founded by Kanō Jigorō in 1882 as a modernized and "scientific" (in other words, sport-like) blend of various martial-arts techniques, Kōdōkan judo had gained an international following by the time of Hitachiyama's trip. Among its notable adherents was President Theodore Roosevelt, who is alleged to have called out the names of judo moves when he watched Hitachiyama wrestle in the East Room of the White House.[111]

Hitachiyama and his supporters had reportedly seen the trip as an opportunity to promote the "global spread of sumo."[112] Sumo historian Ikeda Masao has argued that the effort proved a complete failure, in part because many of the sumo performances consisted only of the *yokozuna* ring-entering ceremony, something that Hitachiyama seems to have regretted emphasizing.[113] Indeed, American press coverage focused a great deal on the spectacular aspects of sumo, including the great bulk of Hitachiyama, with often negative evaluations, and a number of articles deemed sumo inferior to Euro-American forms of wrestling (see Figure 1.3).[114] Nonetheless, Hitachiyama and his wrestlers brought an unprecedented degree of attention to sumo in the United States. American newspapers seemed more than willing to acknowledge it as a sport, and in many cases as the national sport of Japan, with many articles offering details about its history and rules. Hitachiyama's meetings with President Roosevelt, who deemed Hitachiyama a "splendid specimen of physical manhood," were landmark events in the history of sumo's international image and attracted widespread attention.[115] According to an article featured on the first page of the *Washington Post*, Roosevelt had high praise for sumo, declaring it the "most exciting and scientific sport he had ever witnessed."[116] The Japanese press, for its part, seized on these meetings, highlighting the President's positive response in papers and journals throughout the country. The inaugural issue of the adventure magazine *Bōken sekai*, for instance, included a detailed account of Hitachiyama's exhibition in the East Room, noting that the "eyes of all present were filled with awe" upon seeing Hitachiyama "whose body was like a human mountain."[117] Capturing the underlying concern of much of the Japanese coverage, the subtitle of a 15 December 1907 article in the *Fukuoka Nichinichi shinbun* about the White House performance offered readers "The American View of Japanese Sumo."[118] All the attention at home and abroad made Hitachiyama even more popular, and his encounter with President Roosevelt became one of the most enduring elements of his celebrity image.

SUMŌDŌ: HITACHIYAMA AND SUMO AS TRADITION

At the same time that Hitachiyama and others were reshaping sumo to make it more sport-like, they sought to elevate its status as tradition. Much as Yoshida Zenzaemon felt the need to alter sumo to make it appropriate for shogunal audiences during the Tokugawa period, the Meiji-era changes occurring in sumo can be seen as part of the perceived need to establish a level of dignity appropriate for an activity being redefined as the national sport. As exemplified by the early *kōenkai* clubs, the effort to restore the dignity of sumo and its wrestlers was linked in particular to *sumōdō*, a concept that gained currency during Hitachiyama's years as a wrestler.[119] Three interrelated aspects of the concept warrant closer examination because they are so closely connected to Hitachiyama and his stardom: first, *sumōdō* necessitated the appropriation of an acceptable history for sumo; second, it required the reclaiming of sumo's warrior

JAPAN'S "MOUNTAIN OF FAT AND MUSCLE" TO VISIT AMERICA

HITACHIYAMA, CHAMPION OF CHAMPIONS OF ALL WRESTLERS,

TO INITIATE THE WESTERN WORLD IN THE MYSTERIES OF "SUMO" AFTER THE SKILL OF THE SAMORAI

HITACHIYAMA JAPAN'S CHAMPION WRESTLER

Vineyard of Palo Prieto

Figure 1.3 Article in the *San Francisco Call* newspaper announcing Hitachiyama's planned visit to the United States in 1907. It includes several photographs of Hitachiyama and other famous wrestlers of the day, highlighting the wide variety of images available by this point. *San Francisco Call*, 25 August 1907, 7.

heritage; and last, it called for and produced significant changes in the lives and bodily habits of wrestlers themselves.

Appropriating an acceptable past for sumo was not new. Yoshida had done so in the Tokugawa era, and the Meiji period was a time when such appropriations were occurring in many areas of society.[120] In fact, references to sumo's ancient history during these years often relied on Yoshida's own constructed past to bolster their claims. Unlike the great mythmaker Yoshida, Hitachiyama's contribution lay not in the creation of a *new* past for sumo, but in his power to disseminate that history to a large and receptive audience. Over the course of his life, Hitachiyama produced several sumo-related texts, including media pieces explaining sumo's history, illustrated wrestling-technique manuals, and other types of guides for fans. The longest of Hitachiyama's works, *Sumō taikan*, was an encyclopedia of all things sumo, stretching far back into the ancient past.[121] The version of sumo history that it offered readers tracked the origins of sumo to the time of the gods and the emergence of Japan itself. The work appears to have involved a ghostwriter, and all references to sumo during Hitachiyama's own career were limited to an appendix by yet another author. Nevertheless, the star wrestler's "telling" of the well-worn sumo narratives surely added a new layer of appeal for fans. Hitachiyama proved especially successful at sharing this history abroad, since several stories in American papers detailed Hitachiyama's recounting of sumo's ancient past and its uniquely Japanese virtues.[122] The snowball effect of Hitachiyama's celebrity assured that accounts of the long history of sumo would reach a broader audience than they might have otherwise. Hitachiyama's actions in the United States also suggest that he embraced his role in proselytizing that history, which made him a particularly appealing candidate to send abroad as a representative of Japan's national sport.

Hitachiyama's explanations of sumo both at home and during his time abroad often emphasized one particular aspect of the sport's history: namely, its warrior heritage. It was a heritage that he also shared, as many articles pointed out to readers.[123] The rediscovery of sumo's warrior past parallels Japan's renewed popular interest in *bushidō*, the way of the warrior. Such interest reflected two larger changes occurring in Japanese society. For one, the turn to tradition was in part a reaction to the rapid and often overzealous modernization of the early Meiji period, which among other things had led to calls for the abolition of sumo. At the same time, the specific focus on samurai traditions exemplified efforts to solidify a national image grounded in military prowess. In this sense, Japanese victories in both the Sino-Japanese War and the Russo-Japanese War proved powerful catalysts for fostering nationalism and cultural pride. Japan's "surprise" victory over the Russians, in particular, led many in Japan and abroad to credit the nation's warrior spirit.

Ignoring the deep debt that sumo owed to Tokugawa-era commoner society, promoters of *sumōdō*, including founders of several *kōenkai* clubs and Hitachiyama himself, lamented sumo's decline from warriors' art to lowbrow entertainment. Secure in the knowledge that they already had a potential warrior "savior" in Hitachiyama, they argued that the sport needed to be saved, not just from foreigners, but from itself; it needed to be returned to its rightful place as an expression of *bushidō*, reclaimed from the commoner culture that had corrupted its values.[124] Who better to save it than a top wrestler who happened to have a warrior pedigree? In this sense, Hitachiyama's timing was ideal.

Although it went largely unnamed, the increasing popularity of baseball in the late 1890s, was another element driving efforts to reaffirm sumo's relationship with *bushidō*. By the time Hitachiyama and other sumo supporters began making their case, elite baseball enthusiasts at the top schools had already asserted their claim to the nation's warrior legacy.[125] To be sure, *bushidō* was a diverse and often ill-defined concept that could be evoked to serve sumo, baseball, and a host of other causes simultaneously. However, for devotees of sumo the prospect that another sport—perhaps especially one with foreign origins—might become an embodiment of Japan's samurai spirit must have been disconcerting. In such an environment, assumptions that sumo's history and native origins would assure its idealized standing simply would not suffice. The sport's warrior roots had to be excavated and the value and values of *sumōdō* had to be made apparent for all.

Hitachiyama's statements in the United States reveal an intertwined agenda of advocating the ideals of *sumōdō* and situating himself as a key figure in the sport. In an article whose subtitle declared him a "Member of the Samurai," Hitachiyama offered the following history of the sport to a *New York Times* reporter:

> The practice of Sumo, or wrestling . . . was indulged in by the Samurai prior to the introduction of the feudal system. . . . It was not until Tokugawa's feudal reign began that the Japanese began to take an interest in men endowed with extraordinary physical prowess. These men gradually came to be known as "Rikishi" or "Men of Strength," and adopted wrestling as their profession. The Daimyo, or chieftains of different clans, sought the services of these Rikishi, to whom they granted a liberal allowance and whose art they cherished. The practice of Sumo was thus fostered and rapidly attained prosperity and success. Wrestling afterward came to be a public amusement, but the Rikishi were still privileged to receive the treatment accorded to the military class, and were permitted to wear the two swords, which was the mark of the Samurai. This showed that wrestling was regarded as one of the knightly arts.[126]

References to the "knightly arts" here explicitly associated sumo with Nitobe Inazō's articulation of *bushidō* as Japan's form of chivalry. A clear example of invented tradition, Nitobe's English-language work, *Bushido: The Soul of Japan*, was first published in 1900, followed later by multiple editions and a Japanese translation. It achieved widespread popularity and counted among its notable readers Robert Baden-Powell, founder of the Boy Scouts, and President Theodore Roosevelt, who is said to have distributed additional copies to friends.[127] As if to confirm the link between Nitobe's samurai "knights" and sumo, when Hitachiyama first met Theodore Roosevelt, he gave the president a prized sword that the people of Mito had awarded him when he won a tournament. The *New York Times* explained, "Hitachiyama comes of Samurai blood, and it was entirely proper for him to possess such a beautiful and famous weapon," and apparently appropriate for him to give it away as well.[128] Hitachiyama's selective (though not necessarily inaccurate) history of sumo and his choice of gifts for the president reveal his efforts to promote a warrior-centered image of sumo, one that elevated the sport beyond its commoner roots, and one that made him, in particular, the ideal spokesman and representative of Japan's national sport.

The mobilization of *sumōdō* had its most direct impact on the overall self-presentation of wrestlers, who were to be the embodiment of sumo. Concerns about assuring the "dignity" (*hinkaku*) of wrestlers reflected Western-influenced notions about proper public conduct, especially for those who would be representing the nation. Such concerns also reflected older status distinctions that became all the more significant if sumo was to be appropriated as a national symbol representing Japan's idealized warrior past.

Once again, Hitachiyama stood at the very center of the effort to restore the dignity of wrestlers, in large part by changing their public appearance and behaviors. At Hitachiyama's urging in 1909, the Tokyo Sumo Association began requiring that wrestlers wear formal Japanese-style clothing—*hakama* and *haori*—whenever they were outside the sumo ring. According to Hitachiyama's *Sumō hisshō dokugakusho*, published during his tenure as head of the Sumo Association, such clothing was appropriate for wrestlers precisely because they "had been authorized to wear swords in the past," a reference to Tokugawa practices that granted *selected* wrestlers the right to wear swords like the samurai elite.[129] Katō Susumu's study of famous *yokozuna* links Hitachiyama to several other reforms, including a rule prohibiting wrestlers from blowing their noses through their fingers (*tebana*) while in the ring.[130] Hitachiyama also expressed concerns about wrestlers' hair. Whereas most adult Japanese males had discontinued older hairstyles during the 1870s, sometimes with official pressure, wrestlers had continued to preserve their distinctive topknot. Highlighting efforts to distinguish sumo from other popular entertainments, Hitachiyama complained in the magazine *Kabuki* that plays depicting wrestlers needed to give greater attention to proper sumo coiffure because "our *yagura otoshi* hair arrangement is different from the *tokoyama* style used in drama"; according to Hitachiyama, failure to properly tie up the hair made the wrestlers being portrayed appear "small and shabby."[131] In his view, apparently even someone playing the part of a wrestler had to do so in a manner that would not damage the image of the sport.

For those seeking to elevate the status of sumo, especially by connecting it with renewed societal interest and pride in Japan's samurai past, Hitachiyama's lineage made him an ideal figure. But it is also clear that Hitachiyama himself embraced the ideal of the warrior wrestler, mobilizing his family heritage in order to advance this vision of sumo. Hitachiyama's place at the center of efforts to promote *sumōdō* figured prominently in the creation of his celebrity image and reputation as the saint of sumo who allegedly saved the sport from its self-destructive ways. Significantly, Hitachiyama was aided in his attempts to promote his views about sumo by developments in the media, changes that must be taken into account to understand his emergence as a sports star.

Mass-Mediating Sumo

Aside from the sports themselves, no institution has played a larger role in the emergence of sports celebrities worldwide than the mass media. Japan is no exception, and many of the developments in sumo coverage paralleled changes occurring in media treatment of sports in other national settings. Yet it is crucial to see the emergence of sports reporting in Japan as more than an imitation of American or other Western forms. Attention to sumo in the Japanese media reflected both the particularities of sumo's past and the influences of a market-driven need to sell more newspapers, as well as more tickets. In more ways than one, sumo was big, serious business.

A NEW LOOK FOR THE MEIJI PRESS

Considering the wide distribution of woodblock images and other publications during the Tokugawa period, it is not surprising that by 1873 the recently emerged modern press in Japan was reaching a nationwide audience. Already by that point, major papers from Tokyo and Yokohama were being sent to every prefecture in the country. But by the 1890s the Meiji press had developed, in the words of James Huffman, a "new persona," as a nationwide, commercialized, popular press focused on news reporting. The change resulted from increasing urbanization and the establishment of improved communication and transportation networks, including trains, telegraph, mail services, and telephones.[132] The presence of multiple competing periodicals also forced even the most resistant editors to remake their papers to appeal to a broader public or face ruin.[133] Most importantly, changes in journalism reflected changes in readership, including a larger urbanized population that was also increasingly literate, helped in no small part by the establishment and spread of compulsory education beginning in the 1870s. Kuroiwa Ruikō, whose daily *Yorozu chōhō* sought to tap this emerging market, described such readers as "people who are busy, people who work in the daytime and pay their oil bills in the evening, people who need reading that is easy."[134] Sumo was one of the things these new readers wanted to read about.

SUMO COVERAGE

One direct manifestation of the new media attention was the emergence of several specialty magazines and papers, especially during Hitachiyama's lifetime. In 1882, for instance, Takasago Uragorō announced his plan to establish a periodical called *Sumō shinbun*, in response to what he perceived as the decline of sumo.[135] Several other, generally short-lived, sumo papers appeared over the following decades.[136] In 1912, the Sumō dōkō-kai began publishing *Sumō sekai*, which listed Hitachiyama among its consultants (*sōdan'yaku*). Its articles appear to have been aimed at sumo aficionados and included frequent reports and pictures of *kōenkai* among more general coverage of sumo and its wrestlers. In 1914, the newspaper *Kokugi* appeared with claims of promoting *sumōdō*. Providing detailed explanations of the Kokugikan, extensive reports about wrestlers, and general facts about the workings of sumo, *Kokugi*, while still aimed at specialists, offered a more general approach than its immediate predecessor.[137] These specialty journals and newspapers offered important outlets for disseminating sumo-related information and images to fans, and in this sense they played an important role in fostering sumo stardom. The pages of both *Sumō sekai* and *Kokugi*, for instance, were filled with images and accounts of wrestlers, with Hitachiyama, in particular, benefiting from a disproportionate amount of coverage. Such sumo-specific media were also forerunners of the established and long-running sumo magazines of today such as *Ōzumō* and *Sumō*. For the most part, however, early specialty journals and papers were short-lived and attracted only limited attention, especially when viewed in contrast to the mass audiences that sumo coverage in the newspapers was able to reach.

Among newspapers, increased attention to sumo was a key means of boosting circulation, just as sports coverage in the United States had been throughout the last decades of the nineteenth century.[138] This was especially true because sumo had become increasingly popular during the late 1880s, tied to the boom following Meiji Emperor's *tenran-zumō* in 1884 and the nationalistic backlash against overzealous efforts at Westernization. An article in the *Tōkyō Nichinichi shinbun* from 1889 makes it clear that at least for that newspaper, sumo coverage was aimed at more than sumo aficionados. The paper announced plans to replace "uninteresting" over-detailed descriptions of particular sumo techniques used in the matches—several examples of this previous form of coverage appear in the article—with simplified daily reports of winners and losers, since most followers of sumo "took delight only in the facts of wins or losses."[139] By the time Hitachiyama entered sumo in 1891, sumo coverage aimed at a broad readership was practically a given in most major newspapers, and because the majority of people were not able to attend tournaments with any regularity, if ever, the papers served as their primary source of information about the sport and its wrestlers.

Furthermore, as part of their promotion efforts, newspapers became frequent sponsors of sumo and eventually other sports as well. The presence of several journalists among the founding members of the various *kōenkai* attests to the mutual benefits that sumo and the press offered each other. Indeed, Kuroiwa's creation of the Banzai-kai in the spring of 1900 was almost certainly linked to his interest in boosting the sales of *Yorozu chōhō*. In January 1899, *Jiji shinpō*, a rival newspaper, had already awarded a *keshō-mawashi* apron to the wrestler with the best record at that month's tournament, and another rival paper, *Ōsaka Mainichi shinbun*, had done the same for the January 1900 tournament.[140]

To overtake or at least keep up with rivals, editors seized on sumo, and in the process innovated both sumo press coverage and the sport itself. In the end, the awards being offered by the papers produced the "kind of tournament champion that we now take for granted," since rewarding one wrestler necessitated the establishment of clear and quantifiable standards.[141] By 1909, when the *Jiji shinpō* newspaper began regularly awarding trophies to the wrestler with the best record, the new system of evaluating wrestlers' performances was firmly in place. Inadvertently, then, newspapers aided in remolding sumo to be more sport-like.

Much like sports reporting in the United States, in seeking to capitalize on the popularity of sumo, the papers also altered their coverage to be more appealing for fans. One such alteration was the creation of the *hoshitorihyō*, a kind of scorecard for sumo tournaments that allowed readers quick and easy summaries of the various bouts. The first of these appeared after a tournament in 1884, offering newspaper readers a summary of the entire tournament. During the tournament of May 1900, Kuroiwa's *Yorozu chōhō* began printing a daily *hoshitorihyō* that allowed readers to follow the tournament and the wrestlers day by day.[142] The rival paper *Niroku shinpō* was also offering, not coincidentally, daily sumo results by the time of this tournament. Notably, Hitachiyama finished second overall in this tournament and had already emerged as a dominant presence in the sport, and therefore in the press.

The appearance of the *hoshitorihyō* and other innovations in Japanese newspapers overlapped with transitions in sports coverage in the American press, including increased attention to football, the emergence of the baseball box score, and the rise of feature stories on particular athletes.[143] The simultaneity of these developments in American sports journalism and changes in sumo coverage serves as an important reminder that sports coverage in Japan involved more than just a delayed replication of Western methods.[144] Indeed, the evolving Meiji sumo journalism clearly built upon a number of preexisting practices, trends, and concerns, which were already apparent in Tokugawa-era attention to sumo and its wrestlers.

The publication of *banzuke* rankings in newspapers offers an excellent example of both continuities with, and changes from, well-established practices. In the lead-up to the January sumo tournament of 1889, *Jiji shinpō*, for instance, published the *banzuke* for the upcoming tournament alongside those from the previous one held in May 1888.[145] *Banzuke* were nothing new by this point, but two particular changes are worth noting. First, publication in *Jiji shinpō* (and other papers as well) dramatically increased the potential number of readers for these rankings compared to earlier means of distribution such as handbills or programs. Second, the juxtaposition of the two sets of rankings allowed—practically begged—readers to chart the rise and fall of particular wrestlers, creating a kind of graphic mini-narrative of success or failure. A similar *banzuke* published in the *Yomiuri shinbun* in 1900 featured another innovation by offering readers a narrative evaluation (*gaihyō*), or as the article explained, a "telling of the story about the new *banzuke*" (*shinbanzuke ni tsuite monogataru nari*).[146] Individual fans could have created such comparisons and narratives on their own, especially if they had both *banzuke*. Now, however, the newspapers did it for them, making it easier for more fans to keep track of their favorites and have the results interpreted for them as well.

FROM FREAK SHOW TO HUMAN-INTEREST STORY

Sumo coverage also translated long-standing "freak-show" interest in the daily lives and activities of wrestlers into human-interest stories. A story from the *Tōkyō Yokohama Mainichi shinbun* in 1884, for example, detailed how two men entered a restaurant and surprised the owner by devouring 50 bowls of mixed barley and rice and roughly 8.5 gallons (18 *shō* or 32 liters) of sake between them. The owner, as well as the readers, only learned at the end that the two men were wrestlers.[147] This story is but one example of the sensational scandal and daily-life accounts that became known as *sanmen kiji*—literally, "third-page articles," after the position where such stories typically appeared. By the 1890s, these kinds of human-interest and news stories, which were particularly appealing to the emerging new readership, had become the lifeblood of the major newspapers.[148]

It is not surprising, then, that stories about the lives and controversies of various wrestlers also became a staple of sumo reporting, especially for stars like Hitachiyama, whose fame seems to have generated attention exponentially. If this type of coverage built upon Tokugawa-era interest in—and taken-for-granted access to details about—wrestlers, it was also different in several ways. Here again, the mass audience that the newspapers reached was key. Although we have a great deal of information about wrestlers from the Tokugawa period, textual coverage of them was far more sporadic and less abundant than the stories appearing in daily papers, many of which also published evening editions. In other words, the new sumo coverage reflects the emergence of a truly mass media, which conveyed mass information to a mass audience. Even if some of the stories about wrestlers were little more than hearsay or gossip (as seems to have been the case in the *Tōkyō Yokohama Mainichi* article), their publication in the papers transformed them into "news," which, in turn, made them more influential in the production of celebrity images.

SEEING SUMO: EVOLVING VISUAL IMAGES

Visual depictions of sumo wrestlers, another legacy of Tokugawa-era sumo, remained a critical component of the new sumo media. Illustrations of sumo wrestlers figured prominently in several late Tokugawa-era *kawaraban* (news bulletins published as single monochrome broadsheets) that are often described as forerunners of Japan's modern newspapers.[149] However, until the advent in the mid-1870s of a more popular, more commercially oriented press, pioneered by the *Yomiuri shinbun*, Japanese newspapers, like their American counterparts, initially offered readers little in the way of pictures or illustrations.[150] Among the earliest visual depictions of sumo in the *Yomiuri* is an 1899 sketch of the crowd at the tournament, an image perhaps meant to convey to readers the popularity and excitement of the sporting event. Although no wrestlers are portrayed, the illustration appears above several brief articles about contemporary wrestlers, which are listed under the heading "Tales of Wrestlers."[151] Illustrations of two individual wrestlers appeared a year later in 1900. The first included two sketches of the former wrestler Takasago in connection with articles about his death in April; this was followed by an article a month later about the promotion of Umenotani (Hitachiyama's chief rival, who later changed his name to Umegatani Tōtarō) to the rank of *ōzeki*. Although woodblock prints had long depicted matches between wrestlers, it was not until after the turn of the century that illustrations featuring tournament bouts appear to have become a standard feature in newspapers. In 1902, the *Yomiuri* ran two sketches of matches from the first day of the May tournament. Around the same time, illustrations of tournament days also began appearing regularly in other papers, including *Jiji shinpō* and *Asahi shinbun*. The *Asahi* offered particularly detailed visual coverage, highlighting key matches with several series of three or four sequential sketches.[152]

A month before the appearance of the illustrations from the 1902 tournament, the *Yomiuri* Sunday supplement featured two action images of men engaged in "Western wrestling" (*seiyō sumō*). These visual depictions of Western wrestling techniques accompanied an article debating the role of "strength" in Japanese sumo, especially in relation to top wrestlers like Hitachiyama and Umegatani. The Western-style wrestlers appearing in this newspaper highlight one of the ways in which Euro-American notions of sports and body culture were introduced and circulated. Indeed, one of the first images related to sports in the *Yomiuri* was a first-page sketch of the Olympic Stadium and Crown Prince Constantine of Greece, who aided in organizing the first modern Olympic Games in 1896. The illustration appeared just above an article from the series "Tales of Wrestlers," which detailed the outcome of a tournament 23 years earlier.[153] These images of the Olympic Stadium, the crown prince, and the Western-style wrestlers serve as a reminder that readers had visual representations and access to information about Western sports from very early in the history of Japanese sports coverage.

Juxtaposed with sumo and later other forms of sports coverage, such images set up implicit comparisons between Western and Japanese sports and athletes. For example, the Western-style wrestlers depicted in 1902 are nameless, clothed from the waist down, and appear smaller and far less muscled than their sumo counterparts, whose images would have been familiar to many readers. We might say, then, that sumo and its large, well-muscled athletes emerge from this particular visual comparison as the superior of the two, which certainly would not always be the case for sumo or other Japanese sports. In the end, these nameless Western-style wrestlers and the comparisons and contrasts they evoked were most significant as precursors for a much wider variety of Western athletes who came to be featured regularly in the Japanese media, thereby helping to define the images of sports stars in Japan.

Two other developments in the visual representation of sumo demand particular attention: motion pictures and photographs. Motion-picture technology, in the form of Thomas Edison's Kinetoscope, first arrived in Japan in 1896, only two years after public viewings of the Kinetoscope began in the United States. Within a year, several other forms of cameras and projectors arrived in Japan and began offering shows to a curious public. Unlike the Kinetoscope, which only one person could use at a time, the new machines included some that allowed for a large viewing audience.[154]

Sports and recreational activities were among the earliest images captured and displayed using the new medium of film. One early exhibit of the Kinetoscope in 1897, which attracted members of the imperial family and the nobility, included the films "Scenes of School Exercises" and "Scenes of America's Largest Sea Bathing Site."[155] In 1900, viewers in Osaka, Kyoto, and Tokyo had the opportunity to see what were probably the first moving images of sumo, in Tsuchiya Tsuneji's footage of the summer sumo tournament.[156] Another film featuring Tokyo sumo ran at Osaka's Benten-za Theater in October 1907. Highlighting again the ready availability of overlapping images of Japanese and Western sports and athletes, only three months earlier in July 1907, another theater in Osaka had run Western films, including one depicting "Western sumo."[157] With increased popular interest in sumo during the early part of the century, it is likely that other sumo films besides those mentioned here were produced and shown, but documentation for such early motion pictures remains sketchy, as do details about their content. Both Tsuchiya's film and the other sumo film shown in Osaka appeared after tournaments that Hitachiyama missed, so it is entirely possible that he was not depicted. At some point prior to his retirement, Hitachiyama was filmed performing the *yokozuna* ring-entering ceremony, but information about distribution and showings of this film remains unclear.[158] Consequently, the role that such films may have played in fostering Hitachiyama's celebrity—or that his celebrity might have played in the promotion of these films—must be left to the realm of speculation.

Considering the indispensable roles that film and television footage have assumed in sports coverage in modern times, these sumo films appeared at a remarkably early point in the history of sports media worldwide. Like newspapers, films dramatically enlarged the potential audience of sumo. Even though hearing sports, both as part of films and via radio, would not come for years, by allowing people to see the sports, these early films conveyed a far more concrete sense of action and movement than the most well-written articles, sketches, or photographs could provide. Eventually motion-picture footage became an essential component of sports stardom in Japan as elsewhere. But because photos could be reproduced more easily, appeared with more regularity, and consequently reached a wider audience, for Hitachiyama and his contemporaries, it was photographic images that had the greatest impact on their celebrity.

The earliest photograph published in a Japanese paper, a picture of Mt. Bandai erupting, appeared in the *Yomiuri* in 1888. Technological difficulties made the inclusion of photographs in papers difficult until 1904, when the combination of new techniques and the need to cover the Russo-Japanese War motivated several newspapers to begin publishing photographs regularly.[159] The first sumo photograph in the *Yomiuri* was printed in 1906, a picture of the recently promoted *ōzeki* wrestler Komagatake, who was Hitachiyama's disciple (see Figure 1.4).[160] In the various newspaper clippings that the scrapbook collections of the archives of the Japan Sumo Association contain, photographs related to sumo begin appearing with regularity around 1906. Early pictures include shots of the crowds around the ring, stills of individual wrestlers or groups of wrestlers standing, a photograph of Hitachiyama's family, and a plethora of photos related to Hitachiyama's trip abroad in 1907.[161] No doubt because of technological and lighting issues, action shots of wrestlers actually engaged in wrestling were quite rare, with many papers relying on the use of artists' sketches for their visual depictions of matches.[162] By 1908, the scrapbooks reveal an abundance of sumo-related newspaper photos, although the number barely compares to the ubiquitous (and much higher quality) pictures appearing in sumo-specialty papers like *Sumō sekai* and *Kokugi* only a few years later. The latter often included

Figure 1.4 One of the earliest photographs of a sumo wrestler printed in the *Yomiuri shinbun* newspaper. It depicts Komagatake following his recent promotion to the rank of *ōzeki*. *Yomiuri shinbun*, 28 December 1906, 3. Courtesy of Yomiuri shinbunsha.

pictures of wrestlers engaged in traveling or other daily-life activities, shots of wrestlers' family members, photos of geisha, single or group portraits of *kōenkai* club members, and the occasional photograph of a female sumo wrestler. Souvenir photos were often featured in issues of these newspapers and later sports magazines as well. In many instances, the papers claimed to be the sole source for the picture in question, an obvious marketing technique that several Meiji-era newspapers employed to promote themselves.[163]

The "one-of-a-kind" photos appearing in sumo-specialty papers draw attention to the fact that, in addition to the photographs appearing in the press, there were a variety of other sumo-related images circulating in Japanese society. Perhaps because of longer preparation times and different formats, photographs of wrestlers began appearing in mainstream journals well before they did in newspapers. The journal *Taiyō* was featuring high-quality sumo pictures by the late 1890s, including several of Hitachiyama. Picture postcards of wrestlers offered another form of representation; one series of four cards offered views of Hitachiyama from the front, back, left, and right.[164] When Hitachiyama retired, both *Sumō sekai* and *Kokugi* ran extensive series about his life, including several pictures from throughout his childhood and wrestling career. Many of these same photos, or sketches clearly based on them, appeared again in the press upon Hitachiyama's death and continue to be used in biographies, sumo magazines, and other articles about Hitachiyama. The abundance of photographic attention that Hitachiyama received fueled, and was fueled by, his star status. In this sense, he was literally able to capitalize on new ways of being seen.

SUMO STRONGMEN

Because it highlights the intersection of old and new methods of representing the bodies of sumo wrestlers, one final observation about photographs bears mention. Looking at the 1906 *Yomiuri* photo of Komagatake and others as well, one cannot help noticing several differences with older images of wrestlers. The photo itself is dark and blurry, a fact that helps explain why similar pictures did not appear sooner and why action shots of tournament matches were generally not used in newspapers. Compared with older, brightly colored sumo woodblock prints, the decorative *keshō-mawashi* apron suffers especially from the photo's lack of color.

In the photograph, the wrestler Komagatake stands poised much like wrestlers in sumo woodblock prints, leaving one to wonder if wrestlers having their photos taken simply reenacted poses from prints. Despite the similar poses, the differences are telling. Unlike the wrestlers in prints who barely seem to fit the page, the Komagatake of the photograph appears dwarfed by the solid black background. He himself appears large and bulky, but it remains difficult to see any of the musculature of his arms or legs. The exaggerated muscles depicted in the earlier prints and even in the various newspaper sketches made it relatively easy to determine that a wrestler looked not only big but also strong. Thus, when combined with photography, the traditional poses may have reflected bulk, but they proved less effective in conveying a sense of strength to observers.

A potential solution to this problem was the adoption of new poses that could display the wrestlers' muscles more effectively. A series of photographs of the *yokuzuna* Tachiyama, one of Hitachiyama's rivals, published in *Kokugi* in 1914, offers examples of such poses (see Figures 1.5–1.9).[165] Here, in addition to a relaxed frontal shot where Tachiyama stands arms at his side, four other images depict him from the back, side, and front, assuming positions that require him to flex, thereby rendering his musculature far more visible than was the case in the earlier

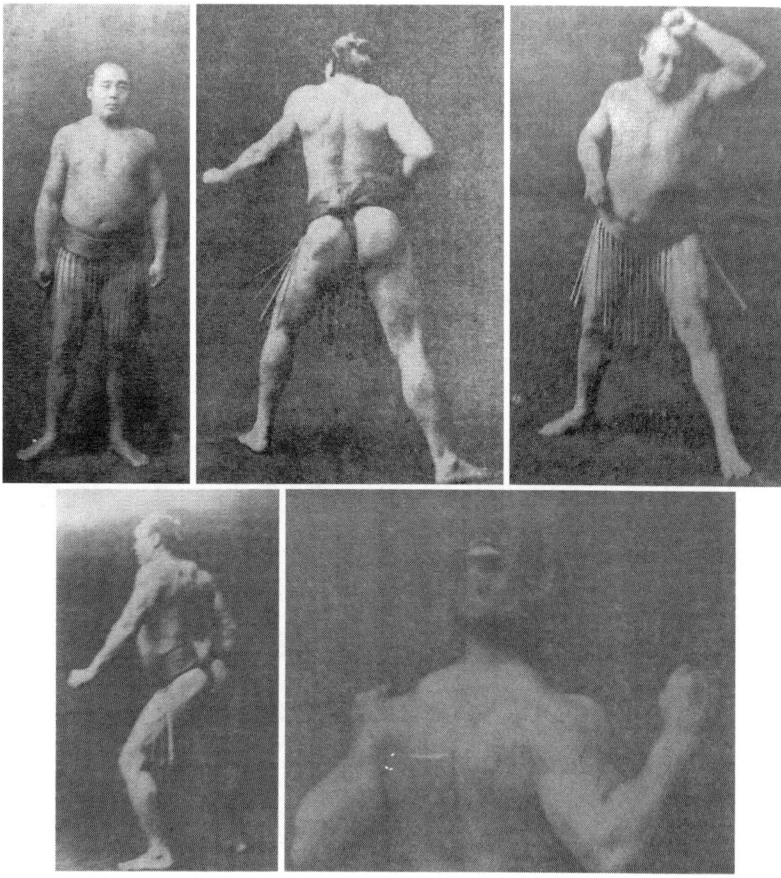

Figures 1.5–1.9 (clockwise, from upper left) Photographs of Tachiyama enacting several poses. These images appeared indivually in monthly issues of *Kokugi*. But all were published together in an article titled, "Tachiyama wa dore dake tsuyoi ka" (How strong is Tachiyama?), *Kokugi*, October 1914, 10. Courtesy of the Sumo Museum.

photograph of Komagatake. Featured in an article that debated how strong Tachiyama was in relation to historical wrestlers, the poses used by Tachiyama suggest the ways in which wrestlers and those depicting them sought to adapt to technological changes that inadvertently made it more difficult to convey the strength for which wrestlers had long been famed. After all, one of the most common Japanese words for sumo wrestler, *rikishi*, literally meant "a man of great strength." The new photographic poses are also strikingly similar to what might be called "strongman poses" of the type made famous by the vaudeville star and bodybuilder Eugene Sandow.

A contemporary of Tachiyama and Hitachiyama, Sandow reached the peak of his fame in Europe and the United States in the early 1900s, having developed a reputation as the "most perfectly developed human male ever to grace the earth."[166] Revealing changing Western attitudes about the nude athletic body—changes that may have helped make the former embarrassment of sumo wrestlers' nakedness less disturbing—Sandow became particularly famous for his poses recreating works of Greco-Roman art, in which he often wore little more than a fig leaf. Sandow's impact on views of the body was far-reaching. After establishing the highly popular *Sandow's Magazine of Physical Culture* in 1898, as well as a series of gymnasiums and fitness centers in Europe, Sandow traveled extensively to promote himself and his bodybuilding techniques, including a visit to Japan in 1905.[167] The roles of Sandow and other Euro-American strongmen as exemplars of the ideal physique may be seen in a Japanese medical expert's 1922 newspaper article on human strength and especially its relationship with sumo. A large photo above the essay displays an unidentified strongman (probably Sandow) resting his closed fist against his forehead in order to display his bulging bicep.[168]

Considering the continuation of more traditional poses for photos and other visual depictions of sumo tournament winners, including the large paintings that hang in stadiums today, it may be that these pictures of Tachiyama striking Sandow-esque, strongman poses are anomalies, taken and offered as special rewards for fans like those purchasing *Kokugi*. The photographs, however, do suggest the ways in which Western practices of viewing and displaying the body reinforced, or perhaps even directly shaped, similar practices in Japan. In this sense, they exemplify the broader evolution of Japanese media coverage of sports, where domestic traditions, practices, and concerns in Japan interacted with incoming international trends and ideas. Such interactions produced ways of talking about and depicting wrestlers that differed dramatically from Tokugawa-era practice and established key precedents for later sports coverage. Without this new media attention and the mass audience it reached, neither Hitachiyama nor any other sports star could have achieved this kind of celebrity status.

Conclusion: Hitachiyama, Japan's First Sports Star?

The present chapter has explored several ways in which Hitachiyama benefited from and took advantage of what the 7 June 1907 *Yomiuri* editorial called the "rich opportunities of the world he arrived in," to become one of Japan's first modern sports stars. When Hitachiyama became a sumo wrestler in 1891, he entered a sport with several well-established institutions, both popular and elite appeal, and a long line of celebrities. In this respect, sumo differed dramatically from such newly introduced sports as baseball, track and field, tennis, boxing, and the modern Olympic Games. One may cite, for instance, the case of baseball. It was only in 1903 that Waseda and Keiō universities instituted regularly scheduled games, forming the basis of what would later become the immensely popular six-university league. The sport did produce some early standout athletes, but none of these players generated the kind of attention that contemporary sumo stars did.[169] Without mass appeal and some form of regular, institutionalized competition, sports like baseball could not yet produce stars like Hitachiyama and his well-known wrestler contemporaries.

Despite its long history, sumo was not immune to changes, and the years preceding and overlapping with Hitachiyama's wrestling career witnessed a number of key transformations. The collapse of the Tokugawa order that had proven beneficial to sumo resulted in the loss of important forms of official patronage, sparking the need for new forms of support like imperial recognition and the organization of *kōenkai* clubs. Imperial patronage in the 1880s boosted the sport's reputation, so that it was already on the rise when Hitachiyama became a wrestler. The emergence of *kōenkai*, with which Hitachiyama was so closely tied, occurred later, at around the turn of the century.

Such patronage proved critical because the influx of Western understandings of sports and body culture, as well as Japan's initial modernization efforts, had threatened the very existence of sumo, which in the eyes of many was a barbaric relic of Japan's past. Although the danger of extinction had passed by the time of Hitachiyama's arrival in the 1890s, his reputation for "saving" sumo is linked to this threat and to consequent efforts to redefine sumo as a sport and elevate its status. Fueled as much by the need to keep attracting fans as it was by perceived challenges from the West, the sportification of sumo through rationalized rankings, increased quantification, and the awarding of championships, coincided with Hitachiyama's career, thereby contributing to his emergence as a sports celebrity. Hitachiyama not only benefited from such changes, but also made his own efforts to reshape global perceptions of sumo, as seen most clearly in his 1907 trip abroad. Because of his own samurai background, Hitachiyama gravitated toward movements to elevate sumo's status, especially by linking the sport to renewed enthusiasm about Japan's samurai past. Hitachiyama's preaching of sumo's history and warrior heritage at home and abroad and his efforts to regulate the bodily habits of wrestlers were both part of his broader effort to elevate the newly dubbed "national sport" by promoting the ideal of *sumōdō*.

Hitachiyama's success benefited to an extraordinary degree from timing, from his emergence just as mass-media networks were developing. Coverage in the emerging media—newspapers, specialty magazines, films, and a variety of visual depictions—built upon preexisting precedents and trends, but the new media also brought sumo and its wrestlers to a wider audience, on a more regular basis than had ever been the case before. Hitachiyama's ability to reach a truly mass audience—nationally and even internationally—is one of the primary factors that distinguishes him from his predecessors and is one of the ways in which Hitachiyama serves as a transitional figure in the history of sports celebrity in Japan.

As much as Hitachiyama benefited from being in the right place at the right time, he was not the only wrestler for whom this was the case. To understand why it was Hitachiyama and not one of his contemporaries who emerged as a dominant figure, we must look more closely at how his image was constructed. The next chapter considers the process by which Hitachiyama's life and career were turned into a "story," and how that story established key precedents for later sports stars.

TWO

The Making of a Self-Made Star: Celebrity Images and the Emergence of a Sports-Star Paradigm

He was more brilliant than the flowers and sharp as a splendid sword.
—Yokoyama Kendō, "Hitachiyama Taniemon"

By the early twentieth century, the rise of the mass media in Japan and abroad made an expanding range of individuals increasingly visible to the Japanese public.[1] While political, military, and social leaders garnered a large share of popular and media attention, so too, did athletes. In May 1903, for instance, Hitachiyama met his rival and fellow *ōzeki* Umegatani in a much-anticipated wrestling bout that, according to rumors, would determine who would become the next *yokozuna*. Covering roughly half a page, the detailed *Asahi* newspaper article about the Hitachiyama-Umegatani match-up offered readers four captioned sketches along with a map, which taken together, illustrated and charted the struggle of the wrestlers throughout the bout.[2] That the *Asahi* would give so much space to a single wrestling match (especially since other matches from the day were also well reported) indicates the significant place of sports and athletes in turn-of-the-century media coverage.

If sports coverage was already noteworthy, if not yet ubiquitous, it was also far from balanced. For a variety of reasons outlined in the previous chapter, sumo and its stars initially generated more press in the early twentieth century than other sports, though sumo's predominance would change dramatically as sports such as rugby, tennis, track and field, and especially baseball were successfully institutionalized and gained a national following. But even in early sumo coverage, certain wrestlers attracted disproportionate attention, reflecting tendencies still apparent in media coverage of sports stars today. Hitachiyama was the sumo "media darling" of his age and remained remarkably popular long after his death. Even when compared with other high-ranking wrestlers, such as his rival Umegatani, who might be expected to have attracted a similar degree of attention, Hitachiyama's appeal remains conspicuous. Time and again he was sought out—and after his death, invoked—to represent and speak for sumo in both the media and society more generally. Why was Hitachiyama so appealing? What made him stand out as one of the most memorable and lauded figures in the history of sumo?

In seeking to answer these questions, it is important to keep in mind that Hitachiyama's story is clouded with the kinds of myths and hagiography that one might expect to find in relation to a wrestler known as the "saint of sumo." Any attempt to uncover the true Hitachiyama, the "man behind the myth," proves fruitless, as almost all sources, including materials dating from his lifetime and his own writings, are the products of efforts to promote particular images of Hitachiyama, the sumo star. Like all sports celebrities, Hitachiyama was as much the product of socially constructed images and representations as he was a "real" person. The various images and representations of Hitachiyama, the factors involved in their production, and their impact serve as the primary focus of this chapter.

For Hitachiyama, the defining feature of his celebrity and key to his popular appeal was his reputation for greatness, an almost constant refrain both during and after his lifetime. Significantly, references to Hitachiyama's greatness reached far beyond the world of sumo specialists and fans, with biographies, children's stories, foreign-language media sources, and a variety of other texts picking up the theme. In this sense, Hitachiyama offers an example of how fame begets fame, a model case of Tyler Cowen's "snowball effects."[3]

Of course, advocates of Hitachiyama's greatness were not content to leave it at a simple assertion. Recurring evaluations of the origins and continuing basis of his fame almost invariably cited three things to justify claims of greatness: his achievements and skills as a wrestler, his excellent physique and strength, and his dignified character. Each of these three elements—skill, body, and character—and their centrality to Hitachiyama's celebrity image is examined below, with particular attention to the ways in which these aspects of Hitachiyama's image were mobilized in the interest of specific causes and agendas.

What tied all these elements together and made Hitachiyama appealing to so many people was the fact that Hitachiyama also made for a great *story*. Exploring the central role of narratives as a means of representing and interpreting Hitachiyama and sports stars more generally, I examine how the heroic, self-made-man narrative that came to define Hitachiyama was as much the product of societal concerns and trends in the production of biographical writings as it was an assessment of Hitachiyama's life and career. Since Hitachiyama was one of Japan's earliest sports stars, the narrative elements employed in crafting his story established important precedents, contributing to the emergence of what I call a sports-star paradigm that shaped—and continues to shape—how later sports celebrities would be viewed and told.

The Great Hitachiyama in Life and Death

In the introduction to his 1988 biography of Hitachiyama, sumo referee Shikimori Inosuke declares Hitachiyama one of the greatest sumo wrestlers of all time. To drive the point home, the two-page introduction, titled "Hitachiyama, a Great Wrestler I Respect," is replete with words and phrases meant to convey greatness—great wrestler, famous wrestler, outstanding wrestler, great man, competent, dignified, refined, pure Yamato man—to list just a few.[4] The theme of the introduction, that Hitachiyama was a great wrestler *and* a great man, is echoed throughout the rest of the book, including a chapter called "Hitachiyama's Death and His Greatness."[5] Concerned as much with proving Hitachiyama's greatness as it is with providing biographical facts, Shikimori's portrait of Hitachiyama easily falls into the category of hagiography. Yet even considering Shikimori's self-acknowledged respect for Hitachiyama and his close connections to sumo as a longtime referee, there is more at work in this glowing biography than the sycophantic musings of an overzealous fan. Shikimori's book reveals not only a great deal of careful research, but also a clear case of preaching to the choir, offering readers a view of the "saint of sumo" that would be as familiar as it was desirable.

Originally published as a twelve-part series of articles in the sumo editions of the magazine *Gurafu NHK*, Shikimori's account of Hitachiyama was aimed at an audience consisting primarily of sumo fans following coverage of professional sumo tournaments.[6] Using the title, "The Saint of Sumo, Hitachiyama Taniemon," the original series ran from March

1986 to July 1988, years that overlapped with the rise of Konishiki, the Samoan sumo wrestler from Hawai'i whose massive size helped propel him rapidly to the second-highest sumo rank of *ōzeki* in 1987. Combined with nostalgia for the "pure" sports of the "good old days," the threat of a foreign "meat bomb" (as some large, non-Japanese wrestlers came to be known) would have made for many willing converts to Shikimori's sermon on the great Hitachiyama. The emergence of a foreign wrestling star like Konishiki also helps explain Shikimori's otherwise out-of-place discussion of Hitachiyama's identity as a "pure Yamato man."[7] Moreover, when the book-length edition of Shikimori's series was released in 1988, its subtitle, *The Hometown "Saint of Sumo" Who Established Modern Sumo*, almost certainly reflected the marketing efforts of its publisher, a local press from Ibaraki, Hitachiyama's home prefecture. From the beginning, then, Shikimori's tale of the great Hitachiyama targeted a variety of readers who might have had special interest in and appreciation for Hitachiyama.

At the same time, Shikimori's account fell in line with a long-standing consensus about the wrestler's greatness. During his lifetime, Hitachiyama was a constant presence in press coverage of sumo. Even in the numerous instances where he did not compete in tournaments, various newspapers carried notes explaining his absence and commenting on the disappointment of fans. Given his status as a *yokozuna*, newspaper accounts understandably referred to him on a regular basis as a great wrestler (*dairikishi*) and frequently included details illustrating his popular appeal throughout Japan.

But in the opinion of many, Hitachiyama was more than an average *yokozuna*. Sakai Shōryō's work, *Gendai jinbutsu no kenkyū* (Study of contemporary figures, 1910), described him as a "perfect *yokozuna*" and perhaps the only wrestler in recent history on par with Tanikaze, the penultimate *yokozuna* of the Tokugawa era.[8] As Sakai's comparative assessments suggest, the star systems employed during Hitachiyama's lifetime were already crafting a celebrity image that defined the wrestler as one of the greatest in the history of sumo.

When Hitachiyama died in 1922, the press was filled with laudatory titles clearly meant to distinguish him from other wrestlers and *yokozuna*: "King of the Sumo World" (*sumōkoku no ōja*), "Champion of the Sumo Kingdom" (*sumō ōkoku no hasha*), or "Giant of the Sumo World" (*kakukai ni okeru kyojin*).[9] The unprecedented nature of the attention Hitachiyama received becomes apparent when compared with press coverage of the death in 1914 of the *yokozuna* Konishiki (after whom the Samoan wrestler was named). Announced with such straightforward titles as "Former Sixteenth Yokozuna Konishiki Dead," Konishiki's passing generated a number of articles and photos, but it was overshadowed by Hitachiyama's retirement as a wrestler during the same year. Unlike Konishiki, both Hitachiyama's retirement and his death led to the publication of long, multi-part biographical articles in several newspapers.[10] In Hitachiyama's case, death was only the beginning.

Offering a reminder that celebrity images often take on a life—and history—of their own, Hitachiyama's reputation for greatness was regularly evoked long after his own lifetime. In 1928, Yokoyama Kendō contributed an essay on Hitachiyama to what might best be described as a "past masters" book, which also included such writers, poets, and actors as Natsume Sōseki, Ozaki Kōyō, Matsuo Bashō, Masaoka Shiki, and Ichikawa Danjūrō. Writing six years after Hitachiyama's death, Yokoyama explained that Hitachiyama's fame was still such that even among those unfamiliar with sumo there were none who did not know his name. Waxing poetic, Yokoyama added, "Truly, for flowers there is the cherry blossom, for sumo there is Hitachiyama."[11]

Ten years later, in December 1938, Suzuki Hikojirō offered readers of the boys' magazine *Shōnen kurabu* a similar view of Hitachiyama. Suzuki's illustrated story used anecdotes from the early years of Hitachiyama's wrestling career to highlight aspects of his character—discipline, bravery, motivation, loyalty, and righteousness—and foreshadow his later greatness. At the end of his story Suzuki reminded young readers that Hitachiyama lived up to his earlier promises and became a *yokozuna* who was "truly without rival, and it is even said that there has yet to be such a strong *yokozuna*."[12] In 1941, Suzuki incorporated the short story into *Hitachiyama Taniemon*, one of several illustrated books on sumo that he wrote for young adults. Suzuki ended this collection of Hitachiyama tales by describing Hitachiyama as a "great wrestler of the Meiji era—nay, a famous *yokozuna* unparalleled in history."[13]

Hitachiyama's postmortem reputation for greatness also made its way into Japan's foreign-language press, as evidenced by the 1941 *Japan Times and Advertiser* article headlined "Hitachiyama Rated Greatest in Sumo," which featured the evaluations of sumo commentator Ikoma Kosho. This article coincided with the peak of fame of Futabayama, another *yokozuna* widely recognized as one of the all-time greats in sumo based on his record-setting winning streak of 69 consecutive bouts. Because it reflects general features of sports-celebrity images and encapsulates dominant elements found in most evaluations of Hitachiyama's greatness in relatively abbreviated form, the article bears quoting at some length:

Why was Hitachiyama so great? The commentator puts down his decision on the basis of Hitachiyama's strength and mastery in defying the "invincible" Tachiyama, second strongest, whose notorious art known as "teppo," or gun charge, was so formidable that no wrestler of those days could withstand it. Tachiyama, also grand champion, comes second. Umegatani II, another grand champion, and Futabayama, the present champion and center of popularity, are both third rank, judging from comments of most experts on the wrestling art.[14]

After examining the "invincible" Tachiyama in detail, the article returns to Hitachiyama, providing more evidence of his overall superiority:

Hitachiyama stood five feet seven and weighed 336 pounds. He had a splendid construction rarely excelled by any other wrestler and, when he went into the ring, there was something really attractive to the spectators. After overriding the ring for 16 years, Hitachiyama retired in 1913 to become the managing director of the wrestling association. In character and strength, he was second to none, and in this respect, he was the greatest wrestler in history. Tachiyama, the greatest rival of Hitachiyama, really admired the immeasurable strength of Hitachiyama and said that when Hitachiyama remained solid in the ring, an opponent would be exhausted when the former thrust his strong left arm under his opponent's right hand and grasped his waist band. The enemy, however strong, could hardly withstand his belly strength. Tanikaze, the first sumo grand champion before the Meiji Era, is venerated by the name "god of sumo," but even Tanikaze might not have been able to overmatch Hitachiyama. Generally speaking, Futabayama would not be an equal rival to Hitachiyama, Ikoma says, but the former might be able to defeat the latter by his skillful foot work.[15]

Resembling the "greatest moments in sports" television programs one might see today, the article offers a nostalgic view of sumo's greats. The evaluations and rankings of the wrestlers here are couched in terms of "elaborate study and careful scrutiny" by putative "experts," whose status as such gives their opinions greater weight than those of an average fan.[16] Yet on closer examination it appears that these experts (Ikoma being the only one mentioned by name) began with a predetermined pool of "great wrestlers" and then relied upon the wrestlers' reputations and popular images to formulate a series of essentially untestable comparisons and observations in order to "prove" what was already a widely held view by this point: Hitachiyama was the greatest. In other words, the experts used their research to give Hitachiyama's existing image their blessing, drawing from, and in the end reinforcing, Hitachiyama's popular reputation.

The article also offers an example of the composite and intertextual nature of Hitachiyama's celebrity. The English-language piece is based on another Japanese newspaper article, which relies on expert evaluations of predetermined great wrestlers.[17] On top of that, it is set against *yokozuna* Futabayama's shocking loss to a low-ranking wrestler in a sumo tournament only a few days earlier, a fact cited in introducing the discussion of the greatest wrestler of all time. In just this one instance, then, we can see multiple layers of representation and interpretation even before the readers had a chance to interpret the information for themselves. Moreover, considering that the newspaper's readership consisted largely of Americans and Europeans with their own cultural and historical biases about sumo and sports, the potential layers of representation and interpretation only multiplied.

Each of the layers in the text also depends to some extent on previous representations to convey meaning and significance. The reference to Hitachiyama's character as "second to none," for example, remains unexplained. The validity of such evidence and, by extension, the overall evaluation that Hitachiyama was the "greatest wrestler in history," assumed some previous understanding of Hitachiyama's character. Such assumptions were based, no doubt, on the prevalence of stories, like those told by Suzuki, that had long emphasized the alleged superiority of Hitachiyama's character.

With its comparisons and differentiations, the article also highlights the star systems inherent in the production and interpretation of Hitachiyama's image. In the end, Hitachiyama's status as the "greatest," according to expert opinion, comes from the fact that he was better than the second-greatest wrestler, his contemporary, the *yokozuna* Tachiyama. During and after Hitachiyama's lifetime, the rivalry between Tachiyama and Hitachiyama cited in the article has generally been viewed as secondary to Hitachiyama's rivalry with Umegatani, who was mentioned in the piece as the third-greatest wrestler. The heights of their careers are frequently referred to in accounts of sumo's history as the "Hitachi-Ume Age," while Tachiyama's glory days are associated with the years following the retirement of both Hitachiyama and Umegatani.

Other comparisons prove equally important for Hitachiyama. Demonstrating the temporally unbounded nature of star systems, the juxtaposition of Hitachiyama and the Tokugawa-era "god of sumo" *yokozuna* Tanikaze sets Hitachiyama up as one of the greatest wrestlers in the entire history of sumo. This comparison with a "god" also defines Hitachiyama as a foundational figure in the sport, someone who might be worthy of the nickname "saint."

The implied and unstated comparisons in the article are equally central to the construction of the image of Hitachiyama. They illustrate the three factors that dominate most evaluations of his greatness: his sumo abilities, his physique, and his character. In the context of Futabayama's humiliating loss, Hitachiyama's assumed superiority to Futabayama implies that he would never disappoint his fans in such a way, since only the skillful footwork of another great like Futabayama *might* be able to defeat him. Furthermore, Hitachiyama's physique, a "splendid construction rarely excelled," is indirectly opposed to that of Umegatani, who, as the article notes in closing, weighed the same as Hitachiyama, 336 pounds (152 kilograms), but at 5 feet 4 inches (163 centimeters) Umegatani stood three inches shorter, making him, in the view of the commentator Ikoma, "one of the most grotesque looking sumo champions."[18] Although Tachiyama was taller than Hitachiyama at 6 feet 2 inches (188 centimeters) he weighed a less impressive 296 pounds (134 kilograms).

Other unstated comparisons between Hitachiyama and Tachiyama prove more significant, especially since the article describes Tachiyama as a "terror to his opponents" and notes that his unbeatable "teppo" technique was eventually banned. In contrast to Tachiyama's use of "illegal" techniques, Hitachiyama's skill in the ring, the article suggests, is linked more closely to pure strength and more traditional techniques such as gripping the *mawashi* or waistband. His skillful use of such techniques allegedly led even his rival Tachiyama to admire him. Contrasted with Tachiyama, Hitachiyama comes across not only as superior for his ability to withstand Tachiyama's ethically questionable technique, but also as more sportsmanlike, a wrestler who was respected rather than feared. In other words, the implicit comparison exemplifies Hitachiyama's superior character, which according to the "careful scrutiny" of "experts on the wrestling art," made him the "greatest wrestler in history."

A Great Wrestler

Obviously not every person, not even every good athlete, can be a sports star. At least a certain degree of talent and recognized accomplishment is essential to garner public attention and respect for one's abilities as an athletic celebrity. By all accounts Hitachiyama was, indeed, a great wrestler. He entered the world of professional sumo in 1891 at the age of seventeen, when he joined the Dewanoumi sumo stable. At the time the stable was under the direction of the retired wrestler Hitachiyama Torakichi, who like Hitachiyama Taniemon was from Mito in Ibaraki prefecture.[19]

Accounts of what brought Hitachiyama to sumo vary. According to some, his uncle introduced him to the sport in Tokyo after Hitachiyama came to the city seeking to further his education. Other accounts, including one of the oldest biographical pieces on Hitachiyama dating from 1899, suggest that he first decided to join the sport while still a boy in Mito, when he witnessed the practice session of a group of traveling wrestlers.[20] This seemingly minor detail proves rather significant, since it raises questions about Hitachiyama's motives for coming to Tokyo in the first place. Did he come for the sake of his education and get sidetracked by a new-found passion, or did he come to pursue that passion from the beginning? In the end, his true motives can never be known for sure, but depending on the story one wanted to tell about Hitachiyama, the flexibility of such details proves advantageous.

In his biography of Hitachiyama, Shikimori makes note of both stories but gives preference to the story about the uncle, including the other version in a parenthetical as an alternate "theory."[21] Shikimori's Hitachiyama was unable to overcome his desire for learning after having to quit school in Mito because of his father's business failure and a household fire. For Shikimori it was only when Hitachiyama realized his true calling, with his uncle's help and urging, that he gave up his admirable original goal of furthering his education in Tokyo.[22] To suggest other-wise would make the "saint of sumo" appear uninterested in education or, worse still, appear to be using education as a pretext for pursuing ulterior motives. The episode contributes to Shikimori's overall portrait of Hitachiyama as not just a great wrestler, but a great, learned, and well-rounded man.

Yanagiwara Ryokufū's short story "Hitachiyama Taniemon" offers a slight variation on Hitachiyama's entry into sumo. Aimed at young adults, the story was published with several other didactic tales of great men in the multi-volume educational series *Shōnen shōjo kyōiku kōdan zenshū* (Collection of educational stories for boys and girls, 1931). In Yanagiwara's account, Hitachiyama proves a very poor student. He is driven to Tokyo not out of his own desire to learn, but as a filial act to satisfy his father's desire that his son improve himself through education. While in Tokyo Hitachiyama performs an amazing feat of strength one day and becomes convinced that he could be a famous *yokozuna*.[23] Hitachiyama's life here serves as a lesson both in filial piety and in using one's natural talents, hard work, and dedication to achieve the goals one has set. The particular emphases in Yanagiwara and Shikimori's accounts reflect not only different readerships but also different agendas, reminding us of the malleability of sports-celebrity images in general.

Although it remains unclear exactly how Hitachiyama came to sumo, records indicate that he made his first appearance as a professional wrestler only months after joining the Dewanoumi stable, wrestling in the 1891 May tournament in Tokyo under the name Onishiyama, a wrestling pseudonym that referenced his hometown of Mito. Over the course of the next several years he moved gradually up the lower ranks of sumo. In 1894, he took the name of his stable master, becoming Hitachiyama Taniemon.[24] While participating in a regional sumo tour in October of the following year, Hitachiyama left his stable in Tokyo to join Nagoya Sumo. At the time, sumo was not organized under one national governing body with uniform rankings and standards. Until the establishment of the All-Japan Sumo Association (predecessor to today's Japan Sumo Association) in the mid-1920s, separate sumo organizations existed around the country, including Nagoya, Kyoto, Osaka, and Tokyo. During Hitachiyama's time, Nagoya and Kyoto sumo served more like amateur feeder organizations for the larger and more prominent Osaka and Tokyo sumo groups.[25] In Nagoya, Hitachiyama rose to the highest official rank of *ōzeki*, but he left after a year to join Osaka Sumo beginning with the September tournament of 1896.[26] With the support of several new patrons he had met while away from Tokyo, Hitachiyama returned to his former stable, rejoining Tokyo Sumo in April 1897.

The specific reasons for Hitachiyama's flight to Nagoya and his activities over the course of his absence from Tokyo are unclear, leaving plenty of room for interpretation. Stories abound, including many that suggest he may have been on poor terms with his stable master, which seems a logical conclusion. Several explanations depict the master as an infamous drunk whose stable existed in little more than name; it supposedly had few wrestlers and lacked a practice area, thus forcing Hitachiyama to travel to another site for his practices.[27] Another account notes that Hitachiyama's troubles with his master were "related to women," an unexplained reference that may reflect other stories about Hitachiyama fathering more than 50 children with multiple women besides his three wives.[28] In a less racy version, a 1903 book on the lives of famous wrestlers cites a leg injury as the original cause of Hitachiyama's failure to return to Tokyo.[29] Sakura Tatsuzan's 1904 biography of Hitachiyama, which was published shortly after he became a *yokozuna*, lists only "inevitable circumstances" as the cause of Hitachiyama's departure from Tokyo and gives almost no details about time spent in Nagoya and Osaka.[30] Suzuki's short story in *Shōnen kurabu* suggests that Hitachiyama fled Tokyo Sumo because he was supposedly unable to overcome his shame after two successive tournaments where he had posted poor records.[31] Shikimori cites money issues as the primary reason that Hitachiyama left Tokyo, but is careful to point to sources that suggest that Hitachiyama was "by nature not greedy." According to Shikimori, the young wrestler ran into financial difficulty only because he had borrowed money to help out a colleague in trouble.[32] Shikimori's apparent need to defend Hitachiyama may stem from an 1899 account that depicts a youthful Hitachiyama who makes off with his stable master's money and is only able to return to Tokyo after a wealthy patron pays off the "debt" of several thousand yen.[33]

Whatever the actual reasons behind Hitachiyama's short absence from Tokyo Sumo may be, the accounts of this period in Hitachiyama's life prove significant for a number of reasons. For one, the variety of reasons itself suggests a certain unease with fitting this period into Hitachiyama's hagiography. After all, why would such a great and promising wrestler cut and run? In this sense, the diverse details also highlight the selective nature of biographical accounts, which in all of these instances were constructed retrospectively after Hitachiyama had already achieved success as a wrestler.[34] The vagueness of Hitachiyama's reasons for leaving allowed those telling his tale to choose, even create, whatever reasons they found appropriate or dismiss those they deemed unsuitable. Finally, although the various biographical portrayals disagree (in some cases dramatically) on the particular cause of Hitachiyama's flight, they all share an understanding that this period was fundamental for his later success, that Hitachiyama would not have been the great wrestler he became if he had not left Tokyo.

Indeed, the short absence from Tokyo Sumo appears in depictions of Hitachiyama as a critical period, especially in terms of physical development and the establishment of important social networks. According to Shikimori, Hitachiyama returned to Tokyo with such increased strength and size that he was like a different person.[35] Suzuki's account suggests one possible cause of the dramatic transformation. Humiliated and mocked by an unwholesome and generally unworthy opponent while away, Suzuki's Hitachiyama vowed to return to Tokyo, become a top-ranking wrestler, and then defeat this foe in the future. "Determined to do so," Suzuki contends, "Hitachiyama devoted himself to training with all his might and became stronger day by day."[36] Sakura's passing references to Hitachiyama's period of what he calls "wandering the provinces" reveal little about physical development, but suggest that these years helped make him famous throughout Japan, since it had been many years since those outside Tokyo were treated to such a promising wrestler. In this way, Sakura offered a veiled comparison of the young Hitachiyama to Tanikaze and Raiden, two Tokugawa-era sumo greats mentioned earlier in his text, who were similarly famous for their nationwide travels.[37]

It was also during this "wandering" period that Hitachiyama first met and established relationships with several powerful patrons. Hitachiyama allegedly swore bonds of brotherhood with the naval officers Yashiro Rokurō, who later became Minister of the Navy, and Hirose Takeo, who was deified as a national war hero following his death in the Russo-Japanese War.[38] He had also met Diet member Kushimoto Kōzō and the banker and business magnate Saburi Kumajirō, both of whom proved instrumental in Hitachiyama's return to Tokyo Sumo. In order to allow Hitachiyama to return to Tokyo unimpeded, Saburi in particular is said to have paid off several of Hitachiyama's debts.[39] In the end, the diverse accounts agree that Hitachiyama returned to Tokyo far more powerful in several ways, and it is this shared emphasis on the *necessity* of Hitachiyama's "wandering" period that allows it to fit within and become a key aspect of his image of greatness.

Although Hitachiyama is said to have achieved wrestling success in Osaka and Nagoya, on his return to Tokyo Sumo, with its different rankings, he had to start again from the bottom, beginning with the May 1897 tournament. By the following year, Hitachiyama had already attracted a loyal following, as evidenced by an article in the journal *Shin shōsetsu* complaining that the Sumo Association's strict adherence to rules about rankings was preventing Hitachiyama from wrestling the top-ranked wrestlers who were his true equals.[40] In January 1899, the bilingual mainstream journal *Seinen: The Rising Generation* included Hitachiyama among those it described as "front rank" wrestlers. Even though he only gained entry to sumo's top division (*makuuchi*) of wrestlers that same month, Hitachiyama merited the reporter's special attention: "The wrestler with the most brilliant record is Hitachiyama, who gained in the last spring match the *Jiji* [*shinpō*'s] ornamental apron for scoring the largest number of victories."[41] Hitachiyama continued his winning ways over the next few years, scoring impressive records in Tokyo Sumo's two annual tournaments. He moved rapidly up the rankings until he achieved the rank of *ōzeki* for the May tournament of 1901.

In the May 1903 tournament, Hitachiyama posted a perfect record, defeating his fellow *ōzeki*, Umegatani, in a much-anticipated bout on the ninth day. Over previous years, the two wrestlers, both of whom had moved quickly up the sumo ranks, had met on several occasions and held nearly equal records against each other. Rumors that the winner would be named the next *yokozuna* had fueled even more interest in the 1903 match. Press coverage, exemplified by the *Asahi shinbun* article described at the beginning of the chapter, was extensive and in some cases quite impressive in its comprehensiveness.

True to rumor, Hitachiyama was awarded the status of *yokozuna* following the tournament, but Umegatani also received this honor. The unusual joint promotion not only contributed to the wrestlers' celebrity images, but also proved to be a brilliant marketing move, since the already popular rivalry could now be billed as a battle of *yokozuna*. As it turned out, many of the two men's later bouts ended in ties or were not held because one or both of the wrestlers were absent. Despite that fact, Hitachi and Ume, as they were often called, counted among the biggest draws during regional tours of sumo, with people anxious to see the stars in action and in person. Their rivalry became one of the most storied in sumo history and made a lasting impression on popular memory, to the extent that a Diet member discussing a piece of finance legislation in 1956 could use the two wrestlers, without explanation, as a metaphor for intense competition.[42]

Hitachiyama remained active as a *yokozuna* until 1914, when he retired from wrestling. But even in retirement Hitachiyama came across as exceptional. After announcing his plans to leave the sumo ring for good, a four-day session of so-called retirement sumo was held at the Kokugikan. As press coverage from the time and Shikimori's later biography pointed out, originally the special series of matches had been planned for three days, which was already a day longer than the custom for an average *yokozuna*, but because of popular demand, an extra day was added.[43] The unprecedented nature of this event both reflected and further contributed to Hitachiyama's reputation as one of sumo's greatest wrestlers.

Over the course of his career, Hitachiyama's win-loss record in the sport's top division was an impressive 150-15, a figure that nonetheless proves misleading, since it does not include the number of bouts missed or the tied and undecided matches that were common in professional sumo at the time. Hitachiyama's career included 24 ties, mostly with fellow top-ranking wrestlers. With a staggering absentee rate of 40.9 percent, the vast majority of Hitachiyama's 131 missed bouts occurred following his promotion to *yokozuna*.[44] Commenting on Hitachiyama's high absentee rate in their examination of changes in quantifying sumo, Allen Guttmann and Lee Thompson note that it did not harm his reputation, adding parenthetically that it is unclear how many absences were the fault of his opponent, because at the time, both wrestlers received a mark of *yasumi*, or "out," in the record. Shikimori offers a similar observation, yet adds that we do not know how many such incidents were the result of opponents who failed to show up because they feared a match-up against Hitachiyama.[45] My own examinations of sumo press coverage from the time reveal that while we may not be able to tell if all of the *yasumi* constituted defaults on Hitachiyama's part, it cannot be denied that in the latter portion of his career he regularly failed to complete a full tournament, disappointing fans and even raising questions about his willingness to engage up-and-coming wrestlers who might defeat him in the ring. One especially daunting opponent was Tachiyama, the wrestler rated as the second best in the *Japan Times and Advertiser* article examined above. In numerical terms, other wrestlers before and since have posted similar or better records than Hitachiyama (including Futabayama, who continues to hold the record for the longest consecutive winning streak), but failed to garner equivalent levels of popular esteem. Considering such factors, it is clear that records alone do not make a sports star.

A Great Body

Drawing from his oft-cited theories on the modernization of sports, Guttmann and his coauthor Thompson have identified quantification and an obsession with records as defining features of modern sports in Japan and elsewhere. Yet with a focus on the "unsurpassed quantified *achievement*," the authors have missed another critical aspect of record-keeping in sports, one that raises fundamental questions about views of modernization: the obsession with facts and details related to the bodies of athletes.[46] It might be easy to take such information for granted or even to dismiss it as mere "facts" documented by modern, record-driven sports cultures. These "facts," however, play a central role in the production of celebrity images, and as the case of Hitachiyama illustrates, despite their ostensibly objective and often quantified nature, details about stars' bodies also prove malleable to the needs of particular causes and circumstances.

Hitachiyama's accomplishments as a wrestler were clearly critical elements of his fame, yet details about his size, his strength, and his general lifestyle were interwoven with accounts of his wrestling achievements. Rooted in earlier Tokugawa-era popular interest in wrestling celebrities, public attention to Hitachiyama's physical attributes and habits—as well as those of later stars—was not new. At the same time, references to Hitachiyama's body point to important changes, including wider availability through mass media, increased emphasis on science and medicine, and intensified governmental interest in the well-being of citizens. Descriptions of Hitachiyama offer a wealth of insights into body culture, or the variety of ways in which people use, think about, and shape their bodies, as well as the socio-cultural and historical factors that influence their bodily experiences.

The first hint that Hitachiyama's physical greatness is more than a simple matter of facts and measures is revealed in its projection backward to the years before he achieved fame, years that are open to a good deal of interpretation. Accounts of Hitachiyama often begin with details about his family, a samurai clan named Ichige, who for several generations had served the important Mito domain as instructors in a variety of military techniques. Born in either late 1873 or early 1874 as the first son of the household, Hitachiyama allegedly possessed exceptional features and build from birth, prompting his father to name him Tani, after a grandfather Taniemon who was famous for his size and strength.[47] As a child, Hitachiyama is said to have quickly surpassed others in these capacities, with some accounts suggesting that he achieved success in school-age amateur sumo, as well as in several martial arts. In the end, repeated tales of amazing feats of strength emerge as defining aspects of Hitachiyama's pre-sumo youth—a reflection, perhaps, of the lack of more objective measures of his size and strength from this early period.

The specifics surrounding such displays of strength vary, offering details of questionable accuracy. Yanagiwara's didactic short story includes an illustrated account of Hitachiyama visiting a shrine and returning the fallen top of a stone lantern to its proper position after four or five men together had been unable to budge it.[48] In a variant account, Hitachiyama's uncle tests the boy's abilities by having him lift several large rocks at Kameido Tenjin Shrine—first one of 165 pounds (75 kilograms), then one of 331 pounds (150 kilograms), and finally a huge rock of 496 pounds (225 kilograms)—all of which Hitachiyama lifted successfully to at least shoulder level.[49] A 1973 series of "factually based" biographical articles on Hitachiyama in *Sumō* magazine includes this story with the slightly more believable figures of 165 pounds (75 kilograms), 254 pounds (115 kilograms), and 413 pounds (187.5 kilograms). In another striking example of overlapping and interwoven layers of representation, this last article, by Ikeda Masao, indicates that after Hitachiyama became a famous *yokozuna*, a local official read about Hitachiyama's earlier feat in a newspaper article and had a plaque inlaid on the now famous rock at the shrine. The marker was destroyed in the war, but members of a local historical group had three stones in the shrine precincts engraved to mark Hitachiyama's famed achievement. The article includes a picture of the engraved stones.[50]

Despite the suspect claims of such accounts, they contain elements that might have rendered them "believable" for many people. The setting of the shrine and the emphasis on lifting heavy objects, and especially rocks, recalls the practice of *chikaraishi* (literally, "strength stone"), which reached its peak of popularity in the early 1800s, but continued at least into the 1920s. The practice varied from place to place, but almost always centered on a strong man's display of his power by lifting heavy stones, which themselves were referred to as *chikaraishi*. Most of the existing stones engraved with names, weights, or other markers designating them as *chikaraishi* are located at shrines or temples. The emergence of the practice as an organized competition is associated in particular with Tokyo, where a list recording the "Men of Strength in Edo" was compiled in 1836.[51] The Edo-Tokyo tradition of *chikaraishi*, together with the fact that Hitachiyama's feat of rock-lifting strength only became significant after he had already demonstrated his strength as a famous wrestler—exemplified by the marking of the stone at the shrine—helps explain why people might have been willing to suspend disbelief about this extraordinary achievement for a young boy. By implicitly situating Hitachiyama as a kind of record holder in a long line of *chikaraishi* practitioners, these stories employ a unique star system that adds further potency to Hitachiyama's reputation for boyhood strength.

Upon his entry into professional sumo, Hitachiyama became subject to another important tradition, the reporting of bodily measurements. At the time of his first sumo tournament, for instance, reports indicate that he was 5 feet 6 inches (170 centimeters) tall, but still relatively thin. This fact has led some to conclude that Hitachiyama was initially dependent on arm strength for wrestling.[52] In addition, the first of many photographs of Hitachiyama dates from around the time he joined sumo. Although he is far from petite, the youth of the early photo bears little resemblance to later pictures of Hitachiyama as *yokozuna*, and hardly appears the hulk one might expect in light of the *chikaraishi* tales (see Figure 2.1). The photo was reproduced frequently in various newspapers and magazines, especially in the weeks following Hitachiyama's retirement and his death. Evoking the image in this widely published photo, Yanagiwara's short story notes that when he entered sumo Hitachiyama "was

間に有り勝な病氣にかゝつて折角の機會を取り逃がすこともあるやうである。從來の教育法は其邊については殆んど自然の淘汰に任かして居るかの傾がある、部屋最負の外科專門の醫學士などは常陸山に向つても奨めもし、之が實行を試みようとして居らるゝ方もあるやうだから、之が實行さるゝ事になれば、有望力士と謳はれたものが中途に頓挫することを從來よりも餘程防禦し得らるゝだらうと考へる

▲力士の禮儀　それから從來の力士は禮儀とか德義とか云ふ事について無頓着なのを以て寧ろ普通性の如く考へても居り、世人も之を看過して居つた有樣であるが、

新弟子當時の常陸山

龜戸天神境内常陸山の力石（是を試して力士となる）

Figure 2.1 Photographs of Hitachiyama at the time he joined professional sumo and the large rock he is credited with lifting in the *chikaraishi* tales. In honor of Hitachiyama's retirement, *Kokugi* ran a multi-part series of biographical articles, which included several photographs depicting Hitachiyama at various stages in life. These images were the first set in that series. *Kokugi*, August 1914, 4. Courtesy of the Sumo Museum.

still thin in body, and not very strong, so master Dewanoumi could not have even imagined that he would become such a great wrestler."[53]

According to Sakura's biography, the soon-to-be stable master's first encounter with the young Hitachiyama resembled the work of a "physiognomist reading someone's fortune" or a "horse trader buying and selling a horse." Based on what he later heard from Hitachiyama's uncle, Sakura's telling replicated the stable master's objectification of Hitachiyama. The biographer offered long explanations of the stable master's careful inspection of Hitachiyama's hair, eyeballs, ears, nose, teeth, the joints in his fingers, arms, legs, shoulders, neck, ankles, toes—every part of Hitachiyama's body. Sakura suggested that the master's careful attention was necessary in order to determine whether Hitachiyama possessed the "various qualifications" that would allow him "to rise above the rest and become a distinguished wrestler." For Sakura, who wrote after Hitachiyama had proven himself by becoming a *yokozuna*, the episode and the stable master's delight with what he saw in Hitachiyama demonstrate, retrospectively, that Hitachiyama was destined for greatness, thanks in large part to his spectacular body.[54]

References to the early period of Hitachiyama's career not only track his improving sumo skills and his fairly rapid ascent to the top ranks, but also offer a parallel narrative of Hitachiyama's bodily development. Reflecting post-fame interest and interpretations, these narratives, like those related to his rank, are clearly teleological in their progression toward the known end point of Hitachiyama's large, yet well-proportioned physique. Nevertheless, several critical points along this predetermined course add drama to tales of Hitachiyama's physical growth. Shortly after he began wrestling, Hitachiyama is said to have succumbed to an illness that caused him to lose weight. He allegedly considered quitting sumo.[55] Of course, Hitachiyama recovered and even gained some recognition for his physique, being selected to serve as one of the special flag bearers representing the sumo wrestlers in ceremonies welcoming home victorious veterans of the Sino-Japanese War.[56] In most accounts, however, it was Hitachiyama's "wandering years" in Nagoya and Osaka that became the key period of transformation for his body, to the extent that even his acquaintances claimed to be surprised by his growth. As one friend observed, "In only two or three years time, he had developed a splendid physique, changed beyond recognition. . . . I heard rumors that he became stronger after going to Nagoya, but as strong as this!"[57]

Only a year after Hitachiyama's return to Tokyo Sumo, the specialty magazine *Sumō shinpō* ran an article praising Hitachiyama: "In terms of his physique, technique, and strength, he surpasses wrestlers of the senior *makuuchi* division and even those of the highest *san'yaku* ranks."[58] At this point Hitachiyama stood 5 feet 7 inches (171 centimeters) and weighed 240 pounds (109 kilograms). A year later in 1899, the journal *Seinen: The Rising Generation* noted that Hitachiyama had "gained in a year 2.870 *kwan* [23.8 pounds or 10.8 kilograms] in weight, and 27 kilo. [60 pounds] in grip." This article offered a wealth of data on sumo's top wrestlers, including the following facts about Hitachiyama: "age, 27; height, 5.70 *shaku* [5 feet 8 inches or 172.7 centimeters]; weight, 30.35 *kwan* [250.9 pounds or 113.8 kilograms]; chest, 3.76 *shaku* [3 feet 9 inches or 113.93 centimeters]; lung capacity, 6000 cub. centim. [366 cubic inches]; grip, 73 kilo. [161 pounds]; upper arm, 1.40 *shaku* [1 foot 5 inches or 42.4 centimeters]; chest expansion, 2.3 *sun* [2.7 inches or 6.97 centimeters]."[59]

Tokugawa-era depictions of wrestlers had often employed measurements of various sorts to convey the impressiveness of their bodies, but the details provided in the *Seinen* article reveal several key differences. For one, these same measurements were initially reported in the *Jiji shinpō* newspaper and subsequently republished in a variety of other media sources, so this information circulated widely, reaching a diverse audience.[60] In fact, an English-language wire service appears to have picked up some of the details from the original *Jiji shinpō* report, and several months later, multiple American papers republished them with notations that they were "Medical Record" stories. Highlighting the co-constitutional, as well as racialized, nature of sports celebrity, these articles begin, "Although the American is willing to concede to the Japanese the possession of a mental capacity almost, if not quite, equaling that of the majority of the white races, he is apt to form a somewhat slighting opinion of him as viewed from a physical standpoint, says the Medical Record." After providing detailed measurements of the wrestlers featured in the *Jiji shinpō* story, the American articles conclude, "There are few wrestlers or pugilists in this or any country who attain these dimensions, and those who have seen some of the best exponents of Japanese wrestling are willing to back them when pitted against the pick of the European or American experts, as it is said that they are as skillful as they are powerful."[61] As these articles suggest, Hitachiyama and his fellow wrestlers were reduced to a series of seemingly objective numbers, but those numbers could be interpreted in completely subjective ways.

Notations in the American articles designating them as "medical" stories point toward another significant change in representations of sumo wrestlers' bodies: increased emphasis on science and medicine. Although Tokugawa accounts had recorded the size of different body parts, especially hands and feet, the purely quantitative evaluation of something like "grip" was new, as were specific measurements for internal organs. References to lung capacity here assume, or perhaps even cultivate, a level of familiarity with human anatomy, as well as an understanding of the importance of lung capacity. These new types of highly specific measurements were not self-reported by wrestlers or journalists; as several of the articles note, the *Jiji shinpō* obtained them with the aid of a medical expert, a certain Dr. Okamoto, the director of Tokyo's Nihonbashi Hospital. Whatever Okamoto's role might have been, his title alone gave the information about the wrestlers added significance and legitimacy. In this sense, the *Seinen* article and others like it exhibit the influence of what historian Susan Burns has described as the "new regime of description and classification" that arose as Japan's public health system took shape in the late nineteenth century.[62] Although far from consistent in its approaches and outcomes, this new system fostered increasingly medicalized understandings of and approaches to the human body in Japanese society. As manifestations of popular interest, the widely publicized representations of wrestlers like Hitachiyama both reflected and helped to promote such changes in body culture.

Quantitative evaluations of Hitachiyama's body, and especially its development, were complemented, and in some ways rendered more concrete, by the availability of photographs from various stages in Hitachiyama's life. After he established his reputation as a wrestler, new pictures of Hitachiyama appeared regularly in the media, and several portraits from his early years as a wrestler were also in circulation during his lifetime. Biographical articles and stories at the time and since employed a wide range of photos. When Hitachiyama retired, for example, the monthly sumo paper *Kokugi* provided readers with a serialized biography, including several pictures from different periods (see Figures 2.2–2.6).[63] In addition to their nostalgic and marketing appeal, photos, especially when presented chronologically, told their own story, one of dramatic physical development. They allowed readers to see Hitachiyama's body transform and take its ultimate shape.

Attention to Hitachiyama's body was not limited to the growth of his belly and improvements in his "grip." Newspapers and other contemporary sources show a marked interest in his diet, his training, his clothing, his health, and other aspects of his personal life, especially after he became a *yokozuna*. As part of the lead-up to major tournaments, reporters for several papers regularly published commentaries detailing their visits to his workout sessions.[64] A sampling of articles included in just two of the many scrapbooks held at the archives of the Japan Sumo Association offers a sense of the popular interest in almost anything having to do with Hitachiyama. One volume includes an article with details about a stomach ailment affecting Hitachiyama, commenting in particular on its impact on his alcohol consumption. The same volume contains an illustrated piece describing and listing specific measurements for the clothing of Hitachiyama and the other two *yokozuna* of the time.[65] The first few pages of the next scrapbook include a description of a medical procedure to deal with the build-up of pus under the nail of Hitachiyama's

Figures 2.2 and 2.3 Second and third photos in the *Kokugi* biographical photo series. *Kokugi*, September 1914, 4; October 1914, 4. Courtesy of the Sumo Museum.

Figure 2.4 Additional portraits of Hitachiyama included with a biographical essay from a special retirement edition of *Kokugi*. These were not part of the photo series featured in later issues. The image of Hitachiyama in Western dress comes from his trip to the United States. *Kokugi*, June 1914, 3. Courtesy of the Sumo Museum.

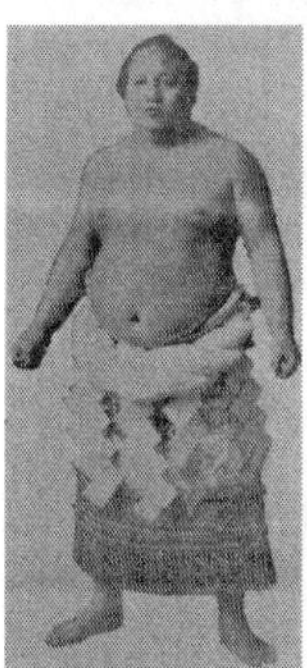

Figure 2.5 (left) Hitachiyama at his peak in the garb of a *yokozuna*. This image was included with several others in yet another *Kokugi* article addressing his retirement from the ring. *Kokugi*, January 1915, 8. Courtesy of the Sumo Museum.

Figure 2.6 (right) A souvenir photo included on the front page of a special retirement edition of *Kokugi*. It depicts Hitachiyama's ring-entering coterie. *Kokugi*, June 1914, 1. Courtesy of the Sumo Museum.

big toe on his left foot, as well as an article reporting that Hitachiyama had been receiving acupuncture treatments for his stomach for three days.[66]

The press was not alone in its documentation of such details. In his biography of Yashiro Rokurō, naval historian Ogasawara Naganari relates several stories of Yashiro's encounters with Hitachiyama as both patron and friend. He describes an incident at a restaurant in which Hitachiyama got stuck entering a restroom because the doorway was too small. Another account portrays Hitachiyama rapidly devouring two box lunches in less time than it took others traveling with him to finish just one.[67] The book *Rekidai yokozuna monogatari* (Tales of *yokozuna* through the ages, 1938) provides biographical entries and comparative analysis of all *yokozuna* to that point. Its chapter on Hitachiyama includes details about his fondness for alcohol, and especially imported whisky, which he allegedly drank from a stein, chugging it down as if it were beer.[68]

The popular fascination with details about Hitachiyama's body and bodily habits continued after his retirement and carried over to his death, resulting in an almost macabre obsession with the wrestler's guts, in the most literal sense. Following Hitachiyama's death, an autopsy was performed not so much to determine the cause of his demise, but because Hitachiyama had previously arranged to donate his body to doctors at Keiō University. The official cause of death was reported as heart failure stemming from the spread of an earlier infection that had started on his left foot.[69] Perhaps because the press had already been covering Hitachiyama's illness in excruciating detail for several days, few articles highlighted the official cause of death. Littered with medical and anatomical terminology, the coverage focused instead on plans for the autopsy—performed in Hitachiyama's home—and especially its findings about the unusual size of Hitachiyama's internal organs. Headlines proclaimed: "An Ideal Body," "Internal Organs All Great," "Organs Developed in Relation to Body," "Organs of a Giant," "Organs 1.5 Times the Average." Most if not all newspapers noted that the percentage of fat in Hitachiyama's body was unexpectedly low, that his heart was double the average size, and that his brain was average in size, but as one paper's subtitle put it, "especially superior."[70] One article reported that Hitachiyama's heart and several other organs would be placed on display at the Medical Department of Keiō University.[71] The autopsy and its results were even mentioned in remarks given by one of Hitachiyama's protégés at his funeral, where the results were evoked to prove the superiority of sumo in promoting physical fitness.[72]

Six years after his death, Hitachiyama's above-average heart became a character in its own right, appearing as a protagonist in a short story by Dr. Masaki Fujokyū. Published as part of a series of children's readers, Masaki's volume included several didactic stories meant to teach youngsters about physiology and hygiene. In "Hitachiyama's Heart," a young boy visits Keiō University, where his father, a doctor there, shows him Hitachiyama's extra-large heart on display. Later that night, as the boy sleeps, Hitachiyama's heart visits to teach him about the circulatory system and about what he needs to do to make sure that he, too, can develop a large, healthy heart. "The heart is the root of life," Hitachiyama's heart explains. The talking organ continues, "If your heart is weak, a long life is impossible. To make your heart strong, you must be sure to get enough exercise." Pointing to the poor, weak heart of a rich man, Hitachiyama's organ preaches the danger of eating too much food without proper exercise and warns about the effects of drinking too much alcohol.[73]

Featuring details about diet and physical fitness, as well as descriptions and labeled illustrations of the human circulatory system, Masaki's story exemplified ongoing efforts to promote public health and bodily awareness in Japanese society. It also points to the ways in which representations of sports stars can sometimes be amenable to the distinctive operations of modern governments, which seek not only to know their citizens in order to mobilize them most effectively, but also to have those citizens discipline and govern themselves. As Jennifer Smith Maguire has pointed out in her application of Michel Foucault's concept of governmentality to contemporary sports, physical culture serves as a key "governmental technology, mobilized to educate citizens in how to manage their own behaviour."[74] Though it was not itself a government publication, Masaki's story highlights the fact that images of sports stars could be usefully employed as a means of teaching people—perhaps especially children—how to live their lives in ways that would be beneficial for a governmentalized state. One need only consider the perennial (and usually contentious) discussions of sports stars as role models to realize that they and their images serve as critical, if indirect, "technologies" for managing modern society.

Masaki's short story drew specific lessons about health and wellness from the available knowledge about Hitachiyama's body, but even without such explicit connections, the overwhelming and invasive coverage of Hitachiyama helped foster a certain degree of bodily awareness and a sense of corporeal norms among readers. If nothing else, detailed descriptions of his "above-average" body parts raised questions about what "average" might be. I would further suggest that coverage of Hitachiyama and other sports stars held the potential for encouraging people to be more forthcoming with information about their own bodies and lives. When people know seemingly every detail about the lives of celebrities, everyday "invasions" into their own personal lives—military or school physicals, anonymous polls, dentists' questionnaires, life-insurance forms, magazine sex quizzes, drug tests, questions about height and weight at a driver's license office—become minor if not "normal." Sports stars alone do not create social and cultural norms, but they play a fundamental, though too often overlooked, role.

At the same time, it is important to recall that the production and consumption of star images operate according to their own systems of logic and allow for multiple, often contradictory, readings. Consequently, the relationship between sports stars and the goals of a governmentalized state are tenuous and fragile. Several well-known sumo wrestlers—and according to one account, even Hitachiyama himself—were deemed unfit for military service, a fact that made them less than ideal role models for a state interested in building a strong, healthy military.[75] Moreover, in Hitachiyama's case the restraint in eating and drinking preached in Masaki's story appears almost satirical when juxtaposed with other popular images of Hitachiyama, the whisky-chugging, ravenous eater. Hitachiyama's own life appears to have been cut short by what many suspect was an untreated case of diabetes. In some ways, then, Hitachiyama's image appears antithetical to what Foucault describes as the purpose of modern governmentality: "the welfare of the population, the improvement of its condition, the increase of its wealth, longevity, health."[76] The selective and intertextual nature of celebrity images allows figures like Hitachiyama to become both a role model and its antithesis, feasibly at the same time, depending on the agendas of those crafting and employing the image. Because they are always polysemic, open to varying interpretations and appropriation by groups and individuals, representations of stars also highlight the potential ways in which "governmental practice can be turned around into focuses of resistance."[77] The overabundance of "facts" about the bodies and lives of sports stars like Hitachiyama, then, prove far less objective and innocent than they might at first appear.

In all these somewhat quirky and at times conflicting details about Hitachiyama's body, there is a clear mixture of awe and admiration. Admiration for Hitachiyama's physique is a constant refrain in much of the material at the time and since. Even a self-professed non-fan declared in the magazine *Kokugi*, "More than his sumo, I love his physique," which he described using words like "spectacular," "flawless," and "ideal."[78] Hitachiyama's great size was also noted abroad. Although much of the press coverage of Hitachiyama's first trip overseas in 1907 focused—often critically—on his bulk, it is particularly striking to find references to Hitachiyama in a woman's account of her life on a rice plantation in South Carolina in the early 1900s. Referring to her encounter with a spider "too large to stand upon a silver dollar," Elizabeth Waties Allston Pringle, writing under the pseudonym Patience Pennington, continued, "I was most reluctant to kill him, for he was doubtless the Hitachiyama of his race."[79] Setting aside the somewhat disturbing comparison of Japanese people to spiders that might need to be exterminated, this seemingly random reference to Hitachiyama's size indicates just how significant this aspect of his image was at home and abroad.

For Hitachiyama, like his Tokugawa-era predecessors and many a sports star after him, his body and what he did with it were as important to his celebrity image as any of his athletic achievements. Yet looking comparatively at his fellow wrestlers, Hitachiyama's height and weight, a respectable 5 feet 8.5 inches (174 centimeters) and 324 pounds (147 kilograms) by the end of his career, do not place him on the top of the charts in either sense. His rivals at the time, Umegatani and Tachiyama, were, respectively, heavier and taller, but this fact did nothing to dampen the popular fascination with Hitachiyama's bodily greatness. And while there is perhaps something to be said for the appeal of his proportionality, we are left with the sense that there was more to Hitachiyama than weights and measures.

A Great Man

Descriptions of Hitachiyama invariably point not only to his status as an exceptional wrestler with a great body, but also to his prominent social standing outside the sumo ring. In the eyes of many, he was a great man, displaying noble character. Four overlapping factors lay at the center of this reputation: social status, connections, education, and legacy. In particular, Hitachiyama stood out among his fellow wrestlers as one of the first professional wrestlers from a former samurai family, and undoubtedly the first of such descent to achieve such a degree of success.

The uniqueness of Hitachiyama's social status was apparent from the beginning, or perhaps more accurately, from before his beginning. Descriptions of Hitachiyama's family lineage figure prominently in tales of his birth and childhood. In themselves, such details are not unusual; biography as a genre practically demands such knowledge, all the more so perhaps in a society influenced by Confucian notions of filial piety. We know, for instance, that his contemporary rival Umegatani was the son of a druggist, and that Tachiyama came from a peasant family.[80] But in Hitachiyama's case, both the length and the level of detail in descriptions of his family background add further notability to the already distinctive fact that he came from an elite lineage. Accounts of Hitachiyama's pre-sumo days frequently include information about his upbringing in not just any samurai family, but one that had a long tradition of service to Mito, a domain directly linked to the Tokugawa shogunate. Hitachiyama's background is further distinguished by the fact that his family acted as trainers and experts in a variety of military techniques. Both his father and uncle were reputedly well-known swordsmen, and his grandfather (or great-grandfather, depending on the account) was a famed archer, known in particular for the great size of his bow.[81] It seems clear from these accounts that Hitachiyama grew up immersed in samurai and especially martial traditions, a circumstance that writers often mentioned directly. Using this background, these biographical accounts, most of which were written after Hitachiyama had already distinguished himself, create the impression that it was predetermined that Hitachiyama would elevate the status of sumo by advocating *sumōdō*, the way of sumo, as a form of *bushidō*, the way of the warrior.

Yet Hitachiyama's reputation as the saint of sumo, as well as his appeal, lies as much in his seeming rejection of this heritage as it does in his embrace of it. It is commonly noted that Hitachiyama's family originally opposed his entry into professional sumo, but through the intercessions of his uncle or cousin (again depending on the account) he finally gained their acquiescence, if not support. Some stories even suggest that Hitachiyama's father had disowned him.[82] Explanations of such familial resistance often point to the fact that when Hitachiyama first sought to enter professional sumo, it was not yet regarded as a distinguished "national sport" (*kokugi*). Instead, sumo was more commonly seen as a kind of lower-class entertainment, and therefore, it was not deemed an appropriate way for the son of a distinguished samurai family to "rise in the world" (*shusse*).[83]

Deciding to pursue a career in sumo despite such resistance and negative attitudes proved significant to Hitachiyama's celebrity image for a couple of reasons. For one thing, it became emblematic of his character because it allowed biographers to depict him as responding to a "higher calling." In this vein, Hitachiyama's entry into the sport came to be portrayed not as the impetuous act of a rebellious young man, but rather as a carefully considered decision to forsake all else in order to do what needed to be done. One biographical account from 1903 suggests that Hitachiyama had already determined as a boy that sumo was more than mere entertainment: "Sumo was truly a matter of technique." At the same time, this account emphasizes Hitachiyama's desire to gain his parents' permission before he would even consider abandoning his studies to pursue a sumo career.[84] Similarly, Sakura's version from a year later highlights the difficulty of Hitachiyama's initial decision to become a wrestler, since it meant certain conflict with his family. In the end, Sakura contends, he could not but "proceed courageously" and become a wrestler, aided by the support of his ex-samurai uncle and aunt.[85] Sakura and others are quick to point out that sumo was not Hitachiyama's only option, that he was on track to enter college and become a political leader or civil servant. But his own family's response had indicated that sumo needed to be saved, and many of these accounts implied that it was Hitachiyama alone, because of his (potentially) great body and his samurai background, who could save it.[86] Hitachiyama's *choice* to enter sumo, then, becomes a necessary and noble sacrifice for a greater good, a sacrifice that foreshadowed—and is often interpreted and retold based upon—Hitachiyama's later reputation as the "saint of sumo," who saved sumo from itself.

Hitachiyama's decision to break with his family heritage and become a wrestler also proved critical to mobilizing fan support for himself and the sport more generally. His embrace of the commoner sport turned him into a "people's samurai" of sorts, boosting his own appeal while also eventually giving him and those who shared his ideals a chance to "educate" fans about what it meant to be a samurai or *bushi* (to use the more common Japanese word).[87] In his 1928 biographical essay, Yokoyama Kendō noted that Hitachiyama's appearance in the ring was often greeted with spontaneous shouts of "*bushi* in the ring!" or "*bushi* sumo!" According to Yokoyama, whether people saw him or only heard about him, they were left with a deep impression of Hitachiyama's *bushi*-like qualities.[88] A year later, Muramatsu Shōfū echoed this claim in a volume devoted to "true stories of hard work and great men," explaining that everyone commented that Hitachiyama "was not a wrestler; he was a true *bushi*."[89]

If Hitachiyama became the people's wrestling samurai, he could also be a particularly worthy champion of the elite, and especially of former samurai. After all, in supporting Hitachiyama, members of the elite were supporting one of their own, someone who presumably shared, or at least was said to have shared, their values. In this sense, Hitachiyama's family background, and especially his samurai roots, played a key role in his ability to establish powerful connections that contributed to his image as a great man. Even before he became closely associated with efforts to organize *kōenkai* patronage clubs, Hitachiyama was remarkably well connected, as exemplified by the support he received during his "wandering" period. It is not far fetched to suggest that Hitachiyama's social background helped ease the way in establishing relationships with military figures like Yashiro Rokurō and Hirose Takeo. Yashiro, in particular, became a lifelong devotee, assuming leading roles in both Hitachiyama's retirement ceremony and his funeral.

Hitachiyama's famous trip to the United States and Europe further highlights the ways in which social standing and connections opened doors for him, especially in view of the fact that Genjiyama's earlier attempt to travel abroad had been denied as potentially too embarrassing. Several years before Hitachiyama announced his plans to travel abroad in 1907, Prince Konoe Atsumaro, the leader of the Japanese House of Peers, had allegedly suggested such a trip, indicating his interest in taking Hitachiyama to the United States and Europe to show off his splendid body. Konoe died in early 1904, so the joint trip never occurred. Nevertheless, both American coverage of Hitachiyama's visit and biographers like Shikimori refer to this story, indicating that the initial impetus for Hitachiyama's travels lay in this powerful political figure's suggestion.[90] Whether or not that was the case, and whether or not the story itself is accurate, such accounts illuminate the fact that Hitachiyama was easily imagined as moving in elite circles.

There is also reason to suspect that Hitachiyama's later meeting with Theodore Roosevelt came about because of similar social connections. While visiting Japan in July 1905, Roosevelt's Secretary of War, William Howard Taft, and the president's daughter, Alice Roosevelt, saw Hitachiyama wrestle and met with him afterwards through the arrangements of former Prime Minister Itō Hirobumi and Army Minister Terauchi Masatake. After these exhibitions, Minister Terauchi is said to have invited the wrestler to his office and thanked him profusely. Various sources suggest that the wrestler, and especially his magnificent body, left a profound impact on Taft (who was himself famous for being large) and Alice Roosevelt, facilitating Hitachiyama's later meeting with President Roosevelt.[91]

Although such episodes point to the important role that elite social networks played for Hitachiyama, they also suggest ways in which these same elites and Hitachiyama himself sought to mobilize his image as a symbol of Japanese strength and masculinity. In proposing his joint trip, for example, Prince Konoe had allegedly declared, "Europeans and Americans tend to slight Japanese as a poor, weak-bodied race, but I would like to show them that Japanese, too, have men with magnificent bodies like *Hitachiyama*."[92] During Taft's visit, Japan was on the brink of agreeing to an armistice with Russia, and less than two months later, the Russo-Japanese War ended with a treaty mediated by Theodore Roosevelt. Japanese officials looked to demonstrate a position of strength during Taft's visit, and in this sense, it was no accident that Hitachiyama, a former samurai and a strong, amply bodied wrestler who was already being called one of the greatest in sumo's history, was introduced to Taft.[93] For Hitachiyama, meetings of this sort, with their implicit suggestion of foreign approval, only added to his already impressive list of acquaintances and accomplishments.

When it comes to connections that bolstered Hitachiyama's celebrity image, his meetings, conversations, and gift exchange with Roosevelt, a foreign head of state, prove difficult to top. Few Americans, let alone Japanese or their sports stars, could be said to have had a similar experience. Considering the unusual nature of Hitachiyama's encounters with the president, the degree of attention that they received in both the United States and Japan is hardly surprising. More importantly, this constantly evoked episode in Hitachiyama's life served as self-confirming evidence that Hitachiyama must be a man of noble character to have merited such a privilege. For Hitachiyama, the honor of meeting an American president was further enhanced by the fact it was Roosevelt whom he was meeting, a man widely hailed in Japan and elsewhere as an exemplar for young people.[94] To an extent, then, Hitachiyama's reputation for being a great man lay in the greatness of the company he kept.

Hitachiyama's reputed ability to move in elite circles at home and abroad was aided not only by his status as a former samurai, but also by a reputation for intelligence. As Muramatsu put it, sumo was a "world full of ignorant people with strength alone," where Hitachiyama was the "sole man of intellect," who also "had the bearing of a gentleman." Because of such qualities, Muramatsu claimed that Hitachiyama counted many intellectuals among his supporters.[95]

Whatever one makes of Muramatsu's assertions, Hitachiyama's desire for learning and the relatively high level of formal education that he received are critical elements of his image. In his biography of the wrestler, Sakura refers several times to the fact that Hitachiyama completed his fourth year of *chūtō gakkō*, the equivalent of a high-school education, and was poised to enter Keiō gijuku (today's Keiō University). Sakura also mentions a comment from Hitachiyama's soon-to-be stable master that in spite of his promising physique, Hitachiyama had the body of someone who "up till now has pursued studies diligently," and would need to train hard to become a wrestler.[96] Other accounts differ, omitting mention of Keiō and the stable master's comments and suggesting that Hitachiyama had actually been forced to quit school because of his family's financial situation.[97] Despite such variations, it is important to keep in mind that whether or not he graduated from *chūtō gakkō*, Hitachiyama's level of education did, in fact, place him among a significant minority. Between 1887 and 1891 an average of only 11,000 students were enrolled in such schools each year, so it is very likely that Hitachiyama was one of the most educated sumo wrestlers of the time.[98] In discussing Hitachiyama's educational background, the accounts by Sakura and many others give particular attention to Hitachiyama's passion for learning and his personal struggle to reach a decision about forgoing further studies. These texts further imply that he had intellectual abilities and a willingness to work hard that would have allowed him to achieve success in whatever field he chose. The point of such portrayals lies, once again, in Hitachiyama's choice to put his intelligence to use by serving (and saving) sumo. As one article published after his death noted, "Hitachiyama was not only a man of physical power, but of a certain grade of intellectual force, thanks to which the prestige [of sumo] was . . . enhanced."[99] With such a strong reputation for intelligence, little wonder that newspapers reporting on Hitachiyama's autopsy felt it necessary to add a qualifying comment about his "especially superior" brain, which unlike the rest of him was only average in size.

In addition to social status, elite connections, and education, Hitachiyama's image as a great man benefited from his contributions to sumo outside his primary role as a wrestler. As shown in the previous chapter, Hitachiyama's image played a fundamental role in movements to change perceptions of sumo, both at home and abroad. But many biographical accounts go a step farther, explicitly asserting that Hitachiyama *made* modern sumo—from the Kokugikan to *sumōdō*. Even the invention and popularization of the "traditional" sumo meal, a stew-like dish called *chanko nabe*, has been credited to Hitachiyama.[100] In these examples, sumo itself becomes Hitachiyama's legacy, a testament to his transformational power, for only a man who was truly great could have made such an impact.

Figure 2.7 A group photograph of all the members of Hitachiyama's stable at the time of his retirement. Hitachiyama is seated in the center of the front row. Hitachiyama's stable was known for being exceptionally large and successful. *Kokugi*, February 1915, 6. Courtesy of the Sumo Museum.

Hitachiyama's willingness and ability to transmit his values and ideals to future wrestlers as well as to those outside the sport further solidified his reputation. His books and travels helped convey what he and others felt was the true nature of sumo, and after retiring he assumed a leading role in the Sumo Association, which gave him a podium to disseminate and enforce his ideals. Hitachiyama was also famous as a trainer, and his stable became one of the most successful in the sport, producing several *ōzeki* and *yokozuna* (see Figure 2.7). The success of Hitachiyama's protégés, commonly attributed to his strict, "*bushi*-like" drilling of young wrestlers, also reflects the fact that Hitachiyama's success and reputation attracted the best young wrestlers, whose own eventual success was linked to Hitachiyama, thereby bolstering his image.[101] In the end, Hitachiyama's activities promoting and building the sport outside the sumo ring were just as important to his image as what he did in the ring as a wrestler, helping assure what Gladys Engel Lang and Kurt Lang have called the "durability of reputation."[102] Like the well-known artists analyzed by Lang and Lang, Hitachiyama had so many powerful friends within and outside the sumo world and had, in their minds, done so much for the sport that his reputation would be—perhaps had to be—protected, projected, and evoked well beyond his lifetime.

A Great Story

For those seeking to convey a sense of Hitachiyama's greatness that went beyond simply asserting the fact, anecdotes and stories were an especially important means of revealing the true character of the man. Hitachiyama himself commented on his life less than one might expect. Although he published several books, no autobiography was among them, and even his encyclopedic work *Sumō taikan* relegated all details about sumo during his lifetime to an appendix written by another person. Hitachiyama's references to himself, often appearing as quotes or interview responses, tended to focus on his sumo, his samurai heritage, or his connections with influential people.[103] But in many ways, Hitachiyama did not need to tell stories about himself; others were more than willing to do so.

Suzuki Hikojirō's children's book, for instance, was basically a series of anecdotes from different periods in Hitachiyama's life, stories that Suzuki hoped would allow readers "to see the whole man."[104] Hitachiyama's daughter, Matsuzawa Hanako, also occasionally wrote articles that promised readers an insider's view of her father. Her writings, which often compared her father and his times with the wrestlers active when she was writing, included stories about how Hitachiyama was extremely strict, if not abusive with his disciples, but generous and caring at the same time, handing spending money to the women of the household and giving candy and fruit to the neighborhood children who practically worshipped him.[105] According to other stories, Hitachiyama was so generous with women and children that he readily accepted financial responsibility when any woman showed up at his door claiming that a child was his. Without bothering to check on the accuracy of such claims, he allegedly acknowledged more than 50 children as his own, a detail omitted in many accounts, including those by his daughter.[106]

A more commonly cited anecdote evoked to convey Hitachiyama's generosity relates to his and Umegatani's promotion to *yokozuna* status. According to what Sakura calls a "heroic tale of the sumo world," the dual promotion was the work of Hitachiyama, who threatened to refuse the honor unless Umegatani was made a *yokozuna* at the same time.[107] Versions of this story were disseminated widely, including one with slightly different details that appeared in the *Yomiuri* newspaper.[108] Although these accounts achieved gospel-like status almost instantly, there is reason to suspect that Hitachiyama might not have been the only one pushing for a joint promotion. Ikeda suggests that leaders of the Sumo Association had been independently considering such a promotion themselves. Their interest in doing so seems logical, since a rivalry between two *yokozuna* held the promise of even greater popular attention—and money—for the sport as a whole.[109] Claims about his generosity aside, Hitachiyama also may have realized that a similarly ranked rival would be good for his own career. Whatever his motivation, it is clear that Hitachiyama's reputation benefited immeasurably from this episode, and all the more so with its constant retelling.

Stories like this one emphasized Hitachiyama's positive attributes, but others in circulation proved less complimentary, a fact that did not stop attempts to interpret them in ways that would benefit Hitachiyama's image. Whereas details about his 50-odd children could be seen as signs of a profligate lifestyle, accounts that mention this particular story use it instead to highlight not only Hitachiyama's generosity and sense of paternal responsibility, but also his virility and status as a sexually appealing "Casanova" (*inpukuka*).[110] Other stories suggest that Hitachiyama had a bad, and potentially violent, temper. A news article from 1910 reported that while seeing off a friend at a train station in Nagoya, Hitachiyama, who was intoxicated, became angry and struck a porter three times. Even though the injured porter filed assault charges, the facts in the article portray Hitachiyama's actions as almost justified: the porter had ignored Hitachiyama's request that he get a policeman to help his (presumably important) friend who had lost his ticket.[111] Hitachiyama may have lost his temper and momentarily forgotten his great strength, but apparently, he was just trying to be a good friend.

The sheer variety of anecdotes about Hitachiyama serves as a reminder that stories and narratives are a primary means for representing and imagining sports stars. Sports as a whole readily lend themselves to and rely upon narratives to convey meanings for both participants and spectators.[112] Background stories about athletes add suspense and interest to the drama inherent in sports, drama that stems from what anthropologist William Kelly has described as sport's "fragile balance of spontaneity and regulation"; sports are rule-bound and highly structured, but at the same time, "not knowing and not being able to predict the outcome of a sporting contest . . . fuels the participant and compels the spectator."[113] As media studies scholar Garry Whannel has observed, sports stars are the actors who make this drama unfold, and the consequent popular attention that they receive makes them both "the producer and the product" of multiple narratives.[114] In Hitachiyama's case, his wrestling career, his body, and his character not only provided the raw material for stories, but also were portrayed in and interpreted through a variety of stories.

In large part, then, Hitachiyama proved successful in attracting both media and popular attention because he provided subject matter that made for good stories. Whether it was his latest winning streak, a look into his extra-large kitchen, or his response to the death of his second wife, people were interested in writing, reading, and hearing about it, and they seem to have become ever more so as his fame grew. Such stories help people make sense of sports stars like Hitachiyama, explaining where they came from, suggesting where they are going, and revealing why they merit attention. Since most people have no access to the actual person, "reading" these star narratives, often by piecing together multiple representations, is the only way to "know" sports stars at all. The highly personal details provided about celebrity athletes foster a kind of intimacy, giving readers a sense that they are somehow involved in a celebrity's life, which in turn generates an apparent need to keep knowing, keep seeing details from that life. Like any good story, those about sports stars draw people in, capturing and maintaining their interest.

At the same time, narratives used to represent and interpret sports stars do more than simply tell about the stars and their exploits. They offer insights about the times and people who produced and consumed them. One feature of Hitachiyama's life story that proved especially revealing of societal expectations and concerns was its role as a potent tale of the self-made man.

The self-made-man narrative associated with Hitachiyama consisted of the following basic elements: first, the young Hitachiyama realized the nature of his gifts of size, strength, and character. Then, driven by the kind of ambition (and according to many accounts, intelligence) that brought him to Tokyo in the first place, he made his own way, even if that meant going against the wishes of his family, or later leaving his stable master. His decisions to do so—never made lightly—were necessary sacrifices in order to achieve personal success and pursue the noble cause of elevating the status of sumo. Next, through perseverance, strenuous effort, and character, he "worked" his way through the ranks to the top (not just once, but several times, when his years in Nagoya and Osaka are taken into account), and at the same time, he improved himself physically, visibly and undeniably achieving success. At this point, his earlier decisions and actions were validated both by this success and by his role in elevating, indeed, *saving*, sumo by imbuing the sport with the values he learned as a samurai son. In the end, Hitachiyama's accomplishments made him, somewhat paradoxically, a filial son, as suggested in accounts that depict his father "shedding tears of joy" after attending a sumo tournament and seeing the popular response and respect that his son received.[115]

As an exemplar of the self-made-man narrative, Hitachiyama's story was far from unique in Japanese society of the time. Marvin Marcus has detailed the rise of a "biography boom" that coincided with Hitachiyama's lifetime. Although only twenty or thirty original biographies were published between 1868 and 1888, the number jumped to over a thousand between 1888 and 1926.[116] Major publishing houses such as Min'yūsha and Hakubunkan played an especially significant role in this boom, with both houses publishing multivolume series on leading Western and Japanese figures. Several of these serial publications were aimed at young readers, including a didactic eight-volume series of both Japanese and Western *risshiden*, or success-story biographies, compiled by Kunikida Doppo in 1897.[117] Since Hitachiyama was only just emerging as a sumo star in the late 1890s, he would not have been included in these early biographical works. But they established key precedents for later works that would feature his tale in similar collections of *risshiden*, including several of the multivolume works cited above.[118] In addition to biographies produced by the publishing houses, newspapers and journals were also quick to pick up biography as a tool for attracting readers.[119] The mass-media interest in biography can be seen in the plethora of Hitachiyama biographies that appeared in newspapers and journals after his retirement and death.

To compile tales of famous figures such as Hitachiyama, biographers drew from and reinforced a number of precedents, models, and ideals. Shoichi Saeki has noted that many early biographies of "national heroes," especially military leaders involved in the Sino-Japanese and Russo-Japanese Wars, employed models of earlier samurai biographies, often explaining the accomplishments of these men "in terms of the *samurai* spirit." He also notes that "*Bushidō* was adopted as a favorite catchword by . . . many of the Meiji biographers."[120] Even though Hitachiyama never proved himself on the battlefield, tales about him made use of similar rhetorical strategies in highlighting his warrior heritage and its role in his (and sumo's) success. As a sumo wrestler, Hitachiyama's story also reflects elements of Tokugawa-era accounts and depictions of sumo stars, as seen in regular comparisons of Hitachiyama to sumo greats like Tanikaze and Raiden.

However, Hitachiyama's narrative of self-made success was perhaps most directly influenced by the Meiji-era ideal of *risshin shusse*, or rising in the world through hard work, perseverance, and character. Meiji usages of the terms *risshin* and *shusse* maintained several older connotations, including the notion that making a name for oneself and rising in the world was a demonstration of filial piety to family and ancestors, but transformations in Japanese society understandably resulted in dramatic changes in understandings of the concept of *risshin shusse*.[121] As an ideal, *risshin shusse* gained wide currency in the early years of Meiji thanks in no small part to Nakamura Keiu's translation of Samuel Smiles' book *Self-Help* (1859), a collection of didactic biographies extolling the rise of several ambitious Western men through perseverance and hard work. Nakamura's translation *Saikoku risshi hen* (1871) was immensely popular and influential in Japan, especially among former samurai and intellectuals, whose educations allowed them access to the complex text.[122] In his study of various *risshin* writings, historian Earl Kinmonth has noted that *Saikoku risshi hen* came to be known as a Meiji-era "holy book" (*seisho*) because of its popularity and influence.[123] Smiles' work, via Nakamura, had a profound impact on later biographical texts in Japan, as indicated by the commonly used term for stories of successful men, *risshiden*. By the time Hitachiyama's biographers were telling the story of his life, the *risshin shusse* ideal of striving for success in the world was already well on its way to becoming what historian Carol Gluck describes as one of the "unquestioned elements" of Japan's "common ideological language."[124] It is little wonder, then, that Hitachiyama's story exemplified key elements of this ideal.

At the same time, Hitachiyama's story of the self-made man reflected changes in interpretations of success since the early Meiji period. During this era, one of the critical factors determining a person's ability to rise in the world was education. Describing the value that both Hitachiyama and his father placed on getting him a proper education, many of the accounts reference this ideal, stressing that both men viewed education as pivotal to Hitachiyama's rising in the world.[125] Sakura explicitly links Hitachiyama's departure for Tokyo to further his education to *risshi*, pursuing his life goal and becoming a "man of even greater promise."[126]

As we know, however, Hitachiyama never continued with his formal education, and in this sense his story pointed to an alternate route for rising in the world, achieving success through sports. This route stood in contrast to earlier ideals, which had associated success with becoming a bureaucratic or military leader. Hitachiyama was emblematic of changes that occurred in the ideal of *risshin shusse* in the latter half of the Meiji-era, especially as opportunities for advancement of any kind became scarce.[127] In this context, late-Meiji accounts of *risshin* shifted their emphasis, implying that succeeding at anything was better than failure in the "proper"

Figure 2.8 Hitachiyama's newly constructed residence and training center. Descriptions of the complex emphasized its above-average size, hinting at both his influence and his wealth. *Kokugi*, December 1914, 10. Courtesy of the Sumo Museum.

pursuits.[128] At the same time, Hitachiyama's story conveyed the sense that even this newly conceptualized means of *risshin* allowed one to be a filial son, a notion that fit well with late-Meiji ideological efforts evoking "familial, communal, and customary verities of the past" as a check to the presumed dangers of too much individualized striving.[129] Similarly, the constant and repeated emphasis on Hitachiyama's samurai qualities was part of broader attempts to use a "modified *bushidō* . . . to stem the tide of materialism," an idea especially popular among those concerned that success was becoming too closely associated with achieving wealth.[130] In part, such anti-materialism helps explain the general lack of attention to the monetary benefits that Hitachiyama's sports stardom provided.[131] Aside from details about expensive habits like drinking imported whisky, which hint at a degree of wealth, few accounts indicate how much money he made from tournaments, patrons, or otherwise (see Figure 2.8).[132] In the prevailing narratives of Hitachiyama's life, the facts that he had risen in the world and proven himself a filial son were of far greater importance. In the minds of Sakura and many others who told his tale, this form of success was seemingly natural, the almost predetermined outcome of "Hitachiyama's extraordinary size and strength combined with his diligence and hard work."[133]

As an accomplished athlete, Hitachiyama was the one who practiced, molded his body, stepped into the sumo ring, and more often than not, emerged victorious. In spite of all his connections and other benefits, Hitachiyama's success was, to a great extent, undeniably his own. The telling of that success was not. In the end, the stories of his rise, which figured so prominently in his image, owed as much to existing—and widely appealing—biographical models and ideals as they did to his "real life." Hitachiyama's story offers a glimpse into the making of a self-made star.

Conclusion: Hitachiyama and the Emergence of a Sports-Star Paradigm

The sports-celebrity image of Hitachiyama that emerged in Japanese society around the turn of the century made him stand out among his fellow wrestlers, helping distinguish him as one of modern Japan's earliest sports stars. Looking at the ways in which Hitachiyama was portrayed, we can also see in the various elements of his image and his story an early manifestation of a sports-star paradigm, a dominant pattern shaping how sports stars are conceptualized, depicted, and interpreted. The three factors so often cited as proof of Hitachiyama's overall greatness—skill, physique, and character—and the self-made-man narratives that defined his life story are all critical elements of a sports-star paradigm.

In the context of sports, the importance given to athletic abilities is understandable, but as Hitachiyama demonstrates, for an athlete to become a sports star, natural-born talent is not enough for narrative purposes. Sports-star narratives place at least as much emphasis, if not more, on a willingness to hone that talent through dedication and hard practice. According to the narrative model, hard work, combined with inborn abilities, results in skills that far surpass fellow athletes, who by implication must not possess the same work ethic—even if that is not in fact the case.

As with Hitachiyama, the bodies of sports stars merit particular attention as another key to their athletic dominance. Heights, weights, training regimens, eating and sleeping habits, and even sexual activity—in short, everything about the athletes and their lifestyles—become relevant and necessary details for an admiring public to understand how and why sports stars achieve success. Stories of bodily development become especially important, and here, too, athletes must develop and mold their bodies, again, through hard work, in order to achieve their "peak." Like Hitachiyama, in conventional narratives the star eventually overcomes a host of perceived bodily inadequacies (Hitachiyama's initial "smallness," for instance) or infirmities (illnesses, injuries, or pain). The ability of sports stars to triumph over their own bodies is emblematic of their athletic dominance. When they prove no longer able to do so, they become the tragic victims of their bodies' inabilities to overcome an inevitable (though for sports stars, often accelerated) human decline. The manner in which a sports star deals with such a decline, especially by knowing when to step down and what to do after retiring, becomes a further indication of distinction.

Hitachiyama's reputation as a great man, like that of other sports stars after him, fed and was fed by his standing as a frequently evoked role model, especially for young people. In addition to values of perseverance and hard work, one of the features that makes sports stars such as Hitachiyama so attractive as role models is the image of devotion that they present, devotion to sports, to nation, and to family. Hitachiyama's effort during and after his wrestling career to train young wrestlers and to elevate sumo exemplifies the sense of personal commitment that sports stars must bring to sports, commitments that go beyond simply achieving their own success. Consequently, in paradigmatic narratives sports celebrities often actively seek to improve their teammates, their sport, and even sports in general. They also willingly and proudly represent their nation, as Hitachiyama did in his well-documented travels and meetings with foreign dignitaries. A sports star's desire to win honor for the country is represented as a primary motivating factor in the drive for success. Depictions of Hitachiyama that emphasize his heritage also illustrate the ways in which success in the sporting realm is portrayed as both consequence and demonstration of an athlete's devotion to family. Success in sports becomes the ultimate proof that a sports star is a filial child. It is not unusual to find the success of athletes in a society linked to their families. We might consider, for instance, the televised inspirational background stories on athletes at the Olympics. However, filial piety and the desire to be a filial child appear so explicitly and with such frequency in narrative accounts of Japanese sports stars that they seem to be almost prerequisites for sporting success and status as a celebrity.

This emphasis on demonstrating filial piety by achieving success figured prominently in the self-made-man narrative that came to define Hitachiyama. Similar narratives of rising in the world through one's own effort are at the very center of the sports-star paradigm. In many ways, it is these kinds of narratives that tie together the particular emphases on skills, bodies, and character, as well as the devotion, hard work, and perseverance necessary to develop these inborn assets to the point of success. For Hitachiyama, and even more so for later sports celebrities, these largely pre-formulated narratives have defined the ways in which stars were evaluated, portrayed, and understood. Still, today, these rhetorical patterns and models continue to dominate representations of sports stars.

The emergence of this sports-star paradigm in Japan beginning in the early twentieth century cannot, of course, be attributed solely to Hitachiyama or those involved in producing his celebrity image. Nevertheless, as an early Japanese sports star whose image resonated with his particular cultural and socio-historical contexts, Hitachiyama attracted widespread popular attention and media coverage and became a role model within and outside sumo. Considering the pioneering role of sumo coverage in Japan's sports media and Hitachiyama's role in that early coverage, his impact on perceptions of later sports stars was all the more pervasive. As the following chapters reveal, depictions of sports celebrities in the wake of Hitachiyama evolved and varied depending on the particular context, but they also maintained the core of the sports-star paradigm that Hitachiyama and his image makers helped put in place.

THREE

"So, Your Daughter Is a Sportsman": Gender Anxiety and Nationalism in the Golden Age of Sports

When I think back four or five years to the time when I began competing . . . I feel like I am living in a completely different age. Girls who participate in sports today are fortunate. When people hear someone say, "Our daughter runs and is going to participate in a meet," they don't call the girl a tomboy or hoyden; such activities have become common things. Instead, you'll hear, "So, your daughter is a sportsman!" We've entered an age when this is a mark of pride among neighbors, mothers, and sisters.

—Hitomi Kinue, "Track and Field"

Among sports fans, commentators, and scholars alike, the 1920s are often regarded as America's "golden age of sports," during which sports as a whole generated unprecedented and increasingly widespread media and popular attention. To a great extent, this booming interest in sports fueled, and was fueled by, the rise of such sporting legends as Jack Dempsey and Gene Tunney in boxing, Babe Ruth in baseball, Red Grange and Knute Rockne in football, Bill Tilden in tennis, Johnny Weissmuller in swimming, and even the famous race horse, Man o' War.[1] If Americans willingly threw themselves into what historian S. W. Pope has called "a popular love affair with the 'golden people of the golden decade,'" they were clearly not alone in doing so.[2] The pages of Japanese newspapers and magazines from this era are littered with depictions of American and

European sporting heroes, highlighting the pervasive global reach of sports and sports stars. During these years, it was not unusual to find Japanese coverage of major American sporting events, such as the World Series or the famous 1926 Dempsey-Tunney boxing match. Sports writers in Japan frequently mentioned names like Weissmuller or Tilden without bothering to explain who these people were, suggesting the extent to which such stars had become familiar to these writers and their readers.[3] Japanese papers and journals also commonly ran feature articles about specific athletes, including baseball stars like Babe Ruth and Ty Cobb, French tennis star Jean René Lacoste, and American decathlete and high jumper Harold Osborn.[4]

Foreign and especially Western sports stars generated a remarkable degree of coverage and interest in Japan, but the bulk of media attention focused on an ever-increasing number of Japanese sports stars, stars who were often directly compared to, and in several instances found to be superior to, their foreign counterparts. The roughly 25 years stretching from the mid-1910s to the late 1930s marked Japan's own golden age of sports, an era of critical development in the institutionalization and popularization of sports. In Japan, as elsewhere, such developments helped foster and were themselves bolstered by the emergence of athletes who achieved national and increasingly international success.

One of the most recognized athletes of Japan's golden age was Hitomi Kinue, a female track star whose athletic achievements both at home and abroad came to be seen as a stunning testament to how far Japanese sports had come in such a short time. Hitomi first attracted national attention in 1923, when she participated in her very first track competition at the age of sixteen and won the long jump by breaking the national record.[5] Until her death in 1931, Hitomi dominated women's track and field in Japan, establishing more than thirty national records in a variety of events. Coupled with her ascendancy at home, Hitomi's success in the realm of international competition helped make her even more famous. Dubbed "The World's Hitomi" (*sekai no Hitomi*), she set her first world record in 1924 and went on to establish several others.[6] In 1926, her performance at the second International Women's Games held in Sweden earned her the all-around individual championship title; two years later at the 1928 Amsterdam Olympics, she became the first Japanese woman to participate in the Olympics and the first to win a medal when she finished second in the 800-meter run. In addition to widespread popular and media attention in Japan, Hitomi's sporting achievements generated significant interest among international media outlets and resulted in numerous requests for her participation in international competitions.[7]

While Hitomi's athletic accomplishments were remarkable in themselves, her gender made them all the more important and noteworthy both at the time and since. As the first Japanese woman who competed successfully at an international level, Hitomi immediately assumed the status of a pioneer; she clearly saw herself as such and worked tirelessly to promote women's sports in Japan. During her lifetime and after, Hitomi was regularly credited with creating and increasing awareness about new opportunities available for female athletes.

At the same time, Hitomi's international achievements and her efforts to encourage more Japanese women to participate in sports initiated a strong undercurrent of concern and criticism. Stories and articles about Hitomi that proudly highlighted her accomplishments also frequently included descriptions of Hitomi's unfeminine appearance and actions. As a well-known sports star and prolific writer, Hitomi figured prominently in raging debates about the so-called "woman problem," a catchphrase for a host of concerns related to marriage, sexuality, work, politics, and shifting gender norms. Betraying anxieties about Japanese masculinity that underlay many of these concerns about women, accounts of Hitomi frequently compared her with Japanese male athletes, suggesting, often explicitly, that Hitomi was showing up her compatriot men who seemed unable to achieve a similar degree of international success. In this sense, Hitomi not only reflected, but also shaped the gender-related tensions and anxieties of her times. This chapter examines Hitomi's emergence as a sports star, focusing on two interrelated aspects of her celebrity that highlight her profound impact on gender relations: her role as an athlete and the controversies surrounding her life, death, and memory.

Hitomi Kinue and Japan's Golden Age of Sports

Before turning to an examination of Hitomi, it is useful to have a better sense of the sports scene in which she became one of Japan's biggest stars. Sumo and its stars dominated the attention of the media and the Japanese public until the mid-1910s, around the same time that Hitachiyama retired from active wrestling. In many ways, it was only at this point that other sports in Japan caught up to (and arguably overtook) sumo in terms of institutionalization and the ability to generate the mass appeal so critical for sports stars. Between 1915 and 1938, for example, a total of 25 national federations were established to provide centralized governance for a variety of sports, ranging from baseball and track to weight-lifting and table tennis.[8] Such institutionalization built upon and further promoted the establishment of extracurricular sports clubs in increasing numbers at schools throughout the country.[9] Baseball clubs, in particular, became widespread at all levels of the educational process, and an extremely popular college baseball league in Tokyo emerged in the 1910s, followed by multiple non-school leagues, including Japan's professional baseball league in the mid-1930s.[10] Japan's golden age of sports also saw important developments for female athletes, including the foundation in 1926 of a national federation to promote and oversee women's sports.[11]

It was also during these years that regular sports competitions became firmly established at local, regional, and national levels, offering increased visibility to Japanese athletes. The earliest national sporting events and their preliminary sub-national rounds emerged in the mid-1910s, when newspapers began sponsoring nationwide tournaments to boost circulation by capitalizing on the sports boom that they themselves were creating. In 1924, the government's Home Ministry established an officially sanctioned national sports tournament called the Meiji Shrine Games.[12] The creation of government-sponsored games reflected, in part, a reaction against such commercialized and popular events as the annual national middle-school baseball tournaments (precursors of today's famous "Kōshien" high-school baseball tournaments) first organized in 1915 by the *Asahi* newspaper company.[13] Women, too, had new opportunities for athletic competition. National "Women's Olympics" were held annually from 1924 to 1935, and women participated in the Meiji Shrine Games from their founding in 1924.[14]

The creation of mass events like these national tournaments and the crowds they attracted encouraged the construction of a number of Japan's most famous, and for their time massive, sporting facilities, including the sprawling Meiji Shrine athletic complex in Tokyo and the famed Kōshien baseball stadium in Hyōgo prefecture.[15] In addition to these large sports venues, radio broadcasts that began in the late 1920s dramatically expanded the size of the audience who could follow events and athletes more immediately than ever before.[16]

Many, if not all, of these domestic developments were intimately connected with the performance of Japanese athletes internationally, especially after Japan began participating in the Olympic Games in 1912 and the YMCA-sponsored Far Eastern Championship Games in 1913.[17] Initially, poor showings abroad led sports enthusiasts and public officials to call for increased preparation, institutional support, and funding. Changes and advances in Japan's domestic sports system, then, were part and parcel of efforts to develop athletes who could compete—and win—at an international level.

Such efforts proved effective, generating a number of athletic successes in international competition during the 1920s and 1930s. During these years, several Japanese male tennis players were among the top-ranked internationally, and the Japanese national tennis team regularly advanced to the highest levels of the international Davis Cup competition.[18] Male and female swimmers won several competitions abroad, especially during the 1932 Olympics in Los Angeles, where the Japanese men's team emerged as a swimming powerhouse, setting several records and winning eleven of sixteen possible medals.[19] As Hitomi's fame indicates, Japan also produced a number of international stars in track and field. In 2000, the Asian Amateur Athletic Association published its rankings of the top Asian track stars of the century, naming three Japanese men and one woman, Hitomi Kinue, to their lists of the top five male and top five female athletes from Asia. Unlike the athletes from other Asian countries, all four of the Japanese stars had been active before World War II.[20]

Japan's international successes in sports generated mixed reactions. From the moment that Western sports were introduced to Japan and other non-Western societies, they had been characterized as universal and necessary elements of modern societies, despite the fact that they were clearly based on Euro-American forms of athletic skill and competition that differed from traditional physical practices found elsewhere. The international achievements of Japanese athletes earned Japan begrudging international recognition, exemplified perhaps most clearly by the contentious decision to allow Japan to host the 1940 Olympic Games in Tokyo, in what would have been the first games outside Europe or America.[21] From the perspective of Western nations, Japanese sporting success and interest in events like the Olympics came to be seen as proof that sports really were universal.

There was, however, much more to the success of Japanese athletes than the natural outcome of the inherent competitiveness and assumed universality of sports. It might be more accurate to see this as a consequence of cultural imperialism that left non-Western athletes two options: athletes could pursue native forms of physical culture and be deemed inferior (or "uncivilized") no matter how much success they achieved, or they could compete according to "universal" standards and hope to overcome their initial disadvantages to demonstrate that they were not inferior by beating the Western athletes at their own game.

In this context, the success of Japanese athletes was a form of resistance, an appropriation of a dominant culture's methods and techniques as a means of challenging that dominance.[22]

But the cultural imperialism of sports involved a co-constitutional relationship where *both* sides defined themselves in opposition to each other. While athletic competitions and successes served as a kind of resistance for Japanese stars, Western athletes and their followers relied on their dominance in sports to define themselves and especially to justify claims of their overall superiority. At the same time, Japan's assertions that Tokyo was the "sports center of the Orient" serve as an important reminder that Japanese, in turn, sought to use athletic success to distinguish themselves from other Asians.[23] Based, as they were, on assumptions about the inferiority and substandard abilities of non-Western, or in some cases non-Japanese athletes, such co-constitutional relationships were inherently unequal and highly unstable.

Consequently, as one of the first non-Western societies to achieve success in sports, Japan may have offered proof of sports' universality and earned a degree of recognition, but it also posed a threat. Though Euro-American athletes continued to hold clear advantages in international competition before World War II, the emerging Japanese stars sparked concerns about a "yellow peril in sports," a fear that Japanese athletes were uniquely unified and driven in their "quest to 'do the rest of the world one better.'"[24] As historian David Welky has noted in his analysis of American press coverage of the 1932 Olympics, the international success of Japanese athletes transformed Japan into more than a fellow Olympic competitor. For America it became a "'menace,' and the country's 'most dangerous rival,' one that threatened to disrupt our very 'peace of mind.'"[25] The anxiety directed at Japan proves all the more revealing considering the fact that Japan's total medal count of 18 for the 1932 Summer Games placed it behind France, Germany, Sweden, Finland, Italy, and the United States, with American athletes alone taking 103 medals—nearly a third of those possible—yet none of these European countries generated the same sense of fear in the American press.[26] To ease and even counter this sense of eminent danger from the Japanese athletes, media coverage in the United States often resorted to exoticizing and trivializing them. Oriental mysticism was portrayed as a key to the success of the Japanese athletes, while repeated references to their small size made them appear less dangerous, if not outright pathetic and worthy of American sympathy. Revealing the racialized nature of such attention, several stories demeaningly dubbed the Japanese competitors "little brown men."[27] Although Japan's aggressive, imperialistic actions toward Manchuria before the 1932 Olympics almost certainly influenced American views, the perceived Japanese athletic threat in this case was not new. In 1913, for example, an article announcing that a Japanese university had invited the University of Washington baseball team for an all-expenses paid trip to Japan bore the racially loaded headline, "The Yellow Peril Again."[28] Whether intended seriously or not, the headline betrayed widespread anxieties about Japan's rising interest and increasing success in sports.

Within Japan, foreign references to a "yellow peril in sports" were a badge of honor. Commenting on one such reference from a European newspaper, an article from the monthly *Taiyō* explained that the notion of yellow peril suggested that the West "feared and admired Japan's astonishing progress in such a short period of time; it is not altogether an unreasonable phenomenon."[29] Nevertheless, writing in 1927, Hashido Makoto, the author of the *Taiyō* article, felt that even though Japan had produced several world-class athletes, the country still had a long way to go before it could truly threaten the dominance of the United States in sports; doing so, Hashido suggested, should be the aim of Japan's next generation of athletes.[30]

With her impressive international victories and record-setting performances, Hitomi Kinue epitomized the kind of athlete who fed both Japanese and Western notions of a yellow peril in sports during Japan's golden age. Such issues worked to Hitomi's advantage by bringing even greater attention to her accomplishments. At the same time, Hitomi benefited from the achievements of other Japanese athletes. Accounts of Hitomi's athletic career, for instance, often highlight the fact that her emergence as a track star coincided with increasing popular interest in track and field generated by Oda Mikio's sixth-place finish at the 1924 Paris Olympics.[31] Oda, who went on to win a gold medal at the 1928 Olympics; a handful of other successful male track stars; and eventually Hitomi all boosted the popularity of track and field in Japan, thereby attracting greater awareness and appreciation of their achievements.

Hitomi also benefited from institutional changes and developments occurring in women's sports, both domestically and internationally. Women's physical education had been part of Japan's school curriculum since the late 1880s, but for several years, physical education for young women was limited primarily to calisthenics, light gymnastics, or various forms of dance. Curricular revisions targeting both boys and girls in the early 1900s led to greater emphasis on sports and competitive games within the classroom and as extracurricular club activities. Hitomi's life coincided with the emergence in the 1910s of several programs or schools specifically established to train young women as physical education instructors.[32] In other words, sports only became (or were still becoming) a standardized part of women's education around the time that Hitomi entered school. Hitomi's status as a sports star also owed a great deal to the rise of new athletic competitions for women during her lifetime. The Japanese Women's Olympics and the Meiji Shrine Games, for example, had only been established in 1924, a year after Hitomi entered the sport of track and field.

It is also important to remember that the creation of these new venues for women's sports in Japan was occurring almost simultaneously with developments taking place internationally. The first International Women's Games were held in Paris in 1922, and it was not until 1928 that the Olympics first allowed women to participate in track-and-field events.[33] In this sense, many of the competitive forums that proved so critical to Hitomi's rise as an international track star became available just prior to or during the course of her career, thereby rendering her achievements possible and far more visible. The simultaneous developments in women's sports at home and abroad also meant that Hitomi entered a relatively level playing field in international competition. We might say, then, that Hitomi's apparent overshadowing of her compatriot male athletes in terms of international success, which was a key facet of her celebrity image, stemmed in part from differing degrees of disadvantage. Japanese men might have had a few years' head start in relation to women, but unlike Hitomi, they faced foreign competition that had an initial advantage of several decades, if not centuries.

From Canal Jumping to the Olympics: A Hard-Working "Lucky Girl"

Much like Hitachiyama, Hitomi achieved success and fame in part because she benefited from the times in which she lived. She also established a lasting reputation as one of Japan's most gifted and accomplished athletes. Hitomi's life, her meteoric sports career, and her tragically premature death at the age of 24 made her a legend. Hitomi's was a story of dramatic struggle, triumph, and tragedy, a story crafted and frequently retold in her autobiographical writings, countless sports articles, biographical accounts, feature films, documentaries, and television dramas.[34] One of the most striking aspects of these various depictions is the extent to which the overall image of Hitomi conforms to the sports-star paradigm that began to take shape in the early 1900s with Hitachiyama. To be sure, the particulars of Hitomi's situation—not least of all her gender—meant that certain aspects of her life and career attracted greater attention and emphasis than was the case with Hitachiyama and other (especially male) athletes. Frequent references to her status as an unmarried, working woman are one such example, as are seeming attempts to offset her unfeminine appearance and her formidable athletic drive and talent with details that highlighted her femininity and suggested that Hitomi was still "just a girl." Despite these significant variations, it is clear that even in Hitomi's own telling of her story, her image as a sports star reflected and was shaped by paradigmatic models and rhetorical patterns external to her own life and career.

For Hitomi, such outside influences are evident from the beginning, as seen in the apparent need to find the roots of her later success in details from her youth. Born in 1907, Hitomi was the second daughter of a poor family from a farming village outside Okayama city. Accounts of Hitomi's childhood often portray and describe her as a tomboy (*otenba*, or *bassai* in the local dialect). One of Hitomi's biographers, Obara Toshihiko, for example, explained that although there were girls her age in the village, Hitomi had mostly male friends and was frequently teased for being a tomboy, especially since she had a reputation for getting into fights.[35] Stretching details to an almost absurd extent, accounts of Hitomi also suggest that her athletic gifts were apparent at a young age. Hitomi was so fast as a child, Obara claims, that she always ended up walking to and from elementary school by herself, even though she set out with her classmates.[36] In another biography of Hitomi aimed at young adults, Manabe Kazuko repeats a story about Hitomi easily jumping over a canal when none of the village boys had been able to do so.[37] Even as a young girl, such accounts seem to indicate, Hitomi was showing up the men in track and field.

In her own writings, Hitomi admits that her father expressed concerns about what he perceived as unfeminine behavior, such as playing in creeks and fishing, but she omits details about early "athletic" accomplishments, as well as the teasing and fights.[38] Such omissions seem logical considering the fact that she was often criticized for a lack of femininity and probably did not want to begin her own narrative by highlighting details that might lend credence to such criticisms. Instead, Hitomi places much greater emphasis on her strong desire to succeed in school. According to accounts of Hitomi's childhood, including her own writings, it was Hitomi's father Isaku who instilled this desire for education and success in his daughter, sacrificing his own needs and those of his family in order to allow Hitomi to achieve an education beyond the elementary years required at the time.[39]

Proving a filial daughter as well as an exemplar of paradigmatic self-made success, Hitomi dedicated herself to schoolwork as an elementary student, which allowed her to enter the prefectural women's higher school (*kōtō jogakkō*, roughly equivalent to high school today), where only one in four women passed the entrance exam, as Hitomi herself pointed out.[40] Hitomi's quest for success through education eventually led her to Tokyo where she graduated from one of Japan's earliest schools for training women's physical education teachers. After graduating in 1925 she received a position as an instructor at a prestigious women's higher school in Kyoto. Later, she entered journalism, becoming one of Japan's first female sports writers in 1926, when she took the position in the sports section of the *Ōsaka Mainichi shinbun* that she held until her death in 1931.

Descriptions of Hitomi suggest that at each point of transition in her education and later her professional and athletic career, she was keenly aware of her duty to her parents. Even at points where she seemed to be taking a path that differed from the one her family planned for her, both Hitomi and her biographers emphasize how she, often with the help of influential men, worked to convince her family that she was doing the right thing. Hitomi's father, for instance, wanted her to attend a women's normal school and become a teacher. He only agreed to Hitomi's pursuit of a career as a women's physical education instructor after the school principal from the women's higher school visited Hitomi's home and told her father that only a school specializing in women's physical education could develop Hitomi's natural abilities and teach her the skills necessary to promote physical education and thereby "develop superior Japanese women" whose bodies would equal those of foreign women.[41] When she took a job as a reporter, it was Kinoshita Tōsaku, a prominent physician, leading eugenicist, advocate of women's sports, and Hitomi's soon-to-be boss at the newspaper, who aided Hitomi in overcoming her father's initial objections, relying in particular on similar claims about Hitomi's ability to be of great service in remaking the women of Japan.[42]

Similar to Hitachiyama, details about Hitomi's education and by extension her intelligence figure prominently in descriptions of her younger years. In her autobiography, for instance, Hitomi includes details about her grades. Nevertheless, her time in school proved all the more significant because Hitomi first became interested in and achieved success in competitive sports during these years.[43] Reflecting both greater educational opportunities and the increased significance of sports in schools compared with Hitachiyama's time, education for Hitomi and other later stars went beyond a matter of character; school itself became the primary conduit for the initial "discovery" and cultivation of unique athletic abilities. In this sense, Hitomi's story points to a subtle alteration in the sports-star paradigm, one that speaks to broader changes in Japanese schools, which assumed an increasingly important role in producing sports stars.

Perhaps it is understandable then that accounts of Hitomi's path to track and field stardom begin not with her first track meet, but with school tennis, which was popular among students at women's schools during this period. Taking up the sport after entering the prefectural women's higher school, Hitomi reportedly "devoted herself to practice," becoming an official member of the school's tennis team in her second year.[44] Later that same year, Hitomi and her doubles partner won a regional championship title. Hitomi continued to play tennis throughout her remaining years at the higher school, becoming known locally as "Tennis Hitomi," famous for her hard work at practice, her unusual height (5 feet 6.5 inches or 169 centimeters), and what her doubles partner described as her forceful, "masculine" (*otokomasari*) smashes.[45]

The success Hitomi achieved in school tennis is often linked directly to her emergence as a track star. Thinking that her proven athletic abilities as a tennis player might help make the school more competitive at a regional track meet sponsored by a local branch of the *Ōsaka Asahi shinbun* newspaper, the school's coaches pushed her to participate, even though she had never competed in the sport before.[46] In most accounts—which were, of course, written retrospectively—this meet during Hitomi's fourth and final year at the women's higher school was a pivotal moment in her life. It was here that she—and the nation—"discovered" her potential in track and field. Surprising everyone, including herself, Hitomi won the long jump by setting a national record. As if to highlight the life-altering significance of this event, Hitomi's autobiographical account reminds readers that this was the same event that she would later win in international competition.[47] Sounding a similar note, Manabe explains that despite Hitomi's amazing achievement at this meet, "Hitomi herself never dreamed that she would become a track athlete breaking world record after world record."[48]

Repeated references to an illness that nearly kept Hitomi from competing at this meet add further drama to this tale of transformational and necessary discovery. Apparently, Hitomi had developed beriberi and received doctor's orders not to engage in strenuous activity. Pointing to her health, Hitomi initially resisted requests that she participate in the track meet. But after her tennis coach and other school officials pressured her about the need to compete "for the honor of your school," Hitomi finally relented, and her history was made.[49]

On the one hand, Hitomi's actions in this case have a semblance of nobility, a willingness to sacrifice her own well-being for some perceived greater good. On the other hand, the seeming disregard for her health, on her own part and that of the adults allegedly advising her, strikes an ominous note, leading one to wonder exactly what kind of greater good was worth such a sacrifice. With the school doctor attending this meet to observe her status, Hitomi emerged from this potential danger point with her health intact.[50] Later in her career, this would not always prove to be the case.

After graduating from the women's higher school in 1924, Hitomi, with the encouragement and assistance of her school principal, decided to enroll in the Nikaidō taisō juku training school in Tokyo. Founded only two years earlier in 1922 by Nikaidō Tokuyo, one of Japan's pioneers in women's physical education, the school focused on training women to be physical education instructors.[51] Although Hitomi entered the program as a successful athlete, Nikaidō was not inclined, at least initially, to encourage Hitomi to pursue competitive sports. In part, Nikaidō's stance reflected her own background in studying and promoting calisthenics and gymnastics for women, generally referred to as women's *taisō*. But Nikaidō's suspicions about sports were also in line with long-standing concerns among physical education promoters about the merits of competitive sports in promoting physical education, especially for women.[52]

No doubt reflecting the influence of Nikaidō's views on sports, records indicate that Hitomi did not engage in track competition for almost a year following her first record-breaking performance in track, missing the first national Women's Olympics and the first Meiji Shrine Games, both held in 1924. Towards the end of that year, however, she was invited back to Okayama to compete in a regional track meet. Allegedly inspired by the recent death of her beloved grandmother and cheered on by her entire family, Hitomi set a world record in the triple jump, making her an instant celebrity. When Hitomi returned to school in Tokyo, Nikaidō reportedly welcomed her as a star, adopting a markedly softer stance on sports, a change no doubt influenced by the increased attention and prestige that Hitomi's success brought to the school.[53]

Hitomi graduated from Nikaidō's school in 1925, having become one of her teacher's top students. For a short time after graduating, Hitomi held a prestigious and well-paid position as a physical education instructor at a women's school in Kyoto. After completing one term, however, the school released her from her contract in order to allow her to travel to Taiwan as Nikaidō's representative. Responding to the request of the Japanese colonial governor-general in Taiwan, Hitomi visited and delivered a series of instructional courses and lectures on women's sports.[54]

Oddly enough, many biographies and even Hitomi's own writings do not mention her time in Taiwan, despite the obvious honor such a trip represented and the fact that she is said to have set several unofficial records during her visit.[55] The specific reasons for such an omission remain unclear. Although it could be a deliberate attempt to obscure Hitomi's relationship with Japanese colonial policies, it could also reflect an effort to make Hitomi's later travels abroad seem more significant. Perhaps Hitomi's trip simply did not go well or proved uneventful. Whatever the reasons, omissions of this sort serve as a useful reminder of the selective nature of such autobiographical and biographical works.

Upon her return from Taiwan in the summer of 1925, Hitomi served as an instructor at Nikaidō's school until April 1926, when she took a position as a reporter for the sports division of the *Ōsaka Mainichi shinbun* newspaper. In addition to providing Hitomi with a livelihood, her work during these years also contributed to her athletic success. As an instructor for Nikaidō, she was able to continue training for track and field and represented the school at the Meiji Shrine Games in 1925, where she won the 50-meter dash and set another world record in the triple jump.[56]

Hitomi's career as a journalist proved even more beneficial to her sports career because it allowed her to maintain her status as a de facto amateur athlete (a key qualification for most international competitions at the time) while providing various forms of support for her athletic career. Hitomi's recruitment as a sports journalist also exemplifies the growth and increasing prominence of the sports sections in newspapers throughout Japan. For the *Ōsaka Mainichi*, Hitomi was a useful PR tool, a "company treasure," especially since the paper was constantly on the lookout for ways to boost circulation at the expense of the rival *Ōsaka Asahi shinbun*.[57] When Hitomi competed abroad, she regularly served as a foreign correspondent. In this role, she wrote several feature stories for the *Ōsaka Mainichi*, and at one point, provided an exclusive interview with Manchurian warlord and sports enthusiast Zhang Xueliang.[58] But the paper's relationship with Hitomi was not one-sided. Accounts from

Hitomi's years as a reporter suggest that she had a full working schedule, but her job with the paper was flexible enough to allow her to maintain an intense training regimen and engage in regular competition. Prior to joining the *Ōsaka Mainichi*, Hitomi had participated in only five track meets, where she competed in a total of five different events. In contrast, from April through August of her first year with the paper, she entered five meets and competed in fourteen different events, setting several national records in the process. Up to the year of her death, Hitomi engaged in similar levels of competition while working for the paper.[59]

One of the meets during Hitomi's first year with the *Ōsaka Mainichi* became one of the most important to her career and sports-star image. In 1926 Hitomi traveled to Sweden to compete as Japan's sole delegate at the second International Women's Games (see Figure 3.1). The support of the paper was central to Hitomi's participation in this international event. Hitomi's boss Kinoshita Tōsaku, head of the newspaper's sports division as well as the director of Japan's national federation for women's sports, encouraged Hitomi to participate and helped with the arrangements for her trip. Two of the paper's reporters accompanied Hitomi for parts of her long trip to Europe via the Trans-Siberian Railroad.[60]

In her debut international competition in Sweden, Hitomi entered six events, four of which were new for her. She placed no worse than sixth in all the events, winning both the long jump and the standing broad jump, finishing second in the discus and third in the 100-yard dash. Her overall performance gave her the all-around individual championship title and placed Japan fifth in the national standings.[61] Hitomi's success bolstered her celebrity status at home, silencing critics who had scoffed at her alleged world-class abilities, claiming that such talk was that of a "frog in a well," since she had never faced any kind of real competition.[62]

Hitomi's performance also made her the new face of Japanese women abroad. Commenting on Hitomi's participation in these games, a German paper noted that Hitomi defied the common perception of demure Japanese women dressed in kimono and wearing high *geta* sandals. The German reporter was "deeply impressed" with the contrast that Hitomi offered from the stereotypical view, displaying a "splendid body no different from those of female athletes from Europe and America."[63] This reporter was not alone in his interest in Hitomi. A local paper in Sweden ran a cartoon drawing of Hitomi under the words "Banzaj [sic] Hitomi" (see Figure 3.2).[64] At a banquet hosted in Hitomi's honor, the Swedish minister of education suggested that Hitomi had helped raise awareness

Figure 3.1 Hitomi Kinue as Japan's sole delegate to the second International Women's Games held in Sweden in 1926. Hitomi's success at these Games established her reputation as one of the top female athletes in Japan and beyond. *The Asahi Sports* 4, no. 19, 15 September 1926, 3.

Figure 3.2 A Swedish newspaper cartoon featuring Hitomi published during the second International Women's Games. Obara, *Hitomi Kinue monogatari*, 92. Courtesy of Obara Toshihiko.

about Japan beyond news of earthquakes and disasters. In his words, "This Olympics opened our eyes to the fact that Japan has sports and that Japan has women like Hitomi."[65] In the United States, the *Los Angeles Times* ran a photo of Hitomi after these Games with a caption that offered a somewhat understated description of Hitomi's achievements: "Japan's champion woman athlete. Miss Hitomi won the standing broad jump at the recent women's Olympiad at Gothenburg, Sweden. She is shown ready to take off for her winning leap."[66] Throughout Hitomi's career, the *New York Times* regularly included articles announcing Hitomi's record-breaking performances, as well as articles announcing when another athlete broke Hitomi's records.[67] Articles in the *Washington Post* cited Hitomi as evidence of "Taller Japanese," as well as changes in Japanese women's fashion.[68] In the words of Furushō Kunio, who produced one of the first biographical accounts of Hitomi in a 1927 volume about female pioneers from all over the world, Hitomi's success at these Games and the international recognition it generated made her "Japan's first international woman."[69]

After returning to Japan in the fall of 1926, Hitomi began what would become almost a second career as a lecturer, delivering speeches throughout Japan about her experiences abroad and themes related to women's sports in general. Sports historian Misawa Mitsuo, perhaps the foremost expert on Hitomi's life, has documented 52 talks that Hitomi delivered between September 1926 and November 1930, including several that she gave overseas.[70] Hitomi's lecturing went hand in hand with her writing, as she began to publish extensively on similar themes. In addition to the work she did for the *Ōsaka Mainichi*, by the time of her death Hitomi had written five books and nearly fifty articles or essays for a variety of publications, ranging from track magazines to popular women's journals.[71]

Through her writings and her speaking tours, Hitomi was able to capitalize on her fame in order to promote women's sports and physical education, often using her own experiences as a means for teaching rules and methods. In her book *Tatakau made* (Up to the competition, 1929), for example, Hitomi offered readers strategies to prepare for and engage in competition, including details about clothing, conditioning, mental preparation, and proper techniques for different track-and-field events. The book used autobiographical descriptions, illustrations and photos of Hitomi, as well as several European and American athletes, to demonstrate exemplary techniques (see Figures 3.3–3.5).[72] Hitomi's more overtly autobiographical writings are also filled with sports-related details, indirectly

Figures 3.3–3.5 (left to right) In several of her works, Hitomi used photographs of herself or other female track stars to demonstrate various events and techniques. These images were used to show the proper form for starting a sprint. Hitomi, *Tatakau made*, 100–103. Courtesy of Sanseidō Co., Ltd.

(though intentionally) educating her readers about sports and athletes in Japan and other countries.[73] Hitomi's writings and speeches reveal the pioneering role she played in fostering women's sports in Japan. They also suggest that Hitomi herself embraced that role, perhaps seeking to become what Kinoshita told her father she could be if she joined the *Ōsaka Mainichi*. On that occasion Kinoshita purportedly said, "Miss Kinue shouldn't be a teacher of a single school, she is the kind of person who should be Japan's teacher of women's sports."[74]

Hitomi's efforts to promote sports did not keep her from pursuing them herself. In fact, Hitomi's dedication to training and competition in spite of all her work and promotional activities came to define her success and her image. Hitomi and her biographers often emphasize the grueling practice leading up to her trip to Europe. Much of Hitomi's personal account of her time in Europe reads like a log of practice routines (or complaints about not being able to practice while on the train) in the weeks leading up to the games in Sweden. The key detail in such accounts is that Hitomi did it all on her own, in the most literal sense: until 1927, when she started training under the sprinter Tani Misago, Hitomi had no coach. She was self-taught and self-trained, "continuing to practice all alone, day after day," according to Manabe.[75] Looking back on this period, Hitomi suggested in her writings that her fear of failing at the Games led her to over-train, in part because she had no coach.[76] Hitomi and her biographers both indicate that she was only able to maximize her talent and her practices after she began working with Tani during what her chapter title calls her "era of practice" (*renshū jidai*), following her return from Europe. Betraying her own insecurities about her training, Hitomi called herself a "lucky girl" (*rakkī gāru*) whose good fortune allowed her to achieve success without proper training. But she was not willing to deny her own role, maintaining that her hard work had also been key to ongoing athletic achievements: "Seeing as I had been given such a great honor, I didn't want to dirty it, and since I was aiming for great progress, I had to work hard. . . . My first winter in Osaka was cold, but no matter how much snow was blowing or rain was falling, I was on the practice grounds."[77] Hitomi's good luck, it seems, only made her want to work harder, and her reputation for success through hard work quickly became central to her image. Pointing to the observations of Oda Mikio and Hitomi's other contemporaries, Hitomi's biographer Misawa has argued that her "strength was the product of long periods of effort," rather than particular natural gifts.[78] In this sense, Hitomi was not only an ideal amateur, balancing work and sport, but also an exemplar of self-made success in sports, offering the implicit suggestion that with enough work, dedication, and perhaps a little luck, almost anyone could do the same.[79]

In the years immediately following Hitomi's trip to Sweden, her achievements in track added to her already celebrated reputation as Japan's premier female athlete. In 1927 and 1928 Hitomi set several national and world records, and in the lead-up to the 1928 Olympics she also broke a British national record at a meet in London (see Figure 3.6).[80] Despite these earlier achievements, Hitomi is perhaps best known for her medal-winning performance at the 1928 Amsterdam Olympics. The standard dictionary *Kōjien*, for instance, includes a definition for Hitomi, which mentions only her medal at the 1928 Olympics.[81] Because of the overwhelming symbolic significance of the Olympic Games to modern society, Hitomi's single medal at the "official" Olympics has generally meant more than her multiple victories at the International Women's Games. The short-lived nature of the International Women's Games has also influenced popular views of Hitomi. In contrast to the Olympics, the Women's Games were only held four times. As Japan's first female medal winner at the Olympics, Hitomi became—and continues to be—a key element of the star system that defined later Japanese women participating in the Olympics. Consequently, Hitomi's image is often invoked at the time of the Olympics, especially when a Japanese female athlete wins a track-and-field event. When Arimori Yūko won a silver medal in the marathon at the 1992 Barcelona Olympics, her achievement was instantly linked to Hitomi, particularly because this was the first medal for

Figure 3.6 Hitomi competing in a track meet in London prior to the 1928 Amsterdam Olympics. Hitomi set a British national record during this meet. In her autobiographical works, Hitomi wrote extensively about her experiences in London and the British athletes she met. *The Asahi Sports* 6, no. 17, 1 September 1928, 5. Courtesy of the Asahi Shimbun Company.

Japanese women in track and field since Hitomi, and because both are natives of Okayama prefecture.[82] It is also common for Japanese television stations to run documentaries on Hitomi (and others) in order to supplement Olympic coverage during the Games.[83] Hitomi's success at the Olympics and the continuing significance of the Games themselves have assured her an ongoing presence in the mass media. At the same time, this coverage has helped turn her single Olympic appearance into the defining event of Hitomi's career.

The seemingly out-of-proportion attention that Hitomi's Olympic medal has received also stems from the oft-repeated story of her quest for this medal, which has become emblematic of Hitomi's drive and determination, as well as her devotion to the Japanese nation. When Hitomi was eliminated in the semifinal heat of the 100-meter dash, an event where she held the world record, she overcame her bitter disappointment. As she later recounted in her autobiography, Hitomi had longed to see the Japanese flag flying and hear the national anthem "Kimi ga yo" at the Olympics: "For me, to think of the flag on that mast and the Kimi ga yo. . . . Recalling how two years earlier in Sweden I had twice sung the Kimi ga yo before 40,000 spectators, and twice the Rising Sun flag had brightened the fall skies of northern Europe, my eyes suddenly became hot."[84] Claiming that she could not return home a failure, Hitomi entered the 800-meter run, a race she had never before run in competition.[85] In a dramatic race where she entered the final lap in sixth place, Hitomi picked off runners one by one during the last lap to finish in second place, only eight-tenths of a second behind the gold medalist.[86] The reporter covering the race for the *Ōsaka Mainichi* hailed Hitomi's come-from-behind, near victory as a testament to the Japanese nation, declaring, "If this isn't a manifestation of the Japanese Spirit [*yamatodamashii*], then I don't know what is."[87] Both Hitomi and the winner, Germany's Lina Radke, collapsed and lost consciousness following the race, and as a consequence, the 800-meter run was not included again as an Olympic event for women until 1960.

Following these Olympics, Hitomi returned to Japan, but according to many accounts found it difficult to return to sports. Facing a busy schedule of presentations throughout the country, her desire to practice waned. Writing several years later, Hitomi noted in one of her autobiographical accounts that she had briefly considered retiring until she received a letter from Alice Milliat, the leader of the Fédération Sportive Féminine Internationale. At that point, Milliat and her federation were in the process of organizing the third International Women's Games to be held in Prague in 1930. Milliat reportedly told Hitomi that she was too young to retire and needed to get back to her practice so she would be ready for the upcoming competition.[88] In narratives addressing this period in Hitomi's career, Milliat comes across as an almost necessary hard-nosed, yet inspiring, coach or teacher, who helps keep the young athlete on the path to further athletic success. Without Milliat, such stories seem to suggest, Hitomi's story might have ended with the Amsterdam Olympics. Of course, Hitomi took Milliat's words to heart, and for better or perhaps ultimately worse, she decided not to retire from sports.

Committed to attending the 1930 Women's Games, Hitomi returned to active practice and competition during 1929, participating in several meets in Japan and overseas, including a joint German-Chinese-Japanese meet held in Northeastern China, where she had the opportunity to meet and interview Zhang Xueliang.[89] Despite her time off, Hitomi appears to have returned to form quickly, breaking national and world records in a variety of events throughout the year. She also began recruiting and training a team of Japanese women who could accompany her to the 1930 Games. As part of her efforts to prepare these young women for international competition, Hitomi organized and directed a training camp that she paid for with the proceeds from her books, two of which were published in 1929. Hitomi's role in leading and funding this training camp, which hosted fifteen women for a two-week period, points to her personal commitment to fostering the development of women's sports in Japan.[90]

The five young Japanese women who joined Hitomi to participate in the 1930 International Women's Games signified both the fruits of Hitomi's efforts and the fundamental changes that had occurred in women's sports in Japan since Hitomi's trip to Sweden four years earlier. Although Hitomi expressed great pride in the effort that these athletes displayed in their first international meet, the athletes themselves proved less than successful. Hitomi scored all of Japan's points herself, with the exception of the 400-meter relay, where Hitomi's anchor leg earned the team a fourth place finish and a single point. Japan placed fourth overall, and Hitomi, to her own disappointment, finished second in the individual standings.[91]

Before returning home after the games in Prague, the Japanese team competed against several other national teams in a series of competitions in Poland, Germany, Belgium, and France. Even though Hitomi had developed a serious cold following the Prague Games, she continued to compete in these meets. Realizing that the Japanese team had very little chance to be competitive without her, Hitomi refused to sit out, even when her fellow teammates begged her to do so on account of her health.[92] Her boss from the *Ōsaka Mainichi*, Kinoshita Tōsaku, who was also a medical doctor accompanying the team in Europe, offered Hitomi medical advice and administered regular injections of painkillers.[93] But without adequate time to rest and recover, Hitomi grew noticeably sicker and weaker. By the last of these international meets in France, Hitomi was, in the words of one French sports paper, "clearly exhausted."[94]

After a long sea voyage, Hitomi and the other women returned to Japan in November 1930. Only days after arriving home, Hitomi returned to the lecture circuit, even though her father had begged her to take time to rest and recover, since she was visibly suffering from exhaustion and illness.[95] In seeking to fulfill her obligations to her employers and continue in her role promoting sports for women, Hitomi took little opportunity to rest or seek medical treatment. By March 1931, her condition worsened dramatically when she began coughing blood and running a high fever.[96] Hitomi was hospitalized in Osaka and diagnosed with pleurisy. She never left the hospital. Doctors were unable to stop the deterioration of her lungs, and on 2 August 1931—the third anniversary of her silver medal performance at the Amsterdam Olympics—Hitomi died of respiratory failure.[97] Such was the unfortunate end of the "lucky girl."

Troubling Hitomi: Martyr, Moga, *or Man?*

By the time of her death, Hitomi's athletic success, speaking tours, and extensive list of publications had made her one of Japan's most famous celebrities. Japanese commentators on "Miss Hitomi" often referred with marked pride to the fact that Hitomi was known worldwide, bringing recognition and prestige to Japan and its sports. Hitomi was a national hero, an example of Japan's rising status in sports and in the world more generally. Hitomi appeared to serve the interests of Japan in other ways as well: her writings and talks often highlighted the value of women's sports to the Japanese nation, especially by producing healthy mothers who would go on to have healthy children. "Why should girls run and jump?" Hitomi asked at the beginning of one essay, answering, "'For the improvement of the maternal bodies that will produce the nation's next generation.' Thinking of it in such ways is surely not mistaken. The spirit of a race and brightness of a country are born of healthy motherhood. We women must bear this awareness and responsibility."[98] Language of this sort would certainly have made Hitomi a welcome ally of eugenicists (such as her boss, Dr. Kinoshita) interested in improving the national body through women's sports.[99] Perhaps because of her professed dedication to the nation, her filial commitment to her family, and her reputation for hard work, educators also saw Hitomi as a potential role model, including selections from her writings in several textbooks, especially those aimed at young women.[100]

At the same time, Hitomi was the subject of much societal debate and concern. The controversies surrounding her were, and continue to be, central to the construction and interpretation of her image as a sports star, proving as significant as her athletic abilities and achievements. Not least among the factors that have made Hitomi a troubling figure was her "premature" death. The tragedy of Hitomi's death became linked in particular to diverse and often conflicting claims about the goals of women's sports, as well as the need for improvements in sports medicine in order to prevent similar incidents in the future.

If Hitomi was controversial in death, she had been no less so in life. Combined with other perceived threats to the power and influence of Japanese men at the time, Hitomi's success in sports contributed to what can be seen as a crisis of masculinity. In some ways, Hitomi proved all the more threatening because she challenged assumptions about male dominance in sports, which often serve as a form of what R. W. Connell has called "exemplary masculinity."[101] Critics—as well as supporters—also highlighted the ways in which Hitomi unsettled societal expectations about women's bodies, femininity, and sexuality. In the years since her death the multiple readings that Hitomi's image allowed for have remained troubling for many, as seen especially in attempts to rescue Hitomi's memory from speculation that she was a lesbian—or possibly even a man.

MARTYR?

Hitomi's death received widespread publicity at home and abroad. Her parents first learned of her death from a radio news broadcast at a train station in Himeji, Japan, when they were on their way to see her in Osaka.[102] The *New York Times* was notified by a special cable and ran an obituary the day after her death. Highlighting Hitomi's youth and including surprisingly detailed information about Hitomi's international competitions and records, her obituary was one of the longest in the *Times* that day.[103] For Hitomi's funeral, a total of 328 telegrams of condolence were received from all over Japan and the world.[104] In September 1932, a year after Hitomi's death, track enthusiasts and physical education supporters in Prague, Czechoslovakia, constructed a monument in the city, memorializing Hitomi's participation in the 1930 International Women's Games, as well as her contribution to women's sports.[105] In Japan, Hitomi's death initiated a wave of articles celebrating her achievements and lamenting the tragic loss of one of Japan's greatest athletes at the tender age of 24. In October 1931, for instance, leading athletes and sports advocates contributed special tributes to Hitomi in the track magazine *Rikujō kyōgi*, which included 20 different essays with titles such as "Hitomi as Epoch-Maker," "This Fighting Spirit," and "My Memories of Hitomi."[106] For the next few years, reports dealing with major national or international women's track-and-field events regularly began by commenting on the sport's great loss.[107] Considering her status as not only an internationally successful sports star, but also a pioneer in women's sports, the elegiac loss and praise associated with Hitomi are understandable.

But Hitomi's death also sparked controversy, especially since it was seen as unexpected or at the very least premature.[108] What were the men and women of Japan to make of her death? What did it mean for the future of sports, particularly for women? In the ensuing struggle to define the causes and significance of Hitomi's death, both supporters and critics offered radically varying interpretations, serving as a telling reminder of the malleability of sports-celebrity images. Hitomi was, simultaneously, a martyr, hypocrite, victim, and proof of the need to curb women's sports. She also became the impetus for promoting and popularizing sports medicine.

Overwork, according to the overwhelming consensus, was the underlying cause of Hitomi's illness and death. But who was to blame for this overwork, and why was Hitomi willing to go to this extreme? In most biographical accounts, Hitomi emerges as a martyr, willingly sacrificing her own desires and in the end her life for the sake of furthering the status of women's sports in Japan. Reflecting this common sentiment, the postscript in Manabe's illustrated biography of Hitomi for children compares Hitomi's life with her famous Olympic 800-meter run. It suggests that Hitomi had given her all in life and collapsed at the finish; that she had overworked and sacrificed herself out of a great "sense of responsibility"; that she "had to do it, for the sake of developing women's sports."[109] In constructing this image of Hitomi, biographers like Manabe did not need to look too far. Hitomi often portrayed herself in this vein in her writings and comments. A biography of Hitomi from a history of pioneering Japanese women, for example, includes a selection from Hitomi's autobiographical book *Supaiku no ato* (Spike tracks, 1929) to highlight Hitomi's dedication to sports and their development in Japan. "There was pain, and there was pleasure, but there was not a day when I did what my own heart or body desired. . . . Apart from my work with my company [*Ōsaka Mainichi shinbun*], I sacrificed everything to go about my training."[110] Highlighting Hitomi's self-sacrifice for a greater good made her death a noble, if still tragic, loss.

But not everyone was willing to accept such an interpretation. Hitomi's death was of particular concern for those in the medical establishment, especially doctors with an interest in promoting their views about sports. A month after Hitomi's death, her former boss Kinoshita Tōsaku offered his thoughts in the mainstream journal *Chūō kōron*. Kinoshita explicitly denied that Hitomi's death had anything to do with sports. It was better to see her case as that of a person who suddenly became gravely and terminally ill, a possibility for even the healthiest person, he pointed out. If anything, he contended, sports had actually improved Hitomi's health and quality of life.[111] Kinoshita also used this essay to explain his views about the best approaches to women's sports and their benefits for health and physical fitness. Reaching out to a popular audience, the article offered a condensed and simplified version of comments Kinoshita had offered in a much longer and more technical essay published the previous year, while Hitomi was still alive, in a special volume on women's sports.[112]

Whether or not Kinoshita's vociferous defense of women's sports in the wake of Hitomi's death reflected his own sense of responsibility in perhaps overlooking the seriousness of Hitomi's illness or fostering her inclination to overwork, it almost certainly indicated his concern, as a eugenicist and women's sports promoter, that Hitomi's death might create a popular backlash against women's participation in athletics.[113] Observations about mothers discouraging their children from pursuing track and field in the wake of Hitomi's death suggest that Kinoshita may have had reason to be concerned.[114] Perhaps more disturbing was an article by another medical expert published in the *Yomiuri shinbun* two months after Hitomi's death. Its title bluntly declared, "The Problem Is Women's Sports: *To Be Avoided During Development*." Although the author, a medical doctor named Iwata Seidō, did not call for an outright ban on sports for women, he raised his doubts about their benefits, citing in particular his concern that excessive practice and competition, especially during young women's menstrual cycles, might damage their "feminine functions." Iwata called for caution and more studies to determine the influence of sports on women's bodies.[115]

Although Iwata's views were more hostile than the majority of medical and sports experts who used the media to communicate their observations on Hitomi's death, Iwata shared an approach with these other experts. They not only admitted the connection between Hitomi's death and sports, but also used her as a teaching tool and a means of pressing for increased medical oversight of athletes. Medical and intellectual debates about the benefits or dangers of sports, especially for women, were not particularly new. Hitomi herself had often directly challenged medical opinions in her writings and talks, but the shocking demise of one of Japan's most well known sports stars brought such discussions to the attention of a much wider audience and provided the previously abstract debates with a concrete and all-too human example.[116]

In October 1931, the *Yomiuri* newspaper, for example, ran a special multi-part series of articles where medical experts (including Iwata) offered their views about the reasons behind and remedies for preventing sports-related deaths like Hitomi's.[117] If there was any doubt that Hitomi was the inspiration for the articles, Azuma Ryōtarō's contribution, which called for improving sports medicine in Japan by using German models, carried the warning: "Do not let Miss Hitomi Kinue's death be in vain!"[118] Azuma's personal memoirs reveal that at the time, he saw Hitomi's death as a wake-up call that sports without medical input could result in potentially dangerous anomalies. Azuma also noted his disappointment that an autopsy had not been performed on Hitomi's body. He argued that whatever the reasons for not doing so, they did not outweigh the potential good such an autopsy could do for sports by explaining not only why Hitomi had died, but why she had been so good.[119] Even in death, it seems, Hitomi could have done more for sports.

Hitomi's death was also directly connected to a later fourteen-part series titled "Sports and Medicine," which ran in the *Yomiuri* newspaper during March and April 1933.[120] Although it had been nearly a year and a half since her death, the series' author, Saitō Kazuo, called upon Hitomi's memory to introduce the series and justify its importance. Like many of Saitō's articles, this first one included an illustration, a headshot of Hitomi, evidently engaged in practice or competition, to judge by the headband.[121] As impetus and inspiration for Saitō's series and the earlier articles by other medical experts, Hitomi's death played a key role in popularizing medical-related views about sports.

Hitomi's death also sparked calls for health examinations of athletes and the establishment of sports medicine, especially since athletes at group institutions like schools were said to be at particular risk of contracting tuberculosis, the disease with which Hitomi's death was widely associated.[122] Although her death was certainly not the only factor, the increased attention to sports medicine and concerns about the health of athletes were no doubt behind Tokyo Imperial University's statement that it would begin to offer medical examinations of athletes from January 1932.[123] In April 1933, the Ministry of Education announced that, starting in August, its sports and physical education section would include a "Sports Medicine Consultation Bureau," which would offer advice and health examinations for athletes as well as those just beginning sports.[124] These changes point to increased state and medical regulation of athletes and their bodies, in the name of "contributing to the healthy development of our national sports scene" and avoiding another Hitomi.[125]

Many of the articles published in the wake of Hitomi's death aimed to teach athletes and non-athletes alike about their bodies and encouraged them to monitor and regulate their own behavior. Even though many of these articles did not cite Hitomi directly, their numbers increased markedly in the initial months following her death. Articles of this kind were often written by doctors and addressed "need-to-know" (*warera no shiraneba naranu*) topics such as the connection between exercise and blood cells, the "Modern Man's Heart," and irregularities in the bones of athletes.[126] One article appearing alongside a series related to Hitomi's death taught readers the warning signs of overwork in athletes.[127] The *Yomiuri* newspaper's "Women's Page" (*fujin no pēji*) a month later included an article that explained which foods and drinks were best and worst for athletes, referring specifically to the advice of a trainer from the New York Giants baseball team, whose autographed photo appeared with the article.[128] This piece might have been aimed at women athletes, but with its baseball references and placement on the women's page it seems even more likely that it was targeting mothers feeding young, male athletes. Another article published on the "Women's Page" less than two years after Hitomi's death invoked the memory of the tragedy with its provocative title: "Among Our Female Athletes, Why Are There So Many Victims?" As it turns out, the "victims" in the article were the high number of young female athletes who had reported "abnormal menstrual cycles" in a recent survey. Echoing Iwata's points from 1931, the article sought to explain why so many female athletes seemed to be affected in this way. In the process it not only provided a warning about the dangers of becoming "abnormal" because of excessive participation in sports or exercise, but also encouraged *all* female readers, including non-athletes, to consider whether or not they, too, were "victims" of abnormality.[129]

Many of the topics that Saitō raised in his 1933 series were aimed at promoting both bodily awareness and self-regulation among his readers. Among his fourteen articles, one featured an illustration of the hand bones of both pitchers and catchers; another used photos of European men to highlight different body types and explain which athletic activities were best suited to each type. The final article in the series included a warning for swimmers about the need to be wary of ear ailments.[130] As Saitō's use of European photos suggests, Western, and especially German, models played a key role in defining how Japanese medical experts saw and sought to regulate and improve the bodies of Japanese athletes. Such would continue to be the case in the years to come, as sports medicine and sports science emerged as powerful, transnational, and often state-supported forces in Japan's effort to achieve sporting success on the global stage.[131]

Hitomi's role in promoting and popularizing sports medicine in Japan appears to have been largely overlooked by history, but her impact was clear. Japanese society may have longed for another internationally successful athlete like Hitomi, but it had to avoid a similar demise. Hitomi's death was tragic, shocking, and controversial, and largely because of that, it empowered Japan's medical experts to push for greater oversight of athletes and raised popular awareness about the "need" for both medical intervention in sports and greater self-regulation. Responding to these perceived needs and demands, the Japanese government itself eventually offered its assistance, in the name of improving Japanese sports and athletes. In this sense, Hitomi's demise, as a negative example, could also serve the needs of the Japanese state, helping to produce not just healthier women, but healthier men. In death, Hitomi had proven a useful and powerful—though extraordinarily versatile—symbol.

MOGA?

If Hitomi's image was useful, it was also threatening, especially during her lifetime. In 1924, the same year that Hitomi gained widespread attention with her first world-record-setting track-and-field performance, she was joined in the national spotlight and imagination by another female star of the era, the so-called modern girl (*modan gāru*), who is better known by the Japanese abbreviation *moga*. Not unlike Hitomi and other sports stars, the "vastly exaggerated image" of the modern girl was as much a media and social construct as it was a depiction of "real" Japanese women at the time.[132] In her idealized form, the modern girl was a drinking, smoking, and flirtatious figure "symbolized by the short skirt worn above the knees, Louise Brooks haircut, rouge, and lipstick; she appeared as a woman who 'struts through the throngs' signifying both sexual and financial independence."[133]

Was Hitomi a modern girl? Even a quick glance at her photos would suggest that aside from her short haircut, she did not exactly fit the stereotypical image, a sense confirmed by written accounts and descriptions. Hitomi was, first and foremost, an athlete, and she often acted and dressed the part. She single-mindedly focused on practice, completely eschewed alcohol for most of her life, and regularly wore sweatbands, shorts, and jogging suits.[134] If Hitomi was not the stereotypical modern girl, she nonetheless came to embody aspects of the socio-historical moment that gave rise to public concern with the *moga*. The modern girl, as historian Harry Harootunian has observed, "was not simply an empty symbol . . . but was the signification of more deeply rooted social and material processes that were threatening to alter the social structure of Japanese society and throw into question the status of traditional forms of morality and claims of authority."[135] One of the main threats signified by the modern girl was what historian Miriam Silverberg has described as

Figure 3.7 A cartoon by Ōtsuki Mamoru from the November 1926 issue of the comic magazine *Manga zasshi*. Suggesting the potentially disruptive nature of Hitomi's athletic pursuits and achievements, the cartoon shows Hitomi leaping over a book labeled *Etiquette for Women* while several women in traditional Japanese dress look on. Shimizu Isao, ed., *Manga ni egakareta Meiji, Taishō, Shōwa*, 207. Courtesy of Shimizu Isao and Newton Press, Inc.

the "militancy" of Japanese women in the 1920s, a militancy "articulated through the adoption of new fashions, through labor in new arenas, and through political activity that consciously challenged social, economic, and political structures and relationships."[136] Hitomi was at the very center of such militant challenges and the sense of concern that they generated. Furushō Kunio, one of Hitomi's earliest biographers, made this point clear in 1927, when he began his account of Hitomi's life with references to "feminism" and several aspects of the "woman problem" (*fujin mondai*) facing Japan at the time.[137] As Manabe wrote in a more recent biography, Hitomi was famous for breaking new ground in sports, but she also pioneered "new ways of living for women."[138]

One of the factors that Furushō and others highlighted was the issue of economic independence. As a single, working woman, Hitomi was an object of particular interest and concern, especially since she seemed less interested in marriage than a woman in her late teens and twenties was *supposed* to have been. On several occasions, Hitomi contributed articles to various journals providing details about her personal and professional life outside of her athletic performances (though both were intertwined with sports). Several of these essays were solicited for special thematic sections of journals, such as the general-interest magazine *Kaizō* or the women's magazine *Fujin saron*, which tackled questions or concerns of the day.[139] In one such article published in 1927 in *Kaizō*, Hitomi was one of several women asked to comment on what she described as the "route to happiness for women." As suggested by her title, "Women Are, After All, Women," Hitomi discussed her own "search" for the best route in sports and the workplace, but concluded with a general affirmation of more traditional notions that women's happiness was ultimately tied to the home, marriage, husband, and children.[140] Hitomi's conclusions may have assuaged the concerns of some—perhaps the activities of women like Hitomi were, after all, only a temporary, pre-marriage issue—but her own unmarried status raised further doubts. In an article published in *Fujin saron* only months before her death, Hitomi bemoaned the fact that she was constantly bombarded with questions about when she was going to marry. As it was, she never gave an answer to the question her title posed, "When Will I Marry?" Thinking about marriage, she concluded, was "troublesome," especially since such thoughts, and by implication marriage itself, distracted her from "concentrating on good work."[141]

As an unmarried woman who seemed to show little interest in changing her status, Hitomi, not unlike the *moga*, seemed to be flaunting her single status as a valid alternative, and therefore challenge, to patriarchal conceptions of the family and motherhood. Hitomi's unmarried status was also troubling because it was something that she had in common with some of the most politically active women at the time, including the well-known suffrage activist Ichikawa Fusae.[142] In the late 1920s and early 1930s, the women's suffrage movement in Japan was at its prewar peak.[143] Hitomi's connection with Ichikawa and suffrage might be little more than coincidence were it not for the fact that Hitomi's sporting accomplishments became linked to the demands for giving women the vote in Japan, even though Hitomi herself never explicitly made the connection. Citing Hitomi's success at the international 1926 International Women's Games, Harishige Keiki's 1927 examination of the Japanese sports scene offhandedly remarked that Hitomi's success and the increased participation of women in sports could be seen as "preparation for women's acquisition of voting rights."[144] By this logic, Hitomi's promotion of sports was also the indirect promotion of political rights. Hitomi was linked to socio-political changes in other ways as well. Hitomi's 1931 *Fujin saron* article discussing her lack of plans to marry, for instance, was preceded in the journal by an essay from her employer Dr. Kinoshita, who suggested, approvingly, that sports fostered the "masculine beauty of women." Kinoshita's article was followed by an article explaining why a recent session of the Japanese Diet had failed to pass a proposal that would have granted women limited voting rights.[145] Although such a combination of articles was certainly open to mixed interpretations, seeing a connection between women's participation in sports and socio-political change—for better or worse, depending on one's view—was not at all difficult.

Indeed, claims linking Hitomi's achievements to suffrage were not as far-fetched as they might at first seem. For one thing, as a newspaper article from 1924 indicated, both women and men often based their opinions on women's suffrage on assumed gender differences and roles.[146] By engaging in and achieving success in a "male" activity like sports, Hitomi raised fundamental questions about the validity of even medically based assumptions about gender. Considering Hitomi's success, some people at the time might easily have begun to wonder why Japanese society seemed to be enthusiastically embracing women as representatives of the nation on the international stage, yet simultaneously continuing to argue that the country's women were not ready to vote for a local elected official. It is also worth noting that connections between women's participation in sports and the granting of women's political rights were not unique to Japan. The progressive American historian Frederic L. Paxson had argued for just such a connection in 1917, three years before the 19th Amendment to the U. S. Constitution was ratified, guaranteeing American women the right to vote.[147] Perhaps Hitomi was, after all, a suffragette in athlete's clothing.

As a symbol of the medley of challenges to Japan's existing gender order, Hitomi may have been all the more disconcerting because her success came in sports, a field of activity (like politics) often viewed as a "male preserve," a kind of "safe zone" that men could turn to "as a proof of masculinity, especially if their gender identity seemed threatened for other reasons."[148] At a time when Japanese women, especially middle-class women, were entering the workforce in increasing numbers, ostensibly rejecting their traditional roles as wives and mothers, and demanding access to the masculine world of politics, Japanese men, or at least their hegemonic roles in the socio-political order, were seemingly under attack (see Figure 3.8).[149] Citing mostly American examples, R. W. Connell has examined the ways in which forms of "exemplary masculinity," including sports, assume even greater importance during historical moments when men's superiority or right to rule appears to be challenged.[150]

The examples of Hitomi and Japanese masculinity in the 1920s and 1930s suggest that for societies "late" in coming to Western-style sports—essentially much of the world outside the United States and

Europe—the role of sports in bolstering masculinity was problematic. In the Japanese case, sports appear to have further contributed to, rather than necessarily countered, concerns about masculinity, in part because notions of masculinity tied to sports and sports stars were embedded in unequal transnational relationships that privileged the West.

For Japanese men, the problems with sports and masculinity began at home. Naturally, most men were not themselves star athletes, and as sports and sports stars became increasingly popular in Japan, some male commentators began asking why Japanese women seemed so interested in sports and whether or not this was a good thing. In his contribution to a 1931 series of articles on "Sports Eroticism," the writer Kataoka Teppei detailed women's fascination with particular stars and cited the case of a girl he knew as proof that young women were beginning to expect their future husbands to be "sportsman-like" (*supōtsuman raiku*).[151] In another magazine, Satō Hachirō began a comic article by talking about how his wife enjoyed accompanying him to sporting events. Following several of his anecdotes about her growing enthusiasm for pretty much any sport, Satō repeatedly added the refrain, "My wife likes sports." By the end of his essay, however, with his wife preparing to go with her friends to see a Keiō University swimming practice the following day, Satō concluded, "Ah, my wife likes sports. No, she likes them a little too much."[152] By highlighting his wife's (and her friends') growing, and implicitly dangerous, obsession with sports and how it superseded the husband-and-wife sports outings that began the article, Satō betrayed, albeit jokingly, anxieties about women losing interest in less athletic men (see Figure 3.9).

If non-athletic Japanese males were beginning to show concern about challenges from Japanese athletes, then the images of Western athletes flooding Japan at the time, along with the athletes themselves in several cases, were potentially more disturbing. Abe Tomoji's 1930 short story about the Japanese-German track meet held in Tokyo the previous year raised the specter of just such a threat. The main character in Abe's story, a married woman with a young daughter of her own, becomes obsessively infatuated with one of the German athletes, Kurt Weiss, after she sees him during the first day of the meet. She secretly attends the second day of the meet and later goes to see the German team's departure, but otherwise does not act on her infatuation. Nevertheless, after accidentally encountering Weiss, up close, in a hotel elevator, she later finds herself imagining that the copy of Leonardo da Vinci's *St. John the Baptist* hanging in her bedroom depicts not St. John, but a naked and

Figure 3.8 Cartoon of unknown authorship from the 1 November 1916 issue of the comic magazine *Ōsaka Pakku*. The English caption reads, "If you would marry with any of the Yuhigaoka school girls' [*sic*] you can be sure to find these useful tools in her dowry." The Japanese caption offers a more detailed list of the tools that attendees of this school for women bring to the marriage, including mountain climbing gear and sports equipment. Shimizu Isao, ed., *Manga ni egakareta Meiji, Taishō, Shōwa*, 146. Courtesy of Shimizu Isao and Newton Press, Inc.

Figure 3.9 Cartoon dating from 1924 by Shimokawa Hekoten from an evening edition of the *Chūō shinbun* newspaper. According to the quotation included in Shimizu Isao's edited collection of cartoons, this young woman thought of the baseball player as an ideal husband during her school days, but she opted to marry for money and now thinks longingly of her school days. Shimizu Isao, ed., *Manga ni egakareta Meiji, Taishō, Shōwa*, 125. Courtesy of Shimizu Isao and Newton Press, Inc.

suntanned Weiss. In contrast to the beautiful, well-muscled Weiss with his light, golden-blond beard, bronze skin, and auburn hair, Abe's main character finds the features and characteristics of the Japanese men in her life (her husband and a young, would-be lover) completely unpalatable. Their beards are "mere trash," her husband's muscles, "like wire and permeated with the stench of cigar."[153]

Some have read Abe's story as a "critique of the presumably arranged and certainly loveless marriage of an older man and a younger women," suggesting that the "story's implications are feminist."[154] Although certainly plausible, such readings fail to explain why the woman's sensual awakening is spurred, not by her potential young lover or even the Japanese athletes, but instead by a foreign sports star. This choice was no accident. By revealing the secret thoughts and desires of an unhappy and dissatisfied woman, Abe's story articulated what some men feared at the time: Japanese men, athletes or otherwise, simply did not measure up when compared with Western men. As if adding insult to injury, the Japanese track team, in the story and real life, lost to the Germans.

The Japanese track loss in 1929 points to the fact that sports had historically been and continued to be a less than effective means for bolstering masculine pride for Japanese men. From almost the moment they were introduced to Japan, sports had been linked to Euro-American manliness and dominance, a linkage that effectively feminized any society without the "universal" of sports.[155] The efforts of Hitachiyama and others to redefine sumo had served as one way in which Japanese sought to overcome their newly determined "effeminate" culture, but many others perceived a need to embrace Western sports and prove their masculinity through victory in international competition. Doing so, however, was an especially difficult task, since European and American athletes maintained a dominant position in international sports. As the comparative charts of body measurements published in one of Saitō's 1933 *Yomiuri* sports medicine articles suggested, Western athletes also maintained a distinct physical advantage.[156] When both the bodies and achievements of Japanese male athletes seemed constantly to fall short in relation to their Western counterparts, any efforts to call upon sports as symbolic proof of male superiority in Japan were shaky at best, and necessarily relied on the supposition that sports and athletic success were the exclusive domain of men.

Hitomi's success effectively demolished the myth of male exclusivity in sports in Japan. When women began making advances in sports in the United States and Europe, they met with strong resistance, but men in those societies could still at least point to their international athletic presence as a form of exemplary masculinity.[157] This was not necessarily the case in Japan. With Hitomi's international sporting success, the star systems that linked her to her compatriot males, many of whom seemed to be struggling internationally, placed Hitomi in a privileged—and consequently threatening—position. Little wonder, then, that many of the articles addressing Hitomi's achievements in international competition expressed a mix of pride and subtle disgust that she was doing better than Japanese men. Commenting on Hitomi's success at the 1926 women's games, one article compared her directly to male athletes, indicating that by thoroughly defeating all her international competition, she had "one-upped" (*hana o akasareta*) the men.[158] A 1928 note on Hitomi in the monthly *Taiyō* offered a detailed list of her accomplishments and suggested that it was no exaggeration to say that from an international standpoint, Hitomi "outshined the men."[159] Mentioning rumors (clearly untrue) that Hitomi was already hard at work in May 1931—she had, in fact, been hospitalized since March—preparing for the 1932 Los Angeles Olympics, one writer wondered if her efforts shouldn't make men "die in shame" (*kishi seshimuru*).[160] As these back-handed comments suggested, Hitomi's athletic success abroad implied that something was amiss with Japanese men. If Hitomi could do it as a woman, why couldn't the men? One of the potential answers to this question—and a potential balm for the egos of Japanese men—was the idea that Hitomi herself might not be what she appeared or claimed to be. Although her certified world records and documented victories might be beyond question, her gender was not.

MAN?

In May 1931, as Hitomi lay dying in the hospital, writer and social critic Murobuse Kōshin penned an article for the women's magazine *Fujin gahō* offering what his title called "A Discussion of Hitomi Kinue." Although Murobuse claimed to know almost nothing about her, he took up the question of Hitomi's gender and her athletic success. Based on his observations and especially the fact that she was unmarried and a "sportswoman," Murobuse suggested that Hitomi was "40 or 50 percent male and 50 or 60 percent female." Although he indicated that most modern people were not 100 percent male or female, he averred that in Hitomi's case, there was a nearly equal percentage of both, so that she was "sexually self-satisfied" and consequently seemed to express "lessened sexual desires towards others." Evaluating Hitomi's success in sports, Murobuse asserted that Hitomi's achievements were the result of the high percentage of male in Hitomi. After restating this point multiple times, he offered readers one final reminder about the *true* nature of Hitomi's success: "Hitomi's 'prestigious records' were not those of a woman, but a man."[161]

It might be easy enough to dismiss Murobuse's observations as ridiculous. Considering his redundancy and his self-congratulatory praise for coming up with such a "fabulous explanation" (*saikō no setsumei*), it is entirely possible that he meant for them to seem so. Murobuse's article, however, does offer a glimpse of how Hitomi was viewed in Japanese society, especially since claims of this sort would not necessarily have struck his readers as far-fetched. Throughout her life and long after her death, societal uncertainties about Hitomi's "true" gender, uncertainties that encompassed not only her biological sex, but also her femininity, her body, and her sexuality, were a defining feature of her celebrity image.

By the time Murobuse wrote, Hitomi's body had long been a subject of attention. Even as a tennis star at her women's higher school, she had been known locally for her unusual height. Details about the bodies of athletes are common, though critical, components of their celebrity images. What made Hitomi's case unusual, however, was the comparison of her body with those of men. Writing in 1926, shortly after Hitomi's successful trip to Europe, Hoshino Tatsui, for instance, provided Hitomi's height and a reference to her big arms and legs as "stronger than those of most men"—all before mentioning her name.[162] In his biographical essay, Furushō Kunio gave Hitomi's height as precisely 5 feet 7.042 inches (5 *shaku* 6 *sun* 2 *bu* or 170.286 centimeters), and added, "If this height were a man's, it would pass [the military conscription physical] splendidly as an artilleryman."[163] Describing Hitomi's muscles and strong limbs, Furushō gushed about the "beauty of her well-proportioned physique," declaring, "It would be difficult to find such proportions, even among a hundred thousand male athletes."[164] Such comparisons, perhaps intended as praise, also served to highlight the fact that in terms of her appearance, Hitomi seemed more like a man (and an impressive man, at that) than a woman.

It is not surprising, then, that sources from the time indicated that people often questioned whether Hitomi was a woman at all. Mentioning these frequent questions in his 1926 article, Hoshino, who was also Hitomi's colleague in the sports section of the *Ōsaka Mainichi* newspaper, offered his readers a gossipy-sounding tidbit as an example. As Hoshino told it, while still a student at the women's higher school, Hitomi had once been mistaken for a man and asked to leave the women's swimming area just as she was about to go in the water.[165] Whether or not the account was true, Hoshino's rather unsympathetic sharing of the story did little to challenge, and may have even reinforced, doubts about Hitomi's womanhood, doubts which Hoshino never explicitly denied.

Hitomi was not entirely alone in having to deal with doubts and concerns surrounding gender. The questions she faced were part of broader, concurrent debates in Japanese society about shifting perceptions of masculinity and femininity as Japanese women challenged traditional gender roles and patterns by entering the workforce in increasing numbers, pursuing new fashions, or taking up politics, dancing, and sports. Hitomi's sports career, moreover, overlapped with the early popularity of the all-female Takarazuka Revue theater. By the 1920s, critics in the print media were describing the women playing male roles, or *otokoyaku*, in this theater troupe as "abnormal, masculinized females, who sported short hair [*danpatsu*] and wore pants."[166] For such critics, the emergence of these androgynous females and their fans evidenced societal disorder and "abnormal sexual desire" and threatened to undermine the alleged stability of traditional gender roles.[167] Emerging from this socio-historical milieu, Hitomi's well-publicized athletic activities and fashion choices understandably raised similar concerns.

At the same time, Hitomi was a female athlete during a period when that category was unusual in Japan. As such she shared much in common with pioneering athletes outside the country as well. Hitomi's reception and treatment in Japanese society bears remarkable similarities to American female stars such as Mildred "Babe" Didrikson and Eleonora Randolph Sears, women who were exceptional athletes and consequently "risked being considered either eccentric, anomalous, or freakish," finding their gender identity subject to doubt.[168] Still today, when female athletes have become common in societies worldwide, tensions remain apparent. As Abigail M. Feder-Kane's study of figure skating has shown, television commentary, official regulations, and costumes undeniably overemphasize the femininity of female skaters (who are still officially called "ladies" in competition) in order to soften, even hide the "athletic prowess required for executing triple-jumps and flying sit-spins."[169] Even in a sport like figure skating, which is popularly viewed as "feminine," for a woman to appear too athletic is to invite being labeled as masculine or dubbed a lesbian.

In Hitomi's case, both she and her biographers felt the need on several occasions to soften and feminize her athletic image. Some of Hitomi's own comments seemed to imply that she eventually wanted to assume a role as a wife and mother, especially when such comments are taken together with her frequent references to women's sports as a means for improving the health of Japan's future mothers.[170] Hitomi's self-professed interest in marriage, however, eventually became, and has remained, a matter of speculation, not only because of the indifference, if not hostility, to marriage she seemed to express in her later writings, but also because of her close relationship with another woman.

Since moving to Osaka, Hitomi had lived together with Fujimura Chō, a female friend who had been one year Hitomi's junior at Nikaidō taisō juku. In 1931, just months before Hitomi's death, stories from two different women's magazines directed their attention, and that of their readers, to certain "unknown facts" about this relationship, promising to reveal Hitomi's "secret story of sexual desire."[171] Relying on common tropes and terminology associated with female same-sex intimacy that would have been familiar to readers at the time, the two stories indicated, in no uncertain terms, that this relationship, or at least Hitomi's role in it, went beyond that of friendship.

Iwaki Shōzō's account, published in two installments in *Fujin kōron*, offered extensive details about Hitomi's job, sports competitions, training, and her lecture tours, all as background for explaining why so much time spent "mixed among men" made her long for the "feminine life" that she was able to experience at home with her attractive and feminine housemate "S-ko."[172] With S-ko assuming responsibility for day-to-day household affairs, their "Sweet Home" (*suīto hōmu*) was "pleasant, pure, and beautiful." According to the article, "S-ko respected, trusted in, and wished the best for Hitomi, and Hitomi felt deep affection and appreciation for S-ko."[173] By contrasting Hitomi's masculine qualities and activities with S-ko's femininity and indicating that this relationship had begun during the time they spent "living together in the dorm at the Nikaidō girls' school," Iwaki employed popular images of schoolgirl intimacy to alert his readers to the "true" nature of this relationship. What Iwaki was describing in *very* thinly disguised terms was not a mutually beneficial and close relationship between friends and housemates, but rather a "female married couple," which newspaper publisher Fukushima Shirō had characterized in 1911 as a harmful form of the female same-sex intimacy popularly associated with students at Japan's girls' schools.[174] Iwaki's choice of the pseudonym for S-ko was also revealing. The capitalized Latin letter "S," as it appeared in this story (as many as six times on one of the article's pages), was also widely used by this time as a "generic signifier for schoolgirl intimacy," both among schoolgirls and in the media.[175] As if to reinforce his "hidden" suggestions, at multiple points Iwaki also refers to S-ko as Hitomi's "same-sex friend S-ko" (*dōsei no tomo* S-*ko*), a seemingly superfluous modifier, no doubt intended to evoke connections between "S" and "same-sex love" (*dōseiai*).[176]

In contrast to Iwaki's comments, the language of Ōsaka Rokusuke's story in the July issue of *Fujin gahō* was far less veiled and bordered on cruel. Ōsaka's story focused almost exclusively on Hitomi's relationship with her housemate, here dubbed Shibata Hatsuko. Ōsaka situated the pair's relationship in the context of questions about Hitomi's lack of interest in marriage and questions about her biological sex. Citing her "MENSTRATION" (misspelled in capitalized Latin letters) as proof, the story noted that Hitomi was in fact a woman, but an "extremely peculiar woman."[177] Ōsaka left little question about his perspective on the relationship, bluntly describing Shibata as "Hitomi's bride" and her "same-sex lover" (*dōsei no aijin*).[178] Ōsaka also peppered his account with stereotypical images associated at the time with female same-sex intimacy. In an imagined conversation between Hitomi and Shibata, the two swore never to marry men and made passing mention of suicide, a reference on Ōsaka's part to several highly publicized scandals involving young women who allegedly swore oaths and committed joint suicides.[179] By citing the connection with suicide, Ōsaka was hinting at the unhealthy and potentially dangerous nature of this relationship. A similar logic was evident in Ōsaka's supposition that Hitomi's current state of ill health was linked to her relationship with Shibata, who had eventually broken their oath and fallen in love with a man Hitomi deemed unworthy.[180] In Ōsaka's telling, Hitomi's body, "the core of a steel rod," was "eaten up" not simply because of overwork, but because of this betrayal in her "life of sexual desire" (*aiyoku seikatsu*).[181]

Despite the differing tones of these two stories, both styled themselves as exposés of what they claimed was the "true" story of Hitomi's love life. By using models and terminology that would have been familiar to many readers and linking these to other well-known aspects of Hitomi's activities and actions, the two authors presented Hitomi's relationship with her housemate as aberrant and offered—in the guise of exposing the truth—an explanation of the causes and significance of something that they themselves had constructed. Stories addressing the nature of Hitomi's sexuality appear to have circulated well beyond these women's magazines and their readers. An *Asahi shinbun* article published the day after her death mentioned a similar story as one of the "interesting episodes" that it highlighted from Hitomi's life.[182] Whether or not readers at the time accepted the veracity of these stories and articles, such "facts" and the questions they raised about Hitomi became one more component of her complex image, further evidence that she had indeed been a troubling, "peculiar woman."

Conclusion: Rescuing Hitomi from Herself

The questions and concerns surrounding Hitomi did not, of course, end with her death. Hitomi has remained a troubling figure, especially for those who would wish to use her complicated image to fit a particular agenda. In the years since her death, Hitomi has understandably continued to be seen as a pioneer and is regularly featured in works addressing prominent women in Japanese history. In the world of sports, she has been held up as an exemplar and inspiration for young female athletes. After marathoner Arimori Yūko won an Olympic medal in 1992, for instance, she cited Hitomi as her role model.[183] Yet for those seeking to celebrate and use Hitomi, the questions raised during her lifetime about her gender and sexuality have often proven problematic, sparking a seemingly constant need to defend and in some cases even re-create her image.

One biographical account published in 1980 as part of a collection dealing with important prewar Japanese women alluded to Hitomi's statements about her desire for a husband and family and ended its brief description by suggesting that Hitomi had never really been troubling at all: "She was an ordinary daughter, filial and loyal to her country."[184] When Oda Mikio and Toda Jun republished a single, abridged version of Hitomi's two autobiographical works in 1983, they found it necessary to include a special editors' note declaring, "Both the popular stories that Kinue was a man and the rumors that she and [Fujimura] Chō were same-sex lovers are completely without basis in fact. All the people who knew Kinue would die laughing [at such stories]."[185] Hardly the most convincing defense, such words point toward the uneasiness that many continued to feel over the questionable status of Hitomi's gender and sexuality.

The 1992 special television drama *Akai inazuma: Hitomi Kinue* (Red lightning: Hitomi Kinue) offers a striking example of rescuing Hitomi's memory.[186] Much like the stories that claimed to reveal the "true" nature of Hitomi's relationship with Fujimura (or S-ko, or Shibata), the drama seeks to expose Hitomi's secret love life. Here though, the story is one of unrequited love not with Fujimura (whose character does appear several times in the drama, almost as a foil), but with Imai Kenji, a well-known male architect who was one of Hitomi's fellow passengers on the Trans-Siberian Railroad during her first trip to Europe. In crafting this "true" story of Hitomi's love life, the drama carefully combined selected details from Hitomi's autobiographical writings, where Imai is, in fact, mentioned several times—along with several of the other men and women Hitomi met on the trip—with facts gleaned from Imai's notes about a handful of letters he mailed to Hitomi. The drama shows the two enjoying their time together in Europe with Hitomi becoming increasingly taken with Imai. As the drama's tale unfolds, Imai seems to have developed a genuine respect for Hitomi as an athlete and as a brave, adventurous young woman willing to venture so far from home, but he remained blind to Hitomi's interest and did not return her affection. After going back to Japan, he soon married. At this point in the drama, Hitomi, now left with a broken heart, never returns to her former self, in sports or life. With the closing scene the drama's narrator—the character who allegedly has found and publicized all these new "facts"—shares his final epiphany with the audience: Hitomi's death was not simply the result of her diseased lungs, but also an outcome of her loss in love. Unlike Ōsaka's oddly similar observations, in the words of the drama's narrator there is no critique of Hitomi, implicit or otherwise, but rather a new certitude about the "truth" of Hitomi's life and death.

Citing the "half-century old, new facts" used in the drama, an article from the weekly magazine *Sandē Mainichi* suggested that this story offered the long-sought answers to questions of whether Hitomi was a man or a lesbian. Hitomi, the article implied, had been rescued from uncertainty, and with her gender identity now safe, she could go back to being just like any girl, with dreams of marriage. Indeed, those reading the article and watching the drama were actively encouraged to recognize this new "fact" about Hitomi and feel particular sympathy for her case: the *real* tragedy of her premature death, they suggest, was that her all-too-normal dreams had gone ultimately unfulfilled. Hitomi had died with a broken heart, "without having been able to grasp happiness as a woman."[187]

Despite the seeming certitude expressed in both the drama and article that these new "facts" offered definitive answers to the questions surrounding Hitomi, perhaps the only thing definite about this new story is that it further complicated Hitomi's image. Though the drama, the *Sandē Mainichi* article, and countless other sources seem intent on doing so, the gender-related tensions surrounding Hitomi cannot be erased; they are an indelible part of her image as a sports celebrity. Any effort to deny or disprove such questions and concerns must necessarily raise them. As one of Japan's greatest sports stars and a pioneer in women's sports, Hitomi cannot be forgotten, nor, it would seem, entirely forgiven. Her image, which has been and continues to be regularly and selectively re-crafted, will persist in generating attention. But even the most concerted efforts to define the "real" Hitomi will remain troubled by the very complexity and malleability that have made her sports-star image—and by extension, those of other stars—so compelling, useful, and powerful in the first place.

FOUR

"Japan's Number One" Goes to War: Baseball, Militarization, and Memory

Not once did he put on airs or act based on his status as a star pitcher. Thinking only of his girlfriend Yūko and his family, he devoted himself to baseball. His simplicity and honesty were beautiful.

—Ikeda Tsuneo, *An Immortal Great Pitcher: Sawamura Eiji*

Sawamura Eiji may have been as simple, honest, devoted, and hardworking as the well-known baseball journalist Ikeda Tsuneo suggested, but what made Sawamura worthy of such adulation in the first place was his status as a sports star, one of Japan's most popular baseball players of the 1930s and 1940s. As a founding member of Japan's professional baseball league and a renowned pitcher with the Tokyo Giants, Sawamura was frequently called "Japan's Number One." The events surrounding his rise to national and even international fame highlight the transnational, co-constitutional processes at work in the production of sports-celebrity images. After a stunning display of his pitching abilities in a series of games against Major League Baseball players who visited Japan in 1934, Sawamura became a national hero, his image inseparably linked to Babe Ruth and other American players. Sawamura was and continues to be the "pitcher who struck out Babe Ruth."

Yet Sawamura's "battles" with American baseball greats, his amazing fastballs (still today considered to be among the fastest in Japanese baseball), and his no-hit games (he pitched a total of three) are only part of his story. He is also the "player who died in the war."[1] In 1944, Sawamura's military transport was en route to the Philippines, when an American submarine torpedoed the boat and sank it, killing all on board. This ill-fated voyage was not Sawamura's first experience in the military. On two previous occasions he had been called to active duty with the Japanese army and dispatched to the front—China in 1938 and the Philippines in 1941. Because of his status as a sports hero, Sawamura's military service attracted widespread media and fan interest. His well-publicized comments and writings about military experiences made the star pitcher a de facto spokesman for the war effort. Challenging common assumptions that baseball's relationship with Japan's wartime state was inherently antagonistic, this chapter examines how Sawamura and other baseball enthusiasts actively promoted the sport's usefulness for a nation at war.

If Sawamura's military career and exploits generated considerable and often laudatory notice during his lifetime, in the multiple retellings of his story since his death, they have been noticeably obscured. Largely ignoring Sawamura's participation in the war effort, his story has been recast in the postwar period as a tragic narrative of wartime struggle and loss. In the aftermath of Japan's lost war, Sawamura, like baseball and Japanese society more generally, has come to be seen as a victim of Japan's aggressive wartime state.

A Bond with America in Life and Death

In 1947, *Nekkyū,* a fan magazine associated with the Yomiuri Giants baseball team, created a new prize for the best pitcher in Japanese baseball, the Sawamura Eiji Award. Highlighting the rapid resurgence of baseball after World War II, *Nekkyū* established the award seeking "to foster accurate coverage of the world baseball situation and contribute to the wholesome development and popularization of our national baseball game" by encouraging good pitchers and "immortalizing the glory and achievements of the extraordinary, great pitcher Sawamura Eiji."[2] The Nippon Professional Baseball league later adopted this privately initiated prize as one of its own official awards.[3] Thanks in part to this award, given annually to the pitcher deemed the best in Japanese professional baseball, Sawamura Eiji continues to play a role in Japanese baseball more than sixty years after his death.

In both Japanese and English commentary and descriptions, the Sawamura Award is often compared with the Cy Young Award, which is presented every year to the top pitchers in Major League Baseball. An English-language description from the Japanese Baseball Hall of Fame, for instance, refers to the Sawamura Award as "Japan's Cy Young

Award."[4] On the surface, descriptions of this sort seem logical, the result of efforts to explain the Japanese award in terms that might be more familiar, especially for non-Japanese. Cy Young, after all, achieved fame as a star pitcher years before Sawamura was even born, and because of the international popularity of Major League Baseball and the annual presentation of an award in his honor, Cy Young's fame has extended well beyond his lifetime and home country.

Closer consideration reveals a more complex picture. For one thing, descriptions of this sort highlight the uneven power relationships inherent in sports and sports celebrity. The Cy Young Award was established in 1956, nine years *after* the first Sawamura Award, yet we do not see references to the Cy Young Award as "Major League Baseball's Sawamura Award," in either Japanese or English. Although neither side "copied" the other, defining the Sawamura Award in terms of Cy Young creates the impression of a Japanese imitation of a Western model. To suggest otherwise by inverting the comparison, even when it might be historically accurate, would be tantamount to sacrilege, since Cy Young holds a privileged position in baseball lore as a foundational star in the history of a quintessentially American sport.

That is not to say that these comparisons are to Sawamura's detriment. In this instance, the comparisons of the two awards draw from Young's symbolic significance to complement Sawamura's reputation, implying that he, like Young, was not only a great pitcher, but also played a pivotal role in the history of baseball. These kinds of postmortem Sawamura/Young pairings are but one of several ways in which Sawamura's image as a sports star in Japan has been constructed specifically in relation to foreign baseball stars. Even though nearly all of the games in his baseball career were played against Japanese teams, it was Sawamura's games against Americans that propelled him to national and international stardom and became a defining aspect of his celebrity.

Ever since his first "professional" baseball games in 1934, Sawamura has been inextricably bound up with America and American baseball players. That year, while Sawamura was still a seventeen-year-old student at a middle school (*chūtō gakkō*, precursor of present-day high school), he was convinced to quit school and join the team of Japanese all-stars who were being organized to play against a visiting group of American Major League players, including such future Hall of Fame stars as Babe Ruth, Lou Gehrig, and Jimmie Foxx. Although it may seem unusual that a seventeen-year-old, middle-school dropout would make a team of national all-stars, two issues help to explain the situation: the status of amateur baseball in Japan at that time and Sawamura's reputation as an amateur star.

BASEBALL IN JAPAN: AN AMATEUR'S GAME

Baseball was first introduced to Japan in the 1870s. Like many other Western sports, it initially attracted attention mostly among Japan's young elite enrolled in the higher schools that would later become the nation's top universities. By the 1890s, the sport had become increasingly popular, especially after the Japanese student baseball club from the First Higher School achieved several lopsided victories against various groups of Americans residing in Japan.[5] By the turn of the century, several of Japan's private universities—most notably Waseda and Keiō—had established baseball clubs and begun holding regular games; and in 1914, Waseda, Keiō, and Meiji universities formed Japan's first intercollegiate baseball league. By 1925, that league had expanded to include three other universities in Tokyo (Hōsei, Rikkyō, and the University of Tokyo).[6]

Alongside these developments at the college level, baseball was also emerging as a popular participatory and spectator sport at lower-level schools throughout Japan. When the new Meiji government officials initiated a system of compulsory education in Japan during the 1870s, they had included physical education, often in the form of Western gymnastics, as part of the new curriculums for both teachers-in-training and their students. Although games and sports, such as baseball, soccer, and tennis, appeared with increasing frequency in primary school curriculums and at local school sports festivals (*undōkai*) during the 1880s, it was extracurricular sports clubs (*undōbu*) that transformed Japan's school sports scene. Inspired partly by the growing popularity of baseball at the college level, middle schools (*chūtō gakkō*) throughout Japan began establishing baseball clubs around the turn of the century.[7] As Hitomi Kinue's school-time athletic experiences in tennis and track and field suggest, other types of schools and other sports followed suit, but baseball quickly outpaced other school sports, thanks in no small part to the media.

In 1915, as part of its efforts to boost circulation by capitalizing on increasing interest in baseball, the *Asahi* newspaper established a national baseball tournament for middle schools. The annual tournament sparked the creation of even more school baseball clubs and eventually attracted hundreds of teams from throughout the country, as well as Japan's colonies. The *Asahi* tournament was remarkably successful, leading to the construction of the famed, 50,000-seat Kōshien Stadium in

Hyōgo prefecture in 1924, as well as the creation of a second middle-school tournament sponsored by the *Mainichi* newspaper beginning that same year.[8]

Newspapers such as the *Asahi* and *Mainichi* were not the only businesses interested in fostering and feeding off the popular frenzy over baseball. Seeing baseball as a means for attracting customers and improving worker-management relations, several businesses, including railways, newspapers, and industrial companies like Yawata Iron and Steel, also sponsored baseball teams in the 1920s, leading to the creation of Japan's industrial league. A number of graduates from college leagues and various middle-school baseball teams went on to play for these industrial teams, where they remained "amateurs" by virtue of the fact that they held at least nominal jobs in the companies for which they played.[9] Efforts to establish a fully professional team in Japan, with players paid explicitly for their skills, were also initiated in the early 1920s by a group of former college players, but the new team proved unsuccessful, failing to attract the best athletes and generating little interest among baseball fans.[10]

As the general lack of interest in Japan's first professional team suggests, it was amateur baseball and especially the college leagues and the annual middle-school tournaments that fueled what had become by the 1920s a national obsession with baseball. Even after the successful establishment of a professional league in the late 1930s, amateur baseball and its players remained the primary focus of baseball-related media coverage up through the end of World War II. Throughout the period, newspapers continued to play a central role in the promotion of amateur and later professional baseball, but they were not the only media outlets covering the new national sport, which was quickly surpassing sumo in terms of both coverage and popularity. The 1910s and 1920s saw the emergence of several baseball specialty magazines, as well as baseball-related films.[11] Beginning with the 1927 radio broadcast of the *Asahi* middle-school tournament at Kōshien Stadium, radio coverage of baseball games also became common.[12] Baseball specialty magazines such as *Yakyūkai*, which was first published in 1911, regularly featured photos and fan sections in addition to numerous articles on games, teams, and individual players. Mainstream journals such as *Chūō kōron* and *Bungei shunjū* also gave regular coverage to baseball and its stars.

With ever increasing media and popular attention, many college and middle-school players became national celebrities. An article from *Bungei shunjū* in November 1930 informed readers about the "star players" (*sutā pureyā*) active in Tokyo's college league that fall. The article offered various levels of detail about the health, practice schedules, and achievements of more than twenty different stars.[13] Suggesting the degree of name recognition that these players had achieved, all of the players in the article were identified only by their family names, and in several instances, the particular school with which they were connected was not mentioned. The fan sections in the baseball magazine *Yakyūkai* regularly featured commentaries about players on different college teams, like one from a Meiji University fan who offered taunting criticisms of the error-filled performances of three stars often praised as a "good defender," a "smart defender," and a "miracle pitcher."[14] Such baseball coverage indicates that team loyalties ran high, especially among university-league fans, and it also clearly reveals that tendencies to single out individual athletes have long played an important role in baseball stardom in Japan. Even middle-school players who showed promise in the national tournament attracted widespread attention. The career paths of such potential stars were the center of much debate in the media and among fans sharing their thoughts in magazines like *Yakyūkai*.[15] Many of these teenage stars continued to generate significant popular interest throughout their baseball careers. This proved to be the case for Sawamura, even though he diverged significantly from the path that many had expected him to take.

WASEDA OR KEIŌ? SAWAMURA AS AN AMATEUR STAR

Sawamura began playing baseball for his elementary school in 1927, at the age of ten, but accounts of his childhood indicate that he had taken up the sport even earlier. His father, it is said, loved the game and wanted his son to play, especially since the boy was small and sickly. According to Suzuki Sōtarō, the author of the best-known biography of Sawamura and a key management figure with the Giants, Sawamura—always the filial son—devoted himself wholeheartedly to the sport, allegedly even forfeiting summer relaxation time with his friends because his father wanted him to practice. Consequently, baseball transformed Sawamura's weak body, and more.[16]

As the son of a poor rural vegetable vendor in Mie prefecture, Sawamura apparently had no plans to continue his education beyond the mandatory elementary level, intending instead to go to Osaka and find work as a business or store clerk.[17] But after Sawamura's pitching abilities were "discovered" when he led his elementary-school team to several victories, middle schools in the area took notice. They recruited this local standout with an eye towards improving their baseball clubs so that they might reach, and possibly win, the national tournaments at Kōshien. In the summer of 1930, Sawamura entered a commercial school (*shōgyō gakkō*) in Kyoto that had been established a year earlier. The school's founder had explicitly declared his intention to form a baseball club that could compete at Kōshien. Sawamura's fastballs and curves promised a bright future for the school and the young pitching phenomenon.[18]

Much like Hitomi Kinue, Sawamura is often said to have possessed extraordinary natural gifts as an athlete, but like a true sports star—or at least one who conforms to a paradigmatic model—he was not content with that and honed his abilities through hard practice. Citing Thomas Edison as an example, Suzuki asserted that Sawamura's achievements and especially his unrivaled speed as a pitcher were the results of "perspiration—waterfalls of sweat" from devoting himself to hard training. According to Suzuki, Sawamura "would run and run and run, until he could run no more. He would throw and throw and throw, until he could throw no more."[19] Together with the benefits of the coaching he received after entering middle school, Sawamura's childhood efforts to improve his natural abilities came to be seen as the key to his early success—success that in the world of middle-school baseball in the 1930s meant winning national tournament games.

In both 1933 and 1934, Sawamura's pitching helped his school earn one of the coveted spots in the *Ōsaka Mainichi*'s spring tournament at Kōshien.[20] In 1934, Sawamura's team also advanced through the qualifying tournaments to reach the final summer tournament, where the team eventually lost in first-round play. Even though his school never won an overall championship, as the team's ace pitcher who regularly struck out more than ten batters a game and also pitched several shutouts, Sawamura began to attract national recognition.[21]

After his school's second appearance at the spring tournament of 1934, articles featuring Sawamura alongside other middle-school stars appeared in national newspapers and baseball magazines. Based on the 1934 spring tournament, a *Yomiuri* newspaper article naming a "National All-Star Team" carried the headline, "Sawamura, Top Pitcher." Highlighting Sawamura's unbelievably fast "speedball," as well as his ability to control his pitches, the article indicated that Sawamura stood out from his fellow middle-school players and had a promising future worth watching.[22] In 1934, the baseball magazine *Yakyūkai* also began taking notice. A June article about key games at the preceding spring tournament described Sawamura as the tournament's "most exceptional" pitcher.[23] A month later, an article featuring twenty middle-school stars "of talent and virtue" listed Sawamura first, praising not only his abilities, but also his work ethic and his humility. Comparing him to previous middle-school greats, the author declared his hope that Sawamura would "remain uncorrupted by the world's applause" and help usher in the "Age of Sawamura" in school baseball.[24] Following the summer tournament in 1934, a reporter from the *Ōsaka Jiji* newspaper contributed an article to *Yakyūkai* in which he lamented the fact that the previous Kōshien tournament had been the last opportunity to see the "amazing pitching" of Sawamura who would be graduating the next spring. The only consolation for the writer was that Sawamura was said to be headed for Keiō where he would continue pitching in Tokyo's college league.[25]

Media observers were not the only ones taking an interest in Sawamura. Beginning in the fall of 1934, the fan sections of *Yakyūkai* frequently included letters and questions from throughout Japan revolving around which college Sawamura would play for after middle school. The magazine's "Readers' Club" pages featured several letters from Waseda fans expressing their delight about rumors that Sawamura had decided to attend Waseda.[26] However, on the "Questions and Answers Page" of several issues, *Yakyūkai*'s answers to fan questions about Sawamura's college plans indicated that he was going to enter Keiō.[27] Sawamura did, in fact, have the option of attending either of these schools, and many suggest that he was leaning toward Keiō. In the end, as a special note from the "Readers' Club" editor pointed out in response to a Waseda fan's letter about Sawamura in December 1934, Sawamura had a third option that had presented itself that autumn. He joined the professional team being organized to play the visiting American all-stars.[28]

In choosing to forgo the more common, and at the time more socially acceptable, college route, Sawamura was opting for a less respected professional team with an uncertain future. His reasons for doing so have generated much debate.[29] One of the most oft-cited factors behind his decision to join the professional team was money—not for himself, allegedly, but for his family who were struggling financially. Accounts written both during and after his lifetime highlight the fact that Sawamura always thought of his family's needs and wants before his own, and used his early earnings to pay for his brother's education.[30] As his father later put it, Sawamura "sacrificed his own will," giving up his desire to go to Keiō in order to provide better opportunities for his family and his younger siblings.[31] Whatever the reasoning, when Sawamura joined the professional team, he also quit middle school, effectively eliminating the possibility of joining any college team. From that point on, his future was tied to that of Japanese professional baseball.

SAWAMURA AND JAPAN GO PRO

In July 1934, Shōriki Matsutarō, the owner of the *Yomiuri shinbun*, announced that his newspaper was planning to bring a team of American baseball stars to Japan in the fall. Three years earlier, Shōriki and his paper had been instrumental in bringing a similar group of American players to Japan, but much to the disappointment of Japanese baseball fans, the 1931 team had not included Babe Ruth, the most well-known and publicized American athlete in Japan.[32] But this time would be different, as the front page of the *Yomiuri* blared to readers on 18 July 1934: "The Great Babe Ruth Is Coming, Along With Current Homerun King Foxx."[33]

When Shōriki set about creating a team to play against the visiting Americans, Sawamura was among the first players he sought to recruit for the Japanese all-star team, in large part because Sawamura had already established a reputation as an outstanding amateur pitcher. But Sawamura ended up on the team for a second key reason. Shōriki and the organizers of the Japanese team were facing recruitment problems because a recent Japanese government regulation had placed new restrictions on games between students and professionals.

In 1932, the Ministry of Education issued what is generally referred to as the "Baseball Regulation Order" ("Yakyū tōsei rei"), which established strict rules governing all levels of student baseball, from elementary to college.[34] Considering the increasing nationalism and militarization of Japanese society throughout the 1930s, it might be easy to look back on this order and see it—as do most standard accounts of baseball history—as an early sign of government interest in curbing the influence of "Western" sports and especially baseball.[35] To do so, however, would be to ignore the actual contents of the order and the context that produced it.

Because it appeared soon after the 1931 visit by the American all-stars, who had played against several college teams or teams consisting of a mix of students and recent graduates, the order is often portrayed as a direct government response to that visit.[36] Although the 1931 games with American professionals probably shaped some aspects of the order (the provisions regulating mixed professional and student games, for instance), plans to draft new guidelines for baseball had begun in 1930, well before the American team came to Japan. The Ministry of Education order explicitly targeted baseball not because it was a Western sport, but because "student baseball served as the very heart of the popular baseball world."[37] In general, the order had less to do with curbing baseball than it did with "cleaning up" the sport and maintaining the amateur status of baseball among students. Consequently, references to gate receipts, acceptable prizes, and appropriate forms of reimbursement abound.[38] The order did limit student participation, but it did so in ways that would seem familiar for many student athletes: for players in elementary school, only students in the fifth year or above, who had parental permission, could participate.[39] At the next level, students needed the authorization of parents and school officials, and anyone who enrolled part-way through the school year had to wait one year to be eligible to play.[40] College players had to have the approval of school authorities, and at all levels, students needed medical authorization.[41] The Ministry of Education requirement that elementary and middle schools limit games, as much as possible, to non-school hours, especially weekends and school holidays, also reflected understandable concerns that the ever increasing number of practices, games, tournaments, and even international tours were beginning to interfere with educational activities.[42]

Anxieties about professionalism and educational impediments were not new to Japan, having both been the subject of countless media debates at various points.[43] Neither were they limited to baseball or unique to Japan. In 1926, alleged concerns about students missing too many classes led the Ministry of Education to forbid student participation in the annual Meiji Shrine Games, which were sponsored by the government's own Home Ministry.[44] In 1929, the Carnegie Foundation released *American College Athletics*, a report providing damning evidence of corruption and abuses in several major college sports programs in the United States. Pressing for several necessary reforms, the Carnegie report received extensive publicity in the United States and may have served as a reference, model, or perhaps even impetus for the Ministry of Education order about baseball in Japan.[45]

For Shōriki, the reasoning behind the Ministry's order did not change the fact that it was going to make it more difficult to put together a team for the Americans to play in 1934. Most of Japan's best players at the time were in the extremely popular college leagues, but because of the regulations affecting student games with professionals, Shōriki and his team organizers saw the need to look elsewhere for potential recruits. The industrial leagues offered one source. So did middle schools, where students like Sawamura, who had not yet entered a university, might be persuaded (and in some cases pressured) to choose an alternative to college, even if it meant leaving middle school before graduating.[46]

The new government policies and the efforts of team organizers to get around them offer a revealing example of the unintended consequences of state-led regulatory efforts. Student players, like Sawamura, who joined the team, simply dropped out of school, which was certainly not what Ministry of Education officials had desired in establishing the new regulations.[47] More significantly, the regulatory measures, in the end, helped spark the emergence of what would eventually become a successful professional baseball league in Japan.

Even before the American players arrived, the Japanese media and especially the sponsoring *Yomiuri* newspaper bombarded fans with pictures, statistics, and biographies of the American team, as well as more general facts about baseball in the United States. Similar, though generally less extensive, coverage was provided for the Japanese team.[48] In addition to media coverage, what was probably the first Japanese book-length biography of Babe Ruth, complete with a guide to Ruth's baseball tactics, was published shortly before his arrival in Japan.[49] With all this build-up, when the American team finally arrived in November, massive crowds greeted the players, and the games attracted sell-out crowds in locations throughout the country.

The activities of the Major League stars and their reception in Japan did not go unnoticed in the United States. Billing the trip as "another American goodwill voyage," American media coverage, though understandably less extensive than that appearing in Japan, reported several details about the trip and the all-stars' games in Japan.[50] Babe Ruth and his popularity in Japan received particular attention in papers throughout the United States.[51] A front-page article from the national weekly baseball newspaper *Sporting News* began its report on the American players' arrival declaring:

> Babe Ruth has come, seen and conquered Japan. It required police reserves to push back the crowd that greeted him on his arrival, along with other members of the American League All-Star team; he had to be guarded every time he stepped out of the hotel to prevent his being mobbed; he autographed so many baseballs that he could no longer write and 65,000 enthusiasts crammed the Meiji Shrine Stadium to see him play in the first game.[52]

But Ruth was more than just a popular attraction; he was "Babe, the Ambassador" who helped the Japanese forget their policy disagreements and made them "go American."[53] Pointing to the transnational, co-constitutional nature of sports celebrity, Ruth's experiences in Japan became a key element of his celebrity image, repeatedly referenced to highlight his appeal and recognition of his greatness.[54]

To no one's surprise, the American team won all sixteen of the games in Japan, often with lopsided scores. Despite such losses, the media coverage makes it clear that Japanese fans and players were enthusiastically embracing not only their American baseball heroes, but also the opportunity to learn from them. This emphasis on the instructional nature of the games no doubt reflected Shōriki's efforts to dampen criticisms about professional baseball by marketing his Japanese all-stars as an "amateur team receiving instruction on baseball skills from the American pros."[55] During and after the tour, Japanese players regularly appeared in the media explaining what they had learned by playing against the American pros. Such articles often explicitly expressed appreciation to various American players for their guidance. Immediately following the Americans' departure, the *Yomiuri* ran several articles where the Japanese team members offered their impressions of the tour.[56] In January 1935, *Yakyūkai* offered a special series of articles on the tour, which included several essays from Japanese players talking about what they had gained from their experience. This series included a group of articles that juxtaposed American comments about the Japanese team with Japanese players' comments about the Americans.[57] Because of the critical role he had played in these games, Sawamura appeared in the January issue of *Yakyūkai* and in a special article the following month. Among other points, Sawamura noted his surprise that even the great Babe Ruth had weaknesses and also expressed appreciation for the feedback he received from American pitchers.[58]

If the Japanese players were eagerly assuming the role of students, American players were just as eager to play the teacher. In doing so, they had the active support of the Japanese press, as indicated by the post-tour articles in *Yakyūkai* and perhaps most clearly by a multi-part series in Shōriki's *Yomiuri* called "The American Players Teach," which ran throughout the tour.[59] Speaking to an attentive audience through the Japanese media, Babe Ruth did not hesitate to scold the Japanese team for overusing its good pitchers, and at one point, Lou Gehrig offered a lecture on two key mistakes that had led to a Japanese loss the previous day.[60]

Premised as it was on understandable assumptions of American superiority, the relationship between the American baseball "teachers" and their Japanese "students" in this case highlights how both sides looked to the other to define themselves. This fact became even more apparent when the assumed stability of the relationship was threatened by none other than the seventeen-year-old pitcher Sawamura. In the tenth game of the tour on 20 November 1934, Sawamura held the American All-Star team to one run, a solo homer by Lou Gehrig in the seventh inning. Over the course of the game, Sawamura allowed only five hits and struck out nine of the American players, including consecutive strikeouts of Charlie Gehringer, Babe Ruth, Lou Gehrig, and Jimmie Foxx during the first and second innings of the game.

Even though the Japanese lost the game 1-0, the team and fans were elated. Many argued that this game offered a sign that Japan could develop a competitive professional league of its own, one that could compete on par with the American big leagues. The overall success of the tour prompted Shōriki to establish a professional team shortly after the Americans departed, a move that was eventually followed with the establishment of Japan's first professional baseball league in 1936. Sawamura was dubbed "Japan's Number One," instantly becoming a national hero and even gaining attention abroad as American papers reporting on the tour quickly picked up on the amazing exploits of the teenage pitcher.

American coverage of the famous game proves revealing as much for what it says as what it omits. The earliest stories in the American press came in the form of a short AP report that was carried with slight variations in newspapers throughout the country soon after the game. Describing the contest as a "pitcher's battle between the veteran Earl Whitehill and 17-year-old Eiji Sawamura," the article acknowledges Sawamura's near shutout, but it erroneously reports that Ruth, rather than Gehrig, hit the game-winning homerun.[61] For Americans, it seems, "the Bambino" had to be the hero, even when he was not. Some versions of the AP story also preface remarks about Sawamura's "brilliant" pitching, with the misleading statement that he had been "recently expelled from Kyota [*sic*] commercial school because he played against professionals."[62] Tellingly, all versions of the AP story completely omit mentions of Sawamura's successive strikeouts, relying instead on vague references that he "tamed the major leaguers' murderers row" or "tamed the major league stars."[63] As a weekly baseball specialty newspaper, *Sporting News* might be expected to offer more accurate and extensive reporting on this close game, but if anything, its coverage, which may itself be based on newswire stories, appears even more dismissive. In a 29 November 1934 article titled, "Japanese Catching On: Ruth's Homer Only Run in Nov. 20 Game as Scores Grow Closer," the baseball paper includes a reference to Sawamura's "commercial college" expulsion but it also fails to mention his nine strikeouts, noting instead that "Sawamura is said to have pitched with all the cunning of an ace big leaguer all the way, save when he made one too good for the Bambino."[64] Such seeming praise for Sawamura was offset later in the article with a demeaning reference to the Japanese as "little brown men."[65] When an article recapping the tour appeared several weeks later in *Sporting News*, the detailed box scores for the two closest games were not among those published.[66] Apparently, if the game was not a blowout for the Americans, no one was going to be reading about it.

For their part, the American players were less than excited about the success of their up-and-coming students. Expressing concern for Sawamura's health, American pitchers informed Sawamura that he was pitching too many curve balls, adding that in the Big Leagues eventually the big-name hitters would figure out how to hit it. While the American players admitted that Sawamura was good, with some even suggesting that with a few more years of practice he could play in the Major Leagues, the Americans, and Ruth in particular, also blamed the sun for their strikeouts. As the story goes, the sun shining in their eyes had made it nearly impossible to see the ball, thus explaining their relatively poor showing against Sawamura.[67] Perhaps understandably, American coverage of the game did not mention this "fact."

Whatever one makes of the "sun was in our eyes" story, from this point on, Sawamura's image as a sports star was linked to his battle with the Americans. When Lou Gehrig died in 1941, for instance, Sawamura was the natural choice to eulogize his one-time rival. A *Yomiuri* newspaper article reporting Gehrig's death featured photographs of both stars. It also included Sawamura's recounting of the famous game in which he made passing mention of the sunshine excuse and offered comments expressing his respect and appreciation for Gehrig's guidance. Referring to Gehrig's game-winning homerun, Sawamura explained that the disappointing turn not only showed him how impressive the American players were, but also made him all too aware that preparing to meet the Americans again would require him to work and practice harder than ever.[68] On the surface, Sawamura's comment reflects good-natured sporting competition—competition that drives all players to be their very best. But there is always more to sports than what appears on the surface.

In describing these imagined future meetings between Japanese and American players, Sawamura used the phrase *sōhasen*, which is often used to describe a championship game, but can also be used, more generally, to mean a "struggle for supremacy." With this fact in mind, Sawamura's seemingly mild comments take on a whole new range of possible meanings, especially when we consider the tense relations between the United States and Japan in June 1941, when this article was written. Only six months later, Sawamura himself would become part of the struggle for supremacy as a soldier participating in Japan's invasion of the Philippines. Even though Sawamura would not have known about his own role in the upcoming battles with the Americans when he wrote the eulogy, his references to the American baseball victory as a wake-up call is suggestive. The perceived need for hard work in order to prepare for a "future Japanese-American struggle for supremacy," was, in fact, very much in line with his frequent observations about the parallels between baseball and his own military experiences, both before and after this date. As it turned out, both Sawamura and baseball proved extremely useful for a nation at war.

From Baseballs to Grenades: Sawamura the Soldier

When Shōriki established a professional team at the end of 1934, Sawamura and several of the other players he had recruited to play against the Americans joined his Greater Japan Baseball Club (Dai Nippon yakyū kurabu). In both 1935 and 1936, Shōriki sent the team to the United States, where it played several games against minor league teams. During the 1935 tour, the team took on the nickname "Giants," the name that the Yomiuri team has used since. Sawamura was especially popular during the tours. According to several local American papers and the writings of the tour's manager, Suzuki Sōtarō, people came to the games just to see the pitching of the "schoolboy" who had challenged the American greats.[69] Highlighting the pivotal role of transnational star systems in shaping Sawamura's sports-celebrity image, during the 1936 tour, several American papers dubbed him "Japan's School Boy Rowe," a reference to Lynwood "Schoolboy" Rowe, the pitcher who had helped the Detroit Tigers win the American League championship in 1934 and the World Series in 1935.[70] Sawamura also attracted the attention of several American baseball teams. Although stories vary widely, it appears that in 1935 a scout for a Major League team tried to trick Sawamura into signing a contract by simply asking him to sign what he thought was an autograph. The trick was revealed, and Sawamura's "kidnapping" avoided.[71] After returning to Japan, Sawamura made his feelings clear about whether he would play for an American team. In the magazine *Shinseinen*, Sawamura explained that although he wanted to play baseball at a professional level, he felt committed to baseball in Japan. He also indicated that he did not want to live in the United States, claiming, "I hate America and could never possibly come to like Americans."[72] The driving force behind his "hatred" appears to have been cultural difference, with language, meals without rice, and arrogant women topping Sawamura's list of things to which he could never adjust.[73]

In any case, the Giants soon had professional competition at home, as six other teams were created to form Japan's first professional league in 1936.[74] Sawamura may have been the "schoolboy" to Americans, but at home he had earlier been billed as "Japan's Number One," and his first seasons in the new professional league seemed to justify the title. In September 1936, Sawamura pitched the first no-hit game in Japanese professional baseball, and in May of the following year, he pitched his, and professional baseball's, second no-hitter. Later, in July 1940, he would pitch his third and final no-hit game, only three months after being discharged from the army. In June 1937, Sawamura became the first pitcher in professional baseball to win twenty games; a month later, he was voted the league's Most Valuable Player, an honor not awarded until that time. With such success, Sawamura and the professional league began to generate significant interest, becoming fixtures in media coverage of baseball. Sawamura became one of the professional league's biggest stars, and many suggested that his popularity helped the league survive.[75] An article from the September issue of the boys' magazine *Nihon shōnen*, for example, used Sawamura's recent MVP award to introduce readers to the professional league.[76] Whenever Sawamura pitched, his name appeared in headlines of articles about the games. By 1937, professional baseball had its own subsection in *Yakyūkai*, and issues that did not include at least one article about or picture of Sawamura had become the exception (see Figure 4.1).[77]

With all this attention focused on Sawamura's baseball achievements and promising career, it is not surprising that his departure from professional baseball would also merit notice. Officially drafted in late 1937, Sawamura entered the military in January 1938, and shortly thereafter was sent to fight in the full-scale war between China and Japan that began in 1937. Sawamura returned to civilian life and baseball in 1940.

Soon after his much-vaunted pitching comeback with the Giants, Sawamura joined his team and the rest of the professional baseball league for a special month-long "Manchuria League" series (Manshū rīgusen). In the weeks preceding the series, several reports in the local Japanese-language newspaper *Manshū Nichinichi shinbun* praised Sawamura's recent

Figure 4.1 "Pitcher Sawamura, Japan's Number One," from the baseball magazine *Yakyūkai* in 1937. The text on the left references both Sawamura's upcoming entry into the military and high expectations for the young pitcher in the autumn baseball season. *Yakyūkai* 27, no. 13 (October 1937): photo section. Courtesy of the Baseball Hall of Fame and Museum.

military service in China, but also expressed the hope that the star pitcher would be back in top form by the time he arrived in Manchuria.[78] Acknowledging the fact that fans had been disappointed with his slow return to baseball, Sawamura himself told *Manshū Nichinichi shinbun* readers on the first day of the series that he was back in shape and "prepared to make amends by demonstrating the spirit of our homefront citizens and pitching magnificent complete games during the Manchuria series."[79]

As it turned out, Sawamura pitched his way to winning records in both 1940 and 1941, but his impressive baseball comeback was short-lived. In the fall of 1941, he was drafted again and dispatched to the Philippines. Returning home in 1943, he was called back to active duty in 1944 and died en route to the Philippines later that year. As both a soldier on the front and a returnee, Sawamura continued to attract attention. The fan sections of *Yakyūkai* regularly included requests for details about when and where he would be joining the military, when he would be coming home, and whether or not he would return to baseball.[80] Both during and after his periods of active duty, Sawamura wrote and spoke about his military experiences in articles, letters, and interviews published in newspapers, general-interest magazines, and especially the pages of *Yakyūkai*. Sawamura's observations about the war and his experiences offer new insights into the role of baseball in military mobilizetion that in many ways belie widely held perceptions about baseball's victimization in wartime Japan.

MAKING BASEBALL PROUD: SAWAMURA'S MILITARY PHYSICAL

On 21 July 1937, just underneath an article highlighting professional baseball statistics from the spring season, statistics that proved Sawamura's status as the top pitcher in the league, readers of the *Yomiuri* newspaper would find a small but important note. As the brief article explained, Sawamura had reported for his military physical the previous day. Standing exactly 5 feet 8.593 inches tall (5 *shaku* 7 *sun* 5 *bu* or 174.225 centimeters) and weighing 148.8 pounds (18 *kan* or 67.5 kilograms), Sawamura passed the military physical "splendidly" with the highest ranking and would now "stand and assume the burden of Japan's crisis."[81] The crisis, of course, was Japan's war against China, and this short article in the paper indicated that Sawamura was going to leave baseball to fulfill his duty to the nation.

The *Yomiuri* newspaper was not alone in its interest in Sawamura's military physical. In an interview published in *Yakyūkai*, Sawamura's father indicated that on the day of the physical the family home had been busy with newspaper people clamoring for pictures. With a hint of paternal pride, he also referred to newspaper articles reporting that Sawamura had done well at the physical and even received special praise from the local commander, who offered to consider the star's desires in selecting his military assignment.[82] As part of a barrage of Sawamura-related articles that followed his second career no-hitter, *Yakyūkai* itself had offered readers the innocuously titled story, "A Day in the Life of Sawamura Eiji," that provided a richly detailed account of the medical exam. The *Yakyūkai* version included Sawamura's results, but went well beyond that, with extended quotations from his alleged conversation with military officers present at the medical exam. After commenting on Sawamura's good physique, the commanding officer explained that he was one of Sawamura's fans, congratulating the pitcher on his accomplishments during the previous season. He then asked, "This time, it's for the sake of the country, but if you serve as a soldier, won't it cause problems for you in baseball afterwards?" To which Sawamura replied, "As a pitcher, I think that shouldering a heavy gun will ruin my arm." Their back and forth continued:

> "As a person who makes a living playing baseball, if you do ruin your arm, you probably won't be able to do your job after your return from military service."
>
> "That will probably be the case, but military service is a duty for the country, so I am not thinking about that kind of thing."
>
> "Yeah, that's a great mindset. But it's not good to lose your profession. If you can, it would be best if you could go back to pitching after you return from service. There are many military classifications besides the infantry. Was there a particular classification you desired?"
>
> "Nothing in particular."
>
> "Good. If that's the case, don't you have a game in Yokohama tomorrow, the 21st, against the Tigers?"
>
> "Yes, that is the case. Tonight I am returning to Tokyo by night train to play."
>
> "Play hard! That will be all."

According to the *Yakyūkai* article, following this discussion with the commanding officer, three military police officers, or *kenpeitai*, realized that Sawamura was present. Forgetting their own earlier calls for silence, the officers confessed that they were all big fans, and proceeded to pepper Sawamura with baseball-related questions and praise for nearly two hours as he and the other draftees waited for the commanding officer to release them. After assembling the would-be recruits for his final evaluations, the commander in the story began by criticizing Japan's young people for failing in their responsibilities to the country by not properly improving their bodies. He then called Sawamura forward and announced, "Everyone, this body is 5 *shaku* 7 *sun* 5 *bu* and 18 *kan*. For Japanese draftees it is really ideal. This man crafted this kind of body through sports. Everyone needs to follow his example closely. That's all!"[83] With that, the commander and the article concluded. What more needed to be said? Sawamura and baseball could be proud.

Whether or not this story reflects the actual events of "a day in the life of Sawamura," the various accounts of the celebrity pitcher's physical results and experiences reveal several ways in which baseball contributed to the war effort. For one, they effectively humanized the military medical exams. Throughout the war, young men all over Japan would undergo similar physicals, but few individuals would have their results shared nationwide. Publishing the details of Sawamura's physical gave the abstract ranking system used for the physical results an identifiable and well-known face and body. And publicizing details of this sort may have helped make the physical seem less invasive on an individual level, or at the very least, may have fostered a sense that individuals had "shared" the experience with the likes of Sawamura. Coupled with tales about Sawamura's hard work and his success in baseball, the article also indicated a means for achieving a similarly high ranking at the military physical: baseball.

Articles about Sawamura's physical also publicized the fact that a star of Sawamura's status was entering the military, making him an excellent role model. Considering that several players at the time sought to avoid the draft by enrolling as university students, the critical importance of Sawamura's alleged willingness to serve, despite the potential threat to his life and career, should not be underestimated. In his later telling of Sawamura's life, the biographer Daidō Bun implied that Sawamura himself would have opted to avoid military service, a detail absent from descriptions of the new draftee's physical. But according to Daidō, the management of the Giants refused to allow any of its players to dodge conscription, insisting, "All men today absolutely must serve in the military one time and receive training."[84] Daidō further suggests that as a superstar, Sawamura realized that any attempt to avoid military service would have had a negative impact not only on his image but also on that of professional baseball in general.[85] In this telling, Sawamura's more or less mandatory entry into the military makes him a martyr who (once again) sacrifices his own desires for others. Whether he truly wanted to or not, Sawamura entered the military in January 1938.

In some ways, Sawamura's experiences were not unlike those of Joe DiMaggio and Ted Williams, who despite their initial resistance, both joined the military in response to increasing public and private pressures about the need to serve the country in a time of war. Williams is said to have initially fought his draft in order to play one final season in baseball to help support his mother before voluntarily enlisting. DiMaggio eventually realized that as long as he failed to enlist, questions about his patriotism would distract attention from his playing, no matter how good he was.[86] In either case, much like Sawamura, both Williams and DiMaggio were seen as potential role models (either positive or negative), and consequently, their military intentions and careers sparked widespread interest.

Figure 4.2 Sawamura Eiji throwing a grenade after entering the military. Sawamura Eiji, "Senjō yori supōtsu nomi o omou: tokui no teryūdan nage," *Yomiuri shinbun*, 5 January 1939, 4. Courtesy of Yomiuri shinbunsha.

CHAMPION OF THE WAR: SAWAMURA'S WARTIME TALES

The day after Sawamura's official entry into the army, the evening edition of the *Yomiuri* newspaper featured a story on the top of its second page quoting "The New Recruit, Sawamura" on how excited he was to try throwing grenades. Citing his strong arm and his excellent throwing control, Sawamura claimed that he would be able to throw grenades farther and more accurately than anyone. Sawamura also assured readers that he would return to baseball as soon as he had fulfilled his military service.[87] Sawamura would prove correct on both accounts. He not only returned to baseball in 1940 (only to be drafted two more times), but also became especially famous for record-setting grenade throws of more than 70 meters. His 83-meter grenade throw, a new Japanese record, was one of the first things that Sawamura mentioned in a letter he sent from the front that was published in the September 1938 issue of *Yakyūkai*.[88] For both Sawamura and those seeking to chronicle his story, the star recruit's unique grenade-throwing abilities were an oft-cited badge of honor and a clear example of how baseball had made Sawamura (and by extension, anyone else who played the sport) a better soldier (see Figure 4.2).[89]

Questions published in the fan sections of *Yakyūkai* suggest that having grown accustomed to reading details about Sawamura as a star athlete, fans remained interested in what was happening to him as a soldier. The media—with Sawamura's aid—tapped and fanned this interest with multiple stories, letters, and interviews addressing his experiences during and after his periods of active duty. Given his status as a (if not the) star of the Yomiuri baseball team, Sawamura understandably received conspicuous attention from that newspaper, but articles relating details of his military experiences appeared elsewhere, especially in the pages of *Yakyūkai*. Years later, Ikeda Tsuneo, the magazine's editor at the time, recalled, "Sawamura was a star, right, so I had reporters running all over the place, writing this or that. Even after he entered the service, we did exclusive interviews and published, as is, the letters he sent from the front."[90] Ikeda's comments indicate that capitalizing on Sawamura's popularity, as both a pitcher and a soldier, was seen as critical for the baseball monthly. With all this diverse media coverage of the athlete-turned-soldier, Sawamura, who wrote several articles and stories himself, emerged as a useful symbol and advocate of the war.

Throughout Sawamura's period of service, media images regularly depicted him in military outfits and gear, providing a constant reminder of his willingness to serve the nation (see Figure 4.3).[91] As if to remind everyone that he was still connected with baseball, photos or articles dealing with Sawamura's military career, including those he wrote himself, almost invariably, if unnecessarily, included the descriptive title "pitcher" somewhere in the title or at least the first few lines. The various reports about Sawamura's time in the service also showed him to be extremely passionate about performing his military duties. In addition to his fondness for throwing grenades, Sawamura professed an enjoyment of long and sometimes grueling marches. His letters and interviews repeatedly expressed both his willingness to sacrifice himself for the "ancestral homeland" and his conviction that Japan would undoubtedly prove victorious.[92] Sawamura also helped foster positive impressions of the military, suggesting in one interview, "My first year as a soldier was hard, but since becoming a second-year soldier, I think military life is fun."[93]

As befitting a role model, Sawamura appeared in the media as intently focused and dedicated to the war. When asked at an interview during his early training whether or not he planned to return to baseball, Sawamura contended that he was not presently thinking about that issue. "Now as a soldier, my mission is to carry out my imperial duty," he was quoted as saying.[94] Although the *Yakyūkai* interviewer noted that these words hinted at Sawamura having been "trained" (*kyōiku sareta*),

Figure 4.3 Titled, "From the Front," this full-page photo from *Yakyūkai* depicted Sawamura and Ogawa, a player from the rival Tigers, posing together in their uniforms after meeting on the front. Their specific location is designated only by two circles. *Yakyūkai* 29, no. 17 (November 1939): photo section. Courtesy of the Baseball Hall of Fame and Museum.

later reports about his experiences in the brutal fighting in China suggest that Sawamura had been an especially receptive trainee. Echoing earlier assertions of his single-minded attention to duty, after returning to civilian life Sawamura noted in an article published in the popular journal *Modan Nippon* that in the course of fighting he rarely, if ever, thought about baseball or even his own well-being: "My mind and body were completely driven by war."[95] Even after injuries sustained in battle in central China in the autumn of 1938 led to a brief hospitalization, Sawamura claimed that he remained focused on the war. Returning to the front, Sawamura served until August 1939, when he was promoted and reassigned to a post back in Japan.[96]

Although Sawamura's own letters and other writings indicate that he did, in fact, think about baseball quite often during his time in the service, and especially during his stay at the hospital, his promotion and his reputation for being a good soldier highlighted the fact that baseball, and any concerns about his future in the sport, did not hinder his commitment to military service. If anything, the opposite was true. Time and again, Sawamura drew connections in his writings between baseball and his military experiences. As a new recruit, he claimed that he struggled less than others in adjusting to the harshness of military life because his body was acclimated to the hard work of training for baseball.[97] His baseball skills and training not only gave him grenade-throwing skills, but also had allegedly made him strong enough to handle even the most grueling marches without lagging once.[98] His training in sports also allowed him to serve as a machine gunner, a task that required great strength and endurance.[99] Sawamura also maintained that baseball taught him the importance of both individual effort and teamwork, and it fostered a strong drive for victory, all of which, he noted, were critical for military success.[100] Asked about his impressions of war and baseball, Sawamura replied that they were the same, and that in both cases you needed a big, strong body. "I want to make my body much, much bigger," he noted.[101] And after returning home from war not once, but twice, Sawamura declared in a 1943 article that his experiences in baseball "saved me from dangerous situations [in China] more times than I could count," and that the "war in the Philippines confirmed the merits of baseball even more clearly."[102] Baseball, according to Sawamura, strengthened his arm and gave him the confidence that allowed him to save not just himself, but his entire unit with effective grenade throwing.[103] Both Sawamura and baseball were heroes, it seems.

For Sawamura, there was no question that baseball and the war effort were compatible. Throughout his time in the military, Sawamura clearly served as baseball's champion, repeatedly making a case for the sport's usefulness to a nation at war. But Sawamura's words and actions left little doubt that he—and baseball—also embraced and championed the war. In this sense, his fame and frequent retellings of his first-hand experiences for popular audiences made him an advocate of nationalism and militarization in Japan. Sawamura's 1943 account of his recent battles against the Americans in the Philippines offers a telling example of how Sawamura and baseball lent support to the war effort.

In October 1941, a year and a half after the army honorably discharged him, Sawamura was drafted a second time. After a year fighting in Japan's initial capture of the Philippines, Sawamura and his unit returned to Japan in January 1943, when he was discharged and once again returned to professional baseball.[104] Much as he had done during and after his time fighting in China, Sawamura shared his war stories from the Philippines with the readers of *Yakyūkai*, which in January 1943 had changed its name to *Sumō to Yakyū* (Sumo and baseball).

The new title reflected several developments. For one, sumo assumed a key role in promoting nationalism and the war, as the "national sport" actively employed and expanded upon many of the precedents established during Hitachiyama's era. But the wartime years were also the peak of fame for the *yokozuna* Futabayama, whose celebrity and record-setting achievements helped carry sumo to new heights of popularity.[105] Ignoring sumo would have been economically detrimental to any magazine, especially one dealing with sports. Given the context, both the increasing space given to sumo in a "baseball" magazine and the eventual decision to change the name seem less than surprising. Fan comments also suggest that the magazine staff was caught between the sometimes conflicting wishes of its readership—some demanded more baseball, but others wanted more sumo. Complicating matters still further was the fact that all publications were facing increased pressure to consolidate because of governmental regulations and officially limited access to paper.[106]

It was in this publishing environment, that *Yakyūkai* (or *Sumō to Yakyū*) once again turned to Sawamaura as a featured contributor for its June 1943 issue. Because he would be killed shortly after being drafted a third time in October 1944, Sawamura's "Memoir of a Fighting Baseball Player," proved to be his last publicized comments about his wartime experiences. In previous interviews and articles, Sawamura had offered readers relatively brief accounts of his experiences, though these were often filled with gripping details about heroic struggles and triumphs.[107] Sawamura's article about his stint in the Philippines was the magnum opus of his wartime tales. At nine pages, it was by far the longest piece that Sawamura authored, including his various baseball articles unrelated to the war. In a magazine where articles longer than five or six pages were rare, Sawamura's war tale would have ranked among the longest in the magazine up to that point. In addition to its length, the article was also a masterpiece of storytelling, a soldier's tale of adventure and heroism. Although this extended "memoir" may have involved the handiwork of a ghostwriter or editor, the article is attributed solely to Sawamura, who is pictured wearing his Giants uniform and preparing to throw a pitch. Whether or not the star himself actually wrote all or even any of it, the story was clearly being marketed as Sawamura's personal battlefield tale, a fact that would not have seemed at all strange to fans who had read his other wartime accounts.[108]

As the memoir unfolds, Sawamura and his comrades repeatedly find themselves in life-or-death situations, only to be saved just in time, often by his grenade throwing. At one point, after being attacked in a roadside ambush, Sawamura and his unit instantly leave their vehicles and fearlessly plunge into the nearby jungle, engaging the enemy in the nighttime jungle warfare at which Japanese soldiers allegedly excel.[109] After another Japanese unit leads the charge that finally overcomes the enemy, Sawamura's only regret is that his unit had not been the first to charge ahead.[110]

These moments of tension and bravado are complemented by scenes of quieter heroism. Sawamura and his fellow soldiers rescue a group of imprisoned Japanese civilians, including women and children, who have been mistreated and given inadequate food and water by the enemy. While playing with the children they had just rescued, the soldiers give away the chocolate they were carrying to these hungry boys and girls. When the children's teacher makes them return the chocolate to the soldiers, who, she says, would need it more than the children do, Sawamura and his fellow soldiers are moved to tears.[111]

But Sawamura and the Japanese soldiers in the article are also moved by the righteousness of their cause, especially upon hearing horror stories about atrocities the Americans have committed. As if recalling his own varied experiences with and observations of Americans, Sawamura notes that one cannot know the "true nature" of a people until seeing them in action on the battlefield: "It would be a great mistake to think that the Americans one saw on the street were the true Americans." On the battlefield, according to Sawamura, "the Yankees" (*yankī*) have proven themselves to be "brutal and inhuman." Sawamura goes on to recount stories he and his fellow soldiers heard about Americans denying food, water, and medical treatment to captured and injured soldiers. He also tells of American attempts to have locals poison the rice that they serve to the Japanese. When the plot fails, the Americans in the story kill all those who failed to carry out their requests, boiling some to death and skinning their bodies. "Such cowardly and brutal techniques," he observed, "are the Yankee way."[112]

Hearing these stories secondhand, Sawamura and his fellow soldiers become filled with hatred for the "Western demons," and now want to kill them even more.[113] By repeating such stories, Sawamura obviously sought to elicit a similar emotional response from readers. As indicated by the portrayals of the inhumane American brutes, soldiers whom Sawamura claimed were far more cowardly than the brave Chinese he had fought earlier in his military career, Sawamura's article was rife with standard wartime propaganda.[114] In contrast to the Americans, the Japanese soldiers appear fearless in the face of death, yet kind to small children. They long for the order to charge, are tough fighters in the jungle, and are skilled with their indispensable weapons, the bayonet and hand grenade, skills and weapons that ultimately bring them victory over their evil foe. "Consequently," Sawamura concludes the article, "as Japanese, it is essential that everyone train in order to understand how to use these two weapons at any time."[115] Earlier in this piece, Sawamura expressed his appreciation to baseball for helping him develop the very same skills that he defined here as critical to the war effort, so that in effect, his closing remarks tell his readers, "To win the war, Play Ball!"

NOT ALONE

Looking at Sawamura's writings and comments, it becomes apparent that he was an advocate of baseball's usefulness to the war and of the war itself, but it is important to note that he was not alone. Fans were as interested in Sawamura the soldier as they were in Sawamura the pitcher, if only because they wanted him to come back and lead the Giants to more victories. Although Sawamura's military experiences received a disproportionate amount of media attention, naturally, other players entered the military throughout the war, and many of them also wrote and spoke about their experiences.

From the earliest stages of Japan's full-scale war with China in 1937, the pages of *Yakyūkai* began including such accounts.[116] Even before this point, one of the magazine's photos from 1935 pictured a half-dressed college star at his military physical, including details about his height, weight, and his physical evaluation, which the caption explained was lower than might have been expected due to chronic inner ear problems (see Figure 4.4).[117] As the war intensified, the number of articles in the magazine related to the military experiences of baseball stars increased—including a series called "Notes of a Returned Player," with installment titles such as "Military Spirit and Baseball" and "Learning the Field Service Code."[118] One such returned pitcher, Shimizu Hideo, paid special tribute to Sawamura, whose baseball comeback following an injury had given Shimizu hope when he received a similar battlefield wound.[119] Also appearing frequently were stories on players, both college and professional, who had died in the war.[120] Coverage of this sort was duplicated in newspapers. The professional baseball association's newsletter also included details about its players turned soldiers, as well as information about and for recent returnees.[121]

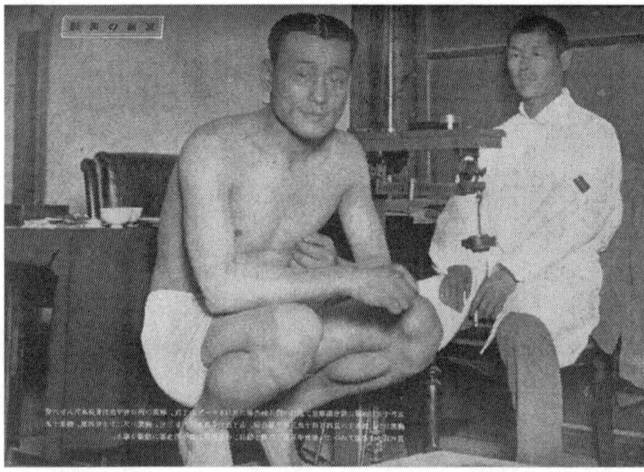

Figure 4.4 A full-page photo of Keiō University baseball star "Babe" Yamashita at his military physical. The caption frames the physical in terms of the famed sports rivalry between Waseda and Keiō. It points out that Yamashita's measurements were good, but chronic inner ear problems resulted in a relatively low *heishu* (third) ranking. In contrast, Olympic pole-vaulter Nishida Shūhei, a Waseda student whose measurements are also reported here, passed with the highest ranking. *Yakyūkai* 25, no. 9 (July 1935): front photo section. Courtesy of the Baseball Hall of Fame and Museum.

Much like Sawamura, many of the players featured in these accounts made specific reference to their baseball background and how it had served them well during their time in the military. Kojima Toshio, for instance, offered a lengthy discussion with several examples describing how the "instincts" (*kan*) he had honed as a hitter had aided him on the battlefield.[122] Promoters and management figures also penned articles for *Yakyūkai* after the outbreak of war with the United States, proclaiming baseball's usefulness in developing both physically and spiritually strong citizens.[123] Suzuki Ryūji, the head of the Japan Baseball Association, emphasized baseball's role as a form of "wholesome entertainment" (*kenzen goraku*) that taught the values of self-sacrifice and teamwork.[124] In his January 1942 "Essay on Wartime Japanese Baseball," the long-time baseball promoter and Giants manager Suzuki Sōtarō raised similar points, listing a sampling of baseball's virtues that included some fourteen physical and spiritual benefits, attributes that "as Japanese boys, everyone should possess."[125] He ended his article with a call to arms: "Japanese baseball people, arise! This is our one-in-a-thousand opportunity. Now is the time that we must give every desperate effort and consider every possible perspective so that we might proclaim the genuine essence of Japanese baseball."[126] In other words, the war was baseball's finest hour.

The nationalistic and militaristic tones so evident in the writings of Sawamura and others demonstrate the ways in which baseball, and by extension other sports, served the Japanese state's efforts to mobilize society for total war. That said, we should be careful not to view Japanese baseball and sports as aberrations that somehow diverged from the otherwise "progressive promise of sport."[127] After all, wedding militarism and nationalism with baseball was certainly not unique to Japan. Baseball and baseball stars in the United States played an equally important role in the American war effort. Several baseball stars were held up as national heroes for joining the military almost immediately after the conflict began. Bob Feller, a young pitching sensation with whom Sawamura was often compared, was lauded for joining the navy within days of the Pearl Harbor attack. Even Babe Ruth, who did not enlist (he was approaching his 47th birthday), proved he could still serve his country by buying $100,000 worth of war bonds.[128] Several players who had visited Japan used their experiences to demean the enemy, including Ruth, who cited his games against the Japanese as proof that they lacked the will to win. According to Ruth's estimate, "The way a man plays in sporting competition is an accurate yardstick of his basic character. American boys never give up until the 'last man is out.' That's why our boys can't lose the war; the Japs won't fight to the bitter end as so many people believe; they'll quit as soon as they start to lose."[129] In March 1943, other baseball figures used their knowledge of Japanese interest in baseball to warn against abandoning the game in the United States: "The Japs so envy us for our baseball prowess and our intense love for the game that to call it off during wartime would be like a tonic to them. I think they would construe it to mean we were becoming panicky or something in this country."[130]

The baseball rhetoric in the American media was no less militaristic, nationalistic, or propagandistic than the materials surrounding Sawamura. More than a year before Pearl Harbor, headlines in *Sporting News* had proclaimed, "Uncle Sam Need Only To Call," and in the first issue following the attack, the baseball weekly announced, "Uncle Sam, We Are At Your Command!"[131] The latter wartime article asserted, "If suspension becomes necessary, the commander-in-chief of the nation has only to say the word, and baseball voluntarily will go 'all out' "; however, it nonetheless offered several preemptive arguments for why baseball should continue: "Both citizen and military morale must be maintained by all possible means, and sports represent one of the most effective of all morale-building agencies." The piece went on: "Born in America, propagated in America and recognized as the National Game, baseball and all those engaged in the sport are Americans first, last and always. . . . None will be found lacking today, for in all the history of baseball there never was a conscientious objector, or a slacker in its ranks."[132] Little wonder, then, that the American baseball press, not only condemned Japanese actions in war as treacherous, but also argued that the "soul of our national game" had never "penetrated their yellow hides."[133] The sport had been an American "gift," and when the "Jap agents of Hell treacherously attacked Pearl Harbor," they had proven the "unworthiness of Japanese to carry on baseball."[134]

But if baseball was thoroughly American, as these articles suggested, that fact did not guarantee its continuation during wartime. By late 1943, Babe Ruth was predicting that the professional game would be halted the following year, and U.S. Senator Scott Lucas of Illinois was compelled to inform his Senate colleagues of his hope that "nothing will be done by any agency of the government which will in any way disturb the continuation of this great American institution."[135] Behind such statements were concerns that professional baseball, a game—being played for profit, no less—was taking men away from military service or work in war factories.[136] It is no mere coincidence, then, that arguments to keep the national sport going during the war emphasized not only baseball's critical role in producing the kind of physical and mental toughness that soldiers would need, but also the sport's importance for maintaining morale at home.[137] In the end, Ruth and others proved wrong, and professional baseball did not become a casualty of the war.

By highlighting the American response to war among baseball fans and supporters in the United States and comparing it to baseball's role in wartime Japan, the point here is not to justify either view. Rather, it is to emphasize the fact that sports and sports stars are amenable to the needs of the state—any state—especially when those needs are related specifically to the bodies of its members. As the postwar reinterpretation of Sawamura's memory reminds us, the images of sports stars are also useful to a society because they are malleable and subject to multiple views.

Memorializing Baseball, Forgetting the War: Sawamura in Postwar Japan

Although Sawamura's own writings and comments point to the fact that he assumed a fairly prominent role in supporting the war effort and promoting baseball's military efficacy, in postwar retellings of Sawamura's life, various aspects of his wartime role are downplayed, and in some instances, altogether missing. In Suzuki Sōtarō's biography of Sawamura, 19 out of 353 pages address Sawamura's military service, and 5 of these pages deal with his death.[138] Writing about Sawamura's military physical and his entry into the army, another postwar biographer, Daidō Bun, quotes at length from the previously mentioned *Yakyūkai* article, "A Day in the Life of Sawamura Eiji," but Daidō makes several significant edits. Sawamura's response that he was not thinking about the potential threat to his career because "military service is a duty for the country" is noticeably absent. Also gone are the commanding officer's comments that Sawamura should do his best to return to baseball, the explanation that the infantry was not the star pitcher's only option, all of the praise for Sawamura's body, and even the encouraging words about the next day's game.[139] The omissions here not only help Daidō construct his case about Sawamura's unwillingness to serve, but also make the military officer appear almost sadistic, as his edited comments now seem to taunt the star about the potential threat to his career. If editing a few lines in this case produced a remarkably different picture of Sawamura and his military experience, then other erasures prove equally, if not more, significant. Overlooking Sawamura's lengthy retelling of his experiences in the Philippines, Daidō's entire description of this period in Sawamura's military service observes with patent falsehood, "It is said that he repeatedly faced death, surrounded by Americans in the jungle, but detailed accounts of his battles do not exist."[140] Another article dealing specifically with Sawamura's war service offers a similarly brief examination of this period, with only vague references to Sawamura saving his surrounded unit with his characteristic grenade throwing.[141]

As attention shifted away from his military experiences, the image of Sawamura that emerged in the years following his death was that of a victim unable to escape the cruel fate of war. Sawamura's story was rendered all the more tragic in postwar reinterpretations because some suggested that his death could have been avoided. Asking why Sawamura was drafted three different times, many people, including his own father, concluded that this would not have been the case if he had only finished middle school and gone on to college, which would have given him a higher status as a draftee.[142] In these tellings, Sawamura's original self-sacrifice for his family proved all the more significant and costly, and perhaps coincidentally offered an implicit lesson about the importance of staying in school.

When addressing the period of Sawamura's military service, postwar accounts have focused especially on the hardships that Sawamura faced as a soldier—marching twelve hundred miles in a single month in China, struggling with potentially career-ending injuries, suffering from a body wracked with malaria, and later facing terrible conditions with barely enough food to eat in the Philippines—all of which he allegedly bore with no complaint.[143] Sawamura's two baseball comebacks in 1940 and 1943 and the hard training that his returns necessitated have also received particular attention. But here again we see the tragic loss of war, for as such accounts point out, Sawamura could never return to his peak pitching form, since his pitching shoulder had been ruined from carrying machine guns and throwing grenades. A pitcher without the ability to pitch was not much use to a baseball team; consequently, in the spring of 1944 the Giants did not renew Sawamura's contract.[144]

In direct contrast to Sawamura's own assertions and those of his superiors, several postwar accounts portrayed Sawamura as less than an ideal soldier. A recent biography of Sawamura aimed at children has him constantly thinking about baseball while fighting in China. In this biography, Sawamura hardly seems to engage in fighting at all, and rather than the devotion to duty that Sawamura repeatedly professed, what motivates him is the oath he made to himself that he would not die before standing on the pitchers' mound as a Giant again.[145] In this version, Sawamura also does not show the least interest in throwing grenades (after all, that would be bad for his arm) and only does so after his military superior, hearing that he had been a pitcher, orders him to throw grenades during his time in the Philippines.[146] Both the children's biography and a book-length fictionalized account of Sawamura's life also create a distinct impression that Sawamura did not want to fight the Americans. The biography, in particular, suggests that his own experiences with the Americans had secretly led him to conclude, "Facing off with that country, we cannot expect to win."[147]

In 1955, the Tōhō movie company released a feature film about Sawamura titled *Fumetsu no nekkyū* (Immortal fireball). A box-office hit that is said to have sparked a baseball movie boom, the film highlighted yet another way in which Sawamura's wartime experience was supposedly tragic. Focusing on Sawamura's relationship with his girlfriend and later wife, Sakai Yūko, the film told a story of star-crossed lovers set against the backdrop of professional baseball and military tensions.[148] Although this aspect of Sawamura's life attracted minimal attention during the war, several postwar accounts pick up on this story, interweaving it with Sawamura's baseball and military career, highlighting in particular Sawamura's repeatedly frustrated attempts to find happiness.[149] Not only did Sakai's well-to-do family purportedly oppose the relationship, but soon after the couple first met and fell in love, Sawamura was drafted for the first time. Even though he returned and the pair was eventually able to overcome the opposition of Sakai's family and marry, Sawamura was drafted again almost immediately thereafter. When he was drafted a third time, Sawamura left both his wife and a newborn daughter.[150] As a manifestly fictionalized account, Kitahara Ryōzaburō's *Sawamura Eiji to sono jidai* (Sawamura Eiji and his era, 1992) offers several private "inside views" of the couple's relationship, including the birth of their child. Kitahara's last depiction of the couple together offers a poignant scene, as Sawamura tells his wife to stop crying and assures her that he will return—he'd gone twice already and come back; he would do it again. This, of course, was not to be.[151]

Looking at such biographical accounts, it seems, then, that Japan's transition from war to peace resulted in a transformation of Sawamura's image. From a champion of the war he becomes its hapless and seemingly unwilling victim. But why? This transformation reminds us of the ways in which celebrity images are constructed—and reconstructed—in relation to changing socio-historical contexts. Reimagining Sawamura in the postwar period suited the needs of both baseball and the Japanese public.

For baseball, the postwar accounts of Sawamura that obscured, if not erased, his own complicity in the war effort were part of a larger postwar reinvention of the sport as a tool for "healing" and rebuilding war-torn Japan and fostering democratic ideals. Under the aegis of the Allied, but essentially American, Occupation of Japan, professional baseball, which had played its last public wartime game on 20 September 1944, was resurrected almost immediately after Japan's surrender. The first postwar professional game was held on 23 November 1945, and by the beginning of 1946 the professional league had reorganized and begun playing a full season.[152] Discussing plans to revive the professional league and develop baseball in Japan more generally, Suzuki Sōtarō provided *Sporting News* with an extended interview, in English. His explanations of baseball in Japan emphasized the respect that he and others held for the American game, observing at one point, "We admired baseball officials and the government in the United States for keeping the game alive during the war. I wish we were as fortunate."[153] As his interview reaching out to an American baseball audience suggests, Suzuki and other postwar Japanese baseball supporters saw baseball as a valuable tool for building bridges between defeated Japan and its conquering American occupiers.[154] Baseball, the quintessentially American sport, was also portrayed as a means of teaching Japan the values of American democracy and peace. As the *Asahi shinbun* explained in announcing plans to revive the national middle-school baseball tournament in 1946, "[B]aseball will help mend young souls twisted by war, and contribute to the development of democratic spirit."[155]

In the postwar period, terms like "democracy," "peace," "revival," and "Japanese-American friendship" were the buzzwords of the day. It simply would not do to recall how only a few short years earlier, baseball and its players had aided the war effort with things like pregame exhibitions of players throwing mock grenades at signs marked "Annihilate the Americans and British" (see Figure 4.5).[156] Many of the most active postwar advocates of baseball's potential contribution to democracy and Japanese-American relations, including figures like Suzuki Sōtarō and Suzuki Ryūji, had themselves earlier declared their convictions about the usefulness of the sport in defeating the Americans in war. In this context, it was far easier, far better, to forget, or at the very least, to recast the story of baseball as a struggle against an oppressive and antagonistic military state, a struggle where the only means for baseball to survive was to go along, however unwillingly.

The postwar re-remembering of baseball's wartime past among Japanese advocates of the sport suited American needs and views of baseball. For the occupiers, from the Supreme Commander, General Douglas MacArthur, on down, baseball and other Western sports offered keys to the reformation of postwar Japan. American baseball propaganda in the wake of Pearl Harbor had often insisted that Japan had never understood the true meaning and spirit of the American game; the occupation, in this sense, was a chance to make sure that they got the game right this time.

American views of baseball's wartime history in Japan as a struggle against a clique of "warlords" also proved critical to postwar reinterpretations of the sport. As early as August 1941, baseball coverage in the United States had already reported on the outcome of this perceived struggle: "The abolition of baseball in Japan by a decree of the war lords."[157] Despite the obvious inaccuracy of the statement—the professional league, after all, continued playing up through 1944—the concept of the warlords and their hatred of baseball took root in the American view of Japanese baseball. Arguments for continuing baseball in the United States during the war often evoked the Japanese ban on baseball for support, as in the case of Senator Lucas, who ended his pro-

Figure 4.5 One of two full pages from *Yakyūkai* featuring pregame "National Defense Grenade Throwing Competitions." According to the description, players from the two teams were dressed in military uniform and attempted to strike targets positioned at various distances. The target was marked with the phrase, "Annihilate the Americans and British." *Yakyūkai* 32, no. 6 (15 March 1942): photo pages. Courtesy of the Baseball Hall of Fame and Museum.

baseball remarks by noting that the "treacherous Japs dropped baseball because it is an American game—another added reason for us to keep the game going."[158] Wartime propaganda, such as the film *Know Your Enemy: Japan,* also picked up on the theme. Mentioning the tours of American players in Japan during the 1930s, it ominously declared, "Baseball was becoming the national sport. . . . The warlords were afraid of baseball and tried to stop it!"[159] The film, in this case, alluded to a right-wing secret society member's attempted assassination of Shōriki Matsutarō, allegedly for his role in sponsoring the American all-star team in 1934. Although investigations into the motives behind the assassination attempt proved them to be far more complex, including allegations that a rival newspaper was involved, American media coverage of the incident focused on baseball and especially Babe Ruth as the cause.[160] Ruth himself reportedly became a special target of Japanese militarists' animosity towards the sport. According to battlefront accounts relayed to the American public, Japanese troops were supposedly charging to their deaths with the battle cry, "To hell with Babe Ruth," a phrase that the *New York Times* suggested should be remembered by envoys signing any peace treaty with Japan.[161]

As the Americans moved toward victory and occupation, stories of these imaginary warlords oppressing baseball fit well with occupation leaders' "wedge policy" of separating the emperor and his people from the "gangster militarists" who had duped the nation and its sovereign into pursuing a disastrous conflict.[162] It comes as no surprise, then, that the myth of the antagonistic warlords remained dominant in American understandings of Japanese wartime baseball, consequently aiding Japanese efforts to reinterpret baseball's past in a similar vein. During the occupation, American press coverage of baseball's reemergence in Japan almost invariably mentioned the government's wartime "ban" of the sport.[163] In spite of clear evidence to the contrary, a recent English-language work on the history of baseball in Japan still maintains this view, claiming, "Military warlords in Japan, disgusted by the American influences of baseball, first tried to 'Japanize' the game, then abolished it altogether."[164] Commenting on the toll of this "military backlash against baseball," which was "alarming but mercifully short-lived," the author concluded, "In terms of emotional victimization, the anti-American, anti-baseball campaign in Japan was similar to the ugly anti-Communist witch-hunt led by Senator Joseph McCarthy in the United States in the 1950s."[165] Based on such historical accounts, many of which cite Japanese sources or experts, it seems clear that Japan's wartime state had it in for baseball, but was this, in fact, the case?

Sawamura's wartime experiences, in particular, suggest that claims of opposition to, and especially bans of, baseball in Japan have been greatly exaggerated. To be sure, the war resulted in dramatic transformations and limitations of all sports in Japan, but such changes were infinitely more complex than simple top-down bans and were often shaped by financial and logistical concerns. Large-scale sporting events, for instance, are not necessarily a good option for cities under constant threat of bombardment.[166] Professional and college baseball also faced severe player shortages as the military draft intensified in the later stages of the war.

In the case of student baseball, decisions in 1942 and 1943 to halt national middle-school baseball tournaments and eventually college league play coincided with the Ministry of Education's curtailment of extracurricular activities in general, including the restriction of school field trips and excursions (*shūgaku ryokō*) in 1940, followed by their complete suspension beginning in 1943.[167]

Furthermore, many of the wartime changes were initiated by sports promoters themselves and were far from consistently enforced. The oft-cited "Japanizing" of baseball, especially the replacement of borrowed English baseball terms with "new" Japanese phrases, serves as a case in point. As early as 1940, professional baseball league leaders adopted new terminology. In this instance, however, they substituted one Japanese word for another, changing, for example, the commonly used word for player, *senshu*, to the more militarized *senshi*, which contained the character for warrior and shared its pronunciation with a word for soldier (*senshi*).[168] The new lingo does not seem to have caught on, as evidenced by the ongoing appearance of the word *senshu* in baseball coverage throughout the war. In 1943, the head of the professional league, Suzuki Ryūji, announced two further reforms: all team uniforms would be changed to the "color of national defense" or khaki (*kokubōshoku*), and all foreign words would be eliminated, including team names and terms like "strike."[169] Many of the Japanese words adopted at this point had been employed in newspapers long before this, especially in the tightly spaced box scores, and the old team names still occasionally appeared in print after this order, suggesting that press censors and even editors found their usage less than dangerous.[170] Although baseball officials certainly received pressure from the military and government to support the war, such pressure was not the only factor driving these kinds of changes.[171] The wartime writings of management figures, such as Suzuki Ryūji and Suzuki Sōtarō, clearly indicate that they wanted professional baseball to serve the war effort in any way possible, and in the end, it was such men, not government officials, who were responsible for instituting the wartime changes. As it turned out, "complete Japanization" (*kanzen Nihon-ka*) could not save the sport.[172] American bombing proved far more successful at abolishing Japanese baseball than the "warlords" had ever been.

The myth of baseball's extreme persecution by the wartime state in Japan has persisted precisely because it has told American (as well as Japanese) advocates of baseball exactly what they wanted to believe about the sport and about themselves—that baseball and all those associated with it are inherently good and could consequently never, in "pure" form, be used for "evil." Such a belief also helps explain why, in contrast to the Japanese case, it has not been necessary to obscure or forget the wartime participation of American baseball stars. For the United States, World War II was a "good war"; for Japan, it was not.

Postwar Japanese efforts to come to terms with responsibility and complicity in a flawed and failed war were at the center of the collective recasting of Sawamura's wartime image. Sawamura and his story exemplify what historian Yoshikuni Igarashi has described in his examination of Japanese war memory as the "tension between the nation's contradictory desires—its desire to forget and it desire to remember the past."[173] In Sawamura's case, this contradictory process of forgetting and remembering the war was particularly apparent in the 1947 creation of the Sawamura Eiji Award and the retirement of his baseball uniform number that same year.

The original announcement in the fan magazine *Nekkyū* about the establishment of the Sawamura prize made it clear that the award and baseball were part of postwar Japan's "wholesome" development and reconnection with international society. Sawamura's role in this process was that of a pioneer and model. The award directly invoked his baseball legacy as a pitcher and its potential to inspire other young men. Sawamura's role as a foundational baseball great was confirmed with the retirement of his jersey, an act explicitly inspired and modeled on the Yankees' retirement of Lou Gehrig's number after his death in 1941. Thus, Sawamura was once again linked to his one-time rival and fellow baseball hero.[174] For both Sawamura and Gehrig, it was their baseball achievements, not their deaths, that earned them such an honor, and Sawamura's wartime role had no place in such honors. Or did it?

Public statements about the Sawamura award "immortalizing" his "glory and achievements" (*eiyo to kōseki*) were linked specifically to his pitching. But for a society that a few years earlier had followed Sawamura's exploits, distinguished service (*kōseki* can denote both), and his glory as a soldier, the absence of references to Sawamura's military service in descriptions of the new award did not preclude the potential for seeing the award or the retirement of his number as a memorialization or even implicit celebration of Sawamura's service and sacrifice as a war hero. Such "secret" praise was perhaps even necessary. As John Dower has noted, "In the eyes of the victors, Japan had no 'departed heroes.' . . . One could hold memorial services for the military and civilian war dead after the defeat, but not praise them for their sacrifices."[175] The occupiers' censoring watchdogs effectively stymied public efforts to honor the dead for their bravery or glory in fighting for their country, seeing such celebrations as part of the militaristic, nationalistic, feudalistic, and propagandistic tendencies that they were trying to eradicate in postwar Japan.[176] From the perspective of the occupiers, openly honoring Sawamura the war hero would have been unacceptable, but Sawamura the baseball hero was welcome—especially if that honor appeared to be modeled on an American hero like Lou Gehrig. In this way, memorializing Sawamura's baseball glory could serve as an acceptable substitute for publicly honoring the wartime deeds and heroism of Japan's war dead.

At the same time, memorializing Sawamura also highlights his—and many of his compatriots'—emerging postwar identity as guiltless victims of the war. This tendency may be seen especially in the pairing of Sawamura with Kurosawa Toshio, the other Japanese player whose number was retired at the same time. Kurosawa lived through the war, but contracted epidemic typhus during the 1947 baseball season and died on 23 June of that year.[177] As Japan's first two players to have their numbers retired, Sawamura and Kurosawa formed a unique star system, one that in 1947 also included Lou Gehrig, who had died as a consequence of the disease that came to bear his name. In both Gehrig's and Kurosawa's cases there could be little doubt that they were innocent and tragic victims of situations beyond their control. Grouped with these two other tragedies of baseball history, the retirement of Sawamura's jersey implied not his active participation in the war, but his own premature and "innocent" death. "Japan's Number One" had become the "player who died in the war."

FIVE

Becoming the Kanmuriwashi: *Ethnicity, Narrativity, and "Spectacular Difference"*

I have admired the *kanmuriwashi*, that soul-stirring great eagle of the South, since I was a child. . . . I believe that I am the *kanmuriwashi* of Okinawa. The *kanmuriwashi* has been designated as Okinawa's National Natural Monument. It inhabits Iriomote Island. The life of the *kanmuriwashi* begins with struggle and ends with struggle. Its way of life is difficult to bear.

—Gushiken Yōkō, *The Ring Is My Battleground*

By late 1979, when Gushiken Yōkō offered his observations about the *kanmuriwashi* in his autobiography, his own name and image had already become inseparable from those of this rare Crested Serpent Eagle, found only in the southernmost islands of Japan's Okinawa prefecture. After an unanticipated knockout victory gave him the World Boxing Association Junior Flyweight title on 10 October 1976, Gushiken, a little-known boxer from Okinawa, became an instant national celebrity. As he went on to defend his world title a record-setting thirteen times, Gushiken came to be known throughout Japan as "Okinawa's Star," the "Kanmuriwashi."

Although there is a good deal of variation regarding the original source of his new nickname, it appears to have gained widespread usage after a special documentary aired on the Tokyo-based TBS television network

Figure 5.1 Gushiken Yōkō in his apartment holding a stuffed *kanmuriwashi*. The Japanese text comments on the bird's fierce reputation and notes that it is Okinawa's National Natural Monument. *Bokushingu magajin* 11, no. 12 (1 October 1981): 23. Courtesy of Baseball Magazine Sha Co., Ltd., and Gushiken Yōkō.

during the New Year holiday in 1977. Titled *Wan ya, kanmuriwashi ni, nain* (I want to be the *kanmuriwashi*), the documentary showed Gushiken hard at work training for his first title defense, which was scheduled for later in January.[1] After this point, "Kanmuriwashi" became a media epithet for Gushiken, reiterated and explained repeatedly in articles and depictions of him (see Figure 5.1). At the same time, as the comments from his autobiography suggest, Gushiken used the *kanmuriwashi* to symbolize and define how he saw and presented himself. Representations of this bird appeared on his boxing robes and shorts, in his accounts of childhood, in his descriptions of himself in the ring, on top of his wedding cake, and still today as the symbol and title of the newsletter of his Tokyo boxing gym.[2]

With both Gushiken and the media endlessly reiterating each other's depictions, the example of the *kanmuriwashi* highlights the intertextuality inherent in the production of celebrity images and suggests the ways in which television coverage of athletes emerged during the late twentieth century as a pervasive means of disseminating and shaping such images from the very earliest stages of sports stars' careers. The *kanmuriwashi* also serves as an important reminder of the complex relationships between individual sports stars and society. As a sports celebrity, Gushiken cannot be viewed as a product solely of his own creation, but neither can he be seen as simply a product of societal construction. He—and by extension other sports stars—plays a part in molding not only his own image, but also the very society that is, in turn, molding it. The present chapter explores this process of mutual molding, especially with respect to Gushiken's role in shaping Japanese perceptions of Okinawa.

In this regard, the *kanmuriwashi* proved an apt symbol for both Gushiken's and Okinawa's relationship with Japan. This rare subspecies of eagle was designated a National Natural Monument in 1972, the same year that Okinawa prefecture rejoined the Japanese nation after having spent 27 years under direct U. S. military occupation.[3] Recognizing this bird from Okinawa as something of value and significance to the nation symbolized a national embrace, perhaps even an appropriation, of Okinawa and its uniqueness. Similarly, Gushiken's status as a world-champion athlete made him a national figure, but like the *kanmuriwashi*, it was his "differentness" as an Okinawan that became one of the defining characteristics of his celebrity image. As one of the first nationally recognized athletes from the prefecture, Gushiken's Okinawan identity sparked intense popular curiosity and attention. With an uncritical eye, it would be all too easy to see such interest in Gushiken as an acceptance and celebration of difference within Japanese society. Gushiken, after all, proclaimed his Okinawan identity in multiple ways and seemed all the more popular for doing so.[4] But, in fact, the popular image of Gushiken presented Okinawan-ness as a kind of non-threatening, "spectacular difference," which not only coexisted with notions of Japanese homogeneity, but also helped mask lingering inequalities and tensions in postwar Japanese society.

A Part of, Yet Apart from, Japan: Okinawa's History of Difference

The centrality of Okinawan-ness in Gushiken's image as a sports star must be viewed in the context of the historically ambiguous status of Okinawa and its citizens within Japanese society. Okinawa's relationship with Japan has long been—and continues to be—complicated and politically charged. After a long period of quasi-independence, the Ryukyu Kingdom was formally annexed by Japan in 1879, becoming Okinawa prefecture.[5] Claims of commonality and shared ancestry aside, the government and people of mainland Japan frequently treated people from Okinawa as backward Japanese who needed to be "modernized" or in many cases, as foreigners who had to be assimilated or "Japanized."

In this context, anything deemed "Okinawan" was subject to criticism and few, if any, "Okinawan" qualities were viewed positively. Within Okinawa, efforts to make Okinawans more like their new Japanese compatriots frequently targeted everyday life and bodily habits. Measures were taken—and in some instances, laws were enacted—to change Okinawan patterns of dress, to combat drunkenness, to encourage people to wear shoes, to stop Okinawans from listening to "strange" music, and to prevent them from performing "backward" dances or "superstitious" religious ceremonies. The Okinawan language was another common target of reform, or perhaps more accurately, elimination. In a fascinating, if not disturbing, example of encouraging people to monitor and police themselves, some schools in Okinawa initiated a practice in which students caught speaking a local dialect other than "proper" Japanese were forced to wear wooden signs, so-called dialect tags (*hōgen fuda*), as marks of their errors. The only way for a student to get rid of the sign was to catch someone else speaking "improperly." Although government officials initiated many reforms in a top-down approach toward assimilation, it is important to realize that large numbers of ordinary Okinawans internalized the view of themselves as "backward" Japanese. Many of the most vocal activists for reform were themselves Okinawan. One local Okinawan newspaper went so far as to suggest, "We must even sneeze as the Japanese do."[6]

Despite such Okinawan efforts to prove their Japanese-ness, discriminatory views and treatment of Okinawans remained common. Okinawans emigrating to the Japanese mainland or to Japan's expanding colonial empire in search of work often faced outright discrimination in employment and housing. Okinawans interested in working in Taiwan, for instance, found themselves excluded from positions whose listings bluntly declared: "Ryukyuans and Taiwanese need not apply."[7] Concerns that Okinawans were not "real" Japanese remained an issue during World War II, as evidenced by tales of Japanese soldiers executing Okinawans as spies simply because they used the local dialect during the Battle of Okinawa.[8] The devastating battle itself laid waste to both the physical environment and the people of Okinawa. It is estimated that one-third of Okinawa Island's pre-battle population, approximately 150,000 civilians, did not survive the conflict, and these figures do not include military deaths and the losses for an unspecified number of forced laborers from Korea.

With the end of the Battle of Okinawa and, shortly thereafter, the war, the situation became even more complicated for Okinawans. The U. S. military separated Okinawa prefecture from Japan in 1945 and governed it directly for nearly three decades. Despite rosy propaganda about turning Okinawa into a "showcase of democracy," from the very beginning, the military maintained almost complete control over the former prefecture and was undeniably more concerned with promoting military ends than fostering democracy, especially after Okinawa came to be seen as a key garrison for the United States during the Cold War. Formally separated from Japan, Okinawa prefecture was renamed the Ryukyu Islands, and relations and travel between Okinawa and the Japanese mainland became difficult. Okinawans going to Japan and Japanese going to Okinawa needed to use passports, go through special quarantine procedures, and, not least of all, receive permission from occupation officials before they could travel. Okinawa's period under American occupation, tumultuous years marked by increasingly frequent Okinawan protests and demands for a return to Japanese control, officially ended on 15 May 1972, when Japan reincorporated Okinawa prefecture into the nation, in a process frequently referred to as "reversion."[9]

Many have argued that in the decades since reversion, Okinawa's position within Japan has remained marginal. Okinawa prefecture has repeatedly posted one of the worst economic records in Japan, and the economy remains heavily dependent on the presence of American military bases. The prefecture continues to host nearly 30 percent of the American bases located in Japan, though it makes up less than 1 percent of Japan's total land area. Despite the growth of tourism-related industries that capitalize on Okinawa's warm climate and sunny beaches, a significant portion of Okinawa's service-based economy is still tied to bars, shops, and prostitution near military bases. Such economic and base-related issues have been exacerbated by lingering notions of Okinawan difference and "backwardness."

Looking specifically at Okinawa during Gushiken's years as world champion, from 1976 to 1981, it is clear that, despite a number of measures taken to promote parity with the mainland and to ease the transition of reversion, the prefecture experienced a kind of reversion shock during the period. Changes in U. S. military spending, especially related to Vietnam, also had a negative impact on Okinawa's economy. So did the "Nixon shocks," which caused major turmoil in financial markets worldwide.[10] During these years, unemployment and inflation in Okinawa jumped dramatically, and the initial gains made in the tourist industry following the easing of travel restrictions between Japan and Okinawa were not sufficient to compensate for these changes. Furthermore, significant social and cultural gaps remained. Until 1978, Okinawans did not even drive on the same side of the road as the rest of Japan. Gushiken himself helped in promoting the transition to driving on the left with print and television ads.[11] Given this context, it is not surprising that Gushiken, with his athletic and monetary successes, was frequently lauded in Okinawa for giving Okinawans hope and pride. As one Okinawan hotel manager reportedly commented even before Gushiken became world champion:

> Even though Okinawa has reverted to the mainland [*hondo*, i.e., Japanese control], there are still gaps on all fronts. To become equal both socially and economically, it seems that it's going to take a lot more time. At least in sports, and especially in boxing, where Okinawa excels, I'd like to feel that Okinawa has caught up to the mainland by producing a world champion so quickly.[12]

Everyone's Hero: Work Hard, Get Rich, Buy Your Folks Something Nice

In light of Okinawa's history, Gushiken's emergence as a world champion assumed particular significance for many Okinawans, something both reflected in and stimulated by the local media, which eagerly embraced the boxer from the moment he claimed the world title. In its initial coverage, for example, the *Okinawa taimusu* newspaper featured the "new champion" on the front page, and articles in the local news section provided the reactions of fans who had been following the fight on television and radio at different locations throughout the prefecture. Under a banner headline proclaiming, "'A World Star' Emerges from Okinawa," the sports page was almost entirely dedicated to Gushiken, including an early "profile" piece that highlighted his natural abilities, hard work, and determination, suggesting that he was a "man born to box."[13] As Gushiken began piling up title defense victories over the next five years, the *Okinawan taimusu* dramatically expanded its reporting on the boxer. Although much of this increased hometown press focused on the fights themselves, including extensive pre- and post-fight commentary, fans figured more prominently as well.

Boxing aside, Gushiken's sports celebrity image, as presented in the *Okinawa taimusu*, was dominated by two themes, both related to his Okinawan fans: his unified—and unifying—support from Okinawans and the positive influence of his success on the prefecture's citizens. Many of the articles, fan letters, commentaries, and photographs suggested, or rather assumed, that even if Okinawans differed in their age, gender, class, political leanings, or place of residence, all were united in their enthusiastic support and appreciation for Okinawa's world champion. An *Okinawa taimusu* report observed that on the night of Gushiken's first title defense "people and cars were sparse" in the prefectural capital of Naha because "most people hurried home where they sat riveted to the television, cheering on the defense with bated breath."[14] Later coverage commented on the growing "Gushiken fever" (*fībā*) among residents of Ishigaki, the historically marginalized island in the prefecture where the boxer had grown up.[15] Other articles pointed out that Okinawans residing in other prefectures organized cheering groups for Gushiken's fights on the mainland.[16] Letters to the editor and published fan comments praising the champion came from throughout the prefecture, representing people from all walks of life, from housewives to politicians. One letter from someone named Uehara Susumu observed proudly that even in the midst of a political campaign in the "politically charged" environment of Okinawa, on the night of the title fight, "all the opposing campaign offices took a break, forgot the election, and as all prefectural citizens should, rooted for Gushiken with all their hearts."[17] Whether or not "all prefectural citizens" actually cheered on the boxer "with all their hearts," Gushiken clearly came to be seen as a heroic figure around whom Okinawans could and should rally.

However, by demonstrating how different Okinawans rallied in support of Gushiken, the various media and popular references also serve as reminders that Okinawa was not unified, but was instead fraught with sometimes dramatic differences. While people in Naha were riveted to their televisions, multiple articles pointed out that devoted fans from Ishigaki, including Gushiken's own family, could only follow the fight on the radio because television broadcasts of the title bouts were not available there.[18] Mentions of Okinawans residing in other prefectures highlighted the fact that many people (including the champion himself) had left and were continuing to leave Okinawa in search of better opportunities in other parts of Japan. Uehara's own letter in the paper suggests that politics were a particularly contentious issue in the prefecture, especially since his main point centered on rumors that some of the campaigns were thinking about using Gushiken to bolster their popular support. Uehara adamantly opposed such an idea, asserting that the boxer's role in the campaign would inevitably alienate people and damage his image as the "Champion for all the prefecture's people."[19] Apparently, fight night unity and Gushiken's power to bring Okinawans together were more tenuous and fleeting than some people hoped. As the almost mythic unity of the struggle for reversion and its promises began to fade into the past, differences within post-reversion Okinawa—differences that had been there all along—were rendered increasingly apparent.[20] Even a sports star as mythic as the "Kanmuriwashi" could not put Okinawa back together for long.

That said, much of the Okinawan media and popular attention to Gushiken and his success credited him with transforming the prefecture's people. The well-known Okinawan writer Nagadō Eikichi went so far as to suggest that with one victory (followed, of course, by a national record-setting string of title defenses), Gushiken had restored Okinawan self-confidence, thereby "eradicating" a nearly 400-year-old "Yamato complex" that had left Okinawans convinced of their inferiority vis-à-vis the rest of Japan.[21] Although less dramatic, variations on the phrase "Gushiken gave Okinawans dreams and hopes" became a recurring theme in references to the star, appearing in articles, letters, and even remarks from politicians at the prefectural assembly.[22] Several letters from the *Okinawa taimusu* also highlighted Okinawan pride in Gushiken, with one letter half-jokingly observing that Gushiken's success had made young Okinawans studying in Tokyo "quite full of themselves."[23] Another letter pointed to a more moderate, though no less heartfelt, response, noting that Gushiken's achievements "inspired and encouraged all Okinawans—those here, those residing in other prefectures, and even those living abroad—giving them all a feeling of pride."[24] For one 38-year-old store manager, however, Gushiken was more than a source of pride and inspiration. After summarizing Okinawa's long history of oppression, the letter writer declared, "But Okinawans never submitted, and surrounded by bright sunshine, red flowers, and emerald green seas, they never lost their cheerfulness either. I see the people of Okinawa in Gushiken."[25] In the view of this writer and many other Okinawans, Gushiken became the very embodiment of the prefecture and the spirit of its people. In other words, the "Kanmuriwashi" and the heights he soared to were thoroughly Okinawan.

At the same time, since Okinawa was once again a part of (though still in many ways apart from) Japan, Gushiken's achievements were cause for national celebration. Gushiken was also Japan's world champion. This factor proved all the more significant because Gushiken held his title longer than any other Japanese boxer before or since, and because at several points during his nearly five-year reign as world champion, Gushiken was Japan's *only* world titleholder, Japan's only example of sustained athletic success at an international level.[26]

In this sense, the boxing-related star systems that shaped Gushiken's sports-celebrity image—star systems that placed him in comparison with both Japanese and international boxers—served to define Gushiken as a worthy symbol of Japan as a whole.[27] And he was, indeed, embraced as such. In 1977, 1978, and 1979, Gushiken was one of six athletes, and the only boxer, selected by sports fans as "Dream MVPs" in national fan-voting contests sponsored by the *Hōchi shinbun*.[28] After Gushiken's national record-setting seventh title defense in January 1979, Gushiken met with Prime Minister Ōhira Masayoshi, fueling rumors that he was being considered for the National Medal of Honor (Kokumin eiyoshō).[29] The award had been established just two years earlier in 1977, when baseball star Oh Sadaharu became the first recipient after setting a new world record for the most career homeruns. Gushiken himself expressed interest in the honor, and his growing string of victories augmented calls for him to become only the third person (and the first Okinawan) to receive the prestigious prize.[30] Popular pressure to honor Gushiken with the award continued through 1981, when he lost his title and shortly thereafter retired from boxing. Even though Gushiken and his supporters failed, in the end, to convince the political establishment that he merited the National Medal of Honor, Gushiken has remained an extremely recognizable and popular figure long after retirement, appearing regularly in the Japanese media and various popular entertainment forums.[31]

How did Gushiken become such a popular figure in Japanese society? There are, of course, multiple aspects of Gushiken's situation that contributed to his appeal—not least of all his uniqueness as an Okinawan, a factor examined in greater detail below. But one of the basic keys to his popularity lies in his paradigmatic sports-star story. From almost the moment of Gushiken's emergence as a national sports star, his overall celebrity image, much like those of Hitachiyama, Hitomi, and Sawamura, emphasized the self-made nature of his success. Early media accounts of Gushiken often portrayed him as a quintessential example of the poor boy who recognized his natural talents, honed them through hard work, and in so doing, achieved great success. Gushiken served as a highly laudable example of what one magazine described as the "legendary hunger of classic 'boxer success stories.'"[32] It was in this sense that the Japanese press most often linked Gushiken, in his early career, to the American movie hero Rocky, who, as these stories pointed out, was poor and could do nothing but fight, eventually rising from nowhere almost solely through his strenuous effort and dedication.[33]

Gushiken's paradigmatic story showed significant variations from those of earlier stars, variations that highlight both the particulars of his situation and developments in Japanese society at the time when his image was being crafted and consumed. Nevertheless, the story of Gushiken's life and career that emerged as dominant shared remarkable similarities with narrative patterns established long before his lifetime. In the end, the sports-star paradigm not only shaped how Gushiken and others explained and understood his celebrity, but also influenced popular perceptions of Okinawa and its differences from Japan, often in ways that ignored or obscured issues related to inequality within Japanese society.

Much as with other sports stars, the influences of paradigmatic models can be seen in the conventional search for the roots of Gushiken's later success in his childhood. One of the defining features of his childhood in biographical retellings was his family's poverty, a factor that becomes all the more significant when juxtaposed with his later monetary success through boxing. Gushiken was the third of four children, born in 1955 on the outlying island of Ishigaki. Gushiken's father Yōkei worked on a fishing boat, and his mother Tsune worked in a number of local industries in order to supplement the family's relatively low income. Accounts of the boxer's childhood emphasize that the family lived in a small thatch-roof house, a fact which serves as a foil for later, widely publicized details about his, and his family's, living situations.[34]

Stories and anecdotes about Gushiken's childhood, including several related by Gushiken himself, suggest that he was spirited and feisty even as a child. Bearing a quarter-sized bald spot as the result of a babyhood fall, Gushiken and his biographers indicate that he was subject to frequent teasing, a matter complicated by tensions on Ishigaki between native residents of the island and postwar immigrants from the main island of Okinawa, a group that included Gushiken's father. The boxer recounts a childhood full of fights or quarrels—often with bigger, older kids and often initiated by Gushiken in response to being called *kanpachi*, a local word for scar. Details highlighting Gushiken's below-average size add further excitement to such accounts of him fearlessly taking on his bullies, stories that point toward the origins of his later reputation for fearlessness in the ring, even when fighting putatively stronger boxers.

In the earliest of several book-length biographies about Gushiken, published in 1977, Ashizawa Seiichi drew attention to Gushiken's small size by detailing his height and weight at the end of each school term, facts that Ashizawa printed alongside averages for Japan and Okinawa at the time. Ashizawa even did the math for his readers, offering precise figures for how much Gushiken fell below the national and Okinawan averages. At one point, Ashizawa speculated about the reasons for Gushiken's "below average" height and weight, suggesting that both heredity and an inadequate food supply (because of his family's poverty) were probably key factors.[35] Hinting at the power that such abstract averages have in shaping individuals' perceptions of their bodies, Gushiken himself claims to have consulted these averages at one point in his childhood to see where he measured up, and was completely shocked and disappointed to find he was well below average. In Gushiken's post-fame view, however, he claimed to be "grateful" for his small size: "Because of my small physique, I became world champion."[36] As this comment suggests, accounts of Gushiken's school years indicate, often directly, that his childhood struggles to overcome adversity in the form of poverty, teasing, and his small size were all blessings in disguise, factors that proved critical to his later success.

Gushiken claims to have been adept at a number of sports as a child, including baseball and running. One of his early goals was to become a famous baseball player, a dream he was forced to give up after repeatedly being denied the opportunity to play baseball for his school's club because of his physique, even though Gushiken claims to have been better than most of the bigger boys who did play.[37] In the end, he quit baseball and joined the ping-pong club, where, according to his autobiography, his "footwork" regularly helped him defeat even the biggest opponents.[38] Throughout elementary and middle school, Gushiken was supposedly known for his speed and love of running. He claims to have won many sprinting contests and recalls that after his first victory in the school's field days, he vowed never to be beaten and "trained" accordingly.[39] Although details of this sort seem a bit far-fetched, they are meant to convey key elements of Gushiken's character that made his later achievements in boxing possible, or perhaps even inevitable. Experience at ping-pong may have helped him develop boxing skills (footwork), but more importantly, these childhood tales show that Gushiken was someone who, even as a boy, was committed to the hard work and training deemed essential for sustained sporting success. Gushiken has also been portrayed as a child and later as a sports star who "hated to lose" (*makezugirai*), a phrase used to describe many of the other sports stars examined in this book. In this sense, Gushiken's unquenchable desire for victory in the field-day races serves as an early indicator of his later achievements.

Unlike Hitomi and Hitachiyama, Gushiken's desire for success did not necessarily cross over from sports to the classroom. Gushiken was far from a good student and failed to pass the entrance exam for the most accessible of the three local high schools on Ishigaki. That said, like the other stars, he did continue to pursue his education, and in the end it was through school that he came to "discover" his true calling: boxing. With the assistance of one of his teachers in Ishigaki, Gushiken gained admission to a private school located in Naha, the prefectural capital, and in 1971 he entered Kōnan High School. However, adding a bit of drama to this paradigmatic tale of discovery, Gushiken himself has noted that he nearly quit school after only a few months, a detail noticeably missing in some of the earlier biographical accounts. Although several retellings report that Gushiken's initial time at Kōnan was not what he had anticipated, his autobiographical comments expand on that point, ostensibly offering readers a view of his thoughts at the time, even though they are clearly being recorded with the benefit of hindsight. Whether the specifics in these retrospective accounts are completely accurate or not, their end result is an even better story that offers further explanation for his rise to sporting greatness.[40]

Gushiken's recountings of the first months of school highlight his homesickness, a feeling aggravated by the fact that he missed the beauty of his home island and therefore came to hate the city of Naha. When I asked Gushiken during our interview if being from Ishigaki made his transition to school more difficult, he did not refer directly to his own experience, but noted that it was common then for people from other islands to be teased: "Because everybody talked a little differently, when islanders [*shima no hito*] came to the main island of Okinawa, they were teased by Okinawans, and when islanders went to the big city, they were also teased a bit. 'What are you an islander!' they might say. Having that said to you was harsh."[41] Other autobiographical references to a lack of friends at school also point to tensions with other students, suggesting that his background as a poor kid from remote Ishigaki made it difficult to get along with "students with good upbringings."[42] Perhaps understandably, Gushiken indicates that the combination of homesickness, a lack of close friends, and harder-than-expected schoolwork led him to return to Ishigaki during his first summer break with plans not to go back to school. So was Gushiken a quitter? As everyone reading about the life of the world champion already knew, the answer, of course, was no. In this sense, details about his inner turmoil at school contribute to Gushiken's sports-celebrity image by demonstrating how he, not unlike Hitachiyama, had achieved success in part through his willingness to face, and ultimately overcome, adversity.

But like other stars, Gushiken did not do it all on his own. His path to sporting fame also necessitated counsel from respected advisors, thoughts of his family, and a little luck. According to Gushiken's autobiography, for instance, the same teacher who had helped him get into Kōnan emphasized Gushiken's obligations to his family and convinced him that he owed it to his mother to continue in school because she was having to work long hours to pay the tuition. The teacher also suggested that joining a school club would help Gushiken make more friends. For readers familiar with Gushiken's later success, his decision to return to school with thoughts of joining a club becomes pivotal. Kōnan, like most Japanese high schools, almost certainly had many club options for would-be members, as school officials at all levels had long advocated, if not outright required, student participation in some kind of extracurricular group.[43] Because of his long-standing interest, Gushiken indicates that he thought about joining the baseball club, but dismissed that idea based on his earlier experiences. As Gushiken tells it, he was at a loss for which club would be best, but in the end, a bit of luck provided the ultimate answer. Shortly after he returned to school, a chance meeting with another Kōnan student from Ishigaki and the latter's promise of free room and board led Gushiken to boxing.[44] Thus, even in an instance where academic abilities are less significant in Gushiken's overall story, school and education remain important enablers of athletic success. The logic of the sports-star paradigm suggests that if Gushiken had not gone on to school, he would not have become a boxer. At the same time, it places emphasis on his desire to fulfill his duties as a good son, something that boxing—at least eventually—allowed him to do.

Prior to this introduction to boxing in high school, Gushiken had little exposure to the sport and even admits thinking that boxing was more or less a pursuit for delinquents.[45] Gushiken was probably not alone in his early assumptions about boxing, since the sport seems to have been widely viewed in this way throughout Okinawa. In 1969, for instance, the head of the amateur boxing association in Okinawa had written an article for the national organization's newsletter, in which he lamented that people in Okinawa thought boxing was simply a codeword for picking fights.[46] As it turned out, the free room and board that Gushiken's acquaintance had promised was contingent on his willingness to take up boxing. Gushiken did so without telling his parents, because he was afraid of what they would think, but at the same time, he rationalized that he was in fact acting with his parents' interest in mind, since they would no longer have to pay his living expenses at school.[47] Such stories imply that even though Gushiken's pursuit of boxing took him in an opposite direction from his parents' wishes, Gushiken remained filial, and would eventually prove all the more so.

Accounts of Gushiken's earliest years in boxing as a school club member emphasize not only his natural gifts, which quickly became apparent, but also his efforts to hone them through hard work and a willingness to dedicate himself wholeheartedly to training. Because of his skills and commitment to practice, Gushiken came to be known during his school years as a "prodigy" and a "practice bug," nicknames he saw as badges of honor.[48] By his third year at Kōnan, he was already dreaming about—and being told that he had a shot at—winning a gold medal at the Olympics, especially after he won the national title at the Inter-High Championship in the mosquito weight class in 1973.[49] Gushiken's success in amateur boxing, much like that of Sawamura in baseball, opened up new educational possibilities. With the support of Okinawa's amateur boxing association, Gushiken was promised a free ride at Takushoku University in Tokyo with the understanding that he would be a member of the university's boxing club in order to train for the upcoming Olympics.[50]

Gushiken's success at the national level also attracted the attention of professional boxing promoters, including Kanehira Masanori, the manager of the Kyōei Boxing Gym, who began pressuring Gushiken to become a professional under his management. Once again for those familiar with Gushiken's future fame, Gushiken's arrival in Tokyo to enter college stands as another pivotal moment in his story, a period that Ashizawa summarizes with the chapter title, "From Gold [i.e., Olympic, amateur medals] to Money" (*kin yori kane e*).[51] The story of Gushiken's entry into professional sports unfolds almost as if this development were "fated." Citing a bill that he received from the school, Gushiken has suggested that the college tuition waiver seemed to have fallen through, though it remains unclear whether this was actually the case. Realizing that his parents could not pay for school, Gushiken felt that he would have to take a part-time job to pay the bill. Working a part-time job, though, would have been difficult, if not impossible, if he was going to be a member of the university boxing club and train for the Olympics. Throughout this period, Gushiken was under constant pressure from Kanehira and one of his former boxing colleagues from Okinawa who had become a professional training at Kyōei Boxing Gym.

Echoing other stars, one of the key factors that influenced Gushiken's decision to enter professional boxing was, at least according to his own account, concern for his family. Gushiken was finally persuaded to become a pro when Kanehira talked to him and reportedly explained, "Winning an Olympic medal is great, but it won't provide you food to eat. If you become a professional champion, you'll make loads of money. You can demonstrate your filial piety to your parents" (*goryōshin ni kōkō ga dekirunda*).[52] Noting that this last statement was particularly effective, Gushiken claims that he immediately thought of his mother's face and made up his mind: he quit college, joined Kanehira's gym, and made his professional debut in May 1974, winning in a four-round decision.[53]

Over the next two years, Gushiken won all of his professional bouts, including a match in January 1976 where he fought in the newly established—and lighter weight—international division of Junior Flyweight. Later, in October 1976, in only his ninth professional fight, Gushiken met the WBA Junior Flyweight champion Juan Guzman, a boxer famed for his strength and knockout punches. With a seventh-round knockout victory, Gushiken took the championship title. This victory made him the first Japanese boxer to gain an international title after only nine professional fights and the first-ever world champion, in any sport, from Okinawa prefecture.[54] Gushiken went on to defend his world title thirteen times, finally losing four and a half years later in 1981, ironically in the only one of his title fights held in Okinawa prefecture. Shortly after the loss, he announced his retirement from professional boxing.[55]

Over the course of his boxing career, Gushiken did, as Kanehira promised, make a lot of money. Unlike most of the sports stars examined in previous chapters, Gushiken's monetary success was a key component of his sports-star image. Gushiken's "fight money" was a subject of frequent media speculation and comment, with some articles specifically listing the growing figures that Gushiken reportedly received for each fight.[56] Offering a kind of salary-based sports-star system, a 1979 article from the *Asashi shinbun* newspaper pointed out that Gushiken topped other wealthy athletes as the only multimillionaire.[57] Despite all the attention given to Gushiken's income, he became famous for fulfilling the latter portion of Kanehira's earlier promise, that is, demonstrating his filial piety to his parents. Gushiken garnered praise for his demonstrated lack of greed, as it became widely known—in part because interviewers frequently brought up the topic—that he was continuing to work his part-time job at a Tokyo *tonkatsu* restaurant and setting aside his winnings

Figure 5.2 Gushiken in front of the new house he had built for his parents using more than 40 million yen of his winnings. *Bokushingu magajin* 9, no. 3 (28 February 1979): 116. Courtesy of Baseball Magazine Sha Co., Ltd., and Gushiken Yōkō.

in order to build his parents a new house. Eventually, he used his "fight money" to build a 45-million-yen (roughly $210,000, at the time) house for his parents in Ishigaki, who thereupon left the thatch-roof house where they had brought up their son (see Figure 5.2).[58] The symbolism hit on familiar themes: not only the value of filial piety and the rewards of hard work, but also the successful incorporation of an impoverished and backward Okinawa (as emblematized by the thatched roof) into the mainstream of the modern nation.

That is not to say that Gushiken did not spend money on himself. Numerous photographs reveal that he lived in a spacious (and consequently expensive) apartment, which was well furnished and equipped with electronics and other consumer goods.[59] One of the most extravagant ways in which Gushiken displayed his new wealth was his wedding ceremony, held just weeks after he lost his world title in March 1981. Attracting particular attention in women's magazines, Gushiken's marriage to Takita Kasumi, a 23-year-old fan and Tokyo office worker, involved an elaborate 400-million-yen (approximately $1.9 million) wedding ceremony. Among the highlights of the event was a wedding cake standing 6 meters tall (nearly 20 feet), which one magazine noted was a record in itself. A *kanmuriwashi* decorated the top of the giant cake.[60]

After the wedding, the media continued to follow the couple, providing details and photos about their 5-million-yen honeymoon to the

United States, their shopping trips, their new Tokyo apartment, the birth of their first child, and their views on child-rearing and household finances.[61] Only a year after his retirement Gushiken also received extensive media coverage in connection with a drugging scandal linked to his former manager Kanehira, who had allegedly doped several of Gushiken's opponents to make it easier for Gushiken to win. The initial reports sparked widespread debates, including vigorous discussions among politicians in the National Diet, about what this scandal meant for Gushiken, for boxing, and for Japan.[62] After an investigation, Kanehira was forced out of Japanese boxing, though he maintained his innocence throughout. Despite almost immediate accusations that Gushiken was a "dirty hero," the champion himself expressed complete shock and denied any knowledge of the doping of his opponents. Whatever the case may be, the scandal appears to have largely disappeared from popular view within a matter of years, leaving little lasting impact on Gushiken's overall image as a record-holding world champion. To this day he continues to appear frequently on television and in a variety of advertisements. In the years since his retirement, Gushiken has received regular media attention, including reports on his multiple (and ultimately failed) attempts to manage his own restaurants, his brief stint as a speedboat racer, and more recently his decision to return to professional boxing in the role of gym owner and trainer at the Shirai-Gushiken Sports Gym in Tokyo.[63]

As previous chapters have shown, the interest in the personal and family life of a sports star was nothing new. However, the media's emphasis on his wealth and monetary accomplishments represented a significant departure from earlier sports stars. In Hitomi's case, her status as an amateur athlete and the strict regulations that pertained at the time virtually prohibited her from making money from her athletic achievements. As a professional sumo wrestler, Hitachiyama depended on his income from the sport to live. However, his own promotion of *sumōdō* may be seen as part of a broader effort to counter increasing societal emphasis on wealth as the most important indicator of success. Instead of monetary achievements, the ideals associated with Hitachiyama stressed the need to bring glory to the sport and nation, as well as honor to one's family. Similarly, Sawamura was active at a time when people all over Japan were being asked to sacrifice for the ongoing war effort—a time, in other words, when discussions about salary would have seemed inappropriate. Moreover, Sawamura played during the earliest stages of professional baseball, a period when the future of the professional league as a whole was still

Figure 5.3 An example of early advertising using sports celebrities. This beer advertisement depicts four *yokozuna*, including Hitachiyama (far right) and Umegatani (second from left). In addition to the names of four different beers, the Japanese repeats the phrases, "The wrestler of wrestlers" and "The beer of beers." *Sumō sekai*, March 1913, 7. Courtesy of the Sumo Museum.

in doubt. Even if Sawamura's salary had been relatively high for the time, it could not compare with that of Japanese ballplayers of the postwar era, when professional baseball became a mainstay of the Japanese sports scene, and insofar as it was sponsored by corporations, even of the economy as a whole.

Like earlier sports stars, Gushiken was very much a person of his time, but times, and especially societal views of monetary success, had changed. Gushiken's years as champion—from the late 1970s through the early 1980s—saw an increase in visible affluence. Growing numbers of Japanese had money to spend on leisure activities such as sports and travel, and on commodities like books, color televisions, and luxury goods. For a relatively small group of celebrities and businessmen, incomes six or more times those of the average factory worker allowed for the kinds of conspicuous consumption, like Gushiken's lavish wedding ceremony, that as historian Gary Allinson notes, "set the tone for the late 1980s" in Japan.[64] As Japanese companies and the economy in general outperformed many global competitors, the period also saw countless references to "Japan as Number One," a notion no doubt supported by the international accomplishments of athletes like the longtime world-champion boxer Gushiken and the homerun world-record-holder Oh Sadaharu.

During the postwar years, professional sports as a whole became central to the media and entertainment industries, particularly in television.[65] Attesting to the importance of sports in the marketing of televisions themselves, Gushiken's image, together with such phrases as, "A brilliant performance needs a brilliant picture," appeared repeatedly in *Okinawa taimusu* advertisements pitching the latest color television models.[66] Such advertising was itself new. Even a cursory comparison of the pages of pre- and postwar journals and newspapers reveals a literal explosion of advertisements (see Figure 5.3) depicting sports stars in the postwar period.[67] By lending his name to products ranging from boxing goods to Kentucky Fried Chicken, Gushiken added yet another facet to his celebrity image and tapped a rich source of wealth, and he was not alone. The other athletes listed alongside him in various salary rankings indicate that many sports celebrities reaped the monetary benefits of these kinds of transformations in Japanese society.

The frequently flaunted successes of such sports stars, who almost invariably attributed their achievements to practice and discipline rather than innate talent, reflected and reinforced societal views of the value of hard work.[68] At the same time, they exemplified and perpetuated the paradigmatic self-made-man narrative that had defined sports-celebrity images since Hitachiyama's emergence at the turn of the century. These myths of sports stars, described in rags-to-riches terms straight out of a Horatio Alger story, implied that, given a willingness to work hard, anyone could become a sports superstar. In keeping with shifting societal perceptions of monetary success, accounts of stars like Gushiken also portrayed sports stardom as an escape route from poverty and a means of achieving the fabulous wealth that served as both an important indicator of Gushiken's self-made status and his primary way of honoring his family. In other words, for athletes active in the postwar Japanese sports scene, *money mattered*, as much as, if not more than, other elements of celebrity image. Nevertheless, behind the exaggerated opulence and swaggering confidence of these success stories, Gushiken's own background suggested that countless Japanese were struggling just to get by, and this had been especially true in Okinawa.

Understanding "Our Okinawa": Gushiken and Spectacular Difference

If Gushiken was a quintessential example of a self-made sports hero, his Okinawan identity also made him distinctive, and, I would suggest, particularly appealing for many fans in both Okinawa and Japan. Among the key factors that contributed to popular interest in Gushiken's Okinawanness were the star systems that defined Gushiken through comparisons with athletes in other sports at the time, especially baseball stars like Oh Sadaharu and Nagashima Shigeo. Gushiken's reign as world champion overlapped with the final years of Oh's baseball career, the years when he became the world-record holder for career homeruns. Media stories relating Oh's latest homerun, his income, or details about his personal life often appeared side by side with reportage on Gushiken. They frequently commented on each other's achievements, expressing profound mutual respect.[69] But the two stars shared more than just coincidental timing. Both achieved international success and were lauded for their hard work and dedication. As the son of a Chinese father and Japanese mother, Oh, like Gushiken, also embodied difference within Japan. Oh's Taiwanese citizenship, moreover, explicitly linked him to a former Japanese colony that, similar to Okinawa, maintained a complicated and often strained relationship with Japan and the United States.[70] For both men, issues of ethnic and national identity were central to their celebrity images.

In other ways, Oh, together with his Japanese teammate Nagashima, served as a critical foil for Gushiken. Both Oh and Nagashima, who had retired in 1974, were extremely popular and influential national sports heroes. Their skill, hard work, and dedication were regularly credited with leading their team, the Yomiuri Giants, to eleven of thirteen victories in the national championships, including nine championships in a row from 1965 to 1973. Oh and Nagashima's years with the Giants are often described simply as the "O-N era" (*O-N jidai*), highlighting their central role in the Giants organization. Thanks in no small part to the team's undeniable dominance of professional baseball and the backing and massive reach of the team's parent company, Japan's largest media and entertainment conglomerate at the time, Oh and Nagashima became Japanese cultural icons, their impact reaching well beyond the world of baseball.[71] Gushiken emerged as a national celebrity against this backdrop of the O-N era. On the one hand, he shared with Oh and Nagashima many of the values that made them famous and especially worthy of recognition, not least of all his emphasis on hard work and dedication as the route to success. On the other hand, Gushiken offered fans something completely different: he was definitively *not* a Tokyo baseball player. In part, then, Gushiken's popularity can be regarded as a reaction against the Tokyo-centricity of the Giants and their media coverage, something that rendered his Okinawan-ness a significant asset.

As one of the first nationally recognized celebrities from Okinawa following the prefecture's reversion to Japan in 1972, Gushiken's growing string of title-defense victories quickly made him one of Okinawa's best-known "products."[72] Almost from the very beginning of his professional boxing career, Gushiken's uniqueness as an Okinawan would have been readily apparent. His family name was the first clue, because unlike most Japanese names, it was written with three Chinese characters, and most people in mainland Japan would have been, at least initially, unsure how to read it.[73] After seizing the title and the attention of the national media, questions about pronouncing his name quickly disappeared, and fans would eventually learn that Gushiken was a very common name in Okinawa.

It also quickly became apparent that Gushiken spoke differently. The famous statement attributed to him in the documentary that helped give him his nickname—"I want to be the *kanmuriwashi*"—connected him with this exotic bird from Okinawa prefecture, but in the minds of those marketing his image to a mainstream Japanese audience, his statement also necessitated a translation. In Ashizawa's biography, for instance, Gushiken's alleged words, "*Wan ya kanmuriwashi ni nain*," are glossed in more "standard" Japanese as "*Ore wa kanmuriwashi no yō ni naritai*" (I want to be like the *kanmuriwashi*).[74] An article from the weekly magazine *Shūkan gendai* published shortly after Gushiken became world champion placed particular emphasis on the fact that he seemed unusually quiet. The article attributed Gushiken's reticence to his "Okinawan accent" (*Okinawa namari*), which made him uncomfortable when he was forced to communicate in a "world that speaks standard Japanese" (*hyōjungo*).[75] The author of the article added that Gushiken's embarrassment stemmed from his "hating to lose" (*makezugirai*), an observation implicitly suggesting that Gushiken would work to overcome this perceived gap between him and the rest of Japan.[76] Gushiken's speech remained a focal point throughout the course of his career, including several well-publicized Japanese-language mistakes that commentators often cited in connection with his Okinawan background.[77] Gushiken often emphasized his linguistic and personal difference by using Okinawan words and phrases to describe himself. In such instances, he often indicated that his sentiments could not be effectively conveyed in "standard" Japanese.[78] Suggesting that media references to Gushiken's choice of words were improving Japanese understanding of Okinawa's unique qualities, several fan letters in the *Okinawan taimusu* praised Gushiken for not forsaking his native tongue.[79]

As Gushiken's use of Okinawan phrases suggests, both he and the media employed his personal connection with Okinawa as a means of distinguishing and promoting his celebrity image. Such displays became particularly apparent in the latter portion of Gushiken's career, after he had established himself as a national superstar with several title-defense victories and increasingly visible displays of wealth. Although the *kanmuriwashi* quickly came to serve as Gushiken's nickname, if not alter ego, depictions of this bird only began to appear with regularity on his boxing shorts—colorfully and elaborately embroidered—around the time of his

Figure 5.4 Gushiken Yōkō in his fifth world title defense fight against Panamanian Jaime Rios on 7 May 1978. Gushiken won with a knockout in the thirteenth round. Note the presence of his nickname and the Japanese flag on his boxing trunks. *Bokushingu magajin* 9, no. 3 (28 February 1979): 22. Courtesy of Baseball Magazine Sha Co., Ltd., and Gushiken Yōkō.

seventh title defense. Before that point, the shorts he wore in title fights had borne his name and nickname (usually in Romanized letters), but the only other distinguishing feature had been a Japanese flag, which, together with the *kanmuriwashi*, would continue to appear on his trunks for the remaining bouts (see Figure 5.4).[80] In his eighth title defense in April 1979, Gushiken again highlighted his connection with Okinawa sartorially when he entered the ring wearing a flashy yellow robe made from an Okinawan fabric that had once been associated with the Ryukyuan royalty and aristocracy. Gushiken's visual displays of Okinawan-ness received high praise from his biographer, Nagadō Eikichi, himself an Okinawan, who saw Gushiken's yellow gown as a symbol of great pride for all Okinawans.[81]

Food also served as a way to demonstrate both Gushiken's and Okinawa's uniqueness. Although Gushiken's part-time job at a *tonkatsu* restaurant early in his boxing career became a critical component of his celebrity image, in 1980 he also became famous for opening his own restaurant in Tokyo's Akasaka district. The establishment received media coverage from a wide variety of sources, including women's journals, entertainment periodicals, and boxing magazines. Eponymously dubbed "Gushiken," the restaurant offered Tokyoites unique Okinawan food and drinks, including the shop's specialty, Okinawa soba noodles, and the prefecture's famous brand of beer, Orion.[82] The mass media connected Gushiken to Okinawa via cuisine in other ways as well. In an article about the soon-to-be wives of several stars, the weekly entertainment magazine *Shūkan myōjō* discussed how these women were preparing for their upcoming marriages, focusing in particular on how they were learning to cook foods that their future husbands favored. In Takita Kasumi's case, the challenge was learning to make the Okinawan dish *gōyā chanpuru*. By noting that this particular meal was "great for fostering stamina," Takita hinted at one of the secrets to Gushiken's success: Okinawan food.[83]

Gushiken was further linked to Okinawa through a variety of advertising and marketing schemes. The back cover of a special edition of the boxing magazine *Gongu*, which had been published in 1980 to celebrate Gushiken's twelfth title-defense victory, bore a full-page advertisement for "Brown sugar: A special product of Okinawa prefecture." The ad featured the question "What is the source of this energy, this power?" superimposed on an image of Gushiken striking a boxing pose (see Figure 5.5).[84] There is probably some room for doubt about the actual role of Okinawan sugar in Gushiken's boxing victories, but sugar was only one of several "Okinawan special products" that Gushiken helped to market. Two years earlier, in 1978, the weekly magazine *Shūkan gendai* announced that Gushiken and Kanehira, his manager, would open a "Ryukyu Folkcrafts" business. Clearly hoping to cash in on the booming interest in Okinawa sparked by Gushiken's celebrity, the business partners planned to sell various Okinawan folk- and handicrafts, including carvings of *kanmuriwashi* (the birds, not the man).[85] Gushiken undoubtedly served as a godsend for Okinawa's *kanmuriwashi*-carving industry, but his biggest impact on marketing came in the travel business.

Accounts and visual depictions of Gushiken often explicitly connected him with the beauty of his home island of Ishigaki. Describing Gushiken for readers, one interview published in 1977 observed, "Gushiken Yōkō comes from the South China Sea—the deep blue sky and white sand beaches. Raised on the island of Ishigaki, which is bathed by the [warm water] Kuroshio Current, this small-framed boxer is a quiet person."[86] In addition to highlighting Gushiken's quiet character and explicitly connecting it with his place of origin, the statement offered readers

Figure 5.5 In addition to a note of congratulation for Gushiken's twelfth successful title defense, this full-page advertisement on the back of the boxing magazine *Gongu* suggests connections between Gushiken's success and "Brown Sugar: A Special Product of Okinawa prefecture." *Gongu*, supplementary issue (July 1980): back cover. Courtesy of Gushiken Yōkō.

a glimpse of paradise through Gushiken. Tales of Gushiken's childhood almost invariably included descriptions of his youth in this island paradise, and Gushiken himself was frequently pictured near the ocean. Such images had captions noting how much he loved and missed Ishigaki's natural environment, or how different Japan's ocean was from that of Okinawa.[87] In the years immediately following Okinawa's 1972 reversion, Gushiken's home island of Ishigaki and Okinawa prefecture in general were beginning to emerge as honeymoon destinations for mainland Japanese. As the result of a kind of celebrity "ripple effect" where anything and everything related to a star becomes important, both Ishigaki and Okinawa received an unprecedented degree of attention as potential tourist destinations. The special Gushiken edition of *Gongu* from 1980, for example, included a five-page article titled, "The Island Paradise That Produced a Boxing Genius." It featured several color photographs of beautiful beaches, coral reefs, tropical flowers, stunning sunsets, and Okinawan-style buildings, alongside brief descriptions of the island and details about important tourist destinations and local specialty products.[88] The article from *Gongu* also noted that the number of tourists to Ishigaki had skyrocketed since Gushiken became champion, and new tourist hotspots had sprung up around Ishigaki, especially Gushiken's childhood home and the famous house he built for his parents.[89] A few years later, visitors to the island were also able to explore the Gushiken Hall of Fame, which opened in 1982 as the first such hall in Japan devoted to a single person.[90] Though perhaps somewhat exaggerated (still today, aside from beaches, there are relatively few tourist attractions to visit in Ishigaki), the island's Gushiken tourist boom reveals one of the pivotal ways in which Gushiken and the media attention he garnered served as a kind of window through which the rest of Japan came to see—literally, in some cases—Okinawa.

The almost obsessive interest in Gushiken as an Okinawan raises questions about oft-cited claims of Japanese homogeneity that are commonly associated with this period, suggesting the existence of parallel and somewhat conflicting discourses on Japanese race and ethnicity.[91] On the one hand, there was an official or intellectual discourse that held that minorities did not exist in Japan, a view exemplified perhaps most clearly by Japan's 1980 report to the United Nations, which explicitly made such a declaration. On the other hand, the focused attention on Gushiken's Okinawan-ness points to a second, more popular discourse that reflected and expressed fascination with difference inside Japanese society. Here, it is worth recalling that Gushiken was not alone in this sense. Oh Sadaharu and several other well-known "Japanese" baseball stars represented diverse ethnic and racial backgrounds. For many fans, the "peculiar fascination of such players" stemmed, in part, from the differences they embodied.[92] Yet many of these baseball stars downplayed their ethnic difference, and in the case of Oh, he was not only born and raised in Tokyo, but also became especially famous for drawing upon quintessentially Japanese cultural forms, such as Zen spirituality, kabuki movements, and *kendō* sword techniques, to achieve his baseball success.[93] In contrast, Gushiken, as numerous articles and letters pointed out, never sought to hide his Okinawan-ness, and in many ways this aspect of his identity served as a central component of his sports-celebrity image. Consequently, popular representations of someone like Gushiken offer an indication of how perceptions of difference played out in the everyday lives of Japanese, and how, in fact, they could easily coexist with a view of Japan as a homogeneous society.

Closer examinations of the ways in which Gushiken's image was used to introduce the culture and history of Okinawa reveal that even though differences and tensions were acknowledged, they were often muted, at times by the very circumstances of Gushiken's story. Focusing on Gushiken's childhood home in Ishigaki, for instance, conveniently hid Okinawa's problems with American military bases. Most of them are located on the island of Okinawa, not on outer islands like Ishigaki. In one sense, attention to Ishigaki, including details about the native-versus-immigrant tensions or the teasing of "islanders" that Gushiken described in relation to his childhood, offered valuable insights about internal differences within Okinawa.[94] At the same time, the coverage related to Gushiken that emphasized Ishigaki had the potential to skew popular perceptions, fostering the impression that all of Okinawa was like Ishigaki as it was pictured in these articles or described by Gushiken. The possibilities for such views to emerge were perhaps all the greater because Gushiken was conflated not with Ishigaki and the differences it represented within Okinawa, but rather with some abstract notion of "Okinawa" and its differences from Japan. A fan's drawing, published in May 1981 in the "Gong Public Square" (*Gongu no hiroba*) section of *Gongu* magazine, is a clear example of such conflation: a sketch depicting the island of Okinawa—labeled as such—appears floating in between Gushiken's head and the characters for his name.[95]

The special television documentary *Waga Okinawa: Gushiken Yōkō to sono ichizoku* (Our Okinawa: Gushiken Yōkō and his family) shows how Gushiken's image became inseparably linked to Okinawa as a whole and how this connection served to mute potentially troubling forms of difference. Originally aired on 22 October 1979, on the national NHK television network, the documentary's reach quickly extended beyond the NHK audience. Shortly after the broadcast, several other media outlets, including popular weekly magazines such as *Shūkan gendai*, picked up themes and facts from the documentary and recycled them in their own articles related to Gushiken.[96] Transcripts of the documentary, which were published in book form in 2003, represent yet another manifestation of the original, now with a prologue and epilogue to tell the rest of the story.[97]

The title of the documentary allows for a certain ambiguity. The "Our Okinawa" (*Waga Okinawa*) found in the main title could be taken to mean either the Okinawa of Gushiken and his extended family, or it could refer more generally to "Our," that is the NHK viewers'—in other words, Japanese people's—Okinawa. In either case, Gushiken is clearly the key to understanding "Our Okinawa." Much like human-interest stories presented during television coverage of the Olympics or other major sporting events, the documentary intersperses scenes from Gushiken's fights and training with details about his childhood and his extended family. Over the course of the program, viewers are introduced to several of Gushiken's relatives. Many of them are only distantly related, but all bear the surname Gushiken, which as the documentary points out, is a common Okinawan name.

The NHK special tells its viewers about several aspects of Okinawan culture, including Okinawan patterns of patrilineal descent, referred to by the word *monchū*. When introducing this word, the transcript for the documentary emphasizes its Okinawan-ness, noting that it is a phrase "unfamiliar to one's [mainland Japanese] ears" (*mimi narenai kotoba*).[98] It quickly becomes clear that "unfamiliar" words abound, as indicated by the frequent use of the *katakana* syllabary used for writing foreign or loan words. The various Okinawan phrases or words written in *katakana* are usually followed by translations and explanations in standard Japanese, drawing attention to Okinawa's linguistic differences.[99] The documentary also illustrates a number of cultural differences, including the practice of *ushīmī* (*seimeisai* in Japanese), an annual event in which extended families all over Okinawa gather in large numbers at their ancestral tombs. In the documentary, this Okinawan practice is explicitly linked to Gushiken Yōkō, not only because the NHK special follows his extended family, but because the event fell on the same day as his eighth title-defense fight.[100] In that sense, the use of Gushiken to introduce this Okinawan custom appears seamless, even providential.

A number of historical facts about Okinawa are also introduced in the documentary. The telling of Gushiken's family history, for instance, notes that the family line stretched back to a late sixteenth-century relative of King Shō Nei.[101] What the program failed to mention was that Shō Nei ruled the Ryukyu Kingdom in 1609 when it was conquered by Satsuma, a feudal domain in southern Japan led by a vassal of the recently established Tokugawa shogunate. Shortly after the documentary aired, a number of boxing and weekly magazines began relating similar facts about Gushiken's family history. However, unlike the NHK program, these magazine accounts not only pointed to Gushiken's descent from the king, but also mentioned Satsuma's invasion, informing readers that in his boxing matches Gushiken was channeling his ancestral anger about the invasion and using it against his opponents.[102] Even though Gushiken's alleged "anger" in these magazine stories stemmed from Okinawa's contentious historical relations with other parts of Japan, historical distance and changed contexts helped to soften potential readings of this anger as "anti-Japanese."

Like the details about King Shō Nei, the NHK documentary glosses over several other touchy historical issues, or omits them altogether because they, conveniently, do not "fit" with the story being told about Gushiken and his family. The sole reference in the program to Japan's annexation of the Ryukyu Kingdom and establishment of Okinawa prefecture describes the event as having resulted from the enforcement of measures to eliminate feudal domains and establish a prefectural system.[103] As it is presented in the documentary, the nineteenth-century remaking of Japan's relations with Okinawa—which many view as a form of colonization—was simply an outcome of modernizing Japan as a whole, or to put it another way, Okinawa's history was really no different from any other prefecture in Japan.

On a similar note, the documentary's discussion of prewar discrimination against Okinawans in mainland Japan mentions only the inability of mainlanders to read the name Gushiken correctly. According to an older woman interviewed about the issue, such discrimination was no longer a problem because, thanks to Gushiken Yōkō's boxing success, everyone in Japan now knew how the name was pronounced.[104] Now that all Japanese knew how to say an Okinawan name, the documentary seemed to imply, a long history of discrimination had been rectified, and neither Okinawans nor Japanese needed to concern themselves with such issues anymore.

References to wartime loss and memory point out that one in four members of the Gushiken family died in the war. Nevertheless, because most of Gushiken's relatives who were interviewed for the documentary had emigrated abroad (primarily to Palau and other islands in Micronesia) and only returned to Okinawa after the war, the documentary offers *no* discussion of the Battle of Okinawa, one of the more contentious issues in Okinawa-Japan relations.[105] Okinawa's postwar history, moreover, is summarized in the narration by the fact that the Gushiken family lost its ancestral village when the U. S. military took over the area as a quarry for materials needed to build bases. This example was one of the documentary's few references to the military bases and the social, economic, political, and cultural effects of the extended American occupation of Okinawa.[106] Similarly, Okinawa's reversion to Japan is grouped with the 1975 Okinawa Ocean Expo, and both are described simply as "world changing" events for postwar Okinawa.[107] Although noting the criticisms of the Expo, which many viewed as a huge disappointment, the

NHK program does not mention similar criticisms about reversion, or Okinawan concerns about the continued presence of several large military facilities in the prefecture.

In the entire documentary, the least muted voice of all is that of Gushiken Yōkō himself. Near the very end of the program, he uses the fairly derogatory Okinawan word *naichā* to refer to mainland Japanese in his declaration, "I cannot lose to a mainlander."[108] This quotation, frequently repeated in the press and in Gushiken's autobiography, is a statement of almost militant difference, so out of sync with the rest of the documentary that it is jarring.[109] And therein lies part of Gushiken's appeal. Gushiken's statement offers a clear example of what theorist Guy Debord has called "purely spectacular rebelliousness," in which "dissatisfaction itself becomes a commodity."[110] For one thing, Gushiken's willingness to make this kind of comment—and be able to back it up—served as an essential part of his image as a world-champion boxer. As an example of biting honesty, Gushiken's declaration displayed his bravado and showed the guts or *konjō*—or as Gushiken himself put it using an ostensibly untranslatable Okinawan word, the *gājū*—for which he was celebrated.[111]

Moreover, makers of the documentary framed the animosity inherent in Gushiken's statement as feeding his "hunger," driving him to work harder than anyone else and serving as his motivating force in the ring. The almost defiant declaration of Okinawan-ness was perhaps more striking because it came at a point when Gushiken's "hunger" was beginning to be called into question. Earlier accounts of his rise had emphasized his poverty and his desire to assist his parents financially as the primary motivations that drove him into the boxing ring in the first place and then pushed him to excel. However, by 1979, when the NHK documentary first aired, the prevalence of details about Gushiken's prize winnings and his lifestyle had made it clear that he was no longer the poor boy from Okinawa attempting to rise in the world. He had already risen. In this sense, it is more than mere coincidence that efforts to link Gushiken's image with abstract notions of Okinawan indignation—and here we might recall the popular assertions about Gushiken's ancestral anger in relation to Satsuma's 1609 invasion—appear with increasing frequency alongside warnings to Gushiken about the dangers of complacency. In 1980, Gushiken himself apparently felt it necessary to reassure his fans that despite monetary success, "I will always be hungry."[112] If Gushiken was no longer a poor boy, he was still the boy from Okinawa, and it was this difference, especially in the latter part of his career, that came to be seen as a key or secret to his athletic success. Gushiken was not simply fighting for the money—if that had been the case, such accounts seem to imply, he would have lost his title much sooner. He was fighting for something higher, something more noble: he stepped into the ring to bring glory to his homeland of Okinawa. Even though at first glance Gushiken's devotion to Okinawa seems to fall at odds with his role as a national hero, the sense of animosity towards "Japan" expressed in his statement actually proved a virtue, because it allowed him to become an extremely successful world champion, and in so doing bring pride and respect to Japan as a whole.

Gushiken's evocations of Okinawa-Japan tensions prove "spectacular" for other reasons as well. For one thing, politics, or more accurately a lack of them, played a significant role in shaping Gushiken's image. Even in the immediate post-reversion period, Okinawa's relationship with Japan was contentious, and a number of high-profile Okinawans, including the prefectural governor, repeatedly criticized Japanese and American treatment of the prefecture and its residents. In comparison, Gushiken, despite his seemingly rebellious comments in the documentary, conveyed a kind of political innocence. He was not questioning reversion or other Japanese policies toward the prefecture. He did not challenge the presence of American bases. Gushiken's apparent lack of interest in such politically charged issues is particularly evident in a 1978 "battle of words" (*tōron*) with the Okinawan rock musician Kina Shōkichi published in the popular weekly magazine *Pureibōi*. Although the bulk of the article features both men discussing their appreciation of Okinawa and their respect for each other, Gushiken appears completely bewildered by Kina's participation in a campaign opposing Okinawa's prefecture-wide transition to driving on the left side of the road like the rest of Japan. From the beginning of the recorded discussion, Kina rails against policies like the traffic change being imposed on Okinawans, while Gushiken simply wonders, "What's all the fuss about? Isn't it strange?" Juxtaposed with Kina, Gushiken appears almost apolitical. In light of well-known details about his behavior and discipline, the boxer also comes across in this case as a model citizen, especially because the article highlights the fact that Kina was known for spending two years in prison on drug-related charges.[113] Gushiken's overall image as a good Japanese citizen further benefited from comments early in his career about his fondness for the national anthem "Kimi ga yo." Various popular sources made much of the fact that Gushiken, unlike most boxers, actually sang the anthem at the beginning of his matches.[114] Although details about Gushiken's respect for the Japanese anthem may appear trivial, they take on added significance in light of Okinawa's recent reunion with the nation.

It is also important to note that Gushiken's famous words about his driving desire to beat "mainlanders" appeared after he had established a reputation as a national star. With his seventh title-defense victory in January 1979, he had already broken the national record, an accomplishment that many believed merited the National Medal of Honor. Gushiken may have been Okinawa's star, but by the time the NHK documentary aired in late 1979 he was also clearly Japan's Okinawan star. Even a striking declaration of difference from Gushiken was unlikely to change that, especially since the claims he made never had to be "tested." Despite the potential for a world-title match against another Japanese opponent, all of Gushiken's title-defense bouts were against non-Japanese.[115] In this way, the star systems that played the most critical role in defining his image, those involving transnational rather than domestic comparisons and rivalries, effectively mediated the potential for conflicting loyalties. There was never a need to choose sides when Gushiken was fighting to keep his title. Gushiken could be a representative of both Japan and Okinawa without particular tension, wearing an Okinawan bird and a Japanese flag on his shorts.

At the same time, Gushiken's statements serve as clear reminders that he himself actively embraced and sought to take advantage of his Okinawan identity. Whether it was discussions about his childhood amidst Okinawa's natural beauty or opening an Okinawan restaurant, Gushiken, the "Kanmuriwashi," did not hide his heritage. Because of his popularity, he became a conduit through which mainstream Japanese audiences could learn about and appreciate Okinawa and its culture.

Much like Gushiken's outwardly rebellious comments in the NHK documentary, popular images of Okinawan associated with Gushiken represented a kind of "spectacular difference" that was not necessarily what it seemed to be on the surface. The differences presented in the documentary revealed an Okinawa with a distinctive culture and history, but one that, when presented through the lens of Gushiken, ultimately hid several points of contention. To be sure, the audience may have been aware of such issues. Nevertheless, the almost deliberate erasures of tension in narratives associated with Gushiken held the potential for fostering illusions that all was well in Okinawa, thanks in no small part to Gushiken, who, among other things, effectively ended the problem of discrimination.

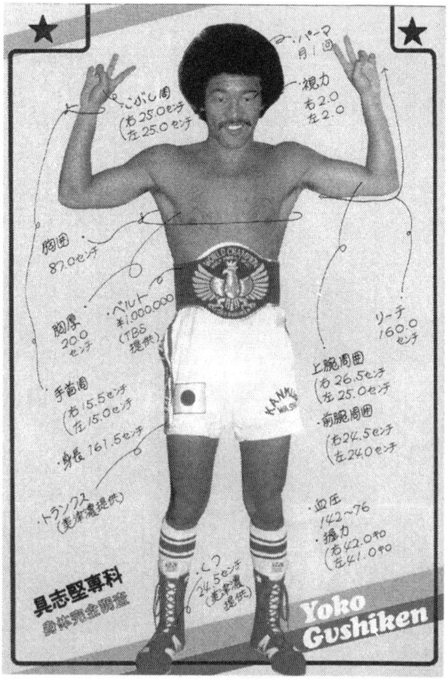

Figure 5.6 This full-page "Comprehensive Bodily Examination" provided readers of *Gongu* magazine with all the important measurements of and details about Gushiken, including his blood pressure (142/76), the names of the sponsors who provided his trunks (Mizuno), shoes (Mizuno, 24.5 cm), and 1 million-yen belt (TBS), as well as the frequency of his hair perms (once a month). The attention to Gushiken's hair was not unique, since his hairstyle became a defining feature of Gushiken's image. *Gongu*, supplementary issue (March 1980): 7. Courtesy of Gushiken Yōkō.

Even more significantly, Gushiken's widespread appeal also helped make Okinawan-ness stylish. As seen in previous chapters, sports stars have long been objectified and reduced to consumable celebrity images, details, pictures, and stories. In postwar Japan, as elsewhere, the advent of television, the ongoing expansion of sports-centered print journalism, and the rising impact of advertising, all combined with the increased societal prominence of sports themselves to take the commodification of sports celebrity to a new level (see Figure 5.6).[116] For Gushiken, whose stardom was explicitly linked to his Okinawan identity, his own commodified image helped transform Okinawan difference itself into a kind of consumable product. Eating Okinawan foods, visiting Gushiken's home island, buying a *kanmuriwashi* statue, or in fact, listening to, reading about, watching, and cheering for Gushiken, Okinawa's star—all became ways for Japanese society to experience Okinawan difference. On the one hand, such consumption held the possibility of contributing to a greater awareness of and perhaps even a newfound respect for diversity within Japan, an appreciation, in this case, for Okinawa's potential contribution to the nation. On the other hand, styles change frequently, and people do not always consume with care and appreciation. The potential problems with manifestations of spectacular difference arise when consumption is taken as evidence for understanding. There are, after all, no guarantees that a person buying a statue of an Okinawan bird or hanging a poster of Gushiken on a wall will consider the broader issues behind the difference they are consuming, especially when those same issues are being downplayed or ignored in other ways. Indeed, there are no guarantees that a month later that bird and that poster will not be replaced by the symbol and picture of another sports hero, who may hail from an entirely different locale. When the heroes fall, so can the places and ideas they represent.

The sports-star paradigm also contributed to the spectacular difference that Gushiken's image presented to popular readers and viewers. The narratives that defined him as a paradigmatic, self-made star served to highlight several ways in which he, as an Okinawan, shared common values with other Japanese, thereby erasing, or at least downplaying, notions of difference. Similar to other Japanese stars, Gushiken was devoted to his family and was able to achieve success through hard work and dedication. In contrast to these important shared values, the image of Okinawa that emerged from Gushiken's story was one of relatively minor, and ultimately consumable, differences, like food and natural environment. Even linguistic differences were not overwhelmingly significant, since they could also potentially be overcome through hard work and practice, or by simply being quiet, as in Gushiken's case.

In many accounts of Gushiken, Okinawan difference also appears closely linked to poverty, an understandable connection considering Okinawa's economic situation during and after Gushiken's childhood. In effect, such linkages create a kind of slippage, with economic class all too easily serving as a stand-in for ethnic difference. A striking example of such slippage can be found in Terayama Shūji's film *Bokusā* (The boxer, 1977). Although one of the two main characters is identified as Okinawan, the film relies almost exclusively on the tropes of dire poverty (which forces him into boxing) and a love of sunshine to portray the character's ethnicity. The only other indication of his heritage comes in a scene where he is introduced to Gushiken (who plays himself in the film) as a fellow boxer from Okinawa.[117] Terayama's film and the various narratives related to Gushiken convey the message that the "real" differences between Japan and Okinawa stemmed from the fact that Okinawans, like Gushiken, were poor. From this perspective, any tensions related to Okinawan ethnic difference would eventually be overcome through economic success. What is more, Gushiken's life story seemed to offer proof that Okinawans could in fact achieve such success on their own. They just had to be willing to work for it, and consequently, any Okinawans who failed to achieve success had no one to blame but themselves.

In the end, the sports-star paradigm not only served to gloss over significant differences between Okinawa and mainland Japan, but also eased the mainland burden of addressing the one issue it did recognize, Okinawa's poverty. By celebrating the success of Gushiken, Okinawa's self-made sports star, all of Japan could take pride in the promise that the rest of Okinawa could also overcome the disadvantages of ethnicity and poverty, through hard work and dedication. Perhaps the national embrace of the "Kanmuriwashi" was not all that it first appeared to be.

Assessing the Spectacular: Gushiken and Okinawa

In his analysis of the modern Olympics as a form of spectacle, anthropologist John MacAloon offers a reminder that the Games, and by extension other manifestations of the spectacular, serve as a "theater of self-delusion." At the same time, he notes that they "generate completely contrary experiences" in which people sometimes "encounter the genuine article."[118] Looking to Gushiken, then, it would not suffice to say that his emerging image simply allowed the Japanese public to dupe themselves, though in many ways that does seem to be the case. Gushiken has had an undoubtedly profound impact on Japanese society, even if that influence did not—indeed could not—ultimately transform and equalize Japan's troubled relationship with Okinawa.

Gushiken's influence is most apparent in the realm of boxing. Gushiken, like other stars, has molded his sport as an athlete, as a commentator, and more recently as a coach. He has also sought to expand the sport's scope by reaching beyond the would-be world champions. Within months of opening his new boxing gym in Tokyo, he began marketing his expertise to both men and women interested in "exercise boxing," employing a diagram-filled article in the weekly magazine *Shūkan hōseki* to promote this "new sport."[119] During our interview, Gushiken also expressed his interest in seeing the development of women's professional boxing, an international trend that he thought would eventually catch on in Japan as well.[120]

Gushiken's impact on boxing, however, extends beyond his role as trainer, a fact most apparent in Okinawa. Including Gushiken, a total of seven boxers from Okinawa prefecture have held world-championship titles, more than from any other prefecture in Japan. Of course, this prefectural success in boxing cannot be attributed solely to Gushiken, especially since Okinawa had already emerged as an amateur-boxing powerhouse by the time he became champion. Yet significantly, many of these world-champion boxers, as well as other Okinawan boxers who never achieved the same degree of success, were frequently cast as the "next Gushiken."[121] These media epithets point to the fact that Gushiken's success popularized boxing in Okinawa and also led many trainers, managers, and promoters to Okinawa in search of "another Gushiken." Even more importantly, Okinawa's boxing successes suggest the ways in which Gushiken changed popular perceptions of boxing among Okinawans. If, as Gushiken and others have suggested, boxing was relatively unknown or viewed simply as fighting among most Okinawans when he first took up the sport in high school, then by the time he retired, his massive popularity transformed the sport's image in the prefecture. Gushiken's success, together with the repeated references to his discipline, his hard work, and his filial piety, not only made professional boxing well known in Okinawa, but also helped make it a completely acceptable and even admirable sport. As comments from Okinawan writers like Nagadō Eikichi and the letters and articles published in the *Okinawa taimusu* suggest, Gushiken had a profound impact on Okinawan perceptions of themselves, well beyond the realm of boxing. Whatever the long-term effects of Gushiken's celebrity might have been, in the context of Okinawa's historical and post-reversion struggles, the "Kanmuriwashi" and his success clearly meant a great deal to many Okinawans.

On the national level, Gushiken's influence on popular perceptions of Okinawan difference remains ambiguous. The spectacular difference that Gushiken came to represent did not preclude the possibility that some fans might, through their consumption of Okinawan-ness, develop a genuine interest and respect for the prefecture, its culture, and its people. Because Gushiken has remained visible in popular culture after his retirement, he continues to serve as a potential vehicle for people to explore, or at least consider, the place of Okinawa within the Japanese nation. However, the problem with popular culture fads and "booms," like those that have sprung up around Gushiken, is that they often go bust, revealing—sometimes painfully so, since yesterday's fad can become the fodder for today's joke—just how superficial understandings of difference really were.[122]

The spectacular difference apparent in images of Gushiken offered a promise of transcendence that it ultimately could not deliver. By eliding tensions and muting some of the most troubling forms of difference, the image of Okinawa that was so central to Gushiken's status as a celebrity made it easy to overlook the root causes of Okinawan difference: a history of discrimination, years of separate and clearly unequal treatment under a repressive American occupation, and a society that continued to be plagued with social, economic, and cultural inequalities. Spectacular difference also fostered the notion that such issues would, eventually, rectify themselves, if only Okinawans would commit to the task at hand. In the meantime, others could applaud themselves for embracing Okinawan-ness as they soaked up the Ishigaki sunshine, sipped their Orion beer, and gazed with reverence on the *kanmuriwashi*, that soul-stirring great eagle of the South.

EPILOGUE

So How Tall Is Ichiro?

He had played baseball all his life. He had approached the sport with a passion and conviction that few of his contemporaries could match. For that, he had his father, a former high school pitcher, to thank. . . . At age seven, the boy, Ichiro, had joined a local youth baseball team, which played on weekends; shortly after that, he asked his father to teach him the proper way to play the game. The father in turn asked his son if he could commit himself to practice every day, to stick without deviation to the endeavor, all the way to the end. Could he promise? The answer was yes.

—Robert Whiting, *The Samurai Way of Baseball*

According to his 2010 ESPN.com player profile, Ichiro Suzuki was born on 22 October 1973, in Kasugai, Japan. He stands 5 feet 11 inches (180 centimeters) tall and weighs 172 pounds (78 kilograms). He bats left, throws right, plays in right or center field, has won thirteen American League awards, and as of 2010, was in his tenth year playing in Major League Baseball (MLB) for the Seattle Mariners. His 2010 salary is given as $18,000,000.[1] Although the information is not included on the ESPN profile, it is widely known that Ichiro is married to former television reporter Fukushima Yumiko, whose lunch boxes and cooking are allegedly delicious, and that he has been involved and caught in at least one extramarital affair.[2] So many records, so many measurements, so many details.

As the preceding chapters have shown, the attention Ichiro has generated as a baseball star is nothing new. Indeed, *history* itself is the simple answer to the seemingly simple question posed in the introduction: why do we know, or at least think we know, so much about these people?

Ways of talking about and depicting sports stars established in earlier periods generated a kind of generic inertia. Combined with the ongoing development of new and often competing media outlets, they have resulted in ever-increasing coverage and attention to the lives and careers of sports stars. Nevertheless, the history of the emergence and evolution of sports celebrity in Japan has been anything but a simple process. At its very heart has been the molding of celebrity images, and those involved in crafting such images—the mass media, agents of the state, biographers, fans, sports promoters, medical specialists, and the stars themselves—have employed representations of sports stars to serve diverse and often contradictory agendas. The resulting images have been highly malleable and polysemic, with a wide range of potential interpretations and uses, and their impact in Japan, as well as other societies, has extended well beyond the realm of sports.

The roots of modern sports celebrity in Japan lie in the Tokugawa period, when sumo emerged as a popular spectator sport and a nascent star system appeared, in which images of individual sumo stars were constructed in relation to other wrestlers. Early *banzuke* ranking sheets and woodblock prints depicted wrestlers in ways that allowed fans to identify and distinguish particular athletes. Agents associated with the emerging mass media of the Meiji era perpetuated, in modified form, earlier representational techniques and practices in their coverage of sumo, but they were also faced with something new. The arrival and diffusion of new Western sports in Japan, along with images and descriptions of non-Japanese athletes, meant that sumo and its stars no longer monopolized sports celebrity. From this time, the celebrity images of sumo wrestlers, as well as those of other Japanese athletes, were increasingly constructed through comparisons and oppositions with a range of both domestic and international sports figures. It was only during the late 1800s, with escalating Japanese interest and participation in sports at home and abroad, that one begins to see the rise of the transnational star systems that have been central to the production and consumption of modern sports-star images.

Combined with Tokugawa-era precedents, these new developments in sports and media played a critical role in the emergence of sumo star Hitachiyama Taniemon, who actively sought to use his fame to reshape domestic and foreign perceptions of sumo. As one of Japan's first modern sports stars, Hitachiyama served as an important link connecting the long line of earlier sumo celebrities with the many sports stars who followed him. Because of his transitional role and widespread popularity, Hitachiyama's celebrity image and the stories explaining his stardom also established precedents and patterns that have shaped depictions and interpretations of later stars. Hitomi Kinue, for instance, the female track and field star active in the 1920s and 1930s, could hardly be more different from Hitachiyama, yet her story maintained many aspects of the sports-star paradigm that took shape during the sumo star's lifetime. At the same time, the mixture of pride and anxiety surrounding Hitomi's life and career exemplifies the polysemic nature of sports-celebrity images, which made it possible for Hitomi to be seen simultaneously as both a national heroine and a potential threat to societal perceptions of gender. Baseball star Sawamura Eiji, whose wartime and postwar images appear almost contradictory, serves as a similar reminder that sports-star images are constructed and often reconstructed in relation to particular sociohistorical contexts. Sawamura's case also illustrates that the influence of the sports-star paradigm and star systems was not limited to nonteam sports, especially since his "battles" with American baseball greats have played a defining role in accounts of his paradigmatic rise to sports stardom. By the time Okinawan boxer Gushiken Yōkō became world champion in the late 1970s, television, advertising, professionalization, increased international competition, and a host of other factors had dramatically transformed the sports scene in Japan since the days of Hitachiyama, resulting in important differences in the boxer's sports-celebrity image. Nevertheless, key elements of the paradigm remained, and Gushiken offers an example of how these lingering elements combine with various star systems to produce not only sports-celebrity images, but also popular perceptions of identity and difference.

As one of Japan's latest international sports superstars, Ichiro Suzuki highlights the ways in which such factors continue to shape the images of sports stars and societies worldwide. Well before Ichiro achieved his current level of fame as a successful player in the MLB in the United States, he had already earned a reputation of superiority vis-à-vis his contemporaries in Japan through repeated record-setting performances and fan recognition.[3] Even Ichiro's now world-famous moniker, unusual in Japanese society where people are rarely referred to publicly by their given names, suggests the centrality of star systems in molding celebrity images. The common usage of "Ichiro" instead of "Suzuki" resulted from a 1994 public-relations effort on the part of his Japanese team, the Orix Blue Wave, to bring greater attention to the team by distinguishing its star, Ichiro, from all the other Suzukis in Japanese baseball (Suzuki is, like Smith, a very common name).[4] After he joined the Seattle Mariners in

2001, American media sources frequently observed that Ichiro insisted on being called only by his given name, something which reportedly made him the only one-name player in the history of American baseball.[5] As it turned out, interest in, and implicit criticism of, Ichiro's unusual name preference were quickly eclipsed by his performances on the field.

Despite Ichiro's earlier success in Japan, it has been transnational comparisons and competition that have driven his emergence as a superstar both at home and abroad. Much like Sawamura Eiji, Ichiro's MLB-level abilities first became apparent, and consequently relevant, during a series of exhibition games against American all-star players in 1996, when his batting performance is said to have sparked the interest of the American coaches and inspired superstar outfielder Barry Bonds to exclaim, "That little shit can really hit the ball."[6] When Ichiro joined the Mariners, he was initially greeted with skepticism in the United States. American uncertainty about Ichiro fell in line with the earlier comment from Bonds, namely, a disbelief that a "little" Japanese man (Bonds, we might note, is famous, or perhaps infamous, for his bulk) could compete effectively in the Major Leagues, no matter how well he had played across the Pacific.[7] In early newspaper coverage, Ichiro was repeatedly described with adjectives like "slightly built," "hardly imposing," "relatively scant," and "gaunt-looking," phrases which were supported by references to Ichiro's reported height and weight: 5 feet 9 inches (175 centimeters) and 160 pounds (73 kilograms).[8] Given such attention to his size, perhaps it is not surprising that Ichiro has allegedly insisted that his measurements were underreported.[9] Indeed, at some point after May 2007, Ichiro's official height received a two-inch boost, so apparently he is no longer "only 5-9."[10] Whatever his actual height might be, it has not prevented Ichiro from exposing the tenuous nature of American assumptions about athletic superiority by becoming a dominant, record-setting figure in American baseball and earning a reputation as one of the top players in the game.

Ichiro's achievements and increasing popularity in the United States did not go unnoticed in Japan. When I first arrived in Japan to conduct research for this project in August 2004, Ichiro was on the verge of breaking an 84-year-old MLB single-season hit record.[11] Ichiro's image was omnipresent in Japan that summer; he seemed to be everywhere, including a welcome reception for visiting American researchers that I attended shortly after my arrival. As part of the general comments of greeting and welcome, one of the Japanese government officials attending the event announced his hope that Ichiro would not only break the record, but also become the kind of hero for American children that Major League greats like Joe DiMaggio had been for him. Like many of the sports stars seen in previous chapters, Ichiro, it seems, had become Japan's unofficial ambassador, a man who could help change Japan's image at home and abroad. Hitachiyama would have been proud.

If those in Japan have clearly looked to Ichiro as a way of redefining themselves, the commentary on Ichiro produced for the benefit of American fans suggests that Americans have done the same. Beyond his well-documented and frequently praised athletic abilities, Ichiro's significance for American audiences lies not only in what he tells them about Japan, but perhaps even more importantly, in what he tells them about themselves. In other words, since both Japanese and Americans employ his image as a kind of lens through which they can define themselves in opposition to the other, Ichiro may be seen as one of the latest manifestations of the transnational, co-constitutional processes that have long stood at the very core of sports and sports celebrity.

A striking example of such processes shaping Ichiro's image can be found in Robert Whiting's book, *The Samurai Way of Baseball: The Impact of Ichiro and the New Wave From Japan* (2004). Aimed explicitly at "North Americans, contemporary fans of Major League Baseball, with little or no knowledge of the Japanese game," Whiting's book was first published in hardcover with a different title—*The Meaning of Ichiro: The New Wave from Japan and the Transformation of Our National Pastime*.[12] As the original title suggested, quite explicitly, Whiting argues that Japanese stars such as Ichiro "had much to offer" MLB, gifts that went well beyond their playing abilities.[13] In the prologue, Whiting observes: "The Japanese may not play baseball with the looseness and joy of the Americans, but they love the game just as much, and they play it as if they mean it. They have a respect for the sport that is sometimes lacking in the U.S."[14] Expanding upon this point, Whiting highlights Ichiro's batting ritual, his respect for equipment, a work ethic that "put his [Seattle Mariners] teammates to shame," and his initial willingness to accept, allegedly without complaint, a relatively low salary of $4 million.[15] In the end, Whiting suggests, all these factors, combined with Ichiro's baseball talent, led American fans to love and respect him as a "throwback to another time" in baseball.[16] At the same time, Ichiro transformed and reinvigorated his fellow teammates. Even young Little League players supposedly began to mimic various aspects of his practice routines and warm-up rituals.[17] Whiting, of course, was not alone in his portrayals of

Ichiro. Many of the points he raised in his 2004 book had been in circulation since Ichiro's first season as a MLB player in 2001.[18]

The point here is not to cast doubt on Whiting's analysis of American interest in Ichiro or to question the overall significance or impact of Japanese stars like him, but rather to highlight how in this particular instance, the images of Ichiro's "strengths" are deployed to demonstrate—and potentially to correct—perceived American weaknesses. For Whiting, a longtime commentator on Japanese baseball, which he frequently portrays as a "different" game from its American counterpart, the contributions of Ichiro and other Japanese stars to baseball in the United States are overwhelmingly positive. After only his first season, sports writers were already describing Ichiro as a "throwback superstar," whose exciting play could take the American game back to its roots.[19] According to many, the positive impact of Ichiro and other Japanese stars has gone beyond the baseball diamond. *BusinessWeek* magazine, for instance, noted that Ichiro's team "dispensed with some outdated notions about baseball marketing by embracing all things Japanese and turning itself into a merchandising dynamo."[20] Whiting and others have also suggested that the popularity of Japanese stars among American fans indicate that Americans can "become global citizens without leaving home."[21]

As demonstrated by the case of Gushiken, however, the popular embrace of difference is not always what it seems. Indeed, a cursory overview of the materials intended to introduce Ichiro to American audiences reveals that others might see a less-than-positive contribution from Ichiro and other Japanese baseball stars. Commenting on the significance of Ichiro's success in his first season of American baseball, the back cover of Rob Rain's book *Baseball Samurais: Ichiro Suzuki and the Asian Invasion* (2001) informs would-be buyers that "American fans are learning what the Japanese already know—these amazing players are *already mapping out* baseball's future, proving that this grand slam Asian invasion is here to stay. . . [*sic*]."[22] References associating Ichiro with an "Asian invasion" of baseball and the "apparent future of the game" were not uncommon during Ichiro's first year in Seattle.[23] His initial success also sparked half-joking remarks about the "sports world turning Japanese," as well as a somewhat more serious article about Japanese interest in American football, which asked, "Having conquered baseball, why not the gridiron?" Among these various references one may detect a contemporary—if softened and perhaps slightly less racially offensive—version of an older idea about an "invasion" of Japanese athletes "mapping out" a secret Japanese agenda with potentially disturbing consequences, something described in the 1930s as a "quest to 'do the rest of the world one better.'"[24] The old "yellow peril in sports" may have a new name: the "Ichiro Effect."[25]

Echoing earlier Japanese pride in response to foreign claims of a "yellow peril in sports," the recent successes of Ichiro and other Japanese sports stars who have garnered international achievements have led some contemporary writers to suggest that the "Japanese sports inferiority complex—the sense that Japanese are not physically or experientially ready for world competition" has been proven false.[26] In October 2004, the Asian edition of *Time* magazine named Ichiro to its list of twenty "Asian Heroes," featuring him on the cover of a special issue and quoting several Japanese fans, including a business executive from Osaka who declared, "Players like Ichiro prove that you can rise to the top even as an outsider."[27] In the words of *Time* magazine, "For Japan, Ichiro has long been a national inspiration, the best example yet that its baseball players (and, by extension, all its athletes) can not only compete with the world's best but triumph."[28] In the eyes of many Japanese, athletes like Ichiro are not just "standing shoulder to shoulder with their overseas peers, [but] in some cases they are leading the way."[29] Perhaps Ichiro and his generation of stars have finally done it.

Looking more broadly at the transnational history of sports celebrity, it becomes apparent that reliance on sports stars to address concerns about not being a "full-fledged, card-carrying member" of the modern world community is an unstable business.[30] Ichiro does not, after all, represent the first instance of claims about Japanese athletes "overcoming" a variety of complexes, yet such overcomings never seem to have been completed, always necessitating the rise of another world-class star to prove the prevailing domestic and international views wrong. How are we to account for the seeming failure of sports stars to guarantee, once and for all, Japan's status in the global community?

Relying on the achievements and success of sports stars to define national identity—indeed, to define any form of identity, national, ethnic, gender, racial, class, or otherwise—is precarious for several reasons. For one, sports stars prove all too *human*. They can and often do fail. They are subject to injury and death, and even if they remain active for an extended period, their bodies show the destructive effects wrought by competitive sports. Still, the humanity of athletes is a key to their celebrity. They represent the human body at its very limits in both form and function, and in that sense, they are simultaneously both human (like everyone else) and exceptional, almost superhuman. The exceptional nature of sports stars itself proves problematic when used to define identities. What happens when the nation, gender, or ethnic group being defined fails to produce the next Hitachiyama, Hitomi Kinue, Sawamura Eiji, Gushiken Yōkō, Ichiro, Michael Jordan, or Lance Armstrong? There are no formulas, no guarantees of continued dominance in the sports arena.

The goal of athletic competition as a whole is to eclipse and to continue doing so: "Faster, Higher, Stronger," the Olympic motto tells us. Achieving enduring athletic success for individual stars, teams, or groups has proven increasingly difficult over time. Even Japan's "national sport" of sumo, the sport of Hitachiyama and countless other Japanese stars, is now dominated by non-Japanese wrestlers.[31] Because of the constant drive in sports to surpass, sports are very much about the immediate, the here and now. Records and the achievements of past stars are critical, but they can cut both ways. Success at an earlier point can add tension and inspire greater interest in the events of the present, but past victories do not necessarily compensate for present failures. The implicit contrasts between previous successes and current failures are just as likely to provoke concerns and to raise the question, "They/we did it then; what's wrong with them/us now?" Such concerns are further aggravated by longstanding inequalities in sports on several levels—the baggage, loosely speaking, of a history of imperialism, cultural and otherwise. In particular, assumptions of Euro-American dominance, upon which the system of international sports was historically built and has long operated, have not completely disappeared. Although non-Western sports stars such as the Japanese athletes examined in this study have, at various points, challenged such assumptions, such athletes have so far proven unable to shake the deep-rooted notions held by both sides.[32] It is almost as if with the passing, or perhaps more accurately the surpassing, of each of these challenges, the global sports system has "reset" itself, easily resorting to old patterns and leaving, at least in Japan's case, the task of achieving a final, perhaps ultimately impossible, "overcoming" to the next wave of athletes.

The sports-star paradigm itself is one of the central factors contributing to the almost cyclical recurrence of the "Japanese sports inferiority complex" and the resulting repeated need to overcome it. Although the paradigm began to take shape in the early 1900s with Hitachiyama and the heroic self-made-man narratives that defined his celebrity, the description of Ichiro's "origins" cited in the epigraph points to a persistence of the sports-star paradigm, in spite of the dramatic transformations in society, sports, and various forms of media coverage since Hitachiyama's day. Just as in Hitachiyama's case—as well as in those of Hitomi, Sawamura, and Gushiken—skill, body, and character are central aspects of

Ichiro's reputation.[33] However, in line with the ideal of a self-made sports star, these "natural gifts" have been deemphasized, becoming secondary within conventional narratives to the dedication, perseverance, and hard work that Ichiro and all of these stars used to hone any inborn abilities or bodily advantages they might have possessed. It is this hard work and dedication, rather than exceptional talent, we are repeatedly told, that allowed sports stars to surpass the average person and their fellow athletes. We may also see in Ichiro another example of how success in sports came to be portrayed as both consequence and proof of an athlete's devotion to family.[34] Furthermore, Ichiro is depicted, both in the United States and Japan, as the embodiment of "distinctly Japanese traits," including respect, loyalty, hard work, and a Zen-like focus—traits that are often connected with stereotypical ideas about the martial arts, the samurai, and Japanese culture in general. These "Japanese traits" have purportedly allowed him to excel abroad and even transform the American game, bringing pride and respect to his nation in the process.[35] Little wonder, then, that the title of the Japanese translation of Whiting's book proudly proclaims: *The Ichiro Revolution: Japanese Major Leaguers and the New Age of Baseball*.[36]

Still clearly at work today in the molding of celebrity images, the sports-star paradigm, with its emphasis on self-made success, in effect downplays the exceptionalness of sports stars. In so doing, it creates the distinct impression that sports stars' achievements can be reduced almost to a simple formula: skill + a lot of hard work + devotion to family and nation = sports stardom. Although I do not question the dedication and hard work of sports celebrities, the fact remains that the vast majority of athletes work hard and are just as devoted, but few ever achieve levels of success comparable with sports stars. By deemphasizing the exceptional abilities and qualities of stars, the sports-star paradigm inadvertently fosters a kind of disjuncture, one that becomes especially significant in the transnational star systems that play a central role in shaping celebrity images. The United States, for instance, has long placed an equally significant emphasis on the ideals of hard work and devotion as fundamental factors in the rise of sports stars.[37] So what happens when two hardworking stars meet up in competition and one must necessarily lose? Does this loss mean that the loser was less dedicated or less hardworking? There are, in fact, no formulas that guarantee success in sports; there are, however, any number of circumstances and factors that come into play in sports competitions and effectively limit the potential for ultimate success. Not least among such factors are several long-standing inequalities—structural, economic, and otherwise—that sports as we know them today have inherited from their past.

Armed with a paradigm that promises a self-made rise in the realm of sports, it is easy to overlook such institutional and human factors when faced, especially in Japan's case, with a seeming inability to make it to the top of the sporting world and remain there. Instead, the problem comes to be seen as one of not working hard enough, or not being prepared enough, and in many instances, the lack of sustainable success in sports seems to perpetuate a belief, like the one mentioned above, that "Japanese are not physically or experientially ready for world competition."[38]

One of the reasons commonly cited for athletic failure—especially in instances when stars' images indicate that they have, in fact, worked hard and prepared with dedication—is a physical inadequacy that comes not from lack of preparation or even human frailty, but from being Japanese. In other words, the failure or success of *individual* sports stars, especially on the international stage, becomes an indicator of *national* bodily effectiveness and, especially in the case of sporting failures, can raise concerns about the need to make all the nation's people stronger and more physically fit. In this sense, sports stars, together with the transnational star systems and paradigmatic models that shape their images, wield an enormous, if unstable, power to influence how people think about and treat their bodies, a power to mold body culture in diverse ways and at multiple levels in a society.

In some instances, the impact of sports stars on body culture is so direct that it is hard to miss. One of the clearest manifestations of such influence may be found in the role of sports stars in promoting various sports by capitalizing on their fame, as seen, for example, with Hitomi Kinue and her active promotion of women's athletics. Hitachiyama assumed a similarly active role advocating his views of sumo, to the extent that he is credited with having saved that sport. As both Hitomi and Hitachiyama indicate, devotion to one's sport and to sports in general often becomes an element of sports stars' celebrity images. Many sports stars assume a direct role in teaching sports by becoming coaches, trainers, or commentators. Both Hitachiyama and Gushiken went on to serve as instructors in their respective sports, and during my interview with Gushiken, the former fighter indicated that one of his primary goals as a trainer is to pass on his knowledge and produce at least one world champion.[39] Sports celebrities frequently retire from active competition at a relatively young age, largely because of the demands that sports place upon their bodies. In fact, this circumstance is one of the factors that differentiates sports stars from other types of celebrities, who need not *necessarily* retire from their primary careers because of age or bodily deterioration. Finding themselves in such a position, sports celebrities often assume second careers as coaches or sports commentators, aided in doing so by their established fame. Inadvertently, then, the inescapable bodily strains that sports inflict upon celebrity athletes allow—perhaps even force—them to take up the role of sports "teachers" later in their lives and thereby exert a profound and direct impact on particular fields of sporting endeavor.

Sports stars also shape body culture in ways that are less direct, but arguably far more pervasive. The popularization of sports medicine in the wake of Hitomi's death, the publication of details about Sawamura's military physical, and comments suggesting that Ichiro helped both Japanese and Americans overcome negative views of small Japanese men, all point to the wide-ranging impact that sports stars exert on body politics. At the same time, sports stars and their image makers generate an overwhelming abundance of "facts" about athletes' bodies and lives: heights, weights, training regimens, statistical comparisons with other stars, eating habits, clothing styles, sexual preferences. This mass of facts, largely taken for granted, nonetheless practically begs a reader or viewer for comparison with himself or herself.

Even if these kinds of comparisons do not always change behavior, they do create a particular form of bodily awareness that can differ radically from one case to the next or from one time to another depending on the representations available for comparison. In this sense, the seemingly insignificant fact that Ichiro might be two inches taller than 5 feet 9 inches really does matter. Giving serious attention to sports stars tells us a great deal about the stars and their sports, but more importantly, it helps us better appreciate how Japanese—and by extension all people—view themselves, as well as their relationship to the nation and the broader world.

Reference Matter

Notes

Introduction

EPIGRAPH. Emi Sui'in, "Dewanoumi o itamu"; quoted in Shikimori, *Hitachiyama Taniemon*, 118–19.

1. The details in this paragraph are based on surveys of the newspaper scrapbooks available at the archives of the Japan Sumo Association. The scrapbooks contain sumo-related clippings from a variety of Japanese papers. On Hitachiyama's death and funeral, see Zaidan hōjin Nihon sumō kyōkai, Newspaper Scrapbook Collection, 198.49:49–81. The press attention to Hitachiyama's passing was unprecedented; the previous deaths of several high-ranking wrestlers generated far less coverage. For further examinations of Hitachiyama's death and the media response, see Chapter 2.

2. At the time, the average annual income in Japan was about 220 yen. For a chart of salaries from the late 1800s through the 1920s, see Smits, "Making Japanese Through War and Peace, Part Two" (accessed 10 September 2008).

3. "Eiyū no matsuro," *Yomiuri shinbun*, 7 June 1907, 1.

4. For a sampling of these "Who's Who" books, see Sakai, *Genzai jinbutsu no kenkyū*, 17–19; Ōsaka Asahi shinbunsha, ed., *Jinbutsu gaden*, 199–200; and Satō, *Gendai hyakunin gō, dai ni*.

5. Shikimori Inosuke's biography of Hitachiyama offers the definitive example of Hitachiyama as the "saint" of sumo; see Shikimori, *Hitachiyama Taniemon*. Portrayals of Hitachiyama as a foundational sumo figure also appear in popular sources, as evidenced by the title of an article from the series, "Stories of Japan's Pioneers" in the weekly magazine *Heibon panchi*. The subtitle reads, "Hitachiyama Taniemon: The Famous Modern Wrestler Who Elevated Sumo to the National Sport and Made the Kokugikan." See Kimoto, "Nippon senkusha monogatari."

6. Throughout this book, I use the terms "sports celebrity," "sports star," or "sports hero" more or less interchangeably. In doing so, I am fully aware that the specific meanings of these terms and their usages have been subject to a great deal of academic debate, which has often been framed in reference to Daniel

Boorstin's now classic study, *The Image: A Guide to Pseudo-Events in America*. For a summary of these debates and an insightful and practical response, see Whannel, *Media Sport Stars*, 40–51.

7. The edited volume *Sports Stars: The Cultural Politics of Sporting Celebrity* addresses the history of sports celebrity in less than three pages that rely almost solely on assumptions like those cited here. Only one of the book's sixteen chapters focuses on a star active before the 1980s (Andrews and Jackson, "Introduction," 6–7).

8. Charles Ponce de Leon's chapter examining American sports stars suggests that the methods of reporting about and the ideals associated with sports stars were still in flux during the early twentieth century (*Self-Exposure*, 241–73).

9. Several scholars have observed that prior to the late 1800s spectators in Britain and the United States tended to relate to teams rather than individual players and that the focus on individual sports stars began to increase dramatically over the course of the twentieth century. For two recent examples, see Rojek, "Sports Celebrity and the Civilizing Process," 683–84; and Smart, *The Sport Star*, 1–3, 16–18, and 37–41.

10. Chris Rojek describes celebrities who predate the mass media as examples of "pre-figurative celebrity," noting that "they were items of public discourse, and honorific or notorious status was certainly attributed to them. But they did not carry the illusion of intimacy, the sense of being an exalted confrère, that is part of celebrity status in the age of mass-media" (*Celebrity*, 19 and 30–32). The present study's examinations of Tokugawa-era sumo wrestlers, who clearly predate mass media, raise interesting questions about Rojek's general characterizations of celebrity.

11. On American views of sports, see Dyreson, "Regulating the Body and the Body Politic."

12. Whitney, "Athletic Awakening of the Japanese," 165–66.

13. My interest in the concept of co-constitution was inspired by graduate-seminar discussions of Manu Goswami's work on Indian nationalism. See Goswami, *Producing India*. For a more philosophical approach to the concept, see Kramer, "Understanding Co-Constitutional Genesis."

14. The presumed authenticity of sports stars is clearly part of popular perceptions, but many scholarly studies of celebrity also emphasize the achieved nature of sports celebrity. Barry Smart's study concludes that the "reality" of sports stars' achievements "is indisputable," a fact that gives sports stars a "quality that is increasingly rare in a world made cynical by the proliferation of image, spin, and artificiality." According to Smart's work, the unique authenticity of sports celebrities gives them an "unrivalled capacity to emotionally lift and inspire spectators and viewers" (*The Sport Star*, 198–99). Although I do not question the "reality" of achievements or the inspirational potential of sports stars, my work demonstrates that the way those achievements are told and interpreted is far from "indisputable" and subject to a great deal of "spin."

15. Dyer, *Heavenly Bodies*, especially ix–x and 1–18. See also Rojek, *Celebrity*, 43–49.

16. Holmes, "Starring . . . Dyer?," 8.

17. Dyer, *Heavenly Bodies*, 5.

18. Daisuke Miyao, *Sessue Hayakawa*, especially 6–15.

19. Dyer, *Heavenly Bodies*, 3.

20. Ibid.

21. With its emphasis on the construction of sports celebrity through a process of differentiation with other stars, my approach to star systems complements the work of others who have employed this concept. If considered at all, comparisons among the various stars—and their societal implications—are secondary concerns for scholars who discuss "star systems." For a pioneering examination of star systems and stardom as products of socio-historical construction, particularly in the context of post–World War II Italy, see Alberoni, "The Powerless 'Elite.'" On star systems and film celebrity, see Gledhill, ed., *Stardom*, especially Part I; see also de Cordova, *Picture Personalities*. In his study of American film stars, Joshua Gamson uses the term "star systems" to describe film-industry institutions and other forms of "celebrity industry" that shape the production of film-celebrity images (*Claims to Fame*, especially 22–28 and 40–48). A similar approach is used to analyze the life and career of David Beckham in Cashmore, *Beckham*. P. David Marshall raises the issue of differentiation in order to highlight institutional differences in how film, television, and music stars are produced and used for various purposes, primarily in the context of contemporary American society (*Celebrity and Power*, especially Chapter 7).

22. "'Nihon no Rokkī' Gushiken Yōkō," 154.

23. Ibid., 156. Gushiken's comment unintentionally highlights a point that most of these comparisons miss: Rocky did lose.

24. Terauchi, "Hakairyoku to reisei pēsu zukuri," 3.

25. Bourdieu, *Distinction*, 291.

26. Dyer's study devotes particular attention to the role of film celebrities in "shoring up the notion of the individual" and serving as "embodiments of the social categories in which people are placed and through which they have to make sense of their lives," points with clear applicability to sports stars (*Heavenly Bodies*, 9–10 and 17–18).

27. Ponce de Leon, *Self-Exposure*, 272.

28. Ibid., 252–54. Joshua Gamson has suggested that popular explanations for the rise of early film celebrities relied on similar paradigmatic notions. According to the circular logic of the classic story of a star's rise: "Greatness is built in, it is who you are. If one works at it, or gets a lucky break, it may be discovered. If it is discovered, one becomes celebrated for it, which is evidence that one had it to begin with" (*Claims to Fame*, 28–33).

29. Brownell, *Training the Body for China*, 10–11.

30. Rojek, "Sports Celebrity and the Civilizing Process," 685.

31. Foucault, "Governmentality," especially 98–103. I offer an expanded discussion in Chapter 2 addressing Foucault's concepts as they relate to sports stars.

32. Eichberg, "'Gefährlich Denken,'" 234; translated and quoted in Brownell, "Thinking Dangerously," 38.

33. See, for instance, the essays in Birrell and McDonald, eds., *Reading Sport*; and in Baker and Boyd, eds., *Out of Bounds*. The essays in these volumes focus

almost exclusively on sports and sports stars in an American context. Although more diverse in their geographical representation, most of the chapters in Andrews and Jackson, *Sports Stars*, examine sports stars in relation to particular national settings, with only five of sixteen essays specifically addressing transnational aspects of sports stardom.

34. There are, of course, a number of biographies of historical sports stars that I am not mentioning. Although many of these works are richly detailed and demonstrate clear research, few of them would be classified as scholarly or academic. In Andrews and Jackson's volume, the only chapter focusing on athletes before the 1980s is Bale, "Nyandika Maiyoro and Kipchoge Keino," 218–30. The Kenyan runners Maiyoro and Keino achieved fame in the 1950s and 1960s. Garry Whannel's rich study of sports-celebrity narratives offers only a brief ten-page chapter summarizing the history of sports celebrity in the United States, Britain, and other parts of Europe ("The Development of Media Sport," in *Media Sport Stars*, 30–39). Perhaps the most detailed account of the history of sports celebrity in the United States is Ponce de Leon's chapter in *Self-Exposure*, 241–73. For a somewhat dated, though richly informative, study of the rise of sports journalism in the United States, see Betts, "Sporting Journalism in Nineteenth-Century America." On the emergence of sports stars in the United States, as well as the social issues contributing to their popularity, see Rader, "Compensatory Sport Heroes." In recent years, a number of scholars have given increased attention to the history of sports in Japan. Although their works have been invaluable resources for me and occasionally touch on issues of sports celebrity, it has not been their primary focus. See, for instance, anthropologist William Kelly's work on baseball, including "The Spirit and Spectacle of School Baseball" and "Blood and Guts in Japanese Professional Baseball." In his dissertation on sumo, anthropologist Kenji Tierney briefly addresses issues of celebrity in his examination of the historical and contemporary significance of sumo in Japanese society (Tierney, "Wrestling with Tradition"). Sports studies specialists Allen Guttmann and Lee Thompson refer briefly to several stars in *Japanese Sports*. Scholars in Japan, too, have given limited attention to the emergence and evolution of sports stars, with much of the existing work addressing celebrity in purely biographical accounts or only tangentially in explorations that tend to focus more on the relation of sports to the media. See, for example, Sugiyama and Kadokawa intarakutibu media, *Terebi supōtsu 50 nen*. The subtitle refers to two specific stars—the professional wrestler Rikidōzan and the baseball player Matsui Hideki—but they serve primarily to illustrate trends and changes in television coverage.

35. Work done on recent non-Western, post-colonial sports stars is a notable exception. See, for example, Bale and Sang, *Kenyan Running*. On cricket and its significance in Pakistani politics, see Corrigan, "Imran Khan." On cricket and Indian nationalism, see Nalapat and Parker, "Sport, Celebrity and Popular Culture." On cricket in the Caribbean, see Beckles, "Brian Lara"; Beckles and Stoddart, eds., *Liberation Cricket*; and C. L. R. James, *Beyond a Boundary*. In the case of Japan, works addressing sports celebrity have tended to focus on baseball and especially recent transnational stars, such as Hideo Nomo who came to the United States

in the mid-1990s. See Mayeda, "From Model Minority to Economic Threat"; and Hirai, "Hideo Nomo." Marketed to a more popular audience, Robert Whiting's recent book exploring Ichiro Suzuki and other Japanese stars in American baseball also falls into this transnational category, as do Whiting's earlier books, which address baseball in Japan and especially the place of foreign players there. See the following works by Whiting: *The Samurai Way of Baseball*; *You Gotta Have Wa*; and *The Chrysanthemum and the Bat*.

36. See, for instance, Archetti, "The Spectacle of a Heroic Life"; and Giardina, "Global Hingis." See also Smart, *The Sport Star*, which considers the transnational dynamics of sports stars, but focuses primarily on athletes in contemporary Britain and the United States.

37. Although celebrity culture itself is often not the object of analysis, a number of scholarly works in English have offered new insights on Japanese popular culture and celebrity. On the imperial family, see Fujitani, *Splendid Monarchy*; and Ruoff, *The People's Emperor*, especially 202–53. On "idols," see Aoyagi, *Islands of Eight Million Smiles*. Music industry stars are discussed in a variety of works, including Atkins, *Blue Nippon*; Condry, *Hip-Hop Japan*; and Tansman, "Misora Hibari." On film stars, see especially Daisuke Miyao, *Sessue Hayakawa*. Miriam Silverberg's study of mass culture touches on several celebrities in Japan, including foreign stars; see *Erotic Grotesque Nonsense*. For two rich studies of "celebrity" female criminals, see Marran, *Poison Woman*; and Johnston, *Geisha-Harlot-Strangler-Star*.

38. Smart, *The Sport Star*, 37–41. In Smart's study, the only reference to Japan and one of the few addressing sports celebrity outside Europe and the United States comes in an endnote, which indicates that unlike the West, a culture of individualism is not a significant feature of modern sports in Japan, or by extension, other non-Western contexts. As evidence for this generalization, he cites the stories of American players described in Whiting, *You Gotta Have Wa*. Quoting Whiting, Smart emphasizes the "concept and practice of group harmony or *wa*" and a consequent lack of Western-style special attention to individual stars as the defining features of Japanese baseball culture (Smart, *The Sport Star*, 41n6). My study's examination of baseball celebrity presents a very different picture.

39. On the emergence and significance of Japan's *otaku* subculture, see Azuma, *Otaku*.

Chapter One

EPIGRAPH. "Eiyū no matsuro," *Yomiuri shinbun*, 7 June 1907, 1. The title could literally be translated as "the end of the road for a hero." The use of the word *eiyū*, or hero, here is the earliest reference in relation to sports that I encountered in the *Yomiuri* newspaper. The term *matsuro* evokes a sense of decline and is linked in particular to the notion of a hero's "last days." The phrase appears at several points in the article.

1. On the announcement, see Shikimori, *Hitachiyama Taniemon*, 72.

2. Cowen, *What Price Fame?*, 14–16.

3. Cuyler, *Sumo*, 21–22.

4. For additional information on alternate attendance and its political, social, and cultural impact, see Vaporis, *Tour of Duty*.

5. On castle towns, see Hall, "The Castle Town and Japan's Modern Urbanization." The segregation in Edo and other castle towns is but one example of the status system, which served as the basis for the social and political organization of Tokugawa society. See Howell, *Geographies of Identity in Nineteenth-Century Japan*.

6. On sumptuary regulations in Tokugawa Japan, see Shively, "Sumptuary Regulation and Status in Early Tokugawa Japan."

7. For a history of publishing in Japan, see Kornicki, *The Book in Japan*, especially 112–223. On commercial publishing and its role in Tokugawa society in particular, see Berry, *Japan in Print*.

8. Furukawa, *Edo jidai ōzumō*, 207; see also Bolitho, "Sumō and Popular Culture," especially 21–23.

9. Bolitho, "Sumō and Popular Culture," 23–24.

10. Nitta, *Sumō no rekishi*, 205–6; see also Guttmann and Thompson, *Japanese Sports*, 21; and Tierney, "Wrestling with Tradition," 42–43.

11. Nitta, *Sumō no rekishi*, 205. On the evolution of techniques and their classification, see Cuyler, *Sumo*, 62–63.

12. Bolitho, "Sumō and Popular Culture," 25.

13. Tierney notes in passing that with the advent of the ring, the bodies of wrestlers changed, "due to the lack of mobility." See Tierney, "Wrestling with Tradition," 43.

14. On the emergence of *toshiyori*, see Bolitho, "Sumō and Popular Culture," 25; and Cuyler, *Sumo*, 72. Sumo elders are an example of what David Howell describes as Tokugawa status groups "created or validated by the state," which "surrendered true autonomy in favor of state legitimation while retaining a measure of control over their internal affairs." See Howell, *Geographies of Identity in Nineteenth-Century Japan*, 35.

15. On the *sumō kaisho*, see Guttmann and Thompson, *Japanese Sports*, 23; and Cuyler, *Sumo*, 72.

16. Furukawa, *Edo jidai ōzumō*, 103.

17. Nitta, *Sumō no rekishi*, 198–99.

18. Cuyler, *Sumo*, 73–75.

19. Bolitho, "Sumō and Popular Culture," 24.

20. Cuyler, *Sumo*, 75–76; see also Guttmann and Thompson, *Japanese Sports*, 23.

21. Bolitho, "Sumō and Popular Culture," 25.

22. Guttmann and Thompson, *Japanese Sports*, 24; Bolitho, "Sumō and Popular Culture," 27–28; and Cuyler, *Sumo*, 78–80.

23. On the evolution of the *yokuzuna*, see Thompson, "The Invention of the *Yokozuna* and Championship System," 176. On invented tradition more generally, see Hobsbawm, "Introduction."

24. Guttmann and Thompson, *Japanese Sports*, 144.

25. On *banzuke* in general, see Cuyler, *Sumo*, 65–68; and Tierney, "Wrestling with Tradition," 27–28 and 47.

26. For references to non-sumo *banzuke*, see Bolitho, "Sumō and Popular Culture," 30.

27. On travel in the Tokugawa period, see Vaporis, *Breaking Barriers*.

28. For depictions of some of these items and more recent sumo-related memorabilia, see Kageyama Tadahiro, *To ni mo kaku ni mo ōzumō*; see also Tierney, "Wrestling with Tradition," 52–53; and Cuyler, *Sumo*, 77.

29. Tierney, "Wrestling with Tradition," 61–62; and Cuyler, *Sumo*, 87–89. Cuyler offers extensive details on Raiden's travels.

30. Yokoyama, *Nihon sumō shi*, 85; quoted in Cuyler, *Sumo*, 85–86.

31. Ueda Akinari, *Tandai shōshin roku*; I use the translation in Bolitho, "Sumō and Popular Culture," 29.

32. Kanzawa, *Okinagusa*; I use the translation in Bolitho, "Sumō and Popular Culture," 29.

33. *Shinpan kasen sumō hyōrin*; I use the translation in Bolitho, "Sumō and Popular Culture," 29.

34. Yokoyama, *Nihon sumō shi*, 86; translated in Cuyler, *Sumo*, 86.

35. The number of matches varied with each tournament; the average is somewhere around nine. A reasonable estimate would put Tanikaze in more than 380 matches, not including draws and other undecided matches.

36. Bolitho, "Frolicking Dragons," 12.

37. Ibid., 17. Many of these measurements were included as inscriptions on prints of these celebrity giants. See, for instance, the prints of Ōzora and another giant named Shakagatake in Bickford, *Sumo and the Woodblock Print Masters*, 34, 69, and 113–14. For additional details about such giants and their representations in prints, see Bickford, *Sumo and the Woodblock Print Masters*, 68–69 and 111–14.

38. Saitō, *Bukō nenpyō*, 104; quoted in Bolitho, "Frolicking Dragons," 17–18. For additional facts on Ikezuki, see Bolitho, "Sumō and Popular Culture," 31.

39. Wrestlers' handprints, including some cast versions, can be found in several areas in the Ryōgoku section of Tokyo today. Visitors often compare their hands with such prints—and I even found myself, almost unconsciously, placing my hand against a print I encountered while conducting research at the sumo museum.

40. Bolitho, "Frolicking Dragons," 18.

41. For a detailed study of sumo-related woodblock prints, see Bickford, *Sumo and the Woodblock Print Masters*.

42. Tierney, "Wrestling with Tradition," 57.

43. Bolitho, "Frolicking Dragons," 18–19.

44. For a discussion of techniques used to create an image of exaggerated emphasis on muscle tone, see Matsunami and Araki, *Shintaikan no kenkyū*, 155.

45. Ibid., 166–67.

46. Ibid., 155–56.

47. Ibid., 163–64.

48. Saitō, *Bukō nenpyō*, 100; quoted in Bolitho, "Frolicking Dragons," 17.

49. For prints and details about depictions of Daidōzan, see Bickford, *Sumo and the Woodblock Print Masters*, 29–31 and 98–102. For additional details on Daidōzan and other oversized children, see Bolitho, "Frolicking Dragons," 18; and Tierney, "Wrestling with Tradition," 48–49.

50. Tierney, "Wrestling with Tradition," 49.

51. Ibid., 41. Tierney highlights several parallels between sumo wrestlers and the other prominent performance-oriented celebrities of the time, including geisha and kabuki actors. See ibid., 43–46.

52. Bolitho, "Frolicking Dragons," 19.

53. Hanley, *Everyday Things in Premodern Japan*, 151.

54. Cuyler's section heading, for example, refers to the "Crisis of the Meiji Era." See Cuyler, *Sumo*, 95–97.

55. Cuyler suggests that sumo wrestlers had been part of a militia from the domain of Chōshū, which opposed the Tokugawa government and helped bring about its collapse; see Cuyler, *Sumo*, 93–94.

56. Smith, "The Edo-Tokyo Transition," 347; for population figures, see graph in ibid., 356.

57. Ibid., 349–50.

58. Harootunian, "The Progress of Japan and the Samurai Class, 1868–1882," 256–57.

59. Tierney, "Wrestling with Tradition," 92.

60. "Koto aru toki ni wa shichōtai ni hairi hōkoku no shi," *Tōkyō Nichinichi shinbun*, 17 February 1885; reprinted in Edamatsu, Sugiura, and Yagi, eds., *Meiji nyūsu jiten*, 3:787.

61. Cuyler, *Sumo*, 98–100.

62. Tierney, "Wrestling with Tradition," 92; and Cuyler, *Sumo*, 100.

63. Tierney, "Wrestling with Tradition," 132–33. On Meiji-era imperial pageantry more generally, see Fujitani, *Splendid Monarchy*.

64. For three accounts of the 1884 event, see Oka, *Kokon sumō taiyō*, 18–24, which includes rich details and a sketch of the tournament site; Miki, *Sumō shiden*, 242–47, which provides details about the audience, the pre-wrestling rituals, and the wrestling itself; and Sawada, *Meiji taitei*, 71–74, which offers information about the color and design of the banners and an extended quote from a *yokuzuna* who performed that day. Notably, Sawada's work includes the imperial tournament alongside several other significant international and national events during the Meiji Emperor's reign.

65. For examples of prints, see Konishi, *Rokumeikan jidai*, 89; and Konishi, *Kenpō happu*, 55.

66. For a print of wrestlers at a special commemorative festival for those lost in the Sino-Japanese War see Konishi, *Nisshin Sensō*, 85. On Meiji's jubilee, see Bickford, *Sumo and the Woodblock Print Masters*, 55. On other state rituals, Tierney, "Wrestling with Tradition," 131–36; and Cuyler, *Sumo*, 100.

67. On the wedding gift, "The Wrestling Matches," *Japan Times*, 7 April 1900, 3; reproduced and available electronically at Klein, *Sumo*, http://history.sumogames.com/newspaper/1900/19000407.htm (accessed 1 July 2010).

68. Donations mentioned in "General News," *Japan Times*, 4 September 1900, 3; reproduced and available electronically at Klein, *Sumo*, http://history.sumogames.com/newspaper/1900/19000904.htm (accessed 1 July 2010). For wrestlers in China, "Japanese Wrestlers' Campaign to North-China," *Japan Times*, 1 June 1901, 2; reproduced and available electronically at Klein, *Sumo*,

http://history.sumogames.com/newspaper/1900/19010601.htm (accessed 1 July 2010).

69. On the Rikugun kaikōsha exhibition, "General News," *Japan Times*, 4 February 1899, 3; reproduced and available electronically at Klein, *Sumo*, http://history.sumogames.com/newspaper/1800/18990204.htm (accessed 1 July 2010). Performance for war veterans pictured in "PHOTOGRAPH OF A WRESTLING MATCH IN TOKYO HELD FOR THE BENEFIT OF WOUNDED JAPANESE SOLDIERS," *Harper's Weekly*, 12 November 1904, 1736; reproduced and available electronically at Klein, *Sumo*, http://history.sumogames.com/newspaper/1900/19041112.htm (accessed 1 July 2010).

70. On Hitachiyama at Sino-Japanese War ceremonies, see Ikeda Masao, "Rekidai Yokozuna Seiden, 33," 149. On Hitachiyama in Korea and Manchuria, see Ishii, "Supōtsu arakaruto," 35.

71. "Tenran-zumō o negai izu." The article notes that it had been nearly twenty years since the emperor himself attended.

72. "Hitachiyama no shitsubō."

73. Katō Takayo, *Meiji jidai no ōzumō*, 287–95.

74. Kelly, "Sense and Sensibility at the Ballpark," 88–89.

75. Raz, *Audience and Actors,* 188–92.

76. Katō Takayo quotes a passage from something designated only as *Sumō taikan* where these groups are referred to as *renchū kenbutsu* (group viewings). The *Sumō taikan* author associates these groups more closely with *engeki* (theater), and they are also distinguished from the warrior patronage enjoyed by sumo (*Meiji jidai no ōzumō*, 287–88).

77. "Hitachiyama-kai no shushi"; quoted in Katō Takayo, *Meiji jidai no ōzumō*, 294.

78. "Hinomoto-kai sōritsu shushi"; quoted in Katō Takayo, *Meiji jidai no ōzumō*, 289–90.

79. "Dōkan-kai setsuritsu no shushi"; quoted in Katō Takayo, *Meiji jidai no ōzumō*, 293–94.

80. "Hinomotokai kaisoku"; quoted in Katō Takayo, *Meiji jidai no ōzumō*, 291.

81. The income for a shop clerk in 1901, for instance, ranged between 15 and 50 yen a year. See "Sociological Mirrors."

82. "Hitachiyama-kai no shushi"; quoted in Katō Takayo, *Meiji jidai no ōzumō*, 295.

83. Ibid., 294–95.

84. "Hinomoto-kai sōritsu shushi"; quoted in Katō Takayo, *Meiji jidai no ōzumō*, 289.

85. Huffman, *Creating a Public*, 243.

86. On Kuroiwa and the Banzai-kai, see Katō Takayo, *Meiji jidai no ōzumō*, 288. Kuroiwa later formed the Oguruma-kai to support the stable of the retired wrestler Araiwa.

87. Hitachiyama with Gojō, *Sumō taikan*. The work was first published in 1909 by Bun'unsha, but was marketed by the well-known publisher Min'yūsha, which appears to have promoted the book widely in the press.

88. A note on the Nagoya Hitachiyama-kai indicates that several people participated in a group trip to view Hitachiyama at the tournament; see *Sumō sekai*, no. 12 (April 1913): 4.

89. On contemporary patronage and *kōenkai*, see Tierney, "Wrestling with Tradition," 263–90.

90. For sumo's transformation into a national embarrassment, see Tierney, "Wrestling with Tradition," 67–93.

91. On the baseball team at the elite First Higher School (Ichikō) and the popular attention it drew, see Roden, "Baseball and the Quest for National Dignity in Meiji Japan."

92. Tierney, "Wrestling with Tradition," 69.

93. Guttmann and Thompson, *Japanese Sports*, 109.

94. This point is frequently included in glosses of Hitachiyama's career. For one example, see Kimoto, "Nippon senkusha monogatari dai jūkyū kai."

95. The tournament in January of 1899 reportedly collected profits of 10,000 yen, a figure said to be the highest in over 40 years. Newspaper reports indicate that profits continued to rise over the next few years. See "General News," *Japan Times*, 25 January 1899, 3; reproduced and available electronically at Klein, *Sumo*, http://history.sumogames.com/newspaper/1800/18990125.htm (accessed 1 July 2010). See also "Wrestling," *Japan Times*, 30 January 1901, 6; reproduced and available electronically at Klein, *Sumo*, http://history.sumogames.com/newspaper/1900/19010130.htm (accessed 1 July 2010).

96. On changes in baseball, see Ponce de Leon, *Self-Exposure*, 249. On American football rules, see Oriard, *Reading Football*, especially 25–56.

97. On sumo's elevation to the status of *kokugi*, see Tierney, "Wrestling with Tradition," 147–212.

98. "Hinomoto-kai sōritsu shushi"; quoted in Katō Takayo, *Meiji jidai no ōzumō*, 289. My translation of the term *sōgi*, literally "heroic art," as "manly art," reflects contemporary Western references to boxing as the "manly art." See Gorn, *The Manly Art*.

99. "Hitachiyama-kai no shushi"; quoted in Katō Takayo, *Meiji jidai no ōzumō*, 294.

100. "Great Wrestling Contest," *Japan Times*, 10 June 1911, 1; reproduced and available electronically at Klein, *Sumo*, http://history.sumogames.com/newspaper/1910/19110610.htm (accessed 1 July 2010).

101. This observation is based on several articles about foreigners' views included in the newspaper scrapbooks at the archives of the Japan Sumo Association. For examples of foreigners' comments, see Zaidan hōjin Nihon sumō kyōkai, Newspaper Scrapbook Collection, 16:7 and 89.

102. "General News," *Japan Times*, 18 June 1899, 3; reproduced and available electronically at Klein, *Sumo*, http://history.sumogames.com/newspaper/1800/18990618.htm (accessed 1 July 2010). "Special Wrestling Matches," *Japan Times*, 26 January 1901, 3; reproduced and available electronically at Klein, *Sumo*, http://history.sumogames.com/newspaper/1900/19010126.htm (accessed 1 July 2010).

103. Dewanoumi, *Sumō hisshō dokugakusho*, 1–2 (citations to reprint edition).

104. Ibid., 4.

105. On *onnazumō* in general, see Tierney, "Wrestling with Tradition," 181–84. Photos of women wrestlers occasionally appeared in the monthly issues of *Sumō sekai* available at the archives of the Japan Sumo Association. Available issues date from May 1912 through February 1915.

106. Shikimori, *Hitachiyama Taniemon*, 88.

107. Comments about Genjiyama's irritation were featured in Kuroiwa's *Yorozu chōhō*; quoted in Ikeda Masao, "Rekidai Yokozuna Seiden 37," 147.

108. Shikimori, *Hitachiyama Taniemon*, 72.

109. Ikeda Masao, "Rekidai Yokozuna Seiden 37," 147–48. Hitachiyama continued the trip alone to Europe and then traveled back to Japan via the Trans-Siberian Railroad.

110. Satake wrote about his experiences in "Beikoku ni okeru wa ga judō."

111. On judo, see Shun Inoue, "Budō"; on Roosevelt's comments, see Tierney, "Wrestling with Tradition," 169.

112. Ikeda Masao, "Rekidai Yokozuna Seiden 37," 147.

113. Ibid., 147–48.

114. For examples from around the United States that have been collected and made available electronically, see Klein, *Sumo*, http://history.sumogames.com/newspaper/1900/1900.htm#1907 (accessed 1 July 2010); and Klein, *Sumo*, http://history.sumogames.com/newspaper/1900/1900.htm#1908 (accessed 1 July 2010).

115. "Roosevelt to See Japanese Wrestle," *New York Times*, 29 September 1907, 4.

116. "EAST ROOM BOUTS: President and Diplomats See Japanese Wrestlers. MARVEL AT HITACHIYAMA," *Washington Post*, 12 November 1907, 1.

117. "Daitōryō to Hitachiyama," 112.

118. "Hitachiyama no daitōryō hōmon," *Fukuoka Nichinichi shinbun*, 15 December 1907, reprinted in Umehara, ed., *Kindai sesō zenshi*, 3:387–89.

119. Guttmann and Thompson, *Japanese Sports*, 139–43. Tierney discusses the concept, but focuses on examples from later periods ("Wrestling with Tradition," 141–44).

120. For examples of such appropriations, see Vlastos, ed., *Mirror of Modernity*; see also Fujitani, *Splendid Monarchy*.

121. Hitachiyama with Gojō, *Sumō taikan*.

122. "Japan's Champion Wrestler Tells Why His Sport Surpasses Our National Game," *Washington Post*, 29 September 1907, SM4; and "JAP WRESTLING ALL THE RAGE: HITACHIYAMA IS CHAMPION OF THE RIGHT SORT: Sport Originated in Feudal Days and Became National One: Army and Navy Hold Frequent Contests: Story of How Early Champion Won Honors and Insignia," *Los Angeles Times*, 30 November 1907, 17. *The Independent* included a lengthy description of sumo allegedly penned by Hitachiyama himself; see Hitachiyama, "Japanese Wrestling."

123. "Roosevelt to see Japanese Wrestle," *New York Times*, 29 September 1907, 4.

124. Katō Takayo, *Meiji jidai no ōzumō*, 287–95.

125. Roden, "Baseball and the Quest for National Dignity in Meiji Japan," 519–20. See also Kiku, "The Japanese Baseball Spirit and Professional Ideology."

126. "Japanese Wrestler to Meet Roosevelt," *New York Times*, 22 September 1907, 6.

127. Nitobe, *Bushido*. References to Roosevelt's appreciation appear in the new preface to the 1905 edition. See Nitobe, author's preface. Bushidō is mentioned at multiple points in Baden-Powell, *Scouting for Boys*.

128. "Roosevelt to see Japanese Wrestle," *New York Times*, 29 September 1907, 4.

129. Dewanoumi, *Sumō hisshō dokugakusho*, 73. Non-samurai, including wrestlers, were sometimes granted the privilege of wearing swords, especially when participating in official business.

130. Katō Susumu, *Rekidai Yokozuna monogatari*, 116–17.

131. Hitachiyama, "Sumō no kami."

132. Huffman, *Creating a Public*, 170–77.

133. Huffman's list of circulation figures for major papers includes fifteen with circulations over 15,000 by 1895; see ibid., 386.

134. Kuroiwa, quoted in ibid., 173.

135. *E'iri jiyū shinbun*, 31 October 1882; cited in Kishino, ed., *Shinpan kindai taiiku supōtsu nenpyō*, 56.

136. *Rikishi shinpō* appeared in 1889, followed by the publisher Maruzen's *Sumō shinpō* in 1897 and a second *Sumō shinbun* in 1904. See Cuyler, *Sumo*, 104; and Kishino, *Shinpan kindai taiiku supōtsu nenpyō*, 86.

137. In addition to multiple issues of *Sumō sekai*, monthly issues 1 through 19 (June 1914–November 1915) of *Kokugi* are available at the archives of the Japan Sumo Association. Statements linking the paper to *sumōdō* appear in *Kokugi*, June 1914, 1.

138. Betts, "Sporting Journalism in Nineteenth-Century America"; for a rich examination of American football coverage, see Oriard, *Reading Football*, 57–133.

139. "Shinbun kiji no kakikata o kairyō," *Tōkyō Nichinichi shinbun*, 10 May 1889; reprinted in Edamatsu, Sugiura, and Yagi, eds., *Meiji nyūsu jiten*, 4:359.

140. On *Jiji shinpō*, see, "Wrestling Matches," *Japan Times*, 5 January 1899, 3; reproduced and available electronically at Klein, *Sumo*, http://history.sumogames.com/newspaper/1800/18990105.htm (accessed 1 July 2010). On the *Ōsaka Mainichi*, see Guttmann and Thompson, *Japanese Sports*, 111.

141. Guttmann and Thompson, *Japanese Sports*, 111.

142. Ibid., 111–12.

143. Ibid. For developments on the American side, see Ponce de Leon, *Self-Exposure*, 241–73.

144. Such simultaneity was not, of course, limited to sports and sports coverage. For examples related to the genre of detective fiction, see Kawana, *Murder Most Modern*, 19–22.

145. "Nijūninen ichigatsu no banzuke," *Jiji shinpō*, 18 January 1889; reprinted in Edamatsu, Sugiura, and Yagi, eds., *Meiji nyūsu jiten*, 4:358.

146. "Shin banzuke gaihyō," *Yomiuri shinbun*, 13 May 1900, 4.

147. *Tōkyō Yokohama Mainichi shinbun*, 21 June 1884; reprinted in Edamatsu, Sugiura, and Yagi, eds., *Meiji nyūsu jiten*, 3:787.

148. Huffman, *Creating a Public*, 239–47.

149. On *kawaraban* as precursors to press, see Huffman, *Creating a Public*, 21–24. On wrestlers in *kawaraban*, see Bickford, *Sumo and the Woodblock Print Masters*, 140–41 and 144–45.

150. Huffman, *Creating a Public*, 89–95. For examples of changes in visual coverage of U.S. football, see Oriard, *Reading Football*, 63.

151. See *Yomiuri shinbun*, 20 May 1899, 4. The illustration here is reminiscent of Tokugawa-era pictures of famous sites, or *meisho*, which often included sumo-related scenes.

152. *Yomiuri shinbun*, 22 May 1902, 5. Several articles in the Japan Sumo Association scrapbooks are labeled to indicate the paper of origin. Both *Jiji shinpō* and *Asahi shinbun* seem to have offered fairly extensive illustrations. For examples, see what are probably *Asahi* illustrations (unlabelled) in Zaidan hōjin Nihon sumō kyōkai, Newspaper Scrapbook Collection, especially 9:164. For a later example of *Asahi* illustrations (labeled as such), see Zaidan hōjin Nihon sumō kyōkai, Newspaper Scrapbook Collection, 11:140 and 149–50. For examples of those from *Jiji shinpō*, see Zaidan hōjin Nihon sumō kyōkai, Newspaper Scrapbook Collection, 11:147.

153. "Sekitori Monogatari," *Yomiuri shinbun*, 13 May 1896, 1.

154. Masumoto, *Supōtsu eizō no episutēmē*, 313.

155. Ibid.

156. Kishino, ed., *Shinpan kindai taiiku supōtsu nenpyō*, 92. The exact date of footage is unknown, but it seems likely to have been from the May 1899 tournament, one that Hitachiyama missed.

157. Kishino, ed., *Shinpan kindai taiiku supōtsu nenpyō*, 106. Specific details about content are not available.

158. This footage is included in a documentary series compiled and first broadcast in 1995 and 1996 by the Japanese broadcaster NHK. The entire series is available on DVD. For Hitachiyama's ring entering, see *Eizō no seiki dai 11 shū*.

159. Huffman, *Creating a Public*, 174 and 283.

160. See *Yomiuri shinbun*, 28 December 1906, 3.

161. Photographs of wrestlers appear regularly in scrapbooks that cover periods after 1906. For shots of the crowd and ring from 1909, see Zaidan hōjin Nihon sumō kyōkai, Newspaper Scrapbook Collection, 12:53. Hitachiyama's family is pictured in Zaidan hōjin Nihon sumō kyōkai, Newspaper Scrapbook Collection, 14:100 (exact date of photograph unknown). Extensive details of Hitachiyama's trip appear in Zaidan hōjin Nihon sumō kyōkai, Newspaper Scrapbook Collection, 16:141 to the end of volume.

162. Zaidan hōjin Nihon sumō kyōkai, Newspaper Scrapbook Collection, 14:43. This volume includes an early picture of a sumo match, which is extremely blurry, making it difficult to see anything. Other pictures of matches appear later and are clearer; see Zaidan hōjin Nihon sumō kyōkai, Newspaper Scrapbook Collection, 16. For the most part depictions of matches from articles in the scrapbook relied on sketches. In some cases, stills of opposing wrestlers were used; see Zaidan hōjin Nihon sumō kyōkai, Newspaper Scrapbook Collection, 12:68.

163. On the variety of "promotion schemes," see Huffman, *Creating a Public*, 321–22.

164. Tierney, "Wrestling with Tradition," 176.

165. Single photos appeared in various editions of *Kokugi*, but all were published together in the October 1914 article, "Tachiyama wa dore dake tsuyoi ka," *Kokugi*, October 1914, 10.

166. Chapman, "Sandow." This website also contains numerous photographs of Sandow posing.

167. Sandow's magazine included articles and advertisements related to Japanese sports. For details on Sandow and Japan, as well as other insights into Sandow's impact on global body culture, see Budd, *The Sculpture Machine*, especially 83 and 88. On Sandow and his appeal for American society, see Kasson, *Houdini, Tarzan, and the Perfect Man*.

168. Yoshida Akinobu, "Ningen no chikara no tsuyosa." The photo is too unclear to declare for certain that it is Sandow, but it is strikingly similar to his famous poses, so it is, at the very least, another strongman using a Sandow-like pose.

169. On Waseda and Keiō, see Guttmann and Thompson, *Japanese Sports*, 83. Robert Whiting has noted the appearance of early baseball stars connected with the First Higher School; see Whiting, *The Samurai Way of Baseball* (previously published by Warner Books in hardcover as *The Meaning of Ichiro*), 53–56 (page citations are to paperback edition). In referring to these early stars, Whiting cites primarily baseball-related sources, but my examinations suggest that these players attracted less attention outside baseball or school circles, unlike many of the top sumo stars of this period.

Chapter Two

EPIGRAPH. Yokoyama, "Hitachiyama Taniemon," 130.

1. For similar media-related developments in the United States, see Ponce de Leon, *Self-Exposure*.

2. See Zaidan hōjin Nihon sumō kyōkai, Newspaper Scrapbook Collection, 11:149. Annotations indicate that the article is from the *Asahi shinbun*, 29 May 1903. In the scrapbook, both the illustration and map have been marked using several different colors. Presumably done by a reader (perhaps even the scrapbook creator), the specific meanings of the colored markings are unclear, but suggest the possibility of a kind of "active reading" that took advantage of the illustrations and map to relive a previous day's match.

3. Cowen, *What Price Fame?*, 14–16.

4. Shikimori, *Hitachiyama Taniemon*, iv–v.

5. Ibid., 113.

6. On the original publication, see ibid., 131.

7. For information on Konishiki and the controversies surrounding him and other foreign wrestlers, see Tierney, "Wrestling with Tradition," 2–4 and 310–47. Hitachiyama was sometimes called the "foreigner" (*ijin*), a nickname that allegedly referred to his light complexion and distinctive facial features. This seemingly odd reference, however, appears to have been associated much more closely with social class and status than it was with race or nationality. References to this nickname often emphasized that Hitachiyama's distinctive features were the

result of his samurai heritage, leaving no question that he was a "pure Yamato man," as Shikimori suggested. For an example of comments about the nickname, see Yamamoto, *Jitsuroku kokon meirikishi hyaku reiden*, 269.

8. Offering a short introduction followed by what amounts to a handwriting analysis, Sakai's "research" examines the signatures of Hitachiyama and his rival Umegatani along with the writing of other members of the contemporary elite, including the military leaders General Nogi Maresuke and Admiral Tōgō Heihachirō (Sakai, *Genzai jinbutsu no kenkyū*, 17–19).

9. See Zaidan hōjin Nihon sumō kyōkai, Newspaper Scrapbook Collection, 198.49:49–81.

10. On Konishiki's death, see Zaidan hōjin Nihon sumō kyōkai, Newspaper Scrapbook Collection, 161.12:86–87. The full title in Japanese reads: *Hatachiyama shisu jūrokudai yokozuna Konishiki.* To avoid confusion, my translation omits the pseudonym Hatachiyama, the name Konishiki used as a retired wrestler. Konishiki is usually counted as the seventeenth *yokozuna*, rather than sixteenth as the article indicates. The celebratory phrases seen with Hitachiyama's death several years later are largely absent in relation to Konishiki, and the articles are far more basic. The vast majority of the articles in this scrapbook volume touch on Hitachiyama's retirement.

11. Yokoyama, "Hitachiyama Taniemon," 129.

12. Suzuki Hikojirō, "Hitachiyama kesshi no sumō," 162.

13. Suzuki Hikojirō, *Hitachiyama Taniemon*, 39.

14. "Hitachiyama Rated Greatest in Sumo," *Japan Times & Advertiser*, 18 May 1941, 8.

15. Ibid.

16. Ibid.

17. The English-language article refers to a Japanese article in the *Hōchi shinbun*, one of Japan's large popular newspapers, which merged the following year (1942) with *Yomiuri shinbun*; see Huffman, *Creating a Public*, 385 and 387.

18. "Hitachiyama Rated Greatest in Sumo," *Japan Times & Advertiser*, 18 May 1941, 8.

19. Shikimori, *Hitachiyama Taniemon*, 15–16.

20. Kamitsukasa, *Sumō shinsho*, 21.

21. Shikimori, *Hitachiyama Taniemon*, 14.

22. Ibid., 13.

23. Yanagiwara, "Hitachiyama Taniemon," 348–54.

24. It is not unusual for sumo wrestlers to have several different wrestling names over the course of their careers, and those names are usually connected to the wrestler's place of origin. In most cases two wrestlers cannot share the same name, so Hitachiyama only took on that name when his stable master assumed the name Dewanoumi, the name of the stable and the name Hitachiyama would use upon his retirement.

25. Cuyler, *Sumo*, 111.

26. As noted in Chapter 1, *yokozuna* did not become the official highest rank until 1909.

27. Kamitsukasa, *Sumō shinsho*, 22; see also Yokohama shinpōsha, *Tōsei rikishi meimeiden*, 11. Shikimori includes details about the master's reputation as a drunk; see Shikimori, *Hitachiyama Taniemon*, 16–17.

28. Wakamori and Kojima, *Ōzumō meirikishi 100 sen*, 139. In a section on Hitachiyama's relationships with women, Shikimori indicates that some believe that before he fled Tokyo, Hitachiyama had been having a secret affair with his stable master's adopted daughter, who later became Hitachiyama's first of three wives. He divorced her after four years and soon after, married a popular geisha. After his second wife died, he married another geisha. See Shikimori, *Hitachiyama Taniemon*, 36–37. Stories about Hitachiyama's allegedly numerous children are included in Hikoyama, *Yokozuna den*, 328. See also Arakawa, "Onnatachi no ōzumō shi 17"; and Shikimori, *Hitachiyama Taniemon*, 36. Both Arakawa and Shikimori reference Hikoyama.

29. Yokohama shinpōsha, *Tōsei rikishi meimeiden*, 12–13.

30. Sakura, *Yokozuna Hitachiyama*, 31.

31. Suzuki Hikojirō, "Hitachiyama kesshi no sumō," 152.

32. Shikimori, *Hitachiyama Taniemon*, 18 and 30.

33. Kamitsukasa, *Sumō shinsho*, 22–23.

34. By the time of the earliest account from 1899, Hitachiyama had already established a reputation as a top wrestler, which is why he was among the selected wrestlers featured in Kamitsukasa's work. Efforts to address this period in Hitachiyama's career offer an excellent example of what Jens Brockmeier calls the "particular retrospective teleology of autobiographical narrative." Brockmeier focuses on autobiographical time and narrative, but several of his points are equally relevant to the genre of biography. See Brockmeier, "Autobiographical Time," 60.

35. Shikimori, *Hitachiyama Taniemon*, 18.

36. Suzuki Hikojirō, "Hitachiyama kesshi no sumō," 152–53.

37. Sakura, *Yokozuna Hitachiyama*, 31.

38. Katō Takayo, *Meiji jidai no ōzumō*, 281. In a biography of Yashiro, naval historian and myth-maker Ogasawara Naganari included notes about Yashiro's patronage of Hitachiyama and detailed several interactions between the men. See Ogasawara, "Hiiki ni sareta Hitachiyama," 160–69. For Hitachiyama's comments about his relationship with Hirose, see Ken'ei sanshi, *Gunshin Hirose chūsa sōretsudan*, 56–59.

39. Kamitsukasa, *Sumō shinsho*, 22; several patrons are discussed in Yokohama shinpōsha, *Tōsei rikishi meimeiden*, 13–14; see also Shikimori, *Hitachiyama Taniemon*, 28.

40. "Jihō," 53–54.

41. See *Seinen: The Rising Generation* II, no. 3 (29 June 1899): 8.

42. Katō Takayo, *Meiji jidai no ōzumō*, 283. For more specifics on the Hitachi-Ume rivalry, see Sakai Tadamasa, "Kinsei daishōbu monogatari." Shikimori comments on Hitachiyama's early fame on the regional tours; see especially *Hitachiyama Taniemon*, 33. Later newspaper reports frequently comment on the popularity (*ninki*) of the two wrestlers. For the politician's comments, see Postwar Diet Records, Session 24 (accessed 1 July 2010).

43. Shikimori, *Hitachiyama Taniemon*, 102. For a sampling of the press coverage of the first day of retirement sumo, see Zaidan hōjin Nihon sumō kyōkai, Newspaper Scrapbook Collection, 161.12:17–37. Although other sumo articles appear throughout, including those about Konishiki's death, the vast majority of material in this volume relates to Hitachiyama's retirement.

44. Analysis based on Shikimori's figures; see especially *Hitachiyama Taniemon*, 22. See also detailed charts of wins and losses in Katō Susumu, *Rekidai yokozuna monogatari*, 131–33.

45. Guttmann and Thompson, *Japanese Sports*, 182; and Shikimori, *Hitachiyama Taniemon*, 22.

46. Guttmann and Thompson, *Japanese Sports*, 3. Italics added.

47. Sakura, *Yokozuna Hitachiyama*, 4; see also Shikimori, *Hitachiyama Taniemon*, 12–13.

48. Yanagiwara, "Hitachiyama Taniemon," 349–53.

49. These details and figures appear in an account from 1903; see Yokohama shinpōsha, *Tōsei rikishi meimeiden*, 8. Shikimori's later biography repeats them (*Hitachiyama Taniemon*, 13). This story is not included in Kamitsukasa's earlier and briefer account.

50. Ikeda Masao, "Rekidai Yokozuna Seiden 33," 147–48. Upon his retirement the sumo specialty magazine *Kokugi* ran a series of biographical essays and also included a photograph of the young Hitachiyama and the now famous rock. See *Kokugi*, June 1914, 2.

51. Guttmann and Thompson, *Japanese Sports*, 39–41. The account of the engraving at the shrine highlights the potential difficulties of using such stones to construct a history of practices like *chikaraishi*.

52. Ikeda Masao, "Rekidai Yokozuna Seiden 33," 148.

53. Yanagiwara, "Hitachiyama Taniemon," 356.

54. Sakura, *Yokozuna Hitachiyama*, 9–10.

55. Ikeda Masao, "Rekidai Yokozuna Seiden 33," 148–49. Shikimori specifically comments on danger to his career; see Shikimori, *Hitachiyama Taniemon*, 17.

56. Ikeda Masao, "Rekidai Yokozuna Seiden 34," 149.

57. Hitachiyama's friend Kimura Shujirō, quoted in ibid., 148.

58. *Sumō shinpō*, quoted in ibid., 149.

59. *Seinen: The Rising Generation* II, no. 3 (29 June 1899): 8.

60. See "Japanese Wrestlers and Their Physical Measurements," *Japan Times*, 27 May 1899, 3; reproduced and available electronically at Klein, *Sumo*, http://history.sumogames.com/newspaper/1800/18990527.htm (accessed 1 July 2010).

61. See "Japanese Wrestlers: Their Physical Development Is Something Truly Remarkable," *San Francisco Call*, 9 January 1900, 10; available electronically at *Chronicling America: Historic American Newspapers*, Library of Congress, http://www.loc.gov/chroniclingamerica/lccn/sn85066387/1900-01-09/ed-1/seq-10 (accessed 1 July 2010). Nearly identical articles from other papers are reproduced and available electronically at Klein, *Sumo*, http://history.sumogames.com/newspaper/1800/18991202X.htm (accessed 1 July 2010).

62. Burns, "Constructing the National Body," 39.

63. Beginning with August 1914 and continuing into the following year, *Kokugi* published numerous photos taken during various stages in Hitachiyama's life and career. Each single edition included multiple pictures.

64. For one example of training in relation to Hitachiyama, see Zaidan hōjin Nihon sumō kyōkai, Newspaper Scrapbook Collection, 17:1. Typically, reporters offered their own observations, but they sometimes included comments from leading wrestlers, or the impressions of notable figures who happened to be attending the sessions.

65. On Hitachiyama's stomach ailment, see Zaidan hōjin Nihon sumō kyōkai, Newspaper Scrapbook Collection, 14:33. On clothing, see ibid., 88. Another article in this volume offers a photo of Hitachiyama's parents and siblings, listing each of their names; see ibid., 100.

66. On Hitachiyama's toe, see Zaidan hōjin Nihon sumō kyōkai, Newspaper Scrapbook Collection, 15:7. On acupuncture, see ibid., 15.

67. Ogasawara, "Hiiki ni sareta Hitachiyama," 164 and 166.

68. Katō Susumu, *Rekidai yokozuna monogatari*, 129–30.

69. Ikeda Masao, "Rekidai Yokozuna Seiden 39," 147. Ikeda mentions complications associated with arthritis, and Shikimori refers to complications from an untreated case of diabetes. See Shikimori, *Hitachiyama Taniemon*, 114.

70. Zaidan hōjin Nihon sumō kyōkai, Newspaper Scrapbook Collection, 198.49:79.

71. Ibid., 75.

72. Funeral speech quoted in Shikimori, *Hitachiyama Taniemon*, 115–17.

73. Masaki, "Hitachiyama no shinzō," 67–70. Throughout his career, Masaki published extensively on matters related to public health. As a side note, it is probable that Masaki had actually seen Hitachiyama's heart. At one point in his medical career he worked at Keiō. For an earlier example of celebrity autopsy results used for purportedly scientific and educational purposes, see Marran, *Poison Woman*, 8–28.

74. Maguire, "Michel Foucault," 306–8. See Foucault, "Governmentality," especially 98–103. For further explanations about Foucault's approach to governmentality, see Colin Gordon, "Government Rationality."

75. For details on one wrestler's failure to meet military physical requirements, see "Military Wrestler," *Japan Times*, 28 December 1900, 3; reproduced and available electronically at Klein, *Sumo*, http://history.sumogames.com/newspaper/1900/19001228.htm (accessed 1 July 2010). Reports also indicate that the *yokozuna* Ōnishiki had failed in his attempts to join the army. See Tittle, *Sumo* (accessed 1 July 2010). Tittle's work cites an unnamed article from the children's magazine *Nihon shōnen* as the original source of this story about Ōnishiki. One of the only references I encountered in relation to Hitachiyama and conscription appears in Kamitsukasa's account from 1899. In a section quoting Hitachiyama's "mother," the wife of his stable master, she offers details about the high level of anxiety in the household and the general understanding that it would be good to secure an exemption from conscription. Apparently she was so concerned about the military prospects of this new promising sumo recruit that she did not eat and offered repeated Buddhist prayers on the day of his physical. Upon his return, Hitachi-

yama reportedly demanded a drink and then explained to the joy and relief of all in the stable, "Well, I was rejected because of qualities unsuitable for a soldier" (*maa, heitai niwa narenai ten de haneraremashita*). What those specific qualities might have been and any further details about his military physical remain tantalizingly unclear, especially in light of the repeated emphasis on Hitachiyama's warrior attributes in later accounts of his life. Notably his sumo "mother" in this retelling was quick to point out that even if he had qualified as a soldier, Hitachiyama's character was such that he would have "risen in the world" (*shusse*) and become a great one. See Kamitsukasa, *Sumō shinsho*, 202–6.

76. Foucault, "Governmentality," 100.

77. Colin Gordon, "Government Rationality," 5.

78. "Taikaku o aisu," 2. The comment is attributed to someone identified only as Dr. Kitazato (Kitazato hakushi).

79. Pennington, *A Woman Rice Planter*, 28 (accessed 2 July 2008). This work is the property of the University of North Carolina at Chapel Hill.

80. Katō Takayo, *Meiji jidai no ōzumō*, 277 and 584–86. On Tachiyama's family background, see Cuyler, *Sumo*, 106.

81. Kamitsukasa, *Sumō shinsho*, 20; and Yokohama shinpōsha, *Tōsei rikishi meimeiden*, 6. See also Katō Takayo, *Meiji jidai no ōzumō*, 279–80; and Shikimori, *Hitachiyama Taniemon*, 12–13. In his account, Sakura talks extensively about Hitachiyama's family's martial heritage, using the first four pages of his relatively short 34-page text to describe the wrestler's place of origin and family background (*Yokozuna Hitachiyama*, 1–4).

82. On Hitachiyama's disownment, see Yokoyama, "Hitachiyama Taniemon," 129; and Muramatsu, *Meijin kushin jitsuwa*, 218.

83. See, for instance, Yokohama shinpōsha, *Tōsei rikishi meimeiden*, 9–10.

84. Ibid.

85. Sakura, *Yokozuna Hitachiyama*, 8–9.

86. See, for instance, Suzuki Hikojirō, "Hitachiyama kesshi no sumō," 161–62. In Suzuki's telling, both Yashiro and Hirose tell Hitachiyama he and he alone can save sumo.

87. Hitachiyama can be seen in some ways as an embodied and commodified form of the versions of *bushidō* articulated by Nitobe Inazō. As Nitobe saw it, his idealized *bushidō* code had once been limited to the warrior elite, but in modern times had come to serve as guiding principles for all Japanese.

88. Yokoyama, "Hitachiyama Taniemon," 129–30.

89. Muramatsu, *Meijin kushin jitsuwa*, 197.

90. For an example of American coverage, see "Jap Wrestling Hero: Champion Hidachiyama [*sic*] Will Visit United States," *Washington Bee*, 12 October 1907, 7; available electronically at *Chronicling America: Historic American Newspapers*, Library of Congress http://www.loc.gov/chroniclingamerica/lccn/sn84025891/1907-10-12/ed-1/seq-7 (accessed 1 July 2010). Examples of other nearly identical articles are available at Klein, *Sumo*, http://history.sumogames.com/newspaper/1900/1900.htm#1907 (accessed 1 July 2010). Shikimori, *Hitachiyama Taniemon*, 70–71. Other top wrestlers also had powerful supporters. Tachiyama,

for instance, was supported by Itagaki Taisuke. Generally speaking, Hitachiyama appears to have had a much wider support network among the elite.

91. Shikimori, *Hitachiyama Taniemon*, 70–71. Contents from Hitachiyama's letter to Taft about his visit were reprinted in several American papers. For an example of press comments on Taft's connection with Hitachiyama's trip, see "Hitachiyana [*sic*] Coming: Jim Jeffries of Japan Will Visit America," *Washington Herald*, 20 August 1907, 2; available electronically at *Chronicling America: Historic American Newspapers*, Library of Congress, http://www.loc.gov/chroniclingamerica/lccn/sn83045433/1907-08-20/ed-1/seq-2 (accessed 1 July 2010). For other similar articles from newspapers throughout the United States, see Klein, *Sumo*, http://history.sumogames.com/newspaper/1900/1900.htm#1907 (accessed 1 July 2010).

92. Prince Konoe quoted in Shikimori, *Hitachiyama Taniemon*, 71. Emphasis in the original.

93. Using wrestlers as a symbol of Japanese strength vis-à-vis foreigners was not a new practice. For several examples of woodblock prints dealing with this theme, see Bickford, *Sumo and the Woodblock Print Masters*, 52–53, 141, and 145.

94. Kinmonth, *The Self-Made Man in Meiji Japanese Thought*, 246–47. As Kinmonth notes, Roosevelt's writings were translated, and several journals emphasized his views of the "strenuous life."

95. Muramatsu, *Meijin kushin jitsuwa*, 197.

96. Sakura, *Yokozuna Hitachiyama*, 4–5, 8, and 15.

97. Yokohama shinpōsha, *Tōsei rikishi meimeiden*, 7; Shikimori, *Hitachiyama Taniemon*, 12–13. Kamitsukasa's account actually suggests that Hitachiyama was forced to leave school and go to Tokyo after his father died of illness (*Sumō shinsho*, 21). According to Kinmonth, *chūtō gakkō* were expensive and the drop-out rate was nearly half (*The Self-Made Man in Meiji Japanese Thought*, 180).

98. Kinmonth compares these averages with those from 1902 to 1906, when 100,000 students enrolled per year (*The Self-Made Man in Meiji Japanese Thought*, 180).

99. Zaidan hōjin Nihon sumō kyōkai, Newspaper Scrapbook Collection, 198.49:75.

100. Kadokura, "Sumo Stew," 70.

101. Many sources refer to Hitachiyama's training sessions for his young followers. Hitachiyama's daughter has written several essays in which she alluded to her father's strict methods. See Matsuzawa, "Chichi Hitachiyama to sumōdō" and "Sumō konjaku banashi." Newspapers and sumo magazines also frequently ran articles on up-and-coming wrestlers from particular stables.

102. Lang and Lang, "Recognition and Renown"; on factors influencing durability of reputation, see ibid., 86.

103. For one of several possible examples, see Emi, *Busō no maki*, 40–43. In this volume on military affairs, Emi includes a quotation of Hitachiyama's account of his childhood relationship with Miura Kaneo, a naval officer who died in the Russo-Japanese War. In the story, Hitachiyama foreshadowed his future achievements with details about his boyhood wrestling prowess, but the story's emphasis, especially as editorialized by Emi, falls on Hitachiyama's sadness over the pre-

mature death of a friend who had seemed destined for greatness in the Imperial Navy.

104. Suzuki Hikojirō, *Hitachiyama Taniemon*, 39.

105. Matsuzawa, "Chichi Hitachiyama to sumōdō," 404–9; and "Sumō konjaku banashi," 62–68.

106. Arakawa, "Onnatachi no ōzumō shi 17," 124.

107. Sakura, *Yokozuna Hitachiyama*, 34.

108. *Yomiuri shinbun*, quoted in Ikeda Masao, "Rekidai Yokozuna Seiden 36," 140.

109. Ibid. Ikeda suggests that the possibility of nominating both wrestlers for promotion was on the table, with Hitachiyama's request simply making the joint promotion more pressing.

110. Arakawa, "Onnatachi no ōzumō shi 17," 124. Shikimori also observes that Hitachiyama had a reputation as a "Casanova," though he questions the veracity of details about Hitachiyama's 55 children. But in both cases Shikimori points to such details as another way in which Hitachiyama was an "exceptional man" (*gōketsu*); see Shikimori, *Hitachiyama Taniemon*, 34–36.

111. "General News: The Wrestler Hitachiyama Charged with Assault," *Japan Times*, 9 April 1910, 6; reproduced and available electronically at Klein, *Sumo*, http://history.sumogames.com/newspaper/1910/19100409.htm (accessed 1 July 2010).

112. A number of scholars have offered examinations on various aspects of the relationship between sports and narrative. See the following: Whannel, "Sports Stars, Narrativization, and Masculinities"; Whannel, *Media Sport Stars*; Kelly, "The Spirit and Spectacle of School Baseball," especially 111–14; Williams, *The Sports Immortals*; Gusfield, "Sports as Story"; Oriard, *Reading Football*, especially 57–133; and Ponce de Leon, *Self-Exposure*, 241–73.

113. Kelly, "The Spirit and Spectacle of School Baseball," 111–12.

114. Whannel, "Sports Stars, Narrativization, and Masculinities," 258.

115. Yokoyama, "Hitachiyama Taniemon," 153. Muramatsu's account of Hitachiyama ends with a similar anecdote (*Meijin kushin jitsuwa*, 218). Sakura includes a lengthy section in his biography detailing the pride-filled response of Hitachiyama's father to his son's success. Noting in particular why he had previously opposed his son's entry into sumo—concerns that sumo might not allow his son to achieve "success" (*seikō*)—the father, here, compiles a list of accomplishments and other points, including comments about sumo's standing as both martial tradition and sport, all of which prove that he had been wrong (*Yokozuna Hitachiyama*, 6–18).

116. Marcus, *Paragons of the Ordinary*, 22.

117. Ibid., 22–23. Kunikida Doppo would later become known as a novelist. As Marcus points out, Kunikida was only one of many Japanese writers who got their start writing biographies.

118. The earliest biographical account of Hitachiyama that I found, a short chapter in Kamitsukasa's book on sumo, was published in 1899 by Hakubunkan. Though he was already a rising star, the self-made-man narrative is far less apparent in this work than in those written just a few years later after Hitachiyama

had achieved much greater success. Many of the later stories about Hitachiyama and other successful men seem to have been aimed particularly at youth, which reflects broader trends in Japanese society at the time. Kinmonth notes that following the Russo-Japanese War a wide range of groups took it as their mission to instruct youth, who, it was feared, might become disillusioned in their quest to rise in the world (*The Self-Made Man in Meiji Japanese Thought*, 245).

119. Marcus, *Paragons of the Ordinary*, 22–23.

120. Saeki, "The Curious Relationship Between Biography and Autobiography in Japan," 79. For additional details on pre-Meiji samurai biography, see Marcus, *Paragons of the Ordinary*, 11–19.

121. Kinmonth, *The Self-Made Man in Meiji Japanese Thought*, 55–58. On continuities in relation to filial piety, see ibid., 75–76.

122. Ibid., 33–35.

123. On the impact and distribution of Nakamura's text, see ibid., 10–11. Before the standardization of textbooks, *Saikoku risshi hen* was frequently used as an ethics textbook in schools, so Hitachiyama himself may very well have encountered it in the course of his schooling. On changes in ethics textbooks, especially as reflections of changing economic and political conditions in Japan, see ibid., 250. For an examination of ethics courses in relation to Meiji ideological debates, see Gluck, *Japan's Modern Myths*, 105–11.

124. Gluck, *Japan's Modern Myths*, 256–57.

125. See, for instance, Yokohama shinpōsha, *Tōsei rikishi meimeiden*, 10; and Sakura, *Yokozuna Hitachiyama*, 4–5. See also Shikimori, *Hitachiyama Taniemon*, 13–14. On education as means to *risshin*, see Gluck, *Japan's Modern Myths*, 104–5 and 163–69. See also Kinmonth, *The Self-Made Man in Meiji Japanese Thought*, 59–80 and 178–202.

126. Sakura, *Yokozuna Hitachiyama*, 5. After the 1880s, going to Tokyo had become synonymous with *shusse*, or one's arrival in the larger world. See Kinmonth, *The Self-Made Man in Meiji Japanese Thought*, 118.

127. On decreased opportunities, especially in the years following the Russo-Japanese War, see Gluck, *Japan's Modern Myths*, 206–7.

128. Ibid., 207. For examples of changing *risshin* accounts, see Kinmonth, *The Self-Made Man in Meiji Japanese Thought*, 162–64.

129. Gluck, *Japan's Modern Myths*, 211. On ideologies of individual success and its critics, see ibid., 204–12.

130. Kinmonth, *The Self-Made Man in Meiji Japanese Thought*, 160.

131. This absence proves all the more striking in comparison with later athletes, such as the boxer Gushiken Yōkō, discussed in Chapter 5.

132. Although I encountered sketches of wrestlers clearly modeled on the various *yokozuna* in multiple beer advertisements during Hitachiyama's career, it is not at all clear that he or anyone else received compensation for these ads. Press coverage indicates that several breweries joined with newspapers in sponsoring prizes at major tournaments, and in at least one case we know that Hitachiyama and several other Tokyo wrestlers held a special two-day series of exhibition matches sponsored by the inventor of Lion Dentifrice tooth powder in June 1900. See "The 'Lion Dentifrice' at Eko-in," *Japan Times*, 2 June 1900, 2; re-

produced and available electronically at Klein, *Sumo*, http://history.sumogames.com/newspaper/1900/19000602.htm (accessed 1 July 2010).

133. Sakura, *Yokozuna Hitachiyama*, 30.

Chapter Three

EPIGRAPH. Hitomi Kinue, "Rikujō kyōgi," 104. It is worth noting that "sportsman" (*supōtsuman*) was used commonly in Japan at the time to refer to both male and female athletes.

1. On "golden ages" as invented traditions in American sports, see Pope, *Patriotic Games*, especially 157–61; see also Ponce de Leon, *Self-Exposure*, 241–45.

2. Pope, *Patriotic Games*, 158.

3. The *Ōsaka Mainichi shinbun* became the first Japanese newspaper to offer coverage of the World Series in October 1923. See Kishino, ed., *Shinpan kindai taiiku supōtsu nenpyō*, 138. In its December 1926 issue, the magazine *Shinseinen* offered a short recap of the Dempsey-Tunney fight, one of the most widely publicized American sporting events of the 1920s. The article included photos of both fighters (Hoshino, "Supōtsu no pēji"). On the fight and its role in the American sports scene, see Pope, *Patriotic Games*, 115–16; and Ponce de Leon, *Self-Exposure*, 241–42. For an example of name-dropping with respect to sports stars, see Hashido Makoto, "Meiji kara Taishō e no supōtsu"; in Hashido's article, Weissmuller, Tilden, and someone called "Padokku" in the Japanized version of his name (perhaps Charles Paddock, a U.S. Olympic sprinter from the early 1920s) are mentioned only by last name and juxtaposed with several Japanese athletes. See also Hirabayashi, "Gendai o shōchō suru mono."

4. Babe Ruth was the only foreign athlete featured in a 22-part series in the *Yomiuri shinbun* about the lives of prominent athletes in their off seasons. All of the articles in the series included photographs of the individual athletes. See "Shīzun gai no hanagata senshu 8: jibun no kikan to shite raku na kimochi de asobu: honruida-ō Bēbu Rūsu," *Yomiuri shinbun*, 8 February 1930, 6. Short feature stories about Cobb, Lacoste, and Osborn, all with photos, appeared in a 1927 series in the journal *Kaizō*. See Oda, "Hashiritakatobi no yūsha Osubōn"; Fukuda, "Rune Rakosuto"; and Miyake, "Tairasu Kabbu-shi." An issue of the children's magazine *Nihon shōnen* from 1937 included articles about the American Olympic diver Katherine Rawls and American tennis player Donald Budge, alongside an article on baseball star Sawamura Eiji; see "Kazarin Rōrusu jō"; and "Debisu Kappu wa dare no te ni."

5. Not unlike Hitachiyama's "discovery" of his sumo abilities, much is made of Hitomi's almost accidental "discovery" of her gift for track and field. This first record, like many at the time, was unofficial, having been set at an unmonitored local event.

6. This first world record went unrecognized by international governing bodies for track and field. Several of Hitomi's later records would receive official international recognition. Because of variations in counting official versus unofficial records, the exact number of Hitomi's records, both national and international, differs in various accounts of her life.

7. Prior to the Amsterdam Olympics in 1928, Hitomi traveled to London, where she trained and competed in several meets. Her achievements there included an official world record in the long jump; see Misawa, "Hitomi Kinue: Sono supōtsu katsudō no chōsa to nenpyō hokan." Records from the Japanese Foreign Ministry also reveal that representatives from Canada's Amateur Athletic Union campaigned, ultimately without success, to bring Hitomi to Canada for the 1930 National Indoor Track Meet; see Gaimushō, "Taiiku narabi ni undō kyōgi kankei zakken dai ikkan, no. 31," Japan Center for Asian Historical Records, http://www.jacar.go.jp/ (accessed 2 July 2010). See also Gaimushō, "Taiiku narabi ni undō kyōgi kankei zakken dai ikkan, no. 48," Japan Center for Asian Historical Records, http://www.jacar.go.jp/ (accessed 2 July 2010).

8. For a complete list with dates, see Guttmann and Thompson, *Japanese Sports*, 130.

9. For further information on school sports, see Yuko Kusaka, "The Emergence and Development of Japanese School Sport," especially 28–31.

10. For more details on baseball, see Chapter 4.

11. Obara, *Hitomi Kinue monogatari*, 67.

12. For a history of the Meiji Shrine Games and especially their connection with the imperial Japanese state, see Irie, *Shōwa supōtsu shiron*.

13. Kelly, "The Spirit and Spectacle of School Baseball," 108–10.

14. Obara, *Hitomi Kinue monogatari*, 47 and 51.

15. On the construction of athletic facilities at Meiji Shrine, see Irie, *Shōwa supōtsu shiron*, 59–64. For the construction dates of Kōshien and other stadiums, see Guttmann and Thompson, *Japanese Sports*, 85.

16. Hashimoto, *Nihon supōtsu hōsō shi*, 11–55. Among other details, Hashimoto's study includes accounts of Japan's early international broadcasts in connection with the Olympics.

17. For encyclopedic coverage of Japan's early participation in these international events see Guttmann and Thompson, *Japanese Sports*, 117–27. For an examination of the Far Eastern Championship Games in the context of Chinese sports, see Morris, *Marrow of the Nation*. Jonathan Kolatch draws extensively from documents related to the YMCA to provide detailed coverage of these games with a particular focus on their role in China's sports history; see Kolatch, *Sports, Politics, and Ideology in China*.

18. Hashido Makoto, "Meiji kara Taishō e no supōtsu," 221. The Japan Tennis Association website offers a history of Japanese tennis in "Nihon tenisu no rekishi," Japan Tennis Association, http://www.jta-tennis.or.jp/JTA/history/history_of_japantennis.html (accessed 2 July 2010).

19. Gems, *The Athletic Crusade*, 42. See also Guttmann and Thompson, *Japanese Sports*, 121–23. Although eighteen medals were awarded, one of the events was a relay, so the most any one country could win was sixteen. Incidentally, Japan won the relay, besting the second-place American team by nearly twelve seconds.

20. "Asia's 'Athletes of the Century,'" 4.

21. These games were later cancelled as a consequence of Japan's ongoing war with China, coupled with the outbreak of war in Europe.

22. Gems discusses how sports served as a form of resistance for Japan, but portrays such resistance as an aberration from the "progressive promise of sport" (*The Athletic Crusade*, especially 41–43). For a further examination of widely held notions that the relationship between Japanese sports (especially baseball) and nationalism represented an "aberration," see Chapter 4.

23. See *Tokyo: Sports Center of the Orient*. This publication was one of the English-language photo albums accompanying Japan's bid for the 1940 Olympic Games. Sports played and continue to play an important, though still largely overlooked, role in Japan's relations with its regional neighbors. Japan was pivotal in shaping China's physical culture and had often, along with Western nations, referred to China as the "sick man of Asia." See Morris, *Marrow of the Nation*, especially 1–16. For observations on how China continues to define itself in relation to Japan and the West, especially in terms of sports, see Brownell, *Beijing Games*, 33–35. The role of sports in Japan's colonial policies in Asia is a topic rich with potential for future research. A Japanese view of baseball in Manchuria during the early 1930s is available in Takamatsu bangarō shujin, "Manshūkoku yakyūbu o kiku." For an example of how the population of Taiwan appropriated baseball as a form of resistance to Japanese colonial rule, see Morris, "Baseball, History, the Local and the Global in Taiwan."

24. For a case from the American press, see Robert Edgreen, "Ichiya Kumagae Is Beginning of 'Yellow Peril' in Sport," *Washington Post*, 18 July 1916, 7. For more examples of the Japanese threat in sports as seen in the American media, see Welky, "Viking Girls, Mermaids, and Little Brown Men," 39–41.

25. Welky, "Viking Girls, Mermaids, and Little Brown Men," 40.

26. Official medal counts are available at International Olympic Committee, "Los Angeles 1932," *The Olympic Games*, http://www.olympic.org/en/content/Olympic-Games/All-Past-Olympic-Games/Summer/Los-Angeles-1932/ (accessed 2 July 2010). If gold medals are used as the primary means of ranking the nations, Japan finished behind France, Sweden, Italy, and the United States. The majority of Japan's medals, gold or otherwise, came in swimming.

27. Welky, "Viking Girls, Mermaids, and Little Brown Men," 39–41. Looking at media coverage related to current Japanese sports stars, I would suggest that this notion of threat, coupled with exoticization and trivialization, remains a common theme in American media representations of Japanese athletes.

28. "The Yellow Peril Again," *Fort Wayne Daily News*, 7 May 1913, 3.

29. Hashido, "Meiji kara Taishō e no supōtsu," 221. For another example of references to the yellow peril in sports as a symbol of Japanese accomplishment, see Gyōda, "Rikujō kyōgi yawa," 237–38.

30. Hashido, "Meiji kara Taishō e no supōtsu," 221–22. Hashido compares Japanese sports to a new store with several great managers, but no young clerks in training.

31. See, for example, Obara, *Hitomi Kinue monogatari*, 51. Also see Yudate, "Supōtsu jinkokki," 226.

32. On women's sports and especially track and field, see Misawa, "Nihon joshi rikujō kyōgi hatten shi," 2–4. See also Guttmann and Thompson, *Japanese Sports*, 92–95.

33. On the first International Women's Games, see Obara, *Hitomi Kinue monogatari*, 66. On women's track and field at the Olympics, see Guttmann and Thompson, *Japanese Sports*, 120.

34. The earliest biographical account I have encountered is Furushō Kunio, *Dai issen ni tateru josei*, 236–55. A more recent biography is Misawa, *Hayate no josei rannā*. In late 1931, Hitomi was the subject of a feature film of which no copies appear to survive. For details on the film, see "Eiga *Hitomi Kinue* kansei," *Yomiuri shinbun*, 15 December 1931, 5. Hitomi has also been the subject of multiple biodocumentaries and dramas on television. For a list of them as of 1998, see Misawa and Takeda, "Hitomi Kinue kenkyū ni kansuru bunken mokuroku." While conducting my research in Japan in 2004 and 2005, several people informed me that they knew who Hitomi was because they had seen a recent television special aired in connection with the Athens Olympics.

35. Obara, *Hitomi Kinue monogatari*, 18–21.

36. Ibid., 20–21.

37. Manabe, *Asayake no rannā*, 12–14.

38. Hitomi, *Supaiku no ato*, 1–2 (all page citations are to the reprint edition, but the reprint appears to be an exact duplicate of the original, including front and back matter).

39. Hitomi, *Supaiku no ato*, 3–4; and Obara, *Hitomi Kinue monogatari*, 20–22.

40. Hitomi, *Supaiku no ato*, 3; and Obara, *Hitomi Kinue monogatari*, 22.

41. Quoted in Obara, *Hitomi Kinue monogatari*, 42. The source for the quotation remains unclear.

42. Kinoshita's discussion with Hitomi's father is quoted in Obara, *Hitomi Kinue monogatari*, 58.

43. For Hitomi's references to her grades, see Hitomi, *Supaiku no ato*, 4 and 19–20.

44. Obara, *Hitomi Kinue monogatari*, 28.

45. Hitomi's tennis partner, Ukita Yoshiko, is quoted in Obara, *Hitomi Kinue monogatari*, 32–33. For more on tennis, see Hitomi, *Supaiku no ato*, 5–20.

46. Hitomi, *Supaiku no ato*, 21–22; and Obara, *Hitomi Kinue monogatari*, 36–37.

47. Hitomi, *Supaiku no ato*, 22.

48. Manabe, *Asayake no rannā*, 20.

49. Hitomi, *Supaiku no ato*, 21–22; Obara, *Hitomi Kinue monogatari*, 36; and Manabe, *Asayake no rannā*, 18–20.

50. Hitomi, *Supaiku no ato*, 22; and Obara, *Hitomi Kinue monogatari*, 36.

51. Nikaidō's school later became the present-day Nihon Joshi Taiiku Daigaku, or Japan Women's College of Physical Education. On Hitomi's entrance to the school, see Obara, *Hitomi Kinue monogatari*, 41; and Hitomi, *Supaiku no ato*, 23–24. For a brief account of Nikaidō, see Obara, *Hitomi Kinue monogatari*, 44. See also the autobiographical account of Nikaidō's stay in England in Nikaidō, *Ashikake yonen*.

52. For similar concerns in relation to women's sports in China, see Morris, *Marrow of the Nation*, especially 112–19. Analogous American concerns from the same general time frame are discussed in Mrozek, "The 'Amazon' and the American 'Lady.'"

53. Hitomi, *Supaiku no ato*, 33–34; and Obara, *Hitomi Kinue monogatari*, 50–51.

54. Hitomi, *Supaiku no ato*, 35–36; and Obara, *Hitomi Kinue monogatari*, 53–54.

55. Hitomi's autobiography makes no mention of the trip. Obara describes it but fails to include it in his timeline of the important events of Hitomi's life (*Hitomi Kinue monogatari*, 288–92). Toda Jun provides the greatest number of details, including several telegraphs detailing record-setting performances and what sound like generally positive experiences in Taiwan (*Kinue koi*, 34). Despite her citation of Obara as a source, Manabe omits Taiwan entirely.

56. Obara, *Hitomi Kinue monogatari*, 55–56.

57. Ibid., 68.

58. Hitomi Kinue, "Uchitoketa atatakai dōshi no taido," *Ōsaka Mainichi shinbun*, 20 October 1929, 4. Also in Obara, *Hitomi Kinue monogatari*, 198–200.

59. Misawa, "Hitomi Kinue: sono supōtsu katsudō," 58–59.

60. Obara, *Hitomi Kinue monogatari*, 67–68; see also Guttmann and Thompson, *Japanese Sports*, 75.

61. Misawa, "Hitomi Kinue: sono supōtsu katsudō," 59. Hitomi offers an extremely detailed account of the competition, including lists of the top finishers in all events (*Supaiku no ato*, 97–171).

62. This criticism is quoted in Furushō, *Dai issen ni tateru josei*, 243–44. The original source is not provided.

63. Quoted in Obara, *Hitomi Kinue monogatari*, 103–4. The German paper is rendered *Tāgeburatto* in Japanese.

64. Image may be found in ibid., 92.

65. Quoted in ibid., 106.

66. "Oh! Yes Oh! Yes," *Los Angeles Times*, 17 October 1926, H2.

67. "100 METERS MARK BROKEN: Miss Hitomi, in Olympic Practice, Timed in 0:12 1–5 at Tokio," *New York Times*, 21 May 1928, 18; "Two World's Sprint Records Are Claimed in Meet in Korea," *New York Times*, 18 October 1929, 38; "Miss Hitomi of Japan Lowers World's Record for 60 Meters," *New York Times*, 21 October 1929, 39; "Miss Hitomi, Japanese Girl, Sets World's Broad-Jump Mark," *New York Times*, 22 October 1929, 40; "Miss Hitomi, Japanese Athlete, Beats Own Broad Jump Mark," *New York Times*, 27 October 1929, S2; "Miss Walsh Helps Polish Team Triumph Over Japanese Group," *New York Times*, 13 September 1930, 19; and "Women's World Sprint Record Equaled by Mlle. Radideau," *New York Times*, 22 September 1930, 23.

68. "Taller Japanese," *Washington Post*, 30 September 1928, SM6; and Inez S. Vaughn, "Modern Styles Invade Japan: The Kimono Retreats Be-fore the Suit and Skirt," *Washington Post*, 15 November 1931, MF-7.

69. Furushō, *Dai issen ni tateru josei*, 238. The title of Furushō's chapter on Hitomi is "Japan's First International Woman." Offering another example of transnational star systems, the chapter on Hitomi is preceded by a lengthy essay on the French tennis star Suzanne Lenglen, who achieved international success and fame in the 1910s. The chapter also refers to the American tennis star Helen Wills, who achieved similar fame in the 1920s.

70. Misawa, "Hitomi Kinue no kōen kōshū katsudō." It is important to note that the talks and exhibitions in Misawa's list are only the ones that he found ref-

erences to in other sources. Hitomi often gave multiple talks at the same location. Some have estimated that the actual number of her talks went well into the hundreds, but such numbers are difficult to verify.

71. For a fairly comprehensive list of writings by and about Hitomi, see Misawa and Takeda, "Hitomi Kinue kenkyū ni kansuru bunken mokuroku," 117–24.

72. Hitomi, *Tatakau made*.

73. Hitomi published two autobiographical books: *Supaiku no ato* and *Gōru ni hairu*. For an example of details about foreign athletes in these works, see Hitomi, *Supaiku no ato*, 85–171, and especially 166–71. Hitomi also wrote countless articles about various aspects of her life. An exemplary article, where she used her experiences to write about her impressions of the world's female athletes, appeared together with several photos of European athletes in the monthly magazine *Kaizō* after her third trip to Europe in 1930. Hitomi, "Sekai joryū senshu no inshō," 21–28.

74. Quoted in Obara, *Hitomi Kinue monogatari*, 58. It is not clear how Obara obtained this quotation.

75. Manabe, *Asayake no rannā*, 37–38.

76. Hitomi, *Supaiku no ato*, 39 and 179–81.

77. For Hitomi's comments on being a "lucky girl" and her hard work, see ibid., 179–81. "Era of Practice" is the title of the third chapter in Hitomi's book. Practice and domestic competition are the overall themes of that chapter (176–287). Hitomi's third chapter includes extensive details about her training regimen, especially in the sections featuring her "training diaries" (*renshū nikki*); see ibid., 217–34 and 237–59.

78. Misawa, "Hitomi Kinue kō," 5.

79. Hitomi herself emphasized her struggle to balance work and training as an "amateur" (*Supaiku no ato*, 212–16).

80. Misawa, "Hitomi Kinue: sono supōtsu katsudō," 59–60. Hitomi discusses her experiences in London and her impressions of British athletes and sports in her autobiography (*Supaiku no ato*, 292–328).

81. *Kōjien*, s.v. "Hitomi Kinue." Oda Mikio, Japan's first gold-medal winner in track and field, is not listed.

82. See, for instance, Guttmann and Thompson, *Japanese Sports*, 221. A documentary from 1996 focused on both Arimori and Hitomi (Misawa and Takeda, "Hitomi Kinue kenkyū ni kansuru bunken mokuroku," 124).

83. As noted above, this was the case in 2004 and 2005 with the Athens Olympics. Several of the documentaries and television programs that Misawa and Takeda list were first aired during Olympic years ("Hitomi Kinue kenkyū ni kansuru bunken mokuroku," 123–24).

84. Hitomi, *Supaiku no ato*, 365; ellipsis appears in original. For similar details see Obara, *Hitomi Kinue monogatari*, 161–64.

85. Hitomi, *Supaiku no ato*, 353–55.

86. For Hitomi's account of the race and its immediate aftermath, see Hitomi, *Supaiku no ato*, 366–70; see also Obara, *Hitomi Kinue monogatari*, 170–72.

87. Quoted in Hitomi, *Supaiku no ato*, 367–68; also quoted in Obara, *Hitomi Kinue monogatari*, 172–73.

88. Hitomi, *Gōru ni hairu*, 1–10 (all page citations are to reprint edition); see also Obara, *Hitomi Kinue monogatari*, 188–89.

89. On Hitomi's experiences in Korea and China, see Obara, *Hitomi Kinue monogatari*, 197–200; for Hitomi's account of her meeting with Zhang, see Hitomi, *Gōru ni hairu*, 27–33.

90. Hitomi, *Gōru ni hairu*, 14–24, 45–53, and 62–72; Obara, *Hitomi Kinue monogatari*, 191–96 and 204–9.

91. Hitomi's description of the 1930 Games are, once again, extremely detailed and include brief descriptions of both the Japanese team and the leading Western athletes; see Hitomi, *Gōru ni hairu*, 56–62 and 111–85; and Obara, *Hitomi Kinue monogatari*, 210–12 and 222–45.

92. In one meet against Belgium, which Hitomi had expected to be an easy victory because Japan had defeated Belgium in Prague, she had planned not to participate. However, when the Japanese team fared poorly, Hitomi became frustrated and entered several events, refusing to allow what she saw as a third- or fourth-rate team to beat Japan (Hitomi, *Gōru ni hairu*, 204–8).

93. Obara, *Hitomi Kinue monogatari*, 254–56.

94. Quoted in ibid., 257. The Japanized name of the paper is *Ōto*.

95. Hitomi's *Gōru ni hairu* ends with her arrival in Japan after the long sea voyage, where she had struggled with frustration after learning via letters and news reports that the Japanese women's team had received rather unsympathetic popular and media responses in Japan (209–56). On Hitomi's state of health and her father's response, see Obara, *Hitomi Kinue monogatari*, 265–69.

96. Obara, *Hitomi Kinue monogatari*, 269–73.

97. Ibid., 273–78. Because an autopsy was never performed, the exact cause of Hitomi's death is disputed. Many believe that she died of tuberculosis.

98. Hitomi, "Joshi to undō kyōgi," 1; for similar remarks, see "Rikujō kyōgi," 103; and *Saishin joshi rikujō kyōgi hō*, 2 (page citations to reprint edition). Based on their frequent appearance in her written work, it seems likely that she also employed these ideas as introductory remarks in her oral presentations.

99. The early promotion of women's physical education and competitive sports were closely linked with the eugenics movement in Japan. Kinoshita, who had a medical degree from Tokyo Imperial University and became the leading authority in the emerging field of sports physiology, played a particularly significant role. He served as head of the Kenbokai, which advocated women's sports from a eugenics perspective, and as founder of the Japan Women's Sports Federation. The Kenbokai was among the sponsors for Japan's first National Women's Olympics in 1924, and after its establishment in 1926, the Japan Women's Sports Federation took the lead in organizing the event (Obara, *Hitomi Kinue monogatari*, 47, 57–58, and 67; Guttmann and Thompson, *Japanese Sports*, 133–34). Anthropologist Jennifer Robertson's examination of eugenics also indicates that several leading figures displayed marked interest in women's sports, including Ikeda Shigenori, who founded the "Legs Society" in 1925 as part of his Japanese Eugenic Exercise Association. Modeled on German youth groups, Ikeda's Legs Society gave particular attention to the physical fitness of women. Despite the overlapping time frame and their clear role in the eugenics movement, Robertson

makes no mention of Hitomi or Kinoshita and gives limited attention to women's sports in general. Robertson, "Japan's First Cyborg?," especially 6–10.

100. Sasaki, ed., *Shinsei shinsen joshi kokugo tokuhon*, 118–28; Haga, ed., *Joshi shinkokubun shinpan kaisei*, 54–64; and Iwai, *Chūgaku kokugo sōgō*, 122–25.

101. On sports as a form of exemplary masculinity, see Connell, *Masculinities*, 54, 80, and 214.

102. Obara, *Hitomi Kinue monogatari*, 278.

103. "Miss Kinuye Hitomi, Athlete, Dies at 24," *New York Times*, 3 August 1931, 17.

104. Manabe, *Asayake no rannā*, 150.

105. In 1932, the *Yomiuri* newspaper featured stories about the monument and its unveiling ceremony ("Hitomi Kinue no kinenhi Purāgu ni tatsu," *Yomiuri shinbun*, 27 August 1932, 5; "Hitomi no kinenhi jomakushiki," *Yomiuri shinbun*, evening edition, 5 September 1932, 2). The sports magazine *Asahi supōtsu* included a photo of the memorial with its article ("Omoide no Purāgu ni kenritsu sareta ko Hitomi Kinue-jō no kinenhi"). See also Obara, *Hitomi Kinue monogatari*, 281–82. This monument continues to be one of the most frequently cited examples of Hitomi's great international reputation, even in death.

106. For a list of these articles, see Misawa and Takeda, "Hitomi Kinue kenkyū ni kansuru bunken mokuroku," 120.

107. An article and cartoon from the *Yomiuri* newspaper in 1932 depicted Hitomi cheering on the Japanese women's Olympic team from "paradise" (*tengoku*); see "Orinpikku konna mondai," *Yomiuri shinbun*, 20 July 1932, 6. For another example of references to the loss of Hitomi in relation to the 1932 Olympics, see Hirose, "Orinpikku de Nihon wa katsu ka," 205. For references in the official report of the Meiji Shrine Games, see Ueda Seiichi, "Joshi kyōgi," 446–47.

108. This is far from unique to Hitomi or Japan. While I was writing this chapter, my local radio station reported the death of an area high-school athlete during a practice. His death led to immediate calls for an investigation and questions about having athletes continue to practice during record-breaking heat waves.

109. Manabe, *Asayake no rannā*, 155.

110. Quoted in Miyao Tomiko, "Hitomi Kinue," 186.

111. Kinoshita Tōsaku, "Joshi no supōtsu to kenkō," 255–58.

112. Kinoshita Tōsaku, "Fujin no taishitsu to supōtsu."

113. My observation about Kinoshita's sense of responsibility is purely conjectural, but he had been with her in Europe when she first became ill. Throughout Hitomi's career, Kinoshita had been one of her most active supporters, actively encouraging her to spread the gospel of sports to the women of Japan.

114. As an introduction to his conference presentation, Itoigawa Yukihiro noted that his mother had previously been trained by Hitomi but became concerned about the potential dangers of track and field after learning of her death ("Emotion Type as Activation and Inhibition Toward Sport Challenge by Gold Medalists").

115. Iwata Seidō, "Mondai na no wa fujin no supōtsu: *hatsuiku tochū wa kinmotsu*," *Yomiuri shinbun*, 8 October 1931, 5 (emphasis in original title).

116. For an example of Hitomi's criticism of medical opinions about women's sports, see Hitomi, *Tatakau made*, 42–43.

117. The *Yomiuri shinbun* series included the following articles: Uramoto Seisaburō, "Nikutai-teki no karō yori mo seishin-teki karō ga mondai (jō)," 6 October 1931, 5; Ogasawara Michio, "Kenkō no ue ni tatsu undō senshu," 7 October 1931, 5; Uramoto Seisaburō, "Nikutai-teki no karō yorimo seishin-teki karō ga mondai (ge)," 7 October 1931, 5; Kawaki Teisuke, "Supōtsu igaku no hitsuyō," 8 October 1931, 5; Iwata Seidō, "Mondai nano wa fujin no supōtsu: *hatsuiku tochū wa kinmotsu*," 8 October 1931, 5; "Undō senshu ni miru karō no jōtai to wa," 8 October 1931, 5; Azuma Ryōtarō, "Supōtsu igaku no michi o hirake mohan to subeki Doitsu no undōkai," 9 October 1931, 5; and Mirusu Bukku, "Kyōgi to taisō no akushu o nozomu," 9 October 1931, 5.

118. Azuma Ryōtarō, "Supōtsu igaku no michi o hirake mohan to subeki Doitsu no undōkai," *Yomiuri shinbun*, 9 October 1931, 5.

119. Azuma Ryōtarō, *Supōtsu to tomo ni*, 198–99. The section on Hitomi's death is dated 1931, but it is not clear whether this was written at that time or later.

120. An article introducing the series and the author preceded its publication; see "Supōtsu igaku," *Yomiuri shinbun*, 28 March 1933, 5. The entire series was written by Saitō Kazuo with articles appearing sporadically from 29 March 1933 through the last on 25 April 1933. Saitō Kazuo, "Supōtsu to igaku," *Yomiuri shinbun*, 29–31 March 1933; 6 April 1933; 8–10 April 1933; 12–13 April 1933; 18–21 April 1933; and 25 April 1933. All articles appeared on page 5.

121. Saitō Kazuo, "Supōtsu to igaku: kenkō zōshin wa tan ni fukusanbutsu," *Yomiuri shinbun*, 29 March 1933, 5.

122. "Hitomi-jō no shi ga shigeki senshu no kenkō shirabe," *Yomiuri shinbun*, 13 August 1931, 7.

123. "Senshu no kenkō shindan Teidai de jisshi," *Yomiuri shinbun*, 15 January 1932, 5.

124. "Supōtsu igaku sōdanjo," *Yomiuri shinbun*, 25 April 1933, 5. This announcement was published the same day that the last of Saitō's articles ran.

125. Ibid.

126. The following articles appeared in the *Yomiuri shinbun*: Sugimoto Ryōichi, "Shūkan ni undō shīzun warera no shiraneba naranu undō to ketsueki no kankei," 5 November 1931, 5; Uchiyama Kōichi, "Supōtsu ni shigeki o motomeru kindaijin no shinzō," 22 January 1932, 4; and Saitō Kazuo, "Undōka no shintai ni miru kokkaku no ijō," 31 January 1932, 4.

127. "Undō senshu ni miru karō no jōtai to wa," *Yomiuri shinbun*, 8 October 1931, 5.

128. Fujimaki Ryōchi, "Undō o suru hito ni wa donna shokumotsu ga kinmotsu ka," *Yomiuri shinbun*, 7 November 1931, 9.

129. "Waga joshi supōtsu senshu ni naze gisei ga ōi?" *Yomiuri shinbun*, 23 June 1933, 9.

130. Saitō's articles for the *Yomiuri* included: "Supōtsu to igaku 9: tōkyū to hokyū de shōkotsu ni sa," 13 April 1933, 5; "Supōtsu to igaku 4: kaku undō ni tekisuru taipu," 6 April 1933, 5; "Supōtsu to igaku 14: undōka ni jūyō na hana," 25 April

1933, 5. The photos are identified with a certain "Kōruraushu," probably Saitō's contemporary Wolfgang Kohlrausch, who was closely associated with the development of sports medicine in Germany.

131. For an example of the role of sports medicine and sports science in Japanese society before and after the 1964 Tokyo Olympic Games, see Ishiko, *Supōtsu to karada*.

132. Harootunian, *Overcome by Modernity*, 23.

133. Ibid. For additional descriptions of the modern girl and an examination of how her image was constructed in and by the media, see Silverberg, *Erotic Grotesque Nonsense*, 51–72. Despite their prominent place in Japanese popular and mass culture, Silverberg makes only passing mention of sports and no references to Hitomi in this work. For an earlier version of her chapter on the modern girl, see Silverberg, "The Modern Girl as Militant," especially 239–55.

134. On Hitomi's general approach to and eventual consumption of alcohol during her long, frustrating return from Prague, see Hitomi, *Gōru ni hairu*, 230–31; see also Obara, *Hitomi Kinue monogatari*, 263. Even if she did not dress like the stereotypical modern girl, Hitomi's adoption of athletic attire would have marked her as definitively "modern," as such clothing for female athletes only became common in her lifetime. For an examination of women's athletic garments, see Hagiwara, "Japanese Women's Sports and Physical Education under the Influence of Their Traditional Costumes."

135. Harootunian, *Overcome by Modernity*, 25.

136. Silverberg, *Erotic Grotesque Nonsense*, 69.

137. Furushō, *Dai issen ni tateru josei*, 236.

138. Manabe, *Asayake no rannā*, 154.

139. In addition to the articles discussed here, Hitomi also wrote an article for the women's journal *Fujin saron* where she traced an average day in her life as a working woman and athlete, interspersed with various observations about working women, dealing with men, and sports ("Onna toshite no watashi no nichijō seikatsu").

140. Hitomi, "Onna wa shosen onna." Several of the other writers, including famous left-wing women's activist Yamakawa Kikue and journalist Miyake Yasuko, were far less conciliatory in their views.

141. Hitomi, "Watashi wa itsu kekkon suru?," 54.

142. Ichikawa was ten years Hitomi's senior and was politically active throughout the prewar and postwar period; among her many activities, she and others formed the Women's Suffrage League (Fusen kakutoku dōmei) in 1924. She and several other single women contributed articles to the magazine *Kaizō* in December 1930 praising the life of a single woman. See Ichikawa, "Dokushin fujin no kien"; and Kitamura, "Dokushin fujin no yase kōei."

143. For details on women's suffrage in Japan, see Garon, "Women's Groups and the Japanese State"; Nolte, "Women's Rights and Society's Needs"; Kathleen Susan Molony, "One Women Who Dared"; Vavich, "The Japanese Woman's Movement"; and Murray, "Ichikawa Fusae and the Lonely Red Carpet."

144. Harishige, "Shōwa no supōtsu kai," 65.

145. Kinoshita Tōsaku, "Josei no motsu danseibi"; and XYZ, "Naze fujin kōminken'an wa tōranakatta ka."

146. The article reports the results of a survey addressing the opinions of female students about women's suffrage. As the title suggests, the overwhelming theme was that women and men were "medically" different, and by extension women should not vote (Ishikawa Watari, "Otoko to onna wa igakuteki ni chigau," *Yomiuri shinbun*, 30 January 1924, 4).

147. Dyreson, "Regulating the Body and the Body Politic," 133.

148. Mrozek, "The 'Amazon' and the American 'Lady,'" 199.

149. For humorous and extremely revealing examples of this perceived threat, see the variety of cartoons compiled in Shimizu Isao, ed., *Manga ni egakareta Meiji, Taishō, Shōwa*, 90–100, 102, 106–15, 125, 141–47, 162–67, and 175–78; a cartoon depicting Hitomi appears as well (207).

150. Connell, *Masculinities*, 54 and 214.

151. The series ran in *Chūō kōron* in July 1931 and included three other articles besides Kataoka's. Kataoka, "Ryōryō aimatsu," 314.

152. Satō Hachirō, "Go-fujin wa supōtsu ga o-suki."

153. Abe Tomoji, "Nichi-Doku taikō kyōgi," 25 (on beards) and 26 (on husbands' muscles). Tanizaki Jun'ichirō's serialized novel *Chijin no Ai* offers an earlier fictionalized example of male insecurity about Japanese women's alleged desire for foreign men, though in this case sports are not a central concern.

154. Guttmann and Thompson, *Japanese Sports*, 151.

155. For several examples, see Roden, "Baseball and the Quest for National Dignity in Meiji Japan."

156. The article includes two charts, one with average bodily measurements of athletes from the Far Eastern Championship Games and the other of average measurements from the Olympics. The differences are not the subject of the article, but they are nonetheless noticeable with even a quick glance at the two charts (Saitō Kazuo, "Dono supōtsu ga tekisu ka," *Yomiuri shinbun*, 31 March 1931, 5).

157. Mrozek, "The 'Amazon' and the American 'Lady,'" 199.

158. Hoshino, "Supōtsu no pēji: Taishō no undō kyōgi," 158.

159. Hashido Gantestu, "Supōtsu geppyō."

160. Yudate, "Supōtsu jinkokki," 226.

161. Murobuse, "Hitomi Kinue ron."

162. Hoshino, "Sekai ni katsuyaku seru Nihon no undōka," 137.

163. Furushō, *Dai issen ni tateru josei*, 238. For more on military conscription and athletes, see Chapter 4.

164. Furushō, *Dai issen ni tateru josei*, 239.

165. Hoshino, "Sekai ni katsuyaku seru Nihon no undōka," 138.

166. On criticism of the androgyny of the *otokoyaku*, see Robertson, "The Politics of Androgyny in Japan," 429. Later critics explicitly linked women's sports and the theater castigating both for their role in the "progressive masculinization and independent-mindedness of Japanese girls and women" (Robertson, *Takarazuka*, 156).

167. Robertson, "The Politics of Androgyny in Japan," 422 and 428–30.

168. Mrozek, "The 'Amazon' and the American 'Lady,'" 205–10. If Hitomi had lived and participated in the 1932 Summer Olympics, she would have competed against Didrikson, who was four years younger. Much like Hitomi had been, Didrikson was frequently subjected to questions about her plans for marriage and her sexual identity even after she married in 1933. For an example of media discussion of "Babe" Didrikson's lack of femininity in her later career as a golfer, see Arthur Daley, "Sports of the Times: Short Shots in Sundry Directions," *New York Times*, 9 April 1948, 30. After dismissing the ability of women, even one as "phenomenal" as "the Babe," to compete successfully against men in sports, Daley observes, "Women are superior to men only in the motherhood department, never in sports."

169. Feder-Kane, "'A Radiant Smile from the Lovely Lady,'" 209. An article discussing Danica Patrick, the IndyCar racing star who posed for the 2008 *Sports Illustrated* swimsuit issue, observes that attempts to fend of the "lesbian label" continue to shape women's sports and especially the efforts of women and sports promoters to present almost hyper-feminine images of female sports celebrities (Zirin, "Edge of Sports," 20).

170. In his biographical essay, Furushō quoted almost all of Hitomi's "Women Are, After All, Women," and at one point, he also praised her for not having lost her "sense of humility as a woman" (*Dai issen ni tateru josei*, 247).

171. Iwaki, "Sabishii Hitomi Kinue"; and Ōsaka, "Supōtsukai no myōjō otsu?"

172. Iwaki, "Sabishii Hitomi Kinue," 1:155. Iwaki includes a detailed physical description of S-ko, whose image contrasts strikingly with that of Hitomi.

173. Ibid., 156.

174. Pflugfelder, "'S' is for Sister," 163.

175. Ibid., 136–37.

176. Iwaki, "Sabishii Hitomi Kinue," 1:155, 2:204.

177. Ōsaka, "Supōtsukai no myōjō otsu?," 55.

178. Ibid., 55 and 57.

179. Ibid., 56. On suicides and scandals, see Pflugfelder, "'S' is for Sister," 150–62.

180. In Iwaki, as well, S-ko falls in love with a disreputable man, a fact that destroys their "Sweet Home." In both stories, Hitomi plays a key role in eventually driving the man off.

181. Ōsaka, "Supōtsukai no myōjō otsu?" 60.

182. *Asahi shinbun*, 3 August 1931, quoted in Miyao Tomiko, "Hitomi Kinue," 180. Iwaki's story was the featured item in an advertisement for *Fujin kōron* (*Yomiuri shinbun*, 25 May 1931, 9).

183. Guttmann and Thompson, *Japanese Sports*, 221.

184. Tachibana, *Nihon no onna*, 208.

185. Oda and Toda, *Honō no supurintā*, 442.

186. Konno, dir., *Akai inazuma: Hitomi Kinue*, first broadcast on 22 November 1992, on Japan's TBS networks. My comments are based on the script, which was published as Konno, *Hitomi Kinue monogatari*.

187. "Hanseiki buri no shin jijitsu," 157.

Chapter Four

EPIGRAPH. Ikeda Tsuneo, "Atogaki," in Suzuki Sōtarō, *Fumetsu no daitōshu*, 356–57.

1. Descriptions of Sawamura in relation to Ruth appear regularly in print sources. When I spoke with Japanese people about Sawamura while completing my research, references to Babe Ruth were among the most common, but he was also regularly described to me as the "player who died in the war." Sawamura is featured as one of several such players in Yomiuri shinbun Ōsaka honsha shakaibu, *Sensō 9: senbotsu yakyū jin* (Baseball figures who died in war).

2. *Nekkyū*, 1947; quoted in Fujita, "Sawamura-shō ni tsuite kangaeru," *Puro yakyū kiroku jānaru*, www.baseball.per.sg/column/200312.htm (accessed 7 August 2006).

3. In 1960, the Nippon Professional Baseball league created a special committee to select the annual winners, who had previously been named based on votes from journalists. For details on the origins of the prize, see Fujita, "Sawamura-shō ni tsuite kangaeru." The "private" nature of the original award might be subject to debate, since the Yomiuri fan organizations have historically been closely connected with the team and its management. On baseball fan clubs, especially in Osaka, see Kelly, "Sense and Sensibility at the Ball Park."

4. Zaidan hōjin yakyū taiiku hakubutsukan, "Sawamura Eiji," *The Baseball Hall of Fame and Museum*, http://english.baseball-museum.or.jp/baseball_hallo/detail/detail_008.html (accessed 2 July 2010). The award is described similarly in Reaves, *Taking in a Game*, 69.

5. Ikei, *Hakkyū Taiheiyō o wataru*, 39–46; Roden, "Baseball and the Quest for National Dignity in Meiji Japan."

6. On the early history of Waseda, see Ikei, *Hakkyū Taiheiyō o wataru*, 49–50. On the six university league and its popularity, see ibid., 102–3; and Kelly, "The Spirit and Spectacle of School Baseball," 106.

7. Guttmann and Thompson, *Japanese Sports*, 90–92. For details on baseball clubs, see Yuko Kusaka, "The Emergence and Development of Japanese School Sport," 24–28.

8. Yuko Kusaka notes that 72 schools participated in the first tournament; by the fourth year of the tournament, the number of participating teams had risen to 410 ("The Emergence and Development of Japanese School Sport," 28). For more on the popularity of middle-school tournaments, see Ikei, *Hakkyū Taiheiyō o wataru*, 102–3; and Kelly, "The Spirit and Spectacle of School Baseball," 108–9.

9. Guttmann and Thompson, *Japanese Sports*, 131–32. For an analysis of the baseball ideology of such "amateur" teams, see Kiku, "The Japanese Baseball Spirit and Professional Ideology," 45–46.

10. On these early professionals, see Ikei, *Hakkyū Taiheiyō o wataru*, 160. See also Kiku, "The Japanese Baseball Spirit and Professional Ideology," 43–45.

11. Kishino, ed., *Shinpan kindai taiiku supōtsu nenpyō*, 108, 114, 124, and 132.

12. Hashimoto, *Nihon supōtsu hōsōshi*, 19–21.

13. Amachi, "Konshū rīgusen to sutā pureyā."

14. Among the many possible examples, see the criticism mentioned here in "Aidokusha kurabu," *Yakyūkai* 30, no. 13, 221, third row.

15. For one example, see Kusaka Reiji, "Chūtō kyūkai shungō nijukketsu." See below for more details on the fame of middle-school players specifically in relation to Sawamura.

16. Suzuki Sōtarō wrote two articles for *Yakyūkai* that offer an early biographical account of Sawamura's life up to 1937. The details noted here are available in "Omoideru mama ni," 7:238–39. Suzuki makes explicit references to Sawamura's filial piety in the article (238). In his later book-length biography, Suzuki expands upon several of the same examples. See *Fumetsu no daitōshu*, on Sawamura's father (16–18) and on Sawamura as a weak child (21–22). Daidō Bun includes many of these same details based on an interview with Sawamura's father (*Puro yakyū gōketsu den*, 16–19).

17. Suzuki Sōtarō notes that Sawamura was especially gifted with the *soroban*, or abacus (*Fumetsu no daitōshu*, 26).

18. Suzuki Sōtarō, "Omoideru mama ni," 7:239–40; for expanded details, see Suzuki Sōtarō, *Fumetsu no daitōshu*, 21–29.

19. Suzuki, *Fumetsu no daitōshu*, 43–44. For more on Sawamura's work ethic as the secret to his success and as an example for all pitchers, see Suzuki Sōtarō, "Yakyū shinpō no dankai," 108–19.

20. For the spring tournament, the newspaper selected teams from the various prefectures based on their records.

21. For a brief summary of Sawamura's Kōshien experiences, see Suzuki Sōtarō, "Omoideru mama ni," 8:232–34. See also Daidō, *Puro yakyū gōketsu den*, 30–32. More extensive coverage is available in Suzuki Sōtarō, *Fumetsu no daitōshu*, 46–60.

22. "Tōshu no zuiichi wa Sawamura," *Yomiuri shinbun*, 14 April 1934, 5.

23. "Kyōto shōgyō 4–0 Sakai chūgaku."

24. Kusaka Reiji, "Chūtō kyūkai shungō nijukketsu," 176–77.

25. Nakagawa, "Kōsenshu o erabu."

26. "Aidokusha kurabu," *Yakyūkai* 24, no. 11, 204, third row; no. 14, 204, first row. The second of these two letters is actually written in response to a previous letter, highlighting the interactive nature of these sections. Despite the time delay, these forums appear not unlike today's web-based bulletin boards. After examining such letters in successive issues of the magazine, it is not unusual to see "dialogues" emerging from issue to issue as fans read and then responded to each other's comments. In many cases the fan letters use Romanized characters to represent the particular school (as in K or KO for Keiō, W for Waseda, M for Meiji, etc.) or spell out the name in Romanized characters (such as WASEDA). Most of these fan letters included the writers' locations and names, which in many cases appeared to be pseudonyms related to the particular writer's love of baseball or a specific team. The prevalence of pseudonyms makes it difficult to say for certain, but the presence of a significant numbers of the names ending with the character *sei* suggests that several of those writing letters were identifying themselves as students. Another common character appearing in the names was *ko*, which literally means child, but is also commonly used in female names. This nomenclature, together with regular comments about "female fans" in these sections, hints that *Yakyūkai* enjoyed a marked degree of popularity among young women, or at least writers seeking to give that impression.

27. "Shitsugi ōtō ran," *Yakyūkai* 24, no. 11, 206, third row, and 207, third row; no. 12, 206, third row, and 207, third row; no. 12, 207, fourth row. Even after Sawamura joined the professional team, fans continued to write well into 1935, asking where he was going to school. See "Shitsugi ōtō ran," *Yakyūkai* 25, no. 1, 206, first row and second through third row, and 207, first through second row; no. 4, 206, first row; no. 5, 206, first through second row.

28. The editor's note follows the Waseda fan's letter. "Aidokusha kurabu," *Yakyūkai* 24, no. 14, 204, first row.

29. For instance, see Suzuki Sōtarō, *Fumetsu no daitōshu*, 61–70; and Daidō, *Puro yakyū gōketsu den*, 34–51.

30. Quoting details he read elsewhere, essayist Fujii Iseji claimed that he was nearly moved to tears upon learning that Sawamura sacrificed his chances of going to Keiō so that he could support his brother's education ("Zuisō," 95–96). Suzuki Sōtarō related an anecdote about Sawamura's trips to the United States: unlike the other players, Sawamura bought no souvenirs for himself, but did get something for his younger siblings ("Omoideru mama ni," 7:238–39).

31. Quoted in Daidō, *Puro yakyū gōketsu den*, 40.

32. See Chapter 3 regarding the popularity of various American athletes, including Ruth, among Japanese fans.

33. *Yomiuri shinbun*, 18 July 1934; headlines quoted in Ikei, *Hakkyū Taiheiyō o wataru*, 129.

34. Issued on 28 March 1932, the full title of the order was "Yakyū no tōsei narabi ni shikō ni kansuru kunrei." A copy of the complete text as well as a lengthy discussion of the reasoning behind the order and the merits of specific points is available in a booklet written by the head of the Ministry of Education, Physical Education Section, that produced the order. See Yamakawa, *Yakyū tōsei no hanashi*.

35. Ikei connects the order specifically to tensions over Manchuria and right-wing nationalism, suggesting increasing government antagonism to sports, even though the Minister of Education was a baseball fan (*Hakkyū Taiheiyō o wataru*, especially 128). Referring to the 1934 arrival of the American baseball team, Guttmann and Thompson explain, "Despite the government's growing opposition to Western sports, a hundred thousand fans lined Tokyo's streets in 1934 to welcome the visiting American players" (*Japanese Sports*, 137). In this case it is not clear what opposition is being described, but the sentence captures widely held views about the status of sports, and especially baseball, in wartime Japanese society. I would suggest that assertions of Japanese government opposition rarely give due consideration to historical context and have been greatly exaggerated, in part because of postwar reinterpretations. This issue is examined in greater detail below with regard to postwar memories of Sawamura.

36. Suzuki Sōtarō gives this impression in his brief mention of the order (*Fumetsu no daitōshu*, 62). See also Ikei, *Hakkyū Taiheiyō o wataru*, 127–28. In English, see Reaves, *Taking in a Game*, 70. Reaves inaccurately indicates that the order was issued during the summer before the 1934 American tour.

37. Yamakawa, *Yakyū tōsei no hanashi*, 188. On the role of well-known amateur baseball advocates in drafting the order, see Blackwood, "Bushidō Baseball?" 12–13.

38. The order includes an entire section devoted to ticket sales and a special requirement that college teams charging admission report the total gate receipts; these facts speak to the extreme popularity of the university league games and events like the tournaments at Kōshien (196–98). It also outlines prize limitations (198).

39. Ibid., 190.

40. Ibid., 194.

41. Ibid., 196.

42. Ibid., 190 and 193. Notably, the order included special provisions for cases where it was not possible to avoid games during school hours.

43. For a brief summary of some of these controversies, see Kelly, "Sense and Sensibility at the Ball Park," 106–7 and 109–10.

44. Kishino, ed., *Shinpan kindai taiiku supōtsu nenpyō*, 145.

45. For an examination of the report, its historical context, and its continuing symbolic significance in efforts to reform American college sports, see Thelin, *Games Colleges Play*, especially 13–37. In its examination of the Ministry of Education order, a history of the Tokyo college baseball league connects the order with the 1929 report, suggesting that it was a good reference, if not impetus, for the Ministry of Education (Tokyo rokudaigaku yakyū renmei, *Shichijūnen no ayumi*, 55–56).

46. Another of the middle-school recruits, Victor Starffin, the son of Russian immigrants in Japan, is said to have been more or less blackmailed with vague threats of his family's expulsion from the country if he did not join the team. For more on Starffin, who went on to a successful professional career, see Sutaruhin, *Roshia kara kita ēsu*. For a brief biography in English, see Reaves, *Taking in a Game*, 70–71.

47. In 1935, when two other students were compelled to leave school in order to join the Japanese professional team preparing to tour the United States, the *Yomiuri* newspaper, which was sponsoring the team, published articles declaring the Ministry of Education regulations "irrational" and the "mistake of the era" ("Jidai sakugono yakyū tōsei" and "Fugōri na tōsei kunrei," *Yomiuri shinbun*, 13 February 1935, 7).

48. The library at the Japanese Baseball Hall of Fame includes a scrapbook collection of newspaper clippings, organized by date, dealing with the emergence of professional baseball in Japan. The general observations here are based on my surveys of the materials in the scrapbooks covering the period before and during the arrival of the American all-star team. See Zaidan hōjin yakyū taiiku hakubutsukan, Newspaper Scrapbook Collection, 1934. Even before the announcement about the American team's trip to Japan, the *Yomiuri* was publishing extensively on the workings of American baseball, including a series of articles by Suzuki Sōtarō in March and April 1934. In addition to introducing baseball rules, structure, and key players, these articles also taught readers American baseball slang. One special series was dedicated solely to Babe Ruth. Photo rosters of both the Japanese and American teams were also published in the paper. Having joined the Japanese team, Sawamura was also the subject of an article ("Zen-Nihon daihyō yakyū chīmu sobyō 8," *Yomiuri shinbun*, 15 October 1934, 5).

49. Ōe Shinkichi, *Yakyū-ō Bēbu Rūsu*. Ōe is listed as a translator, but the original book he was translating is not clear. It may have been Ruth's own book *How to Play Baseball* (1931). Ōe's book included an advertisement for a special Babe Ruth trivia contest (the book, of course, contained the answers) in which the winner would receive an autographed baseball.

50. For one example, see the extensive details provided in "All Japan Ready to Hail Ruth and His Team of Stars," *Sporting News*, 18 October 1934, 3.

51. For two examples, see "65,000 Watch Ruth Lead Mates to Triumph in Tokyo by 17 to 1," *New York Times*, 5 November 1934, 25; and "Japan Greets Ruth, Players: Baseball Entry Attracts 100,000 But Admirals Still Talk Oil," *Amarillo Globe*, 2 November 1934, 1.

52. "Ruth Conquers Japan," *Sporting News*, 8 November 1934, 1.

53. "Babe, the Ambassador," *Sporting News*, 15 November 1934, 3.

54. See, for instance, "Baseball Honors Babe Ruth Today," *New York Times*, 27 April 1947, S2; and Ruth's obituary in "Babe Ruth, Baseball's Greatest Star and Idol of Children, Had a Career Both Dramatic and Bizarre," *New York Times*, 17 August 1948, 14.

55. Sano, "Shōwa no puromōtā," 407. For more on the ostensibly "amateur" ethos of early Japanese professional baseball teams, see Kiku, "The Japanese Baseball Spirit and Professional Ideology," 46–49.

56. See especially a series of articles that ran for several days, beginning with "Nichibei yakyūsen kaiko zadankai," *Yomiuri shinbun*, 4 December 1934, 5.

57. "Zen-Beigun Nihon inshōroku." See also Nakamura Takanori, "Amerika-gun no inshō."

58. On the surprising revelation that Ruth had weaknesses, see Sawamura, "Dai-Bēbu Rūsu ni datte ana wa aru." On Sawamura's overall experience as a member of the Japanese all-star team, see Sawamura, "Zen-Nihongun no purēto o funde."

59. See pointers on pitching in "Beikoku senshu wa oshieru 5," *Yomiuri shinbun*, 14 November 1935, 5.

60. Bēbu Rūsu, "Sugoi Sawamura no kyōkyū," *Yomiuri shinbun*, 14 November 1934, 5. Gehrig's evaluations are cited in Suzuki, *Fumetsu no daitōshu*, 93.

61. In the *New York Times* the story ran as "Ruth's Home Run Tops Japanese, 1-0," *New York Times*, 21 November 1934, 24. The story ran under different titles and with edited text in multiple papers nationwide. For a few representative examples, see "Battle of Pitchers," *Oshkosh Daily Northwestern*, 20 November 1934, 14; "Bambino's Homer Wins," *Bismarck Tribune*, 20 November 1934, 6; and "Pitcher's Battle Depends on Ruth to Bang Homerun," *Mason City Globe-Gazette*, 20 November 1934, 12.

62. See "Battle of Pitchers," *Oshkosh Daily Northwestern*, 20 November 1934, 14. Notably, the *New York Times* version did not mention the expulsion, but referred to the school he had previously played with; see "Ruth's Home Run Tops Japanese, 1-0," *New York Times*, 21 November 1934, 24.

63. "Murder's row" mentioned in "Battle of Pitchers," *Oshkosh Daily Northwestern*, 20 November 1934, 14. "Major league stars," in "Ruth's Home Run Tops Japa-

nese, 1-0," *New York Times*, 21 November 1934, 24. Other articles cut these references entirely.

64. "Japanese Catching On: Ruth's Homer Only Run in Nov. 20 Game as Scores Grow Closer," *Sporting News*, 29 November 1934, 2.

65. Ibid.

66. Daniel M. Daniel, "Ruth Averaged .408 on Japanese Tour," *Sporting News*, 7 February 1935, 2.

67. The *Yomiuri* featured a lengthy article on the game including Ruth's complaint about the sun. "Nichibei yakyū daijussen (Shizuoka): Sawamura murui no dekibae," *Yomiuri shinbun*, 21 November 1934, 5. For a detailed description of the game and both the Japanese and American responses, see Suzuki Sōtarō, *Fumetsu no daitōshu*, 75–91. For a shorter account in English, see Reaves, *Taking in a Game*, 69. Reaves has the game on the 18th rather than the 20th. Among Sawamura's comments published in *Yakyūkai*, the pitcher noted, "After the game was over, [Vernon 'Lefty'] Gomez and the others gave me all kinds of advice and criticism that essentially came down to the fact that my pitching was still immature. That assessment is pretty much a given" (Sawamura, "Zen-Nihongun no purēto o funde," 133).

68. Sawamura Eiji, "Mabuta ni ukabu yūshi," *Yomiuri shinbun*, 4 June 1941, 6.

69. The games were often featured on the sports pages of local papers. For one example that includes details about Sawamura's game against the American all-stars, see "Blues-Japs," *Wisconsin-State Journal*, 11 June 1935, 13. A photo and a brief description of Sawamura appeared on the sports page in "Tokyo Ace," *Modesto Bee and News-Herald*, 6 March 1935, 22. Suzuki frequently published articles in Japan and had also been instrumental in organizing the 1934 tour by Babe Ruth and other American stars. Because of his English-language skills, and his familiarity with the American media, it seems highly plausible that many of the articles in local papers were based on press releases that he wrote, a fact that might account for some of the repetitive descriptions in the articles. Japanese papers also covered the team extensively during both tours. For a 1935 article suggesting that Sawamura was so popular that a game had to be halted because of fan requests for autographs, see "Sainzeme," *Yomiuri shinbun*, 10 June 1935, 7. Suzuki Sōtarō, *Fumetsu no daitōshu* goes into further detail about Sawamura's popularity on the American tours (118–19) and mentions a key game against the San Francisco Seals where Sawamura proved unable to strike out Joe DiMaggio, who was playing his last season with the Seals before joining the Yankees (132–34).

70. Articles from the latter part of the 1935 tour include references to Sawamura as "Nippon's Schoolboy Rowe" ("Blues-Japs," *Wisconsin-State Journal*, 11 June 1935, 13). Japanese articles also made this connection ("Sainzeme," *Yomiuri shinbun*, 10 June 1935, 7). But the nickname was featured more regularly and prominently in 1936. See, for instance, "Japanese and Coast Team Will Play at Home Field: Sawamura, the 19-Year-Old School Boy Rowe of Nippon, Is Situated to Work Against Acorns: Games Start at 2:30 P. M.," *Modesto Bee and News-Herald*, 14 March 1936, 23. The banner headline topping the sports page reads, "Oaks and Tokyo Giants Will Open Series To-day." Details included in at least one article

suggest that Suzuki may have come up with, or at the very least promoted, several nicknames to market the team to the American audience. See "Japanese Nine Follows U.S. Traditions: Famous Team to Play Here: Tokyo Players Have Names Taken from List of U.S. Stars," *Amarillo Globe*, 17 April 1936, 13. In addition to introducing the Japanese players, the article notes that the Japanese team charged a high fee, a fact used to justify the high ticket prices for this series.

71. Suzuki Sōtarō indicates that it was the St. Louis Cardinals that tried to sign Sawamura (*Fumetsu no daitōshu*, 158–60). Ikei, citing Suzuki's memoirs, claims it was the Pittsburgh Pirates (*Hakkyū Taiheiyō o wataru*, 156–57). In English, references to Sawamura often involve the Pirates because this is what is mentioned in Robert Whiting's best-selling works on Japanese baseball (*You Gotta Have Wa*, 44). Teams on the West Coast had apparently also expressed an interest (Sawamura, "Boku no nayami"). Several American papers also mentioned that scouts were trying to woo Japanese players. For example, see "Tokyo Giants Boast Several Diamond Stars: Members of Japanese Team Are Sought by Major League Clubs," *Ogden Standard-Examiner*, 23 May 1935, 10.

72. Sawamura, "Boku no nayami," 258.

73. Ibid. Sawamura's main critique of American women was the fact that it was considered bad to fix one's shoelaces in their presence. Writing in 1937, Suzuki Sōtarō hinted that Japanese baseball was lucky the Sawamura did not speak English, because that was the main thing that prevented him from joining an American team ("Omoideru mama ni," 7:235).

74. Ikei, *Hakkyū Taiheiyō o wataru*, 159–64.

75. On Sawamura's popularity and its benefits for professional baseball, see Suzuki Sōtarō, *Fumetsu no daitōshu*, 230. These comments also appeared regularly during Sawamura's lifetime. For one example, see Shiro kyūji, "Sawamura tōshu chūmonchō."

76. "Sawamura tōshu saikō shukun senshu ni erabaru."

77. The coverage of professional teams in *Yakyūkai* was still dwarfed by that given to college teams and players. Sawamura attracted a disproportionately large amount of attention in the professional sections. In the July 1937 issue, four out of the twenty pages on professional baseball were devoted specifically to Sawamura, not including other articles where he was mentioned. See *Yakyūkai* 27, no. 10 (July 1937).

78. The Japanese Baseball Hall of Fame scrapbook collection includes several *Manshū Nichinichi shinbun* articles about this series. See Zaidan hōjin yakyū taiiku hakubutsukan, Newspaper Scrapbook Collection, 1940, Manshū rīgusen. For articles mentioned here, see "Kyojin-gun no meitōshu Sawamura no tōjō wa Manshū rīgusen no koro," *Manshū Nichinichi shinbun*, 15 May 1940; and Suzuki Sōtarō, "Shokugyō yakyūdan midokoro," *Manshū Nichinichi shinbun*, 30 May 1940. Given his popularity it may be more than coincidental that Sawamura's comeback occurred before the trip. At the very least, pressure from fans and the press for his quick return seems to have been intense. The Giants had previously played exhibition games in Manchuria and Korea in 1936. See Suzuki Sōtarō, *Fumetsu no daitōshu*, 234–39.

79. "Iyoiyo Manshū rīgu kaimaku," *Manshū Nichinichi shinbun*, 30 July 1940, in Zaidan hōjin yakyū taiiku hakubutsukan, Newspaper Scrapbook Collection, 1940, Manshū rīgusen.

80. "Shitsugi ōtō," *Yakyūkai* 27, no. 14, 205, second row; *Yakyūkai* 28, no. 5, 142, second through third row; *Yakyūkai* 30, no. 6, 185, second row; no. 13, 223, first through second row; *Yakyūkai* 31, no. 5, 122, third through fourth row; *Yakyūkai* 32, no. 21, 159, fourth row; *Sumō to Yakyū* 33, no. 3, 150, third row.

81. "Sawamura tōshu kōshu gōkaku," *Yomiuri shinbun*, 21 July 1937, 4.

82. Mizutani, "Puro Yakyū No. 1 Sawamura tōshu katei hōmon ki," 263.

83. "Aru hi no Sawamura Eiji," 220–21. The article followed several others on Sawamura's pitching and preceded an essay on Sawamura's "likes."

84. Quoted in Daidō, *Puro yakyū gōketsu den*, 116.

85. Ibid., 116–17. This image of the unwilling Sawamura sacrificing himself for the sake of baseball is also picked up in a fictionalized version of his life; see Kitahara, *Sawamura Eiji to sono jidai*, 228–30. This idea is also mentioned briefly in Yomiuri shinbun Ōsaka honsha shakaibu, *Sensō 9*, 42.

86. On DiMaggio, his decision to enlist, and the attention it received, see Cramer, *Joe DiMaggio*, 198–208. On Williams and several other players, see Montville, *Ted Williams*, 99–105.

87. "Shinpei-san Sawamura-kun," *Yomiuri shinbun*, 11 January 1938, evening edition, 2.

88. Sawamura, "Senjō kara: Sawamura tōshu no tegami." Naturally, measurements of this sort would have involved the use of practice grenades.

89. During his military training, Sawamura received a special commendation after throwing a grenade 78 meters. Suzuki notes that Sawamura's achievements and those of other baseball players were widely publicized, "delighting fans because they linked the effectiveness of baseball to the war" (Suzuki Sōtarō, *Fumetsu no daitōshu*, 315). References to grenade throwing are standard in biographical accounts of Sawamura and also appear regularly in Sawamura's own retellings of his battle experiences. In most cases, Sawamura makes an explicit connection between pitching and grenade throwing; see, for instance, Sawamura, "Senjō yori supōtsu omoi o omou: tokui no teryūdan nage," *Yomiuri shinbun*, 5 January 1939, 4.

90. Ikeda Tsuneo, quoted in Yomiuri shinbun Ōsaka honsha shakaibu, *Sensō 9*, 43.

91. Pictures of Sawamura in uniform often accompanied articles, and in at least one instance, the picture itself became part of the reason for and subject of the article. See Kawabe (*tokuhain*), "'Yakyū' to 'kentō' no akushu," *Yomiuri shinbun*, 14 December 1938, evening edition, 1. A photo of Sawamura and another player were also among the full-page photos included in *Yakyūkai*; see *Yakyūkai* 29, no. 17 (November 1939): photo section.

92. For comments on Sawamura's enjoyment of long marches and throwing grenades, as well as a cavalier attitude toward death and injury, see Morishita (*tokuhain*), "Tetsuwan rokujū mētoru," *Yomiuri shinbun*, 11 September 1938, 7. For an example of Sawamura's willingness to die and certainty of victory, see Sawamura, "Senjō kara: Sawamura tōshu no tegami," 172.

93. Ōi, "Kikan no Sawamura tōshu kaikenki," 172.

94. Sadohara, "Sawamura tōshu o heiei ni tou," 177.

95. Sawamura, "Sensen yori futatabi tōshuban ni kaerite," 464 (page citations are to reprint edition).

96. Ibid., 463–64. Sawamura made similar claims about not having time to think about baseball in another article published a month earlier in *Yakyūkai*: Sawamura, "Tōshuban e no akogare." Suzuki Sōtarō indicates that Sawamura later told him that he had been relieved that the injury did not affect his pitching hand (*Fumetsu no daitōshu*, 318–20). Sawamura's injury in this hard-fought battle was also featured in the professional baseball association's newsletter *Renmei nyūsu* ("Sawamura tōshu: Ōbetsuzan de funsen").

97. Sadohara, "Sawamura tōshu o heiei ni tou," 176.

98. Sawamura, "Sensen yori futatabi tōshuban ni kaerite," 463. Sawamura's superior officer also cited the connection between baseball and Sawamura's military abilities in Morishita (*tokuhain*), "Tetsuwan rokujū mētoru," *Yomiuri shinbun*, 11 September 1938, 7.

99. Ōzaki, "Sawamura tōshu hōmonki," 200.

100. Sawamura and Sasazaki, "Kikan ni yūshi sensō to supōtsu o kataru," 378 (page citations are to reprint edition).

101. Ōi, "Kikan no Sawamura tōshu kaikenki," 172. Sawamura's emphasis on the need for a strong body for baseball was not new; in an interview published before he entered the military, Sawamura emphasized the importance that efforts "to build the body" (*karada o tsukuru koto*) played in his pitching regimen. See Shuhō Saburō, "Puro no NO. 1 Sawamura tōshu to ichimon ittō."

102. Sawamura, "Tatakau yakyū senshu no shuki," 97.

103. Ibid., 98–99.

104. For details on Sawamura's first discharge in April 1940 and return to baseball shortly thereafter, see Suzuki Sōtarō, *Fumetsu no daitōshu*, 330–38. It is worth noting that soon after his return to baseball, Sawamura pitched his third career no-hitter in July 1940. Despite this brilliant game, he never achieved the same level of pitching that he had enjoyed before entering the military. Many assume that this was the result of having thrown so many grenades, which ended up injuring his arm. For information about Sawamura being redrafted and his service in the Philippines, see Suzuki Sōtarō, *Fumetsu no daitōshu*, 341–43.

105. Futabayama, mentioned briefly in Chapter 2, is one of the best-known and most successful wrestlers in the modern history of the sport. For more on sumo and the war, see Tierney, "Wrestling with Tradition," 190–207.

106. Details on wartime regulations and the impact of censorship on the mass media, including magazines, is available in Kasza, *The State and the Mass Media in Japan, 1918–1945*, especially 194–231.

107. One of the longest was a three-page article published in *Yakyūkai* as a "diary" of his war experiences in China in early 1938. Details in the article indicate that Sawamura wrote it—probably retrospectively—while hospitalized for injury; see Sawamura, "Senjō nikki."

108. Aside from length, the presence of several stock propaganda stories and some jarring contrasts with his other writings lead me to suspect that another unknown person was heavily involved in crafting this account.

109. Sawamura, "Tatakau yakyū senshu no shuki," 98.
110. Ibid., 100.
111. Ibid., 93–94.
112. Ibid., 95–96.
113. Ibid., 96.
114. Ibid., 92.
115. Ibid., 100.
116. See, for instance, Sadohara, "Senshō hakui no yūshi"; Kageyama Bunzō, "Mihara senshu senjō hiwa"; Fujii, "Nankai-gun Iwamoto shushō o heiei ni tou"; "Senjin dayori (ni)"; and "Kikan shita yakyū senshu no zadankai."
117. *Yakyūkai* 25, no. 9 (July 1935): front photo section.
118. Kageura, "Kikan senshu no shuki"; and Kojima, "Kikan senshu no shuki."
119. Shimizu Hideo, "Futatabi tōshuban ni tatte," 88–89.
120. Sagita, "Kyūkai meisenshu no sange," parts 1 and 2.
121. The scrapbook collection at the Japanese Baseball Hall of Fame includes articles from the *Yomiuri* and other newspapers related to the military activities of various players throughout the war. For example, an article from an unspecified Nagoya newspaper, discusses the war injury of the Giant's star catcher. See "Meihoshu ittōhei chi daruma," 9 September 1937, in Zaidan hōjin yakyū taiiku hakubutsukan, Newspaper Scrapbook Collection, 1937.
122. Kojima, "Kikan senshu no shuki," 78–79.
123. Kōno, "Beikoku-shiki yakyū [*kanji* glossed as "Amerika nizumu"] o tomurau"; Suzuki Sōtarō, "Senji Nihon yakyū ron"; and Suzuki Ryūji, "Nihon yakyū no shin dōkō."
124. Suzuki Ryūji, "Daitōa sensō to Nihon yakyū no shimei," 124–25.
125. Suzuki Sōtarō, "Senji Nihon yakyū ron," 127.
126. Ibid., 131.
127. In a chapter examining sports in Japan as a form of American cultural imperialism, sports historian Gerald Gems asserts, "Japanese nationalism thus superseded the progressive promise of sport and led to the use of sport as a resistive force" (*The Athletic Crusade*, 43). Gems raises similar points throughout the chapter, which also perpetuates long-standing stereotypes about the unique links between sports in Japan and *bushidō*. Even though Gems also discusses the hypocrisy of American claims concerning democracy, equality, and liberty, the chapter leaves a strong overall impression that Japan's approach to sports skewed from some more acceptable and "correct" way (30–44). For similar examples, see Guttmann and Thompson, *Japanese Sports*, especially 137–39 and 155–60; and Abe, Kiyohara, and Nakajima, "Fascism, Sport and Society in Japan."
128. For several examples, see Crepeau, "Pearl Harbor," 71. The early portion of Feller's professional career overlapped with that of Sawamura, who was one year older than Feller. The parallels between the two are striking. Like Sawamura, Feller was recruited at a young age and went on to pitch three career no-hit games. He was also one of the first pitchers in American baseball to win twenty or more professional games before the age of 21 (Sawamura did so in Japan at the age of 20). Feller survived the war and continued pitching into the mid-1950s. For comparisons, see Suzuki Sōtarō, *Fumetsu no daitōshu*, 14–18 and 37–39. For details

on Feller, including his military experience, see Van Meter Memories, Inc., *Bob Feller Museum*, http://www.bobfellermuseum.org/ (accessed 2 July 2010).

129. Babe Ruth, quoted in "Ruth Called Turn on Japs' Foldup Spirit When Losing," *Sporting News*, 6 September 1945, 4. Although Ruth's comments, cited here after the war ended, are portrayed as accurate, the experiences of many Japanese and Americans, and even the rationale for the use of nuclear weapons, contradict his "understanding" of Japanese battlefield psychology.

130. "Baseball Men Warn Against Dropping Game Lest Japanese Morale Benefit from Move," *New York Times*, 26 March 1943, 23.

131. "Uncle Sam Needs Only To Call," *Sporting News*, 5 September 1940, 5; "Uncle Sam, We Are At Your Command," *Sporting News*, 11 December 1941, 4.

132. "Uncle Sam, We Are At Your Command," *Sporting News*, 11 December 1941, 4.

133. "It's Not the Same Game in Japan," *Sporting News*, 18 December 1941, 4.

134. J. G. T. Spink, "Looping the Loops," *Sporting News*, 1 January 1942, 1.

135. "Babe Ruth, Baseball's Greatest Star and Idol of Children," *New York Times*, 17 August 1948, 14; and "Baseball 'Absolutely Essential' To Our Morale, Senate Is Told," *New York Times*, 16 November 1943, 31.

136. For an example of wartime criticism of baseball among legislators, see "Baseball Should Be Ruled Out with Racing, Says Military Affairs Committee Chairman," *New York Times*, 19 January 1945, 27. Although it may be atypical, a letter to the sports editor published in the *New York Times* was highly critical of both "baseball conducted for profit" and arguments that the sport was necessary for morale (Robert Legier, "Letters to the Sports Editor: No Room for Baseball," *New York Times*, 20 February 1943, 18).

137. Crepeau, "Pearl Harbor," 71–72. For an examination of baseball's role in the American war effort, see Bullock, *Playing for Their Nation*.

138. Suzuki Sōtarō, *Fumetsu no daitōshu*, 21, 313–15, 318–21, 329–31, 341–43, and 349–53; the last five pages (349–53) of the book explain how Suzuki learned of Sawamura's death, his visit to Sawamura's grave marker, and his conversations with Sawamura's family after his death.

139. Daidō, *Puro yakyū gōketsu den*, 114–15.

140. Ibid., 127.

141. Ikei, "Daitōshu Sawamura Eiji no senreki," 114. Sawamura's experiences in the Philippines are also omitted in a volume on baseball players who died in the war, which gives only the dates and the fact that he told his parents that he would come back uninjured and did so (Yomiuri shinbun Ōsaka honsha shakaibu, *Sensō 9*, 47–48).

142. Sawamura Kenji, quoted in Daidō, *Puro yakyū gōketsu den*, 48. This issue is also raised in other sources. See Ninomiya, "Kyojin-gun wa Sawamura Eiji o suteta ka," 188–89; and Kitahara, *Sawamura Eiji to sono jidai*, 228–29.

143. On the marching and malaria, see Ogura, *Sawamura Eiji monogatari*, 116. These references to Sawamura's experiences in the Philippines can be found in a fictionalized account of Sawamura's life and sound more like the experiences of later fighting in the Philippines than what Sawamura described in the early phase of the conflict. See Kitahara, *Sawamura Eiji to sono jidai*, 258.

144. Suzuki Sōtarō, *Fumetsu no daitōshu*, 330–38 and 343–49. See also Ogura, *Sawamura Eiji monogatari*, 118–27 and 132–37; and Kitahara, *Sawamura Eiji to sono jidai*, 239–53 and 258–68. In focusing on Sawamura's injuries and his efforts to return to baseball, these accounts evince a selective use of their subject's own writings, since Sawamura often wrote about his struggles to make a comeback, with full acknowledgment that he would not be the same player as he had been before the war.

145. Ogura, *Sawamura Eiji monogatari*, 116–19.

146. Ibid., 129.

147. Ibid., 152. See also Kitahara, *Sawamura Eiji to sono jidai*, 256–57.

148. *Nekkyū* is literally "hot ball," but even though the English term "fireball" may also unintentionally evoke Sawamura's death, fireball is a more common slang term in English for pitchers, like Sawamura, with amazing speed, as exemplified by the phrase "fireball reliever." For details about the film and its reception and influence, see Tanuma, *Nichibei yakyū eiga kinemakan*. During my research, the film was not yet available on video or DVD, and I was unable to find a copy of the original to view. My comments are based on Tanuma's observations and similar descriptions of the film available on an online movie database affiliated with the Japanese film magazine *Kinema junpō*; see Kinema junpōsha, "Arasuji: *Fumetsu no nekkyū*," *Goo eiga*, http://movie.goo.ne.jp/movies/PMVWKPD24199/story.html (accessed 2 July 2010).

149. Coverage during Sawamura's lifetime gave some attention to his parents and siblings, but most of it, along with his own comments, centered on his pitching, his physical well-being, or his military exploits. Aside from occasional details about his personal likes and dislikes, there appears to be relatively little information about his life outside baseball, including relationships with women.

150. The story is complicated still further because Sakai actually ran away from her parents and traveled to the home of a family member living in Manchuria. Around the same time, Sawamura returned from China and was reassigned to duty in Japan. For more on their relationship, see Suzuki Sōtarō, *Fumetsu no daitōshu*, 264–66, 279–83, 299–305, 321–27, and 338–42.

151. In Kitahara's fictional account Yūko proves to be an extremely supportive wife (*Sawamura Eiji to sono jidai*, especially 273–76).

152. Several college games had already been played by this point, including a Tokyo league alumni game that took place in front of a packed stadium on 28 October 1945 (Ikei, *Hakkyū Taiheiyō o wataru*, 195). The dates for postwar revival provided in Guttmann and Thompson, *Japanese Sports*, 170.

153. Red Parton, "Japanese Plan to Resume Pro Ball Next Spring," *Sporting News*, 22 November 1945, 9.

154. The *New York Times* cited Japanese newspapers' demands for a revival of baseball as a means of "promoting understanding between the Japanese and Americans." See "Return of Baseball Is Sought in Japan," *New York Times*, 16 September 1945, 5. For similar statements, see Suzuki Ryūji, quoted in Reaves, *Taking in a Game*, 82–83.

155. *Asahi shinbun*, 21 January 1946; quoted in Guttmann and Thompson, *Japanese Sports*, 163–64.

156. See *Yakyūkai* 32, no. 6 (March 1942): photo section.

157. "Sport Falls as Dictators Rise," *Sporting News*, 28 August 1941, 4.

158. "Baseball 'Absolutely Essential' To Our Morale, Senate Is Told," *New York Times*, 16 November 1943, 31. A similar comment appeared in "Baseball Men Warn Against Dropping Game Lest Japanese Morale Benefit from Move," *New York Times*, 26 March 1943, 23.

159. Capra and Ivens, dirs., *Know Your Enemy: Japan*.

160. "Overseas: 'Some Crank,'" *New York Times*, 24 February 1935, E1; "Killing by Zealots Frequent in Japan," *New York Times*, 26 February 1936, 9; "Japan and Babe Ruth," *New York Times*, 4 March 1944, 12; and "Babe Ruth, Baseball's Greatest Star and Idol of Children," *New York Times*, 17 August 1948, 14. Several of these articles inaccurately report that the attempted assassination was successful. A hagiographic English-language biography of Shōriki cites only anti-Americanism and the connection between Babe Ruth's visit as the reason for the attack (Uhlan and Thomas, *Shoriki*, 111–12). For details on the attack and investigation, see Sano, "Shōwa no puromōtā," 407–8.

161. "Japan and Babe Ruth," *New York Times*, 4 March 1944, 12. This story, often linked to the Shōriki assassination attempt, was reported widely and is frequently included in descriptions of Ruth and his career and in his obituary: "Babe Ruth, Baseball's Greatest Star and Idol of Children," *New York Times*, 17 August 1948, 14. Given the linguistic differences involved, stories about Japanese soldiers using these battle cries raise intriguing, and perhaps ultimately unanswerable, questions about the accuracy of such battlefield accounts.

162. Dower, *Embracing Defeat*, 277–301, and especially 282–85.

163. "Return of Baseball Is Sought in Japan," *New York Times*, 16 September 1945, 5; "Japanese Plan 1946 Resumption of Important Baseball Leagues," *New York Times*, 29 September 1945, 20; and "Japan Revives Baseball Loop," *New York Times*, 10 November 1945, 18. See also Red Parton, "Japanese Plan to Resume Pro Ball Next Spring," *Sporting News*, 22 November 1945, 9. In Parton's article, Suzuki Sōtarō clearly indicates that baseball continued well into the war, but the article still gives the impression, especially in the case of school baseball, that the government banned the sport.

164. Reaves, *Taking in a Game*, 78. Much is also made of changes in team names. In addition to adopting Japanese names that used *kanji* instead of loan words written in *katakana* (though they often had the same meaning), team names also allegedly began to employ the ostensibly militarized term *gun*, as in soldier or unit, after the outbreak of war with the United States. In point of fact, *gun* was associated with team names from the very early stages of baseball, including middle-school, college, and professional teams. Militarized baseball language, including references to "battles" and "invading" teams, had long been common in Japanese and English. One might recall, for instance, references to Sawamura's famous 1934 "pitching battle."

165. Reaves, *Taking in a Game*, 79. The claims about the emotional toll and comparison with the red scare here are completely unsubstantiated, if not absurd.

166. Attacks of this sort were, of course, never a serious issue in American preservation of baseball during the war.

167. Kishino, ed., *Shinpan kindai taiiku supōtsu nenpyō*, 173, 175, 177, and 179.

168. Ibid., 172. American coverage was already discussing linguistic changes in Japanese baseball in November 1940, just after this initial round of changes; "Brief Bits of Gossip: Game Changes in Japan," *Sporting News*, 7 November 1940, 10. These details were repeated and recast as precursors of the warlords' ban in "Sport Falls as Dictators Rise," *Sporting News*, 28 August 1941, 4. During the war the linguistic changes in other sports were cited as demonstrations of Japanese irrationality, though several of the sports mentioned in the article had regularly used Japanese names before the war. See "Nothing about 'Sockyu' in Japan's Sport Names," *New York Times,* 6 March 1943, 17.

169. Kishino, ed., *Shinpan kindai taiiku supōtsu nenpyō*, 178. Explanations of the orders were included in the section of *Sumō to Yakyū* devoted to news from the professional baseball league ("Renmei dayori," 106–7).

170. In his essay from June 1943, Shimizu Hideo refers to several of the teams using their old names, and the *Sumō to Yakyū* editors apparently did not feel the need to address the issue ("Futatabi tōshuban ni tatte," 88).

171. In his postwar descriptions of wartime baseball, longtime professional baseball umpire Shima Hidenosuke indicates that army officials regularly summoned Suzuki Ryūji, as leader of the league, asking that professional baseball demonstrate support for the war in various ways. In Shima's view, Suzuki and other league officials did not want to do as requested, but felt that they had no choice. As one example, Shima recounts an army request that the league open games by having players throw practice grenades at dummies in the outfield wearing the labels America, Britain, and China. Quoting the thoughts of league officials, Shima explains that they resisted because the idea was foolish and would destroy the players' throwing abilities, but to placate the military they offered instead to have players perform gun drills before games. After describing this incident, Shima suggests that if they had followed the original request, some of the baseball people might have been treated as criminals later, presumably by the occupation forces. Shima's defense of wartime baseball figures, however, fails to explain why some teams in the league did, in fact, adopt a very similar pregame ritual in the early stages of war with the Americans. Although it was not dummies in the outfield, as noted above, pictures of grenade throwing at signs labeled with the names of these enemy nations appeared in *Yakyūkai* as early as March 1942. Perhaps some in Japanese baseball were lucky that Americans were firmly committed to the idea that the game had been "banned." See Shima, *Puro yakyū shinpan no me*, 57–63.

172. "Renmei dayori," 106.

173. Igarashi, *Bodies of Memory*, 12. For another examination of Japanese societal efforts to deal with wartime guilt and responsibility by forgetting or reassigning blame, see Dower, *Embracing Defeat*, 485–521.

174. Suzuki Sōtarō, *Fumetsu no daitōshu*, 330. Suzuki cites the retirement of Babe Ruth's number as part of the inspiration for honoring Sawamura in the same way. Yet Ruth's number was not retired until 1948, a year after Sawamura's. The unequal power relationships inherent in such star systems reveal themselves in such counter-historical assertions.

175. Dower, *Embracing Defeat*, 487.

176. On censorship of public expressions of grief and mourning, see ibid., 415–19. On general approaches to mourning and honoring the war dead in occupied Japan, see ibid., 485–96.

177. On Kurosawa, see Hōchi shinbunsha, "Eikyū ketsuban [4] Kurosawa Toshio," *Supōtsu Hōchi*, http://hochi.yomiuri.co.jp/contents/giants/number/kurosawa.htm (accessed 2 July 2010). Kurosawa's death was representative of the day-to-day struggles with starvation, poverty, filth, and disease that plagued Japan in the immediate postwar period. On disease and starvation, see Dower, *Embracing Defeat*, 89–104. Typhus was only one of several communicable diseases reportedly afflicting more than 650,000 people from 1945 through 1948. According to official figures 99,654 people died as a consequence of such diseases; for figures, see Dower, *Embracing Defeat*, 103.

Chapter Five

EPIGRAPH. Gushiken, *Ringu wa boku no senjō da*, 209–11.

1. In popular accounts, Gushiken is often credited with coining the name when he mentioned his desire to be like the bird he remembered from childhood. The first book-length biographical account about Gushiken, which is titled *Okinawa's Star Gushiken Yōkō: I Am the Kanmuriwashi*, gives this impression, even though this work mentions the documentary; see Ashizawa, *Okinawa no hoshi Gushiken Yōkō*. Boxing and other popular magazines are more explicit in attributing the nickname to Gushiken; see Nagadō, "'Chiisana kyojin,'" 85; and "Shōgeki no sutā ningen bunkai shirīzu," 46–47. Gushiken himself suggested in an interview conducted in the journal *Hanashi no tokushū* that one of the producers associated with TBS (the network that aired the documentary and Gushiken's fights) suggested the nickname; see Yazaki, "Sūpā sutā kenkyū 2," 55. Gushiken confirmed this fact when I interviewed him in 2004, noting that he was grateful to the TBS producer for suggesting the name that had become so important to him; Gushiken, interview by author, 30 November 2004. In any case, the documentary seems to have played the most critical role in popularizing the nickname, and both Gushiken and the media quickly adopted it. Details about the documentary are found in Ashizawa, *Okinawa no hoshi Gushiken Yōkō*, 179.

2. The official website of Gushiken's gym includes images of the gym's journal, *Kanmuriwashi faito*; see Shirai Gushiken supōtsu jimu, *Official Website*, http://www11.ocn.ne.jp/-sgs13/top.html (accessed 1 July 2010).

3. The *kanmuriwashi* is sometimes called the Ryukyu Serpent-Eagle; its scientific name is *spilornis cheela perplexus*. In 1977, it was reclassified as a National Special Natural Monument, something similar to an endangered species in the United States. For a brief description and photograph, see the website of the Kyushu Forestry Management Division at Kyūshū shinrin kanrikyoku, "Kanmuriwashi," *Kyūshū shinrin kanrikyoku*, http://www.rinya.maff.go.jp/kyusyu/policy/business/conservation/corridor/kisyou/9-kanmuriwasi.html (accessed 1 July 2010).

4. Nagadō Eikichi, himself Okinawan, makes such a point in arguing that Gushiken was an important and heroic symbol for Okinawans (*Bokusā PART II*, 10).

5. For a history of Okinawa prior to World War II, see Kerr, *Okinawa*. First published in 1958, Kerr's work remains one of the only comprehensive histories of Okinawa in English and is often cited in Japanese-language histories as a source. For a more recent examination of Okinawa's period of quasi-independence from 1609 to 1879, see Smits, *Visions of Ryukyu,* which focuses primarily on intellectual history, but offers several new perspectives on the nature of Ryukyu-Japan-China relations during this period.

6. From the *Ryūkyū shinpō* newspaper, quoted in Rabson, "Assimilation Policy in Okinawa," 140. Rabson offers several examples of both top-down and bottom-up efforts to assimilate Okinawa (138–43).

7. For more on discrimination, assimilation, and efforts to "pass" as Japanese, see Christy, "The Making of Imperial Subjects in Okinawa," 141–69. For position announcements, see 150.

8. The execution of Okinawans as spies is one of several frequently cited examples of the Japanese military's mistreatment of Okinawan civilians during the Battle of Okinawa. See Ōta, *Okinawa*, 170–71. For an overall view of the Battle of Okinawa and especially its impact on Okinawan civilians, see 74–177.

9. For a general overview of the occupation years and the reversion movement in Okinawa, see Nakano and Arasaki, *Okinawa sengoshi*. In English, the majority of studies dealing with postwar Okinawan history have focused on aspects of international relations in the occupation and reversion. For an English-language history that combines an examination of American and Japanese policies toward Okinawa with some details about Okinawa's postwar political, social, and cultural history, see Kensei Yoshida, *Democracy Betrayed*. For a richly detailed study of early occupation policies, see Obermiller, "The United States Military Occupation of Okinawa." For an examination of protest and resistance as key elements of Okinawan history and identity, see Tanji, *Myth, Protest and Struggle in Okinawa*.

10. In connection with economic issues, the "Nixon shocks" refer to the 1971 decision of President Richard Nixon to take the United States off the gold standard. Because it was a unilateral act, it had significant, largely negative, repercussions in global financial markets. The phrase also refers to Nixon's decision to visit communist China in 1972 without notifying Japan, much to the "shock" and chagrin of the Japanese government.

11. On the history of Okinawa after reversion, and especially its discontents, see Arasaki, *Okinawa gendaishi*, especially 20–78. On the change in traffic patterns, see 70–73. Gushiken appeared in print advertisements for the driving change in local papers in Okinawa; see "Rainen 7 gatsu 30 nichi. Okinawa no kōtsū ga kawaru hi," *Okinawa taimusu*, 14 October 1977, 4. I have also seen a television commercial that depicts Gushiken using left and right jabs to demonstrate which side of the road cars and people should use after the transition. For an excellent analysis of the economic and social situation of postwar Okinawa, see Purves, *The Ryukyu-Okinawa History & Culture Website*, http://www.niraikanai.wwma.net (accessed 1 July 2010). Several works have examined the still tense contemporary relationship of Japan, the United States, and Okinawa, including Hein and Selden, eds., *Islands of Discontent*; Johnson, ed., *Okinawa*; Johnson, *Blowback*, 34–64; and Inoue, *Okinawa and the U.S. Military*.

12. Quoted in Ashizawa, *Okinawa no hoshi Gushiken Yōkō*, 38.

13. "Gushiken, Sekai Chanpion ni," *Okinawa taimusu*, 11 October 1976, 1; "Yattā sekai ichi," *Okinawa taimusu*, 11 October 1976, 9. The sports page includes multiple articles with a banner heading that reads, "Okinawa kara 'sekai no hoshi' tanjō," *Okinawa taimusu*, 11 October 1976, 6. The brief biographical profile appears on the same page in "Purofiru: chanpion Gushiken Yōkō 'tame' ni umaretekita otoko."

14. "Gekitō, kusen ni hiyahiya terebi o mae ni sakan na seien," *Okinawa taimusu*, 31 January 1977, 9.

15. "Takamaru Gushiken fībā Ishigaki kara taikyo ōendan," *Okinawa taimusu*, 7 March 1981, 15.

16. "Nanado habataku *kanmuriwashi* kaijō no kenjinkai yan'ya no dai ōen," *Okinawa taimusu*, 8 January 1979, 9.

17. Uehara Susumu, "Dokusha kara: chanpion o senkyosen ni dasanai de," *Okinawa taimusu*, 7 June 1980, 4.

18. This point was mentioned nearly every time Ishigaki fans or Gushiken's family were discussed. One article written following Gushiken's ninth title defense concluded with a call to rectify the fact that his mother had not been able to see her son fight ("Konban no wadai: kyūkaime no bōei," *Okinawa taimusu*, 30 July 1979, evening edition, 1).

19. Uehara Susumu, "Dokusha kara: chanpion o senkyosen ni dasanai de," *Okinawa taimusu*, 7 June 1980, 4. The rumors about Gushiken's possible involvement in the campaigns had been mentioned on the front page of the paper only a few days earlier ("Senkyo purizumu," *Okinawa taimusu*, 5 June 1980, 1).

20. For several examples of diversity and tensions within Okinawa's post-reversion "community of protest," see Tanji, *Myth, Protest and Struggle in Okinawa*, 106–76; see also Inoue, *Okinawa and the U.S. Military*, especially 98–156.

21. Nagadō, *Bokusā Gushiken Yōkō to seishun gunzō*, 192–93.

22. Although it appeared frequently throughout his career, this phrase became even more common in the immediate aftermath of Gushiken's loss of the title. For one example of an article, see "Gushiken no kiseki," *Okinawa taimusu*, 10 March 1981, 8. For fan letters with similar phrases, see Ishihara Shōke, "Dokusha kara: Gushiken ni reiden o!" *Okinawa taimusu*, 22 March 1981, 4; and Nashiro Hakajirō, "Dokusha kara: Gushiken-kun yo gokurōsan," *Okinawa taimusu*, 18 March 1981, 5. On comments from politicians at the prefectural assembly, see "Kisha no memo: ōja chiru—ni kengi mo namida," *Okinawa taimusu*, 10 March 1981, 1.

23. Ishihara Shōke, "Dokusha kara: chiisana kyojin Gushiken Yōkō," *Okinawa taimusu*, 14 April 1979, 10.

24. Nashiro Hakajirō, "Dokusha kara: Gushiken Yōkō-kun o tataeru," *Okinawa taimusu*, 8 June 1980, 6.

25. Itō Tsutomu, "Dokusha kara: chanpion ni Okinawa o mita," *Okinawa taimusu*, 1 November 1979, 4.

26. Six different Japanese boxers held world titles during Gushiken's tenure as world champion. All lost the title within a year, and three failed to defend their title even once; see "Nihon bokushingushi nenpyō" in Wārudo bokushingu hen-

shūbu, ed., *Nippon Sports Mook 31*, 192–93. Articles from a variety of magazines often specifically described Gushiken as Japan's sole (using phrases like *yuiitsu* or *tada hitori*) world champion.

27. Most of Gushiken's title fights received brief mention in the *New York Times*, where he is almost invariably described as "Yoko Gushiken of Japan," with no mention of Okinawa. See as one example, "Gushiken of Japan Keeps Junior Flyweight Crown," *New York Times*, 31 January 1977, 14.

28. By this point, *Hōchi shinbun*, which had once been an independent newspaper, was part of the Yomiuri media conglomerate and focused primarily on sports-related news. See "Fan ga eranda 'yume no MVP,'"; and "Fan ga erabu 'yume no MVP,' kimaru."

29. See, for example, coverage from the *Okinawa taimusu*, which includes a photo of Ōhira examining Gushiken's hands: "Ureshii shōri hōkoku," *Okinawa taimusu*, 8 January 1979, evening edition, 3.

30. The first two recipients were Oh and the composer Koga Masao. For recurring references to the award in relation to Gushiken, see "Kokumin eiyoshō o nerau: Gushiken no 'gōgoroku'"; "Kokumin eiyoshō o nerau: Gushiken no V12 chōsen"; and "Waido tokushū: eikō no otokotachi no fuan." Articles in the *Okinawa taimusu* also referred to popular support for honoring Gushiken; see "Konban no wadai: tōkon 'V12,'" *Okinawa taimusu*, 3 June 1980, evening edition, 1.

31. On two different occasions during my stay in Japan, I turned on the television and was surprised to see Gushiken as one of the featured guests on the comedy talk shows that are common on both daytime and primetime television in Japan. On the evening when I was first introduced to Gushiken in November 2004, at a restaurant in Tokyo, several people came over to shake his hand and have their pictures taken with the "champion."

32. Takasaki, "Takasaki Mieko no iro iro taidan 10," 58.

33. Ibid.; see also the Introduction to the present study.

34. Gushiken, *Ringu wa boku no senjō da*, 28–33.

35. Ashizawa, *Okinawa no hoshi Gushiken Yōkō*, 51–61. For Ashizawa's speculation on the causes of Gushiken's below-average size, see 55–56.

36. Gushiken, *Ringu wa boku no senjō da,* 35.

37. Ibid., 31 and 35–36; and Ashizawa, *Okinawa no hoshi Gushiken Yōkō*, 60–61.

38. Gushiken, *Ringu wa boku no senjō da*, 36; and Ashizawa, *Okinawa no hoshi Gushiken Yōkō*, 60–61.

39. Gushiken, *Ringu wa boku no senjō da*, 32; and Ashizawa, *Okinawa no hoshi Gushiken Yōkō*, 61–62.

40. In an interesting parallel, Hitomi had also contemplated quitting school while she was training to become a physical education teacher, only to decide she owed it to her family to finish (see Chapter 3). On this period in Gushiken's life, his personal struggles with life in high school, and his introduction to boxing, see Gushiken, *Ringu wa boku no senjō da,* 37–56; and Ashizawa, *Okinawa no hoshi Gushiken Yōkō*, 87–92. Ashizawa generally skips this exploration of Gushiken's first months at school and jumps right to his introduction to boxing. In his biographical account of the boxer, Nagadō also omits such details, focusing instead on how Gushiken learned about the boxing club. Perhaps mistakenly, Nagadō goes so far

as to assert that after arriving in Naha, Gushiken "never once thought 'I want to go back to Ishigaki'" (*Bokusā Gushiken Yōkō to seishun gunzō*, 48–53).

41. Gushiken, interview by author, 30 November 2004. The connotations of the term *shima no hito* here appear similar to the American slang words "hick" or "redneck." Biographical accounts by Ashizawa and Nagadō do not address these kinds of tensions with other students.

42. "Watashi to sensei: Gushiken Yōkō," *Asahi shinbun*, 16 February 1991, 29. For a similar account of his early months at school, see Gushiken, *Ringu wa boku no senjō da*, 44–46.

43. On extracurricular clubs in Japanese schools, see Cave, "*Bukatsudō*."

44. Gushiken, *Ringu wa boku no senjō da*, 51–56.

45. Ibid., 55.

46. See Nakamoto, "Zen-Nihon shakaijin senshuken taikai o oete," 3. The essay was written to indicate the assumed importance that Okinawa's participation in a recent national sports competition would play in changing Okinawan attitudes toward boxing. In one of the many seeming inconsistencies that marked the years of American control, Okinawan athletic teams regularly participated in Japanese national sporting events, beginning as early as 1952. For a brief examination of the history of sports in postwar Okinawa, see Frost, "Creating the Sporting Nation."

47. Gushiken, *Ringu wa boku no senjō da*, 55–56.

48. Ibid., 71.

49. Ibid., 58–72. For additional details of Gushiken's amateur career, including comments from his coaches and fellow boxers, see Ashizawa, *Okinawa no hoshi Gushiken Yōkō*, 87–114.

50. For details about the scholarship, the particulars of which remain somewhat unclear, see Gushiken, *Ringu wa boku no senjō da*, 74–76; and Ashizawa, *Okinawa no hoshi Gushiken Yōkō*, 111–19.

51. Ashizawa is using a play on words, since both *kin* and *kane* use the same Chinese character (*Okinawa no hoshi Gushiken Yōkō*, 85). Gushiken's chapter dealing with this period poses a question for its title, "Gold Medal or Go Pro?" ("Kin medaru ka puro iri ka?"); see Gushiken, *Ringu wa boku no senjō da*, 73. This same theme of gold versus money appears in other shorter biographical essays as well.

52. Gushiken, *Ringu wa boku no senjō da*, 83.

53. Ibid., 81–84. For additional information about Gushiken's decision to become a professional boxer, see Ashizawa, *Okinawa no hoshi Gushiken Yōkō*, 117–20. Ashizawa gives much less attention to Gushiken's concern about his family and greater emphasis to his anguish about breaking his promises to people in Okinawa.

54. For extensive details about this fight and Gushiken's resulting celebrity status, see Ashizawa, *Okinawa no hoshi Gushiken Yōkō*, 13–42.

55. For a brief overview of Gushiken's overall career, as well as details concerning other champions from Okinawa, see "Gushiken Yōkō to Okinawa no chanpiontachi," in Wārudo bokushingu henshūbu, ed. *Nippon Sports Mook 31*, 150–52.

56. For one example, see an interview published in the weekly magazine *Shūkan shōsetsu* emphasizing Gushiken's sexual "virginity" (*dōtei*) and his earnings of

100 million yen from his fifth title-defense fight ("Taitoru bōei no Nihon kiroku o mezasu dōtei chanpion," 122). In 1978, an article in the *Asahi shinbun* described Gushiken as a "100-million-yen boxer" ("Hito to wadai 1978 (6): ichiokuen bokusā Gushiken Yōkō," *Asahi shinbun*, 28 December 1978, 12). A 1979 article from a weekly magazine expressed surprise that Gushiken was not among the top ten on a published list of Japan's highest paid athletes ("Igai ni hikui (?)[*sic*] Gushiken no shūnyū," 31). An article from August noted that Gushiken was catching up to Oh Sadaharu in terms of income ("Ō (Kyojin) o nuita Gushiken Yōkō no kasegi," 19). Another article later in 1979 employed the epithet "V10, 300-million-yen hero" to describe Gushiken ("Gushiken Yōkō (24) no shirarezaru ketsuzoku," 38). Details about the percentages of Gushiken's winnings going to his manager are included in "Hitotsu no shiai 'hassenman-en' Gushiken no zaisan kanri hō," 19.

57. "Toppu o hashiru keirinkai 79: kasegi de miru puro supōtsu: okuman chōja wa Gushiken dake," *Asahi shinbun*, 26 December 1979, 15.

58. There are multiple examples in the popular media about Gushiken's work at the *tonkatsu* restaurant; see, for instance, "Akumade mo muyoku na sekai chanpion"; and "Tonkatsuya no sara arai kara chanpion e." An article in the mainstream journal *Chūō kōron* noted that Gushiken sent most of his fight money home to his parents ("Jinbutsu kōsaten," 46–47). For details about the house Gushiken built for his family, see, for example, "Sada Masashi, Yazawa Eikichi to wa koko ga chigau: Gushiken Yōkō (24) no 'nari agari,'" 52.

59. See, for instance, "Chanpion no shiro."

60. Details and photos of the wedding appeared in several popular magazines aimed at both male and female readers. See "'Gushiken Yōkō' 4-oku-en kekkonshiki ga kutta 'daipanchi'"; and "Saisutāto e ai no chikai." The most detailed descriptions and photographs can be found in women's specialty magazines; see especially, "Kobushi de kachitotta hanayaka na kadode." It is entirely possible that the cake was made from plastic or rubber and was not designed to be eaten. Large inedible cakes became common wedding decorations around this time. It is worth noting that the wedding was not Gushiken's first appearance in women's magazines, which had frequently featured photos depicting the previously "eligible bachelor" both inside and outside the ring, including a less than discreet shot of Gushiken in a shower turned slightly away from the camera and holding a small towel, thereby avoiding full-frontal nudity; see "Sa chanpion Gushiken Yōkō: Charenji! V12."

61. On their honeymoon, see "Gushiken fusai hanemūn kanzen tsuiseki." On their new married life, see "Teishu kanpaku!? Achira ga tsuyosugite"; and "Pin kara kiri made shiawase." On the birth of their first child and their child-rearing ideas, see, for instance, "Mama wa shikkari! Papa wa oro oro," 57–58. On the household finances of Gushiken and several other celebrities, see "Keizai & shumi."

62. The controversy generated a great deal of initial coverage. The popular weekly magazine *Shūkan bunshun* broke the story and ran a five-part series beginning on 11 March 1982. For an overview of the controversy, see Saki, *Eiyū*, 6–28. Various Japanese newspapers, including the *Okinawa taimusu*, ran stories as well. The drugging scandal and its implications were discussed during at least two dif-

ferent committee meetings during the 96th session of the National Diet. See Postwar Diet Records, Session 96, Shūgiin hōmu iinkai 6 gō, 5; and Postwar Diet Records, Session 96, Shūgiin yosan iinkai 2 gō, 22. (accessed 1 July 2010).

63. On one of his restaurants, see "Moto yūmei puro supōtsu senshu ga keiei-suru mise no aji"; on his speedboat racing career, see "POWER BOAT"; on his initial plans to open a gym in Tokyo, see "Pīpuru."

64. Allinson, *Japan's Postwar History*, 138–39.

65. On the connection between sports and television, see Partner, *Assembled in Japan*, 162–66 and 237. For information on early sports broadcasts, see Guttmann and Thompson, *Japanese Sports*, 168.

66. I encountered several advertisements for televisions featuring the champion; for one example, see *Okinawa taimusu*, 3 April 1979, 7. In many instances these ads appeared at the bottom of the sports page, and a number included notes of congratulations on Gushiken's latest title defense.

67. My comments on advertisements are based on my own observations during my survey of various pre- and postwar media sources. In the course of my research, I encountered only a handful of advertisements in the prewar period that featured identifiable athletes—most did not include images of people at all and those that did featured illustrations or sketches of abstract figures. In contrast, with Gushiken, I encountered advertisements for cars, televisions, curry, watches, boxing goods, travel agencies, restaurants, airlines, elevators, printing companies, and numerous other products and services, most of which prominently featured his picture and a statement from the "champion" himself. I have not seen Gushiken's commercial for Kentucky Fried Chicken, but he mentioned the advertisement during my interview with him on 30 November 2004.

68. Tsurumi, *A Cultural History of Postwar Japan, 1945–1980*, 69.

69. The night Gushiken won the title was the same night that Oh tied Babe Ruth's record for career homeruns. An article about the accomplishment was one of the only other major stories featured on the *Okinawa taimusu* sports page reporting Gushiken's initial world-championship victory ("Ō 714-gō, Rūsu to narabu," *Okinawa taimusu*, 11 October 1976, 6). Oh broke Hank Aaron's record in 1977 to become the world-record holder. An example of their comments about each other can be found in a series of "conversations" (*taidan*) between Gushiken and other Japanese sports stars, including Oh, republished in 1981 as part of the Gushiken commemorative edition of a popular boxing magazine ("Honshi o kazatta chō sūpā sutā taidan shijō saigen daijesuto," 107–10).

70. Like the other stars examined in this study, Oh's life story reflects multiple elements of the sports-star paradigm. He has provided several autobiographical accounts, including one in English. In Japanese, see Ō Sadaharu, *Boku to hōmuran*; Ō Sadaharu, *Ō Sadaharu no nikki*; Ō Sadaharu, *Kaisō*; and Ō Sadaharu, *Ō Sadaharu*. In English, see Oh and Falkner, *Sadaharu Oh*. For an insightful analysis of Oh's life story and his famous "oriental" training methods, see Kelly, "Learning to Swing."

71. Kelly, "Blood and Guts in Japanese Professional Baseball," 105–7. Of the two stars, Nagashima, who was Japanese, was undoubtedly more popular and remains one of the most respected baseball players in Japanese history. Analysis of the impact of Oh and Nagashima on Japanese popular culture is available in Hol-

den, "ReDotPop," *PopMatters.com*, http://www.popmatters.com/columns/holden/010108.html (accessed 1 July 2010).

72. As a national celebrity, Gushiken was preceded by Minami Saori, a singer from Okinawa who gained national fame just prior to reversion and remained popular through the early 1970s. Gushiken's years as champion overlapped with the national emergence of both Kina Shōkichi, an Okinawan rock musician, and Akamine Ken'yū, an Okinawan pitcher who was drafted by the Yomiuri Giants in 1976 and played several seasons with the team.

73. Kanehira claimed in 1980 that he had originally contemplated a different "ring name" for Gushiken, but after consulting with an expert who evaluated people's potential based on their names, he opted to go with Gushiken's family name instead (Kanehira, "Gushiken Yōkō no himitsu," 58–59).

74. Ashizawa, *Okinawa no hoshi Gushiken Yōkō*, 177.

75. Shimizu Tetsuo, "Shin Nipponjin kenkyū," 172.

76. Ibid.

77. Whether the media attention to these mistakes is read as endearing or insulting depends, of course, on how one perceives Gushiken overall. In one *Okinawa taimusu* article, for instance, such mistakes were portrayed as endearing ("Konban no wadai: shōbu no sekai," *Okinawa taimusu*, 9 March 1981, evening edition, 1). For several examples drawn from throughout Gushiken's life, see *Chocchune: Gushiken Yōkō*.

78. See, for instance, NHK ākaibusu bangumi purojekuto, "Waga Okinawa," 200.

79. See, for example, Shimoji Shigeru, "Dokusha kara: Gushiken V10 ni omou," *Okinawa taimusu*, 2 November 1979, 10; and Uehara Susumu, "Dokusha kara: chanpion o senkyosen ni dasanai de," *Okinawa taimusu*, 7 June 1980, 4.

80. See photographs from his various title fights in Bēsubōru magajinsha, *Tobe kanmuriwashi*, 7–38.

81. Nagadō, *Bokusā PART II*, 8–10.

82. After its opening, the restaurant was often pictured in boxing magazines, but it also appeared in a write-up in a women's magazine ("Gushiken Yōkō-san no o-mise 'Gushiken,'" 181). See also an earlier promotional photo and description from the entertainment magazine *Asahi geinō* ("Rensai 80: Kengyō hanjō watashi ga shujin").

83. This article appears to have been reporting on the content of a previous television program, a common practice in many weekly entertainment magazines. "Mirai no okusama no o-tenami haiken," 179.

84. *Gongu*, July supplementary issue (1980): back cover.

85. "'Fukugyō' o hajimeta Gushiken no fuan bubun," 41.

86. Takasaki, "Takasaki Mieko no iro iro taidan 10," 58.

87. For instance, see Kōdansha, *Gushiken Yōkō shashinshū*, 89; and Bēsubōru magajinsha, *Tobe kanmuriwashi*, 74.

88. "Ishigaki-jima ryojō: tensai bokusā o unda rakuen no shima," 51–55.

89. Ibid., 54; and Saki, *Eiyū*, 3–6 and 28.

90. Saki, *Eiyū*, 3–6 and 28.

91. For a summary of references to Japan's homogeneity, especially in connection with Okinawa, see Obermiller, "The Okinawan Struggle over Identity, Historical Memory, and Cultural Representation," 12–13. To be sure, there were strains within popular discourse that were quite close to the "official" position, and as I argue here, even the seeming popular embrace of difference was not always a challenge to such positions. A number of scholars have sought to debunk official and intellectual proclamations of Japan's homogeneity, resulting in several studies that highlight the long-standing, continued presence and struggles of various minority groups in Japan. See Denoon and McCormack, eds., *Multicultural Japan*; Dikotter, ed., *The Construction of Racial Identities in China and Japan*; Weiner, ed., *Japan's Minorities*; Gladney, ed., *Making Majorities*; Morris-Suzuki, *Re-inventing Japan*. In contrast, popular discourse, which acknowledged and even appears to have celebrated differences, has garnered much less attention.

92. Kelly, "Blood and Guts in Japanese Professional Baseball," 101–2.

93. For examples of players downplaying their ethnic difference, see ibid., 109. Similarly, the well-known Western-style professional wrestling star Rikidōzan, who became a national hero in the late 1950s, was from Korea. Although there were frequent rumors about his background, the wrestler claimed to be from Japan, and his Korean ancestry was erased from his public image. For an examination of Rikidōzan, see Igarashi, *Bodies of Memory*, 122–29. Gossip about athletes allegedly hiding their non-Japanese background still appears occasionally in sports coverage today. On Oh's "Japanese" training techniques, see Kelly, "Learning to Swing," especially 272–75. Practicing batting with a sword became a key component of Oh's sports-celebrity image, as evidenced by its seemingly out-of-place mention in comments from one of the writers who introduced Ashizawa's biography of Gushiken. The writer was comparing the work ethics of the two stars. Terauchi Daikichi, "Hakairyoku to reisei pēsu zukuri," foreword to Ashizawa, *Okinawa no hoshi Gushiken Yōkō*, 3.

94. In discussions of Okinawan history and contemporary society, such issues are too often overlooked, even among academics focusing their scholarly gaze on the prefecture.

95. Teratani, sketch, "Gongu no hiroba," 155.

96. "Gushiken Yōkō (24) no shirarezaru ketsuzoku 1,500-nin no haran banjō," 38–41.

97. The analysis that follows is based on the transcripts. See NHK ākaibusu bangumi purojekuto, "Waga Okinawa," 155–203.

98. Ibid., 166. Comments from one letter to the *Okinawa taimusu* indicate that residents of Okinawa also saw and paid close attention to the documentary, though we might assume that the words and cultural elements were less "unfamiliar" for them. See Shimoji Shigeru, "Dokusha kara: Gushiken V10 ni omou," *Okinawa taimusu*, 2 November 1979, 10.

99. Presumably, similar explanations or subtitles were used in the broadcast version.

100. NHK ākaibusu bangumi purojekuto, "Waga Okinawa," 166–69.

101. Ibid., 173–74.

102. In addition to the previously cited November 1979 article from *Shūkan gendai*, an excellent example of claims about Gushiken's righteous anger aiding him in the ring can be found in Ashizawa, "Gushiken bokushingu no shinzui wa Okinawajin no ikari da."

103. NHK ākaibusu bangumi purojekuto, "Waga Okinawa," 170.

104. Ibid., 176–77.

105. Ibid., 187–90.

106. Ibid., 196–97.

107. Ibid., 197.

108. Ibid., 200.

109. For examples of repetitions, see Gushiken, *Ringu wa boku no senjō da*, 220. Here Gushiken uses the less derogatory word, *yamatonchū*. Many popular magazines published variations of the quote. See, for instance, Ashizawa, "Gushiken bokushingu no shinzui wa Okinawajin no ikari da," 56. Ironically, Ashizawa switches the terms. He has Gushiken declaring that he will never lose to an *uchinanchū*, which Ashizawa glosses as a "mainlander," but *uchinanchū* is, in fact, the word that many Okinawans use to refer to themselves.

110. Debord, *The Society of the Spectacle*, 38. An example of mainstream capitalistic appropriation of dissatisfaction in American popular culture can be seen in so-called grunge music of the 1980s and 1990s.

111. NHK ākaibusu bangumi purojekuto, "Waga Okinawa," 190.

112. An example of Gushiken's frequently repeated statements confirming his "hunger" can be found in "Sada Masashi, Yazawa Eikichi to wa koko ga chigau," 48–49. For further commentary from Gushiken about the dangers of losing one's reason to fight, see "HERO INSIDE," 40–43.

113. Kina continued his music career, but has also become a peace activist and politician. "Okinawa no futari no 'senshi' tōron," 32–36. Gushiken's image as an "apolitical" Okinawan shares several similarities with O. J. Simpson, whose racial crossover appeal during his early career owed a great deal to the fact that he was "un-militant" at a time known for the "revolt of the black athlete" (Johnson and Roediger, "'Hertz, Don't It?'" 40–73).

114. At one point, unbeknownst to Gushiken, one of the television networks captured his rendition with a microphone and broadcast it. Asked about the incident in an interview, Gushiken noted his embarrassment but also declared, "Yeah, I sing. I can relax, and I really like Japan's national anthem" (Sawa, "Sawa Tamaki no 'otoko' taidan," 60). In more recent years, the Japanese flag and anthem have proven far more controversial for other Okinawans, who argue that they are symbols of Japanese imperialism and historical mistreatment of Okinawa. For several examples, including a famous flag-burning incident at a national sports event held in Okinawa in 1989, see Field, *In the Realm of a Dying Emperor*, 33–104.

115. Several of Gushiken's pre-title fights had been against mainland Japanese boxers, but these fights, by and large, receive minimal attention in accounts of his rise. Even his inter-high victories as an amateur garner little discussion in relation to Gushiken's alleged desire never to lose to a mainlander.

116. In addition to television coverage, which began in 1951, by 1960 Japan had seven daily newspapers devoted to sports; see Guttmann and Thompson, *Japanese Sports*, 166 and 168. Sports were also covered in regional sports papers, specialty magazines, and books, and were given increased space in the mainstream and popular press as well. For a summary of similar media developments and their impact on sports celebrity in Britain and the United States during the same time period, see Whannel, *Media Sport Stars*, especially 33–38.

117. Terayama, dir., *Bokusā*.

118. MacAloon, "Olympic Games and the Theory of Spectacle in Modern Societies," 273.

119. "Ekusasaizu bokushingu ni chōsen suru," 212–18.

120. Gushiken, interview by author, 30 November 2004.

121. For one example of the "second-generation *kanmuriwashi*," see "Tobe! 'kanmuriwashi nisei' Tokashiki Katsuo," front photo section. The *Asahi shinbun* described this same boxer, who was also from Okinawa and had become world champion in late 1981, as "Okinawa's next star following Gushiken" ("Tokashiki hatsuchōsen de ōza," *Asahi shinbun*, 17 December 1981, 17).

122. For examples of how Gushiken has become the subject of jokes, some of which border on cruel, see *Chocchune*. Gushiken's role in the production of this book is not completely clear. His gym's website advertises the book, and it begins with a note allegedly written by Gushiken. In this greeting, Gushiken explains that he has made many mistakes and knows that people find them amusing. That, he asserts, does not bother him because, thanks to his upbringing in Ishigaki, he has a laid-back personality, one he describes using the Okinawan word *tēgē* (*Chocchune*, 4–5).

Epilogue

EPIGRAPH. Whiting, *The Samurai Way of Baseball*, 1–2 (page citations are to paperback edition).

1. ESPN.com, "Ichiro Suzuki Stats, News, Photos," *ESPN.com*, http://sports.espn.go.com/mlb/players/profile?playerId=4570 (accessed 25 June 2010).

2. For one reference to the "curry rice balls that his wife, Yumiko, makes for him before every game," see Bob Sherwin, "The Natural Is Swinging for Fame," *New York Times*, 6 April 2008, SP 2. For more on Ichiro's personal life, including various hobbies and personal preferences, see David Shields, "Being Ichiro," *New York Times*, 16 September 2001, Magazine, 50. For additional details on Ichiro's relationship with his wife, see Whiting, *The Samurai Way of Baseball*, 22–23, 32–33, and 38.

3. For a detailed charting of Ichiro's baseball career and achievements in Japan, see Komatsu, *Ichirō intabyū*, 167–91.

4. Whiting, *The Samurai Way of Baseball*, 16.

5. Ichiro's one-name moniker generated frequent comments in the news media. For two examples, see Chuck Johnson, "Suzuki: Mariners' Star Import Japanese Batting Champ Is Ready to Succeed in Seattle," *USA Today*, 21 February 2001, 8C; and Rod Beaton, "Ichiro's Star Rises Beyond Baseball World," *USA*

Today, 10 July 2001, 2C. For one of the most thorough discussions of Ichiro's name, including historical comparisons, see Murray Chass, "Seattle's Suzuki Ready to Excel By Any Name," *New York Times*, 3 March, 2001, D3. It is not unusual in such comments to see Ichiro's name choice compared with famed soccer player Pele.

6. Barry Bonds, quoted in Whiting, *The Samurai Way of Baseball*, 20.

7. Whiting, *The Samurai Way of Baseball*, 26.

8. For "slightly built," see Murray Chass, "Seattle's Suzuki Ready to Excel By Any Name," *New York Times*, 3 March, 2001, D3; for "hardly imposing," Chuck Johnson, "Suzuki: Mariners' Star Import Japanese Batting Champ Is Ready to Succeed in Seattle," *USA Today*, 21 February 2001, 8C; for "relatively scant," Mark Zuckerman, "Tokyo West: Japanese Infusion Huge Reason for Mariners' Unbelievable Start," *Washington Times*, 30 May 2001, B1; and for "gaunt-looking," Sam Howe Verhovek, "Japan's Baseball Idol Wins Fans in Seattle," *New York Times*, 24 April 2001, A1. All of these articles include details about his height and weight.

9. Whiting, *The Samurai Way of Baseball*, 26.

10. The last article I found listing Ichiro's height at 5 feet 9 inches appeared on 16 May 2007, though his weight was listed as 170 pounds at that time (Jon Saraceno, "Ichiro Changes Perspective: Mariners [*sic*] Star Is Trying to Fulfill His Needs," *USA Today*, 16 May 2007, 1C). Articles that list his height after this point use the 5 feet 11 inches measurement also reported on the ESPN player profile mentioned above.

11. For brief references to Ichiro's successful record chase and the response in Japan, see Frederick with Sekiguchi, "Ichiro Suzuki: Heavy Hitter," 44; for a Japanese analysis of American debates about the significance of Ichiro's record, see Okuda, "Ichirō '262-hon' ni Beikoku 'dairongi,'" 118–20. See also Whiting, *The Samurai Way of Baseball*, 272.

12. For information on Whiting's intended audience, motivations behind the book, and mentions of supplementary material and corrections in the paperback version, see Whiting, *The Samurai Way of Baseball*, xi. The alternate title is listed on the copyright page of the paperback edition (iii). Hardcover copies with the original title can be found in several libraries and are still available for purchase. Whiting makes no mention about the change of title in the book itself or in his notes. The new title may reflect efforts to boost sales by linking the book to Whiting's earlier, best-selling books about what he calls "samurai baseball." At the same time, the change in the subtitle from "transformation of our national pastime" to "impact" offers a far more "neutral" assessment, hinting at concerns that American fans might be initially less receptive to outright declarations that these Japanese stars were transforming "our" game.

13. Whiting, *The Samurai Way of Baseball*, xvii.

14. Ibid., xvii.

15. Ibid., 34–36.

16. Ibid., 33.

17. Ibid., 34–35.

18. Articles often raised one or more of these points, especially those employing a more biographical perspective, including David Shields, "Being Ichiro," *New York Times*, 16 September 2001, Magazine, 50; and Rick Weber, "The Importance of Being Ichiro," *Scotland on Sunday*, 30 September 2001, 40. Many of these same points are also included in a short, glossy, photo-filled biographical account that emphasizes Ichiro's success in the major leagues and begins with an introduction titled, "Like Mike," which draws lengthy and in some cases unusual comparisons between Ichiro and NBA superstar Michael Jordan (Lazenby, *Ichiro*, 6–13). Yuka Nakamura's detailed analysis of Ichiro-related coverage in the *Seattle Times*, the *Mainichi Daily Newspaper*, and *Sports Nippon* offers several other examples ("The Samurai Sword Cuts Both Ways.").

19. For example, see Jack Todd, "Ichiro Is Throwback Superstar," *The Gazette* (Montreal, Quebec), 24 October 2001, E1; and Dan Daly, "Mariners' Ichiro Leads Baseball's Newest Wave," *Washington Times*, 17 May 2001, B1.

20. Greene with Belson, "The Mariners Catch a Tsunami," 98.

21. Whiting cites the opinion of Shawn Wong, an Asian-American professor of English at the University of Washington (*The Samurai Way of Baseball*, 41). Daisuke Matsuzaka's first season with the Boston Red Sox sparked similar popular responses; see Gordon, *Nihonjin ga shiranai Matsuzaka mejā kakumei*. It is perhaps worth noting that Ichiro's success was portrayed as a potential benefit for Asian-Americans; see David Shields, "Being Ichiro," *New York Times*, 16 September 2001, Magazine, 50; Alan Schwartz, "Ideas & Trends: In the Spirit of Koufax," *New York Times*, 9 September 2001, Week In Review, 6; and Patricia Wen, "Finding New Heroes Asian-Americans Take a Quiet Pride in Successes in the Athletic Arena," *Boston Globe*, 27 April 2001, A1.

22. Rains, *Baseball Samurais*, back cover. Emphasis is added.

23. On "Asian invasion," see Chuck Johnson, "Suzuki: Mariners' Star Import Japanese Batting Champ Is Ready to Succeed in Seattle," *USA Today*, 21 February 2001, 8C; and "Ichiro The Latest Super Hero For Seattle," *Toronto Star*, 13 May 2001, sports section. On the "apparent future of the game," see Art Spander, "The Sun Also Rises on America's National Pastime," *Sunday Herald*, 6 May 2001, 15.

24. Welky, "Viking Girls, Mermaids, and Little Brown Men," 39–41. One of the quotations in praise of the author that appears in Whiting's book also refers to the Japanese "invasion." Another mentions the "near-maniacal" nature of Japanese players' pursuit of the game; both are quoted in Whiting, *The Samurai Way of Baseball*, i.

25. See Jeff Blair, "Japanese Players Long Way from Home," *Globe and Mail* (Canada), 12 May 2001, S5. This article cites the "Ichiro Effect" to explain why significant numbers of Japanese players were beginning to appear at tryouts for North American baseball teams below the MLB level.

26. Masujima, "How Japanese Athletes Are Changing Japan's Image at Home and Abroad," 4. On Japanese coverage of Ichiro's first season, much of which raises similar points, see Nakamura, "The Samurai Sword Cuts Both Ways," 473–76.

27. Frederick with Sekiguchi, "Ichiro Suzuki: Heavy Hitter," 44.

28. Ibid. Parenthetical statement included in the original.

29. Masujima, "How Japanese Athletes Are Changing Japan's Image at Home and Abroad," 2. Whiting cites Masujima and several other examples as proof of Ichiro's positive impact on the Japanese mindset (*The Samurai Way of Baseball*, 42–49).

30. Masujima, "How Japanese Athletes Are Changing Japan's Image at Home and Abroad," 1.

31. The last Japanese-born *yokozuna*, Takanohana, retired in 2003. According to the official *banzuke* ranking for the May 2010 sumo tournament, four of the top six wrestlers were not Japanese, including the sole *yokozuna* and three of the five *ōzeki*. See "Gogatsu basho banzuke," *Ōzumō,* updated April 2010, http://sumo.goo.ne.jp/hon_basho/banzuke/ban_1.html (accessed 1 July 2010).

32. The success of the Chinese national team at the 2008 Beijing Olympics, especially in leading the gold medal count, raises intriguing possibilities. As of this writing, however, it remains too soon to tell whether these achievements will unsettle the kinds of long-standing trends in sports mentioned here, or whether Chinese athletic success, like Japan's one-time dominance of swimming, may fall from the leader board and all but disappear from broader global sporting memory. It is also worth noting that China's "surprising" success sparked extensive discussion in the American media, including efforts to downplay its significance or suggest that Chinese athletes are mindless servants of the state who do not enjoy what they do and are forced into hard training despite potential health risks. For one example, see Barbara Demick, "China's Gold Medals Came at a High Price," *Los Angeles Times*, 26 August 2008, http://www.latimes.com/sports/la-fg-hardship26-2008aug26,0,2347697.story (accessed 2 July 2010).

33. In November 2004, the cover of the monthly Japanese men's magazine *Brutus* featured Matsui Hideki, a widely popular Japanese player for the New York Yankees, declaring, "Matsui Isn't a Superstar Just Because He's Good at Baseball." The theme of the monthly issue was "Be a Gentleman," clearly suggesting that the secret to Matsui's stardom lies in the fact that he is a "gentleman" (*shinshi*). See Fujiwara, "Matsui Hideki ga sūpāsutā nano wa yakyū ga umai kara dake dewa arimasen," 34–39 and cover.

34. Ichiro offers several examples of his relationship with and respect for his father in Komatsu, *Ichirō intabyū*, 113–23.

35. Unexplained, and generally stereotypical references to samurai, Zen, eastern philosophy, and swords were readily apparent in coverage of Ichiro during his first year with the Mariners. For a handful of examples, see David Shields, "Being Ichiro," *New York Times*, 16 September 2001, Magazine, 50; Chuck Johnson, "Suzuki: Mariners' Star Import Japanese Batting Champ Is Ready to Succeed in Seattle," *USA Today*, 21 February 2001, 8C; Bill Charland, "In Baseball, 'Ichiro' Translates 'Wow!'" *Christian Science Monitor*, 22 June 2001, 12; and Hiroshi Osedo, "Japan Finds Electrifying New Exports," *Courier Mail* (Queensland, Australia), 14 July 2001, 21. Similar references are also employed in several books about Ichiro, including Rains, *Baseball Samurais*; Shields, *"Baseball Is Just Baseball"*; and Lazenby, *Ichiro*. Interestingly, after Lazenby describes Ichiro as a "samurai, those ancient Japanese warriors revered for their heart and discipline and skill with a sword," he

also notes that "Michael [Jordan], too, has been something of a Zen warrior" (Lazenby, *Ichiro*, 8). Apparently, then, Ichiro was really just being "Like Mike" by being a samurai. As the revised title of his book suggests, Whiting also employs similar images in his later examinations of Ichiro. On Ichiro being distinctly Japanese, see the comments of Shawn Wong, quoted in Whiting, *The Samurai Way of Baseball*, 41. On Ichiro's Zen-like qualities and the connection to martial arts, see Whiting, *The Samurai Way of Baseball*, 34–37. As noted in Chapter 3 of this study, the emphasis on Oriental mysticism as a device for explaining the success of Asian athletes is not new and continues to play a role in how such athletes are portrayed. During the World Baseball Classic held in March 2006, the press gave particular attention to the fact that Ichiro played for the Japanese national team (Matsui did not) and that Ichiro was unusually emotional on that occasion (he is generally famed for his stoicism). Ichiro allegedly declared the Japanese victory, "probably the biggest moment of my baseball career." See Alan Schwarz, "Matsuzaka's Pitching, Ichiro's Hitting Lead Japan to Inaugural World Baseball Classic Title," *Baseball America*, 20 March 2006, http://www.baseballamerica.com/today/news/060320wbcfinal.html (accessed 2 July 2010).

36. Whiting, *Ichiro kakumei*.

37. See Ponce de Leon, *Self-Exposure*, 241–73.

38. Masujima, "How Japanese Athletes Are Changing Japan's Image at Home and Abroad," 4.

39. Gushiken Yōkō, interview by author, 30 November 2004.

Bibliography

Abe Ikuo, Yasuharu Kiyohara, and Ken Nakajima. "Fascism, Sport and Society in Japan." *International Journal of the History of Sport* 14, no. 2 (August 1997): 187–99.

Abe Tomoji. "Nichi-Doku taikō kyōgi." *Shinchō* 27, no. 1 (January 1930): 17–26.

"Aidokusha kurabu." *Yakyūkai* 24, no. 11 (September 1934); *Yakyūkai* 24, no. 14 (December 1934); and *Yakyūkai* 30, no. 13 (July 1940).

"Akumade mo muyoku na sekai chanpion." *Hōseki GEM* (December 1976): 57.

Alberoni, Franceso. "The Powerless 'Elite': Theory and Sociological Research on the Phenomenon of the Stars." Trans. by Denis McQuail. In *Sociology of Mass Communications: Selected Readings*, ed. Denis McQuail, 75–98. Harmondsworth, UK: Penguin, 1972.

Allinson, Gary D. *Japan's Postwar History*. Ithaca, NY: Cornell University Press, 1997.

Amachi Shun'ichi. "Konshū rīgusen to sutā pureyā." *Bungei shunjū* (November 1930): 78–81.

Andrews, David L., and Steven J. Jackson. "Introduction: Sport Celebrities, Public Culture, and Private Experience." In *Sport Stars: The Cultural Politics of Sporting Celebrity*, ed. David L. Andrews and Steven J. Jackson, 1–19. London: Routledge, 2001.

——, eds. *Sport Stars: The Cultural Politics of Sporting Celebrity*. London: Routledge, 2001.

Aoyagi, Hiroshi. *Islands of Eight Million Smiles: Idol Performance and Symbolic Production in Contemporary Japan*. Cambridge, MA: Harvard University Asia Center, 2005.

Arakawa Kakuo. "Onnatachi no ōzumō shi 17: Ichige Nobuko + Hiroko-san." *Ōzumō* 32, no. 12 (December 1986): 124–26.

Arasaki Moriteru. *Okinawa gendaishi*. Tokyo: Iwanami shoten, 1996.

Archetti, Eduardo P. "The Spectacle of a Heroic Life: The Case of Diego Maradona." In *Sport Stars: The Cultural Politics of Sporting Celebrity*, ed. David L. Andrews and Steven J. Jackson, 151–63. London: Routledge, 2001.

Arimoto Takeshi. "Kokyō/keiro: Hitomi Kinue no tabi to sōgū—Ietebori, Amusuterudamu, Puraha." In *Orinpikku sutadīzu: fukusū no keiken, fukusū no seiji*, ed. Shimizu Satoshi, 194–216. Tokyo: Serika shobō, 2004.

"Aru hi no Sawamura Eiji." *Yakyūkai* 27, no. 12 (September 1937): 220–21.

Ashizawa Seiichi. "Gushiken bokushingu no shinzui wa Okinawajin no ikari da." *Gongu*, March supplementary issue (1980): 54–56.

———. *Okinawa no hoshi Gushiken Yōkō: wan ya kanmuriwashi*. Tokyo: Deirī supōtsu jigyōsha, 1977.

"Asia's 'Athletes of the Century.'" *News IAAF: The Official Newsletter of the International Amateur Athletic Federation*, no. 41 (May 2000): 4.

Atkins, E. Taylor. *Blue Nippon: Authenticating Jazz in Japan*. Durham, NC: Duke University Press, 2001.

Azuma, Hiroki. *Otaku: Japan's Database Animals*. Trans. by Jonathan E. Abel and Shion Kōno. Minneapolis, MN: University of Minnesota Press, 2009.

Azuma Ryōtarō. *Supōtsu to tomo ni*. Tokyo: Ōbunsha, 1953.

Baden-Powell, Robert. *Scouting for Boys*. London: C. Arthur Pearson, Ltd., 1908.

Baker, Aaron, and Todd Boyd, eds. *Out of Bounds: Sports, Media, and the Politics of Identity*. Bloomington, IN: Indiana University Press, 1997.

Bale, John. "Nyandika Maiyoro and Kipchoge Keino: Transgression, Colonial Rhetoric and the Postcolonial Athlete." In *Sport Stars: The Cultural Politics of Sporting Celebrity*, ed. David L. Andrews and Steven J. Jackson, 218–30. London: Routledge, 2001.

Bale, John, and Joe Sang. *Kenyan Running: Movement Culture, Geography, and Global Change*. London: Frank Cass, 1996.

Beckles, Hilary. "Brian Lara: (Con)testing the Caribbean Imagination." In *Sport Stars: The Cultural Politics of Sporting Celebrity*, ed. David L. Andrews and Steven J. Jackson, 243–56. London: Routledge, 2001.

Beckles, Hilary and Brian Stoddart, eds. *Liberation Cricket: West Indies Cricket Culture*. Manchester, UK: Manchester University Press, 1995.

Berry, Mary Elizabeth. *Japan in Print: Information and Nation in the Early Modern Period*. Berkeley, CA: University of California Press, 2006.

Bēsubōru magajinsha. *Tobe kanmuriwashi: Gushiken Yōkō no subete*. Tokyo: Bēsubōru magajinsha, 1979.

Betts, John Rickard. "Sporting Journalism in Nineteenth-Century America." *American Quarterly* 5, no. 1 (Spring 1953): 39–56.

Bickford, Lawrence. *Sumo and the Woodblock Print Masters*. New York: Kodansha International, 1994.

Birrell, Susan, and Mary G. McDonald, eds. *Reading Sport: Critical Essays on Power and Representation*. Boston, MA: Northeastern University Press, 2000.

Blackwood, Thomas. "Bushidō Baseball? Three 'Fathers' and the Invention of a Tradition." *Social Science Japan Journal* 11, no. 2 (November 2008): 223–40.

Bolitho, Harold. "Frolicking Dragons: Mythic Terror and the Sumo Tradition." In *Sport: Nationalism and Internationalism*. The Australian Society for Sports History, no. 2, 2–22. Campelltown, NSW, Australia: The Australian Society for Sports History, 1987.

——. "Sumō and Popular Culture: The Tokugawa Period." In *The Japanese Trajectory: Modernization and Beyond*, ed. Gavan McCormack and Yoshio Sugimoto, 17–32. Cambridge, UK: Cambridge University Press, 1988.

Boorstin, Daniel. *The Image: A Guide to Pseudo-Events in America*. New York: Harper & Row, 1961.

Bourdieu, Pierre. *Distinction: A Social Critique of the Judgement of Taste*. Trans. Richard Nice. Cambridge, MA: Harvard University Press, 1984.

Brockmeier, Jens. "Autobiographical Time." *Narrative Inquiry* 10, no. 1 (2000): 51–73.

Brownell, Susan. *Beijing Games: What the Olympics Mean to China*. Lanham, MD: Rowman & Littlefield, 2008.

——. "Thinking Dangerously: The Person and His Ideas." In *Body Cultures: Essays on Sport, Space and Identity*, by Henning Eichberg, ed. John Bale and Chris Philo, 22–44. London: Routledge, 1998.

——. *Training the Body for China: Sports in the Moral Order of the People's Republic*. Chicago, IL: University of Chicago Press, 1995.

Budd, Michael Anton. *The Sculpture Machine: Physical Culture and Body Politics in the Age of Empire*. New York: New York University Press, 1997.

Bullock, Steven R. *Playing for Their Nation: Baseball and the American Military during World War II*. Lincoln, NE: University of Nebraska Press, 2004.

Burchell, Graham, Colin Gordon, and Peter Miller, eds. *The Foucault Effect: Studies in Governmentality*. Chicago, IL: University of Chicago Press, 1991.

Burns, Susan L. "Constructing the National Body: Public Health and the Nation in Nineteenth-Century Japan." In *Nation Work: Asian Elites and National Identities*, ed. Timothy Brook and Andre Schmid, 17–49. Ann Arbor, MI: University of Michigan Press, 2000.

Capra, Frank, and Joris Ivens, dirs. *Know Your Enemy: Japan*. 63 min. 1945. Videocassette.

Cashmore, Ellis. *Beckham*. Cambridge, UK: Polity Press, 2002.

Cave, Peter. "*Bukatsudō*: The Educational Role of Japanese School Clubs." *Journal of Japanese Studies* 30, no. 2 (Summer 2004): 383–415.

"Chanpion no shiro." *Bokushingu magajin* 9, no. 3 (28 February 1979): 105–10.

Chapman, David L. "Sandow: The Man Who Made the World Mad for Muscle." *Sandow Museum*. 2001. http://www.sandowmuseum.com/sandowtwo.html (website discontinued)

Chocchune: Gushiken Yōkō: nōnai fantajī. Tokyo: Wani bukkusu, 2005.

Christy, Alan. "The Making of Imperial Subjects in Okinawa." In *Formations of Colonial Modernity in East Asia*, ed. Tani E. Barlow, 141–69. Durham, NC: Duke University Press, 1997.

Condry, Ian. *Hip-Hop Japan: Rap and the Paths of Cultural Globalization*. Durham, NC: Duke University Press, 2006.

Connell, R. W. *Masculinities*. Berkeley, CA: University of California Press, 1995.

Corrigan, Peter. "Imran Khan: The Road from Cricket to Politics." In *Sport Stars: The Cultural Politics of Sporting Celebrity*, ed. David L. Andrews and Steven J. Jackson, 231–42. London: Routledge, 2001.

Cowen, Tyler. *What Price Fame?* Cambridge, MA: Harvard University Press, 2000.

Cramer, Richard Ben. *Joe DiMaggio: The Hero's Life*. New York: Touchstone, 2000.

Crepeau, Richard C. "Pearl Harbor: A Failure of Baseball?" *Journal of Popular Culture* 15, no. 4 (Spring 1982): 67–74.

Cuyler, P. L. *Sumo: From Rite to Sport*. New York: Weatherhill, 1985.

Daidō Bun. *Puro yakyū gōketsu den (jō)*. Tokyo: Bēsubōru magajinsha, 1986.

"Daitōryō to Hitachiyama." *Bōken sekai* 1, no. 1 (January 1908): 112.

"Debisu Kappu wa dare no te ni." *Nihon shōnen* 32, no. 9 (September 1937): 270.

Debord, Guy. *The Society of the Spectacle*. Trans. by Donald Nicholson-Smith. New York: Zone Books, 1995.

de Cordova, Richard. *Picture Personalities: The Emergence of the Star System in America*. Urbana, IL: University of Illinois Press, 1990.

Denoon, Donald, and Gavan McCormack, eds. *Multicultural Japan: Palaeolithic to Post-Modern*. New York: Cambridge University Press, 1997.

Dewanoumi Taniemon. *Sumō hisshō dokugakusho*. Tokyo: San'yūdō shoten, 1923. Originally published 1918.

Dikotter, Frank, ed. *The Construction of Racial Identities in China and Japan: Historical and Contemporary Perspectives*. Honolulu, HI: University of Hawai'i Press, 1997.

Dower, John W. *Embracing Defeat: Japan in the Wake of World War II*. New York: W. W. Norton & Company, 1999.

Dyer, Richard. *Heavenly Bodies: Film Stars and Society*. New York: St. Martin's Press, 1986.

Dyreson, Mark. "Regulating the Body and the Body Politic: American Sport, Bourgeois Culture, and the Language of Progress, 1880–1920," in *The New American Sport History: Recent Approaches and Perspectives*, ed. S. W. Pope, 121–44. Urbana, IL: University of Illinois Press, 1997.

Edamatsu Shigeyuki, Sugiura Tadashi, and Yagi Kōsuke, eds. *Meiji nyūsu jiten*. Tokyo: Mainichi komyunikēshonzu, 1983–86.

Eichberg, Henning. *Body Cultures: Essays on Sport, Space, and Identity*. Ed. John Bale and Chris Philo. London: Routledge, 1998.

——. "'Gefährlich Denken.' Über Rationalität und Angst in der Sportwissenschaft," *Stadion* (1990): 234. Trans. and quoted in Susan Brownell. "Thinking Dangerously: The Person and His Ideas." In *Body Cultures: Essays on Sport, Space and Identity*, ed. John Bale and Chris Philo, 22–44. London: Routledge, 1998.

Eizō no seiki dai 11-shū: JAPAN: Sekai ga mita Meiji Taishō Shōwa. Produced by NHK hōsō. 75 minutes. NHK entāpuraizu: 2005. DVD.

"Ekusasaizu bokushingu ni chōsen suru." *Shūkan hōseki* (30 November 1995): 212–18.

Emi Sui'in. *Busō no maki: gunji shōsetsu*. Tokyo: Hakubunkan, 1904.

——. "Dewanoumi o itamu." *Sumō zasshi*. Quoted in Shikimori Inosuke. *Hitachiyama Taniemon: kindai sumō o kakuritsu shita kyōdo no kakusei*, 118–19.

ESPN.com. "Ichiro Suzuki Stats, News, Photos." *ESPN.com*. 2010. http://sports.espn.go.com/mlb/players/profile?playerId=4570

"Fan ga erabu 'yume no MVP,' kimaru." *Shūkan Yomiuri* (20 January 1980): 171–73.

"Fan ga eranda 'yume no MVP.'" *Shūkan Yomiuri* (24 January 1979): back photo pages.

Feder-Kane, Abigail M. "'A Radiant Smile from the Lovely Lady': Overdetermined Femininity in 'Ladies' Figure Skating." In *Reading Sport: Critical Essays on Power and Representation*, ed. Susan Birrell and Mary G. McDonald, 206–33. Boston, MA: Northeastern University Press, 2000.

Field, Norma. *In the Realm of a Dying Emperor: Japan at Century's End*. New York: Vintage Books, 1993.

Foucault, Michel. "Governmentality." In *The Foucault Effect: Studies in Governmentality*, ed. Graham Burchell, Colin Gordon, and Peter Miller, 87–104. Chicago, IL: University of Chicago Press, 1991.

Frederick, Jim, with Toko Sekiguchi. "Ichiro Suzuki: Heavy Hitter." *TIME Asia* 164, no. 15, special edition (11 October 2004): 44.

Frost, Dennis J. "Creating the Sporting Nation: Okinawa and Kokutai." Paper presented at the Graduate Student Conference on East Asia at Columbia University. New York, NY. 2003.

Fujii Iseji. "Nankai-gun Iwamoto shushō o heiei ni tou." *Yakyūkai* 28, no. 15 (November 1938): 187–89.

———. "Zuisō: Kyojin-gun Sawamura tōshu." *Yakyūkai* 31, no. 21 (October 1941): 94–96.

Fujita Keiji. "Sawamura-shō ni tsuite kangaeru." *Puro yakyū kiroku jānaru*. December 2003. http://www.baseball.per.sg/column/200312.htm (website discontinued)

Fujitani, Takashi. *Splendid Monarchy: Power and Pageantry in Modern Japan*. Berkeley, CA: University of California Press, 1996.

Fujiwara Shin'ya. "Matsui Hideki ga sūpāsutā nano wa yakyū ga umai kara dake dewa arimasen." *Brutus* (November 2004): 34–39.

Fukuda Tadanosuke. "Rune Rakosuto." *Kaizō* 9, no. 8 (August 1927): 75.

"'Fukugyō' o hajimeta Gushiken no fuan bubun." *Shūkan gendai* (13 April 1978): 41.

Funabashi Seiichi. *Sumō ki*. Tokyo: Besubōru magajinsha, 1982.

Furukawa Miki. *Edo jidai ōzumō*. Tokyo: Yūzankaku, 1968.

Furushō Kunio. *Dai issen ni tateru josei*. Tokyo: Kinseidō, 1927.

Gaimushō. "Taiiku narabi ni undō kyōgi kankei zakken dai 1-kan, no. 31: honpō 'Orinpikku' senshu Kanada kyōgikai shutsujō kankei." 28 November 1929. Reference code B04012464100. Ajia rekishi shiryō sentā. http://www.jacar.go.jp/

———. "Taiiku narabi ni undō kyōgi kankei zakken dai 1-kan, no. 48: 'Mirurosu asurechikku asoshiēshon' no Hitomi Kinue shōsei kankei." 6 November 1929. Reference code B04012465800. Ajia rekishi shiryō sentā. http://www.jacar.go.jp/

Gamson, Joshua. *Claims to Fame: Celebrity in Contemporary America*. Berkeley, CA: University of California Press, 1994.

Garon, Sheldon. "Women's Groups and the Japanese State: Contending Approaches to Political Integration, 1890–1945." *Journal of Japanese Studies* 19, no. 1 (Winter 1993): 5–41.

Gems, Gerald. *The Athletic Crusade: Sport and American Cultural Imperialism*. Lincoln, NE: University of Nebraska Press, 2006.

Giardina, Michael D. "Global Hingis: Flexible Citizenship and the Transnational Celebrity." In *Sport Stars: The Cultural Politics of Sporting Celebrity*, ed. David L. Andrews and Steven J. Jackson, 201–17. London: Routledge, 2001.

Gladney, Dru C., ed. *Making Majorities: Constituting the Nation in Japan, Korea, China, Malaysia, Fiji, Turkey, and the United States*. Stanford, CA: Stanford University Press, 1998.

Gledhill, Christine, ed. *Stardom: Industry of Desire*. London: Routledge, 1991.

Gluck, Carol. *Japan's Modern Myths: Ideology in the Late Meiji Period*. Princeton, NJ: Princeton University Press, 1985.

Gordon, Andrew. *Nihonjin ga shiranai Matsuzaka mejā kakumei*. Tokyo: Asahi shinbunsha, 2007.

Gordon, Colin. "Government Rationality: An Introduction." In *The Foucault Effect: Studies in Governmentality*, ed. Graham Burchell, Colin Gordon, and Peter Miller, 1–51. Chicago, IL: University of Chicago Press, 1991.

Gorn, Elliott J. *The Manly Art: Bare-Knuckle Prize Fighting in American*. Ithaca, NY: Cornell University Press, 1986.

Goswami, Manu. *Producing India: From Colonial Economy to National Space*. Chicago, IL: University of Chicago Press, 2004.

Greene, Jay, with Ken Belson. "The Mariners Catch a Tsunami." *BusinessWeek* no. 3738 (25 June 2001): 98.

Gusfield, Joseph. "Sports as Story: Content and Form in Agonistic Games." In *The Olympics and Cultural Exchange: East/West and South/North*, ed. Kang Shinpyo, John MacAloon, Roberto DaMatta, 207–38. Seoul: Institute for Ethnological Studies, Hanyang University, 1987.

"Gushiken fusai hanemūn kanzen tsuiseki: Nyū Yōkū hen 1." *Shūkan myōjō* (16 April 1981): front photo section.

Gushiken Yōkō. Interview by author. 30 November 2004. Tape recording. Shirai-Gushiken supōtsu jimu. Tokyo, Japan.

———. *Ringu wa boku no senjō da*. Tokyo: Kōdansha, 1979.

"'Gushiken Yōkō' 4-oku-en kekkonshiki ga kutta 'daipanchi.'" *Shūkan Shinchō* (19 March 1981): 156–59.

"Gushiken Yōkō (24) no shirarezaru ketsuzoku 1,500-nin no haran banjo." *Shūkan gendai* (15 November 1979): 38–41.

"Gushiken Yōkō-san no o-mise 'Gushiken.'" *Shufu no tomo* (January 1983): 181.

Guttmann, Allen. *From Ritual to Record*. New York, Columbia University Press, 1978.

Guttmann, Allen, and Lee Thompson. *Japanese Sports: A History*. Honolulu, HI: University of Hawai'i Press, 2001.

Gyōda Shigeharu. "Rikujō kyōgi yawa." *Shinseinen* 8, no. 3 (February 1927): 236–41.

Haga Tadahito, ed. *Joshi shinkokubun shinpan kaisei*. Tokyo: Fuzanbō, 1937.

Hagiwara, Miyoko. "Japanese Women's Sports and Physical Education under the Influence of Their Traditional Costumes." In *Civilization in Sport History*, ed. Shigeo Shimizu, 257–69. Kobe: Kobe University, 1987.

Hall, John Whitney. "The Castle Town and Japan's Modern Urbanization." In *Studies in the Institutional History of Early Modern Japan*, ed. John W. Hall and Marius B. Jansen, 169–88. Princeton, NJ: Princeton University Press, 1968.

Hanley, Susan B. *Everyday Things in Premodern Japan: The Hidden Legacy of Material Culture*. Berkeley, CA: University of California Press, 1997.

"Hanseiki buri no shin jijitsu: *Akai inazuma: Hitomi Kinue* ga aishita hito." *Sandē Mainichi* (29 November 1992): 154–58.

Harishige Keiki. "Shōwa no supōtsu kai." *Bungei shunjū* (March 1927): 61–70.

Harootunian, Harry D. *Overcome by Modernity: History, Culture, and Community in Interwar Japan*. Princeton, NJ: Princeton University Press, 2000.

——. "The Progress of Japan and the Samurai Class, 1868–1882." *Pacific Historical Review* 28, no. 3 (August 1959): 255–66.

Hashido Gantestu. "Supōtsu geppyō." *Taiyō* 34, no. 2 (February 1928): 249.

Hashido Makoto. "Meiji kara Taishō e no supōtsu." *Taiyō* 33, no. 8 (June 1927): 221–22.

Hashimoto Kazuo. *Nihon supōtsu hōsō shi*. Tokyo: Taishūkan shoten, 1992.

Hein, Laura, and Mark Selden, eds. *Islands of Discontent: Okinawan Responses to Japanese and American Power*. Lanham, MD: Rowman & Littlefield, 2003.

"HERO INSIDE: Gushiken Yōkō no muteki muketten do o zenkakudo chekku." *GORO* (28 February 1980): 40–43.

Hikoyama Kōzō. *Yokozuna den*. Tokyo: Bēsubōru magajinsha, 1953.

Hirabayashi Hatsunosuke. "Gendai o shōchō suru mono." *Chūō kōron* 44, no. 1 (January 1929): 150–52.

Hirai, Hajime. "Hideo Nomo: Pioneer or Defector." In *Sports Stars: The Cultural Politics of Sporting Celebrity*, ed. David L. Andrews and Steven J. Jackson, 187–200. London: Routledge, 2001.

Hirose Kenzō. "Orinpikku de Nihon wa katsu ka." *Chūō kōron* 47, no. 3 (March 1932): 205.

Hitachiyama. "Japanese Wrestling." *The Independent . . . Devoted to the Consideration of Politics, Social and Economic Tendencies, History, Literature, and the Arts* 68, no. 3068 (19 September 1907): 684.

"Hitachiyama no shitsubō." *Sumō sekai*, no. 4 (August 1912): 3.

Hitachiyama Taniemon. "Sumō no kami." *Kabuki*, no. 117 (1910): 108–9.

Hitachiyama Taniemon, with Gojō Tamekoto. *Sumō taikan*. Tokyo: Bun'unsha, 1909.

——. *Sumō taikan*. Tokyo: Hitachiyama-kai, 1914.

Hitomi Kinue. *Gōru ni hairu*. Tokyo: Isseisha, 1931. Reprinted in *Supaiku no ato/Gōru ni hairu*. Denki sōsho, vol. 154. Tokyo: Ōzorasha, 1994.

——. "Joshi to undō kyōgi." In *Katei kagaku taikei*, vol. 26, ed. Kagawa Toyohiko, 1–225. Tokyo: Katei kagaku taikei kankōkai, 1930.

——. "Onna toshite no watashi no nichijō seikatsu." *Fujin saron* (September 1929): 4–8.

——. "Onna wa shosen onna." *Kaizō* 9, no. 2 (February 1927): 80–82.

——. "Rikujō kyōgi." In *Fujin kōron daigaku: supōtsu hen*, ed. Chūō Kōronsha, 103–41. Tokyo: Chūō kōronsha, 1931.

——. *Saishin joshi rikujō kyōgi hō*. Tokyo: Buntendō shoten, 1926. Reprinted in *Joshi taiiku kihon bunkenshū*, ed. Kataoka Yasuko, vol. 11. Tokyo: Ōzorasha, 1995.

——. "Sekai joryū senshu no inshō." *Kaizō* 12, no. 12 (December 1930): 21–28.

——. *Supaiku no ato*. Tokyo: Heibonsha, 1929. Reprinted in *Supaiku no ato/Gōru ni hairu*. Denki sōsho, vol. 154. Tokyo: Ōzorasha, 1994.

——. *Tatakau made*. Tokyo: Sanseidō, 1929.

——. "Watashi wa itsu kekkonsuru?" *Fujin saron* (May 1931): 52–54.

"Hitotsu no shiai 'hassenman-en' Gushiken no zaisan kanri hō." *Shūkan Shinchō* (7 February 1980): 19.

Hobsbawm, Eric. "Introduction: Inventing Traditions." In *The Invention of Tradition*, ed. Eric Hobsbawm and Terence Ranger, 1–14. Cambridge, UK: Cambridge University Press, 1983.

Hōchi shinbunsha. "Eikyū ketsuban [4] Kurosawa Toshio." *Supōtsu Hōchi*. http://hochi.yomiuri.co.jp/contents/giants/number/kurosawa.htm

Holden, T. J. M. "ReDotPop: Mediations of Japan: The O-N Series." *PopMatters.com*. 8 January 2001. http://www.popmatters.com/columns/holden/010108.html

Holmes, Su. "Starring . . . Dyer?: Re-visiting Star Studies and Contemporary Celebrity Culture." *Westminster Papers in Communication and Culture* 2, no. 2: 6–21.

"Honshi o kazatta chō sūpā sutā taidan shijō saigen daijesuto." *Bokushingu magajin* 11, no. 12 (1 October 1981): 107–10.

Hoshino Tatsui. "Sekai ni katsuyaku seru Nihon no undōka." *Shinseinen* 7, no. 13 (November 1926): 136–39.

——. "Supōtsu no pēji: Demupushī yaburu." *Shinseinen* 7, no. 14 (December 1926): 172–75.

——. "Supōtsu no pēji: Taishō no undō kyōgi: Reimei jidai no sekai no butai e." *Shinseinen* 8, no. 6 (May 1927): 156–61.

Howell, David. *Geographies of Identity in Nineteenth-Century Japan*. Berkeley, CA: University of California Press, 2005.

Huffman, James L. *Creating a Public: People and Press in Meiji Japan*. Honolulu, HI: University of Hawai'i Press, 1997.

Ichikawa Fusae. "Dokushin fujin no kien." *Kaizō* 12, no. 12 (December 1930): 80–81.

"Igai ni hikui (?) [*sic*] Gushiken no shūnyū." *Asahi geinō* (17 May 1979): 31.

Igarashi, Yoshikuni. *Bodies of Memory: Narratives of War in Postwar Japanese Culture, 1945–1970*. Princeton, NJ: Princeton University Press, 2000.

Ikeda Masao. "Rekidai Yokozuna Seiden 33: Hitachiyama Taniemon den (ichi)." *Sumō* 22, no. 10 (October 1973): 146–49.

——. "Rekidai Yokozuna Seiden 34: Hitachiyama Taniemon den (ni)." *Sumō* 22, no. 11 (November 1973): 146–49.

——. "Rekidai Yokozuna Seiden 36: Hitachiyama Taniemon den (yon)." *Sumō* 23, no. 1 (January 1974): 139–41.

——. "Rekidai Yokozuna Seiden 37: Hitachiyama Taniemon den (go)." *Sumō* 23, no. 2 (February 1974): 146–49.

——. "Rekidai Yokozuna Seiden 39: Hitachiyama Taniemon den (shichi)." *Sumō* 23, no. 4 (April 1974): 146–49.

Ikeda Tsuneo. "Atogaki." In *Fumetsu no daitōshu: Sawamura Eiji*, by Suzuki Sōtarō, 353–57. Tokyo: Kōbunsha, 1982.

Ikei Masaru. "Daitōshu Sawamura Eiji no senreki." *Rekishi to jinbutsu* 11, no. 10 (September 1981): 108–15.

——. *Hakkyū Taiheiyō o wataru*. Tokyo: Chūō kōronsha, 1976.

Imamura Yoshio. *Nihon taiiku shi*. Tokyo: Fumaidō, 1970.

Inoue, Masamichi S. *Okinawa and the U.S. Military: Identity Making in the Age of Globalization*. New York: Columbia University Press, 2007.

Inoue, Shun. "Budō." In *The Culture of Japan as Seen through its Leisure*, ed. Sepp Linhart and Sabine Frühstück, 83–93. Albany: SUNY Press, 1998.

International Olympic Committee. "Los Angeles 1932." *The Olympic Games*. Official Website of the Olympic Movement. http://www.olympic.org/en/content/Olympic-Games/All-Past-Olympic-Games/Summer/Los-Angeles-1932/

Irie Katsumi. *Shōwa supōtsu shiron: Meiji Jingū Kyōgi Taikai to kokumin seishin sōdōin undō*. Tokyo: Fumaidō shuppan, 1991.

Ishii Tsuneo. "Supōtsu arakaruto: Sumō sekai o tsukutta Hitachiyama no kyōjō." *Shūkan Asahi* 80, no. 1 (3 January 1975): 35.

"Ishigaki-jima ryojō: tensai bokusā o unda rakuen no shima." *Gongu*, July supplementary issue (1980): 51–55.

Ishiko Toshihiro. *Supōtsu to karada*. Tokyo: Iwanami shoten, 1983.

Itoigawa Yukihiro. "Emotion Type as Activation and Inhibition Toward Sport Challenge by Gold Medalists." Paper presented at XI European Congress on Sport Psychology. Copenhagen, Denmark. 22–27 July 2003.

Iwai Yoshio. *Chūgaku kokugo sōgō (chūgakkō dai ichi gakunen zenki yō)*. Tokyo: Futaba, 1961.

Iwaki Shōzō. "Sabishii Hitomi Kinue." 2 parts. *Fujin kōron* (June 1931): 149–59; (July 1931): 201–11.

James, C. L. R. *Beyond a Boundary*. Durham, NC: Duke University Press, 1993.

"Jihō." *Shin shōsetsu* 3, no. 7 (June 1898): 53–54.

"Jinbutsu kōsaten: Gushiken Yōkō." *Chūō kōron* 93, no. 7 (July 1978): 46–47.

Johnson, Chalmers. *Blowback: The Costs and Consequences of American Empire*. New York: Henry Holt and Company, 2000.

——, ed. *Okinawa: Cold War Island*. Cardiff, CA: Japan Policy Research Institute, 1999.

Johnson, Leola, and David Roediger. "'Hertz, Don't It?' Becoming Colorless and Staying Black in the Crossover of O. J. Simpson." In *Reading Sport: Critical Essays on Power and Representation*, ed. Susan Birrell and Mary G. Mcdonald, 40–73. Boston: Northeastern University Press, 2000.

Johnston, William. *Geisha-Harlot-Strangler-Star: A Woman, Sex, and Morality in Modern Japan*. New York: Columbia University Press, 2005.

Kadokura, Tania. "Sumo Stew." *Saveur* 62 (November 2002): 68–75.

Kageura Masaru. "Kikan senshu no shuki: Guntai seishin to yakyū." *Sumō to yakyū* 33, no. 17 (September 1943): 76–79.

Kageyama Bunzō. "Mihara senshu senjō hiwa." *Yakyūkai* 27, no. 15 (December 1937): 228–29.

Kageyama Tadahiro. *To ni mo kaku ni mo ōzumō*. Tokyo: Nanbāwan, 1985.

Kamitsukasa Shōken. *Sumō shinsho*. Tokyo: Hakubunkan, 1899.

Kanehira Masanori. "Gushiken Yōkō no himitsu." *Ushio* (January 1980): 58–59.

Kanzawa Sadamoto. *Okinagusa*. Sumo-related sections reproduced and available electronically at Tsubota Atsuo. "Shiryōko." *Sumō hyōronka no pēji*. 1996. Revised June 2008.
http://www.ep.sci.hokudai.ac.jp/~tsubota/chrono/okinagu.html

Kasson, John J. *Houdini, Tarzan, and the Perfect Man: The White Male Body and the Challenge of Modernity in America*. New York: Hill and Wang, 2001.

Kasza, Gregory J. *The State and the Mass Media in Japan, 1918–1945*. Berkeley, CA: University of California Press, 1988.

Kataoka Teppei. "Ryōryō aimatsu." *Chūō kōron* 46, no. 7 (July 1931): 313–16.

Katō Susumu. *Rekidai yokozuna monogatari*. Tokyo: Hakubunkan, 1938.

Katō Takayo. *Meiji jidai no ōzumō*. Ōzumō kanshiki taikei 4. Tokyo: Kokumin tairyoku kyōkai, 1942.

Kawana, Sari. *Murder Most Modern: Detective Fiction and Japanese Culture*. Minneapolis, MN: University of Minnesota Press, 2008.

"Kazarin Rōrusu jō." *Nihon shōnen* 32, no. 9 (September 1937): 270.

"Keizai & shumi: saifu mo shumi mo tsuma ni makasete fūfu enman." *Shufu no tomo* (October 1983): 152–53.

Kelly, William. "Blood and Guts in Japanese Professional Baseball." In *The Culture of Japan as Seen Through Its Leisure*, ed. Sepp Linhart and Sabine Frühstück, 95–112. Albany: SUNY Press, 1998.

———. "Learning to Swing: Oh Sadaharu and the Pedagogy and Practice of Japanese Baseball." In *Learning in Likely Places: Varieties of Apprenticeship in Japan*, ed. John Singleton, 265–85. New York: Cambridge University Press, 1998.

———. "Sense and Sensibility at the Ball Park: What Japanese Fans Make of Professional Baseball." In *Fanning the Flames: Fandoms and Consumer Culture in Contemporary Japan*, ed. William W. Kelly, 79–108. Albany, NY: SUNY Press, 2004.

———. "The Spirit and Spectacle of School Baseball: Mass Media, Statemaking, and 'Edu-tainment' in Japan, 1905–1935." In *Japanese Civilization in the Modern World XIV: Information and Communication,* Senri Ethnological Studies, No. 52, ed. Umesao Tadao, William Kelly, and Kubo Masatoshi, 105–16. Osaka: National Museum of Ethnology, 2000.

Ken'ei sanshi [pseud.]. *Gunshin Hirose chūsa sōretsudan*. Tokyo: Daigakukan, 1904.

Kerr, George H. *Okinawa: The History of an Island People*. Revised edition. North Clarendon, VT: Tuttle Publishing, 2000.

"Kikan shita yakyū senshu no zadankai." *Yakyūkai* 30, no. 12 (June 1940): 86–94.

Kiku, Koichi. "The Japanese Baseball Spirit and Professional Ideology." In *Japan, Sport and Society: Tradition and Change in a Globalizing World*, ed. Joseph Maguire and Masayoshi Nakayama, 35–54. London: Routledge, 2006.

Kimoto Itaru. "Nippon senkusha monogatari dai 19-kai: Hitachiyama Taniemon: Kokugikan of tsukuri sumō o kokugi ni takameta kindai no meirikishi." *Heibon panchi* (16 June 1975): 102–6.
Kinema junpōsha. "Arasuji: *Fumetsu no nekkyū* (1955)." *Goo Eiga.* http://movie.goo.ne.jp/movies/PMVWKPD24199/story.html
Kinmonth, Earl H. *The Self-Made Man in Meiji Japanese Thought: From Samurai to Salary Man.* Berkeley, CA: University of California Press, 1981.
Kinoshita Hideaki. *Supōtsu no kindai Nihonshi.* Tokyo: Kyōrin shoin, 1970.
Kinoshita Tōsaku. "Fujin no taishitsu to supōtsu." In *Fujin kōron daigaku: Supōtsu hen*, ed. Chūō kōronsha, 17–68. Tokyo: Chūō kōronsha, 1931.
——. "Josei no motsu danseibi." *Fujin saron* (May 1931): 26–35.
——. "Joshi no supōtsu to kenkō." *Chūō kōron* 46, no. 9 (September 1931): 248–58.
Kishino Yūzō, ed. *Shinpan kindai taiiku supōtsu nenpyō.* Tokyo: Taishūkan shoten, 1986.
Kitahara Ryōzaburō. *Sawamura Eiji to sono jidai.* Tokyo: Tokyo shoseki, 1992.
Kitamura Kaneko. "Dokushin fujin no yase kōei." *Kaizō* 12, no. 12 (December 1930): 82–83.
Klein, Rowan. *Sumo—A Historical Perspective.* Revised June 2008 http://history.sumogames.com
"Kobushi de kachitotta hanayaka na kadode." *Shūkan josei* (4 April 1981): front photo section.
Kōdansha. *Gushiken Yōkō shashinshū: Taitoru macchi.* Tokyo: Kōdansha, 1980.
Kojima Toshio. "Kikan senshu no shuki: Senjinkun ni manabu." *Sumō to yakyū* 33, no. 16 (August 1943): 75–79.
"Kokumin eiyoshō o nerau: Gushiken no 'gōgoroku.'" *Shūkan Shinchō* (5 July 1979): 145.
"Kokumin eiyoshō o nerau: Gushiken no V12 chōsen." *Shūkan Bunshun* 22, no. 10 (6 March 1980): 26.
Kolatch, Jonathan. *Sports, Politics, and Ideology in China.* New York: Jonathan David Publishers, 1972.
Komatsu Narumi. *Ichirō intabyū: Attack the Pinnacle!* Tokyo: Shinchōsha, 2001.
Konishi Shirō. *Kenpō happu.* Vol. 10 of *Nishiki e bakumatsu Meiji no rekishi.* Tokyo: Kōdansha, 1977.
——. *Nisshin sensō.* Vol. 11 of *Nishiki e bakumatsu Meiji no rekishi.* Tokyo: Kōdansha, 1977.
——. *Rokumeikan jidai.* Vol. 9 of *Nishiki e bakumatsu Meiji no rekishi.* Tokyo: Kōdansha, 1977.
Konno Tsutomu, dir. *Akai inazuma: Hitomi Kinue.* First broadcast on TBS television network. 22 November 1992.
——. *Hitomi Kinue monogatari: dorama supesharu (kadai).* Osaka: Mainichi hōsō, 1992.
Kōno Atsushi. "Beikoku-shiki yakyū o tomurau." *Yakyūkai* 32, no. 7 (April 1942): 113–19
Kornicki, Peter F. *The Book in Japan: A Cultural History from the Beginnings to the Nineteenth Century.* Leiden: Brill, 1998.

Kramer, Eric Mark. "Understanding Co-Constitutional Genesis." *Integrative Explorations: Journal of Culture and Consciousness* 1, no. 1 (February 1993): 1–7.

"Gogatsu basho banzuke." *Ōzumō*. Updated April 2010. http://sumo.goo.ne.jp/hon_basho/banzuke/ban_1.html

Kusaka Reiji [pseud.]. "Chūtō kyūkai shungō nijukketsu." *Yakyūkai* 24, no. 9 (July 1934): 176–77.

Kusaka, Yuko. "The Emergence and Development of Japanese School Sport." In *Japan, Sport and Society: Tradition and Change in a Globalizing World*, ed. Joseph Maguire and Masayoshi Nakayama, 19–34. London: Routledge, 2006.

"Kyōto shōgyō 4–0 Sakai chūgaku." *Yakyūkai* 24, no. 8 (June 1934): 142.

Kyūshū shinrin kanrikyoku. "Kanmuriwashi." *Kyūshū shinrin kanrikyoku*. 2008. http://www.rinya.maff.go.jp/kyusyu/policy/business/conservation/corridor/kisyou/9-kanmuriwasi.html.

Lang, Gladys Engel, and Kurt Lang. "Recognition and Renown: The Survival of Artistic Reputation." *American Journal of Sociology* 94, no. 1 (July 1988): 79–109.

Lazenby, Roland. *Ichiro: The Making of an American Hero*. Chicago, IL: Triumph Books, 2002.

MacAloon, John J. "Olympic Games and the Theory of Spectacle in Modern Societies." In *Rite, Drama, Festival, Spectacle: Rehearsals Toward a Theory of Cultural Performance*, ed. John J. MacAloon, 241–80. Philadelphia: Institute for the Study of Human Issues, 1984.

Maguire, Jennifer Smith. "Michel Foucault: Sport, Power, Technologies, and Governmentality." In *Theory, Sport, and Society*, ed. Joseph Maguire and Kevin Young, 293–314. Amsterdam: JAI, 2002.

"Mama wa shikkari! Papa wa oro oro: sutā fūfu no kosodate." *Shūkan myōjō* (10 June 1982): 55–59.

Manabe Kazuko. *Asayake no rannā: mijikai jinsei no zenryoku shissō shita Hitomi Kinue*. Illus. by Kosaka Shigeru. Kyoto: PHP kenkyūjo, 1984.

Marcus, Marvin. *Paragons of the Ordinary: The Biographical Literature of Mori Ōgai*. Honolulu, HI: University of Hawai'i Press, 1993.

Marran, Christine L. *Poison Woman: Figuring Female Transgression in Modern Japanese Culture*. Minneapolis, MN: University of Minnesota Press, 2007.

Marshall, P. David. *Celebrity and Power: Fame in Contemporary Culture*. Minneapolis, MN: University of Minnesota Press, 1997.

Masaki Fujokyū. "Hitachiyama no shinzō." In *Kodomo seiri eisei monogatari*, 58–71, vol. 69 of *Shōgakusei zenshū*. Bungei shunjūsha, 1928.

Masujima, Midori. "How Japanese Athletes Are Changing Japan's Image at Home and Abroad." *Japan Foundation Newsletter* XXIX, no. 1 (October 2001): 1–6.

Masumoto Naofumi. *Supōtsu eizō no episutēmē: bunka kaishaku gaku no shiten kara*. Tokyo: Shinhyōron, 2000.

Matsunami Kenshirō and Araki Yūji. *Shintaikan no kenkyū: utsukushii shintai to kenkō*. Expanded edition. Tokyo: Senshū Daigaku shuppankyoku, 1991.

Matsuzawa Hanako. "Chichi Hitachiyama to sumōdō." *Chūō kōron* 55, no. 6 (June 1940): 404–9.

——. "Sumō konjaku banashi: chichi Hitachiyama no omoide." *Shōsetsu shinchō* 7, no. 8 (June 1953): 62–68.

Mayeda, David Tokiharu. "From Model Minority to Economic Threat: Media Portrayals of Major League Baseball Pitchers Hideo Nomo and Hideki Irabu." *Journal of Sport & Social Issues* 23, no. 2 (May 1999): 203–17.

Miki Aika. *Sumō shiden*. Tokyo: Shokōsha, 1901.

"Mirai no okusama no o-tenami haiken." *Shūkan myōjō* (26 October 1980): 179.

Misawa Mitsuo. *Hayate no josei rannā: Hitomi Kinue sanka*. Tokyo: Fumaidō shuppan, 2005.

——. "Hitomi Kinue kō." *Nihon Joshi Taiiku Daigaku kiyō* 5 (October 1975): 1–12.

——. "Hitomi Kinue no kōen kōshū katsudō." *Taiikushi kenkyū* 19 (March 2002): 43–56.

——. "Hitomi Kinue: sono supōtsu katsudō no chōsa to nenpyō hokan." *Nihon Joshi Taiiku Daigaku kiyō* 33 (March 2003): 60.

——. "Nihon joshi rikujō kyōgi hatten shi: dai 2-ji sekai taisen shūketsuji made." *Nihon Joshi Taiiku Daigaku kiyō* 6 (November 1976): 1–15.

Misawa Mitsuo and Takeda Hajime. "Hitomi Kinue kenkyū ni kansuru bunken mokuroku." *Nihon Joshi Taiiku Daigaku kiyō* 28 (March 1998): 123–24.

Miyake Taisuke. "Tairasu Kabbu-shi." *Kaizō* 9, no. 8 (August 1927): 76.

Miyao, Daisuke. *Sessue Hayakawa: Silent Cinema and Transnational Stardom*. Durham, NC: Duke University Press, 2007.

Miyao Tomiko. "Hitomi Kinue." In *Kunan to eikō no senkusha*. Vol. 11 of *Kindai Nihon no josei shi*, ed. Enchi Fumiko, 186. Tokyo: Shūeisha, 1981.

Mizutani Ryōichi. "Puro yakyū No. 1 Sawamura tōshu katei hōmonki." *Yakyūkai* 27, no. 13 (October 1937): 262–65.

Molony, Barbara, and Kathleen Uno, eds. *Gendering Modern Japanese History*. Cambridge, MA: Harvard University Asia Center, 2005.

Molony, Kathleen Susan. "One Woman Who Dared: Ichikawa Fusae and the Japanese Women's Suffrage Movement." Ph.D. diss., University of Michigan, 1980.

Montville, Leigh. *Ted Williams: The Biography of an American Hero*. New York: Doubleday, 2004.

Morris, Andrew D. "Baseball, History, the Local and the Global in Taiwan." In *The Minor Arts of Daily Life: Popular Culture in Taiwan*, ed. David K. Jordan, Andrew D. Morris, and Marc L. Moskowitz, 175–203. Honolulu, HI: University of Hawai'i Press, 2004.

——. *Marrow of the Nation: A History of Sport and Physical Education in Republican China*. Berkeley, CA: University of California Press, 2004.

Morris-Suzuki, Tessa. *Re-inventing Japan: Time, Space, Nation*. Armonk, NY: M. E. Sharpe, 1998.

"Moto yūmei puro supōtsu senshu ga keieisuru mise no aji." *Shūkan gendai* (26 September 1992): front photo section.

Mrozek, Donald J. "The 'Amazon' and the American 'Lady': Sexual Fears of Women as Athletes." In *The New American Sport History: Recent Approaches and Perspectives*, ed. S. W. Pope, 198–214. Urbana, IL: University of Illinois Press, 1997.

Muramatsu Shōfū. *Meijin kushin jitsuwa*. Meiji Taishō jitsuwa zenshū. vol. 4. Tokyo: Heibonsha, 1929.

Murobuse Kōshin. "Hitomi Kinue ron." *Fujin gahō* (May 1931): 92–93.

Murray, Patricia. "Ichikawa Fusae and the Lonely Red Carpet." *Japan Interpreter* 10, no. 2 (Autumn 1975): 171–89.

Nagadō Eikichi. *Bokusā Gushiken Yōkō to seishun gunzō*. Tokyo: Banseisha, 1979.

——. *Bokusā PART II: Gushiken Yōkō to Okinawa no kenjitachi*. Tokyo: Banseisha, 1980.

——. "'Chiisa na kyojin': Gushiken Yōkō monogatari." *Bokushingu magajin* 11, no. 12 (October 1981): 82–90.

Nakagawa Nobuyuki. "Kōsenshu o erabu." *Yakyūkai* 24, no. 12 (October 1934): 150–51.

Nakamoto Seiji. "Zen-Nihon shakaijin senshuken taikai o oete." *Nichiren kōhō: Nihon amachua bokushingu renmei*, no. 14 (1 May 1969): 3.

Nakamura Takanori. "Amerika-gun no inshō." *Yakyūkai* 25, no. 1 (January 1935): 18–19.

Nakamura, Yuka. "The Samurai Sword Cuts Both Ways: A Transnational Analysis of Japanese and US Media Representations of Ichiro." *International Review for the Sociology of Sport* 40, no. 4 (2005): 469–82.

Nakano Yoshio and Arasaki Moriteru. *Okinawa sengoshi*. Tokyo: Iwanami shoten, 1976.

Nalapat, Abilash, and Andrew Parker. "Sport, Celebrity and Popular Culture: Sachin Tendulkar, Cricket and Indian Nationalisms." *International Review for the Sociology of Sport* 40, no. 4 (2005): 433–46.

NHK ākaibusu bangumi purojekuto. "Waga Okinawa: Gushiken Yōkō to sono ichizoku." In *Yume to wakamonotachi*, vol. 1 of *NHK ākaibusu: yomigaeru jidai no kioku*, 155–203. Tokyo: Futabasha, 2003.

"Nihon-gun Zen-bei inshō roku." *Yakyūkai* 25, no. 1 (January 1935): 38–43.

"'Nihon no Rokki' Gushiken Yōkō: afutā 'FIGHT' no korui no seishun." *Purēbōi* (14 June 1977): 154.

Nihon tenisu kyōkai. "Nihon tenisu no rekishi." 2000. http://www.jta-tennis.or.jp/JTA/history/history_of_japantennis.html

Nikaidō Tokuyo. *Ashikake yonen: Eikoku no shōgakkai*. Tokyo: Tōkyō hōbunkan, 1917.

Ninomiya Seijun. "Kyojin-gun wa Sawamura Eiji o suteta ka." *Gendai* (September 1993): 186–93.

Nitobe Inazō. Author's preface to *Bushido: The Soul of Japan: An Exposition of Japanese Thought*. Tenth revised edition. New York: G. H. Putnam's Sons, 1905.

——. *Bushido: The Soul of Japan: An Exposition of Japanese Thought*. Philadelphia, PA: Leeds and Biddle, 1900.

Nitta Ichirō. *Sumō no rekishi*. Tokyo: Yamakawa shuppansha, 1994.

Nolte, Sharon H. "Women's Rights and Society's Needs: Japan's 1931 Suffrage Bill." *Comparative Studies in Society and History* 28, no. 1 (October 1986): 690–714.

Obara Toshihiko. *Hitomi Kinue monogatari: joshi rikujō no akatsuki no hoshi*. Tokyo: Asahi shinbunsha, 1990.

Obermiller, David Tobaru. "The Okinawan Struggle Over Identity, Historical Memory, and Cultural Representation." *Japan Foundation Newsletter* XXVII, no. 3–4 (March 2000): 12–13.

——. "The United States Military Occupation of Okinawa: Politicizing and Contesting Okinawan Identity, 1945–1955." Ph.D. diss., University of Iowa, 2006.

Oda Mikio. "Hashiritakatobi no yūsha Osubōn." *Kaizō* 9, no. 8 (August 1927): 74.

Oda Mikio and Toda Jun. *Honō no supurintā: Hitomi Kinue jiden*. Okayama: Sanyō shinbunsha shuppankyoku, 1983.

Ōe Shinkichi. *Yakyū-ō Bēbu Rūsu*. Tokyo: Bonjinsha, 1934.

Ogasawara Naganari. "Hiiki ni sareta Hitachiyama." In *Kyōshō Yashiro Rokurō*, 160–69. Tokyo: Seikyōsha shuppanbu, 1932.

Ogura Hajimu. *Sawamura Eiji monogatari: minami no umi ni kieta ēsu*. Tokyo: Sa E Ra shobō, 1987.

"Oh (Kyojin) o nuita Gushiken Yōkō no kasegi." *Shūkan shinchō* (9 August 1979): 19.

Oh Sadaharu. *Boku to hōmuran: 756-gō e no michinori*. Tokyo: Shūeisha, 1977.

——. *Kaisō*. Tokyo: Keibunsha, 1981.

——. *Oh Sadaharu*. Tokyo: Nihon tosho sentā, 2000.

——. *Oh Sadaharu no nikki*. Tokyo: Nihon bunka shuppan, 1977.

Oh Sadaharu and David Falkner. *Sadaharu Oh: A Zen Way of Baseball*. New York: Random House, 1984.

Ōi Masao. "Kikan no Sawamura tōshu kaikenki." *Yakyūkai* 29, no. 17 (November 1939): 172.

Oka Keikō. *Kokon sumō taiyō*. Tokyo: Kōgyokudō, 1885.

"Okinawa no futari no 'senshi' tōron: Gushiken Yōkō vs Kina Shōkichi." *Purēbōi* (15 August 1978): 32–36.

Okuda Hideki. "Ichirō '262-hon' ni Beikoku 'dairongi.'" *Yomiuri uīkurī* (24 October 2004): 118–20.

"Omoide no Purāgu ni kenritsu sareta ko Hitomi Kinue-jō no kinenhi." *Asahi supōtsu* 10, no. 25 (15 November 1932): 24.

Oriard, Michael. *Reading Football: How the Press Created an American Spectacle*. Chapel Hill, NC: University of North Carolina Press, 1993.

Ōsaka Asahi shinbunsha, ed. *Jinbutsu gaden*. Tokyo: Yūrakusha, 1907.

Ōsaka Rokusuke. "Supōtsukai no myōjō otsu? Fuki no byōshō ni aru Hitomi Kinue." *Fujin gahō* (July 1931): 54–60.

Ōta Masahide. *Okinawa: sensō to heiwa*. Tokyo: Nihon Shakaitō chūō honbu kikanshikyoku, 1982.

Ōzaki Sumio. "Sawamura tōshu hōmonki." *Yakyūkai* 30, no. 13 (July 1940): 199–201.

Partner, Simon. *Assembled in Japan: Electrical Goods and the Making of the Japanese Consumer*. Berkeley, CA: University of California Press, 1999.

Pennington, Patience [pseud. Elizabeth Waties Allston Pringle]. *A Woman Rice Planter*. Illus. by Alice R. H. Smith. New York: Macmillan, 1914. Electronic edition available at *Documenting the American South*. http://docsouth.unc.edu/fpn/pringle/pringle.html

Pflugfelder, Gregory. "'S' is for Sister: Schoolgirl Intimacy and 'Same-Sex Love' in Early Twentieth-Century Japan." In *Gendering Modern Japanese History*, ed. Barbara Molony and Kathleen Uno, 133–90. Cambridge, MA: Harvard University Asia Center, 2005.

"Pin kara kiri made shiawase." *Josei jishin* (7 May 1981): front photo section.

"Pīpuru: nengan no jimu setsuritsu Gushiken Yōkō." *Shūkan bunshun* (3 November 1994): 53.

Ponce de Leon, Charles L. *Self-Exposure: Human-Interest Journalism and the Emergence of Celebrity in America, 1890–1940*. Chapel Hill, NC: University of North Carolina Press, 2002.

Pope, Steven W., ed. *The New American Sport History: Recent Approaches and Perspectives*. Urbana, IL: University of Illinois Press, 1997.

——. *Patriotic Games: Sporting Traditions in the American Imagination, 1876–1926*. New York: Oxford University Press, 1997.

Postwar Diet Records. Session 24. Shūgiin yosan iinkai bunkakai 4 gō. 1956 February 23. Hatsugensha 141/150 (Yamamoto Katsuichi), 19. Available at *Kokkai kaigiroku kensaku shisutemu*. http://kokkai.ndl.go.jp/

——. Session 96. Shūgiin hōmu iinkai 6 gō, 24 March 1982. Beginning with hatsugensha 20/70 (Yokoyama Toshiaki), 5. Available at *Kokkai kaigiroku kensaku shisutemu*. http://kokkai.ndl.go.jp

——. Session 96. Shūgiin yosan iinkai 2 gō, 19 April 1982. Beginning with hatsugensha 247/422 (Narazaki Yanosuke), 22. Available at *Kokkai kaigiroku kensaku shisutemu*. http://kokkai.ndl.go.jp

"POWER BOAT: Pawā bōto ni kakeru Gushiken daini no jinsei 'Kanmuriwashi Rēshingu.'" *Mekanikku magajin* (February 1985): 22–25.

Purves, John Michael. *The Ryukyu-Okinawa History & Culture Website*. Updated 2010. http://www.niraikanai.wwma.net

Rabson, Steve. "Assimilation Policy in Okinawa: Promotion, Resistance, and 'Reconstruction.'" In *Okinawa: Cold War Island*, ed. Chalmers Johnson, 133–48. Cardiff, CA: Japan Policy Research Institute, 1999.

Rader, Benjamin G. "Compensatory Sport Heroes: Ruth, Grange and Dempsey." *Journal of Popular Culture* 16, no. 4 (Spring 1983): 11–22.

Rains, Rob. *Baseball Samurais: Ichiro Suzuki and the Asian Invasion*. New York: St. Martin's Paperbacks, 2001.

Raz, Jacob. *Audience and Actors: A Study of Their Interaction in the Japanese Traditional Theatre*. Leiden: Brill, 1983.

Reaves, Joseph A. *Taking in a Game: A History of Baseball in Asia*. Lincoln, NE: University of Nebraska Press, 2002.

"Renmei dayori." *Sumō to yakyū* 33, no. 9 (May 1943): 106–7.

"Rensai 80: kengyō hanjō watashi ga shujin: Gushiken Yōkō (bokusā)—Okinawa soba 'Gushiken.'" *Asahi geinō* (7 February 1980): photo section.

Robertson, Jennifer. "Japan's First Cyborg? Miss Nippon, Eugenics and Wartime Technologies of Beauty, Body and Blood." *Body & Society* 7, no. 1 (2001): 1–34.

——. "The Politics of Androgyny in Japan: Sexuality and Subversion in the Theater and Beyond." *American Ethnologist* 19, no. 3 (August 1992): 419–42.

——. *Takarazuka: Sexual Politics and Popular Culture in Modern Japan*. Berkeley, CA: University of California Press, 1998.

Roden, Donald. "Baseball and the Quest for National Dignity in Meiji Japan." *American Historical Review* 85, no. 3 (June 1980): 511–34.

Rojek, Chris. *Celebrity*. London: Reaktion Books, 2001.

——. "Sports Celebrity and the Civilizing Process." *Sport in Society* 9, no. 4 (October 2006): 674–90.

Ruoff, Kenneth J. *The People's Emperor: Democracy and the Japanese Monarchy, 1945–1995*. Cambridge, MA: Harvard University Asia Center, 2001.

Ruth, Babe. *How to Play Baseball*. New York: Cosmopolitan Book Corp, 1931.

"Sa chanpion Gushiken Yōkō: charenji! V12." *Shūkan myōjō* (18 May 1980): front photo section.

"Sada Masashi, Yazawa Eikichi to wa koko ga chigau: Gushiken Yōkō (24) no 'nari agari.'" *Shūkan posuto* (25 January 1980): 48–52.

Sadohara Yoshio. "Sawamura tōshu o heiei ni tou." *Yakyūkai* 28, no.5 (March 1938): 175–77.

——. "Senshō hakui no yūshi: Nakayama Kyojin-gun hoshu imonki." *Yakyūkai* 27, no. 15 (December 1937): 225–27.

Saeki, Shoichi. "The Curious Relationship Between Biography and Autobiography in Japan." In *New Directions in Biography: Essays*, ed. Anthony M. Friedson, 73–82. Honolulu, HI: Published for the Biographical Research Center by the University of Hawai'i Press, 1981.

Sagita Shigeo. "Kyūkai meisenshu no sange." 2 parts. *Yakyūkai* 31, no. 1 (January 1941): 129–31; no. 4 (February 1941): 146–48.

"Saisutāto e ai no chikai." *Shūkan myōjō* (9 April 1981): front photo section.

Saitō Gesshin. *Bukō nenpyō*. Tōyō bunkō, no. 116. Ed. Kaneko Mitsuhara. Tokyo: Heibonsha, 1968.

Sakai Shōryō. *Genzai jinbutsu no kenkyū*. Tokyo: Shunbodō, 1910.

Sakai Tadamasa. "Kinsei daishōbu monogatari: Umegatani Hitachiyama no kan." *Ōzumō* 7, no. 4 (April 1961): 92–93.

Saki Ryūzō. *Eiyū: Gushiken Yōkō den*. Tokyo: Shūeisha, 1983.

Sakura Tatsuzan [Sakura Magozō]. *Yokozuna Hitachiyama*. Tokyo: Self-published, 1904.

Sandow Museum
http://www.sandowmuseum.com/sandow2001.html (website discontinued)

Sano Shin'ichi. "Shōwa no puromōtā: Shōriki Matsutarō." *Bessatsu Bungei shunjū* no. 196 (July 1991): 396–430.

Sasaki Nobutsuna, ed. *Shinsei shinsen joshi kokugo tokuhon*. Tokyo: Yukawa kōbunsha, 1937.
Satake Nobushirō. "Beikoku ni okeru waga judō." *Undō sekai*, no. 1 (1908): 49–52.
Satō Gisuke. *Gendai hyakunin gō*. Vol. 2. Tokyo: Shinseisha, 1902.
Satō Hachirō. "Go-fujin wa supōtsu ga o-suki." *Kaizō* 14, no. 10 (October 1932): 210–17.
Sawa Tamaki. "Sawa Tamaki no 'otoko' taidan: dai 21-kai." *Shūkan gendai* (24 November 1977): 58–62.
Sawada Bushō. *Meiji taitei*. Tokyo: Teikoku gunjin kyōikukai, 1912.
Sawamura Eiji. "Boku no nayami." *Shinseinen* 17, no. 1 (January 1936): 258–59.
——. "Dai-Bēbu Rūsu ni datte ana wa aru." *Yakyūkai* 25, no. 1 (January 1935): 142.
——. "Senjō kara: Sawamura tōshu no tegami." *Yakyūkai* 28, no. 13 (September 1938): 171–73.
——. "Senjō nikki." *Yakyūkai* 29, no. 4 (February 1939): 259–61.
——. "Sensen yori futatabi tōshuban ni kaerite." *Modan Nippon* (September 1940). Reprinted in *Shōwa dai zasshi: senchū hen*, 462–64. Tokyo: Ryūdō shuppan, 1978.
——. "Tatakau yakyū senshu no shuki." *Sumō to yakyū* 33, no. 11 (June 1943): 92–100.
——. "Tōshuban e no akogare." *Yakyūkai* 30, no. 15 (August 1940): 200–201.
——. "Zen-Nihongun no purēto o funde." *Yakyūkai* 25, no. 3 (February 1935): 132–34.
Sawamura Eiji and Sasazaki Takeshi. "Kikan ni yūshi sensō to supōtsu o kataru." *Ōru yomimono*, September 1940. Reprinted in *Bungei shunjū ni miru supōtsu Shōwa shi*, 371–78. Tokyo: Bungei shunjū, 1988.
"Sawamura tōshu saikō shukun senshu ni erabaru." *Nihon shōnen* 32, no. 9 (September 1937): 271.
"Sawamura tōshu: Ōbetsuzan de funsen." *Renmei nyūsu* (25 September 1938): 15.
Schwarz, Alan. "Matsuzaka's Pitching, Ichiro's Hitting Lead Japan to Inaugural World Baseball Classic Title." *Baseball America*. 20 March 2006. http://www.baseballamerica.com/today/news/060320wbcfinal.html
Seinen: The Rising Generation II, no. 3 (29 June 1899): 8.
"Senjin dayori (ni)." *Yakyūkai* 29, no. 11 (June 1939): 257.
Shields, David. *"Baseball Is Just Baseball": The Understated Ichiro*. Seattle, WA: TNI Books, 2001.
Shikimori Inosuke. *Hitachiyama Taniemon: kindai sumō o kakuritsu shita kyōdo no kakusei*. Tsuchiura, Ibaraki: Tsukuba shorin, 1988.
Shima Hidenosuke. *Puro yakyū shinpan no me*. Tokyo: Iwanami shoten, 1986.
Shimizu Hideo. "Futatabi tōshuban ni tatte." *Sumō to yakyū* 33, no. 11 (June 1943): 88–90.
Shimizu Isao, ed. *Manga ni egakareta Meiji, Taishō, Shōwa*. Tokyo: Kyōikusha, 1988.
Shimizu Tetsuo. "Shin Nipponjin kenkyū: rensai dai 14-kai: 'hyakunen ni hitori no ōmono dā' Gushiken Yōkō (21) no majime sugiru shusse monogatari." *Shūkan gendai* (4 November 1976): 170–75.

Shinpan kasen sumō hyōrin. Sumo-related sections reproduced and available electronically at Tsubota Atsuo. "Shiryōko." *Sumō hyōronka no pēji*. 1996. Revised June 2008.
http://www.ep.sci.hokudai.ac.jp/~tsubota/chrono/s_hyourin.html

Shirai-Gushiken supōtsu jimu. *Official Website*. Updated May 2010.
http://www11.ocn.ne.jp/~sgs13/top.html

Shiro kyūji [pseud.]. "Sawamura tōshu chūmonchō." *Yakyūkai* 27, no. 12 (September 1937): 220.

"Shitsugi ōtō ran." *Yakyūkai* 24, no. 11 (September 1934); 24, no. 12 (October 1934); 25, no. 1 (New Years Edition 1935); 25, no. 4 (March 1935); 25, no. 5 (April 1935); 27, no. 14 (November 1937); 28, no. 5 (March 1938); 30, no. 6 (March 1940); 30, no. 13 (July 1940); 31, no. 5 (February 1941); 32, no. 21 (November 1942); and *Sumō to yakyū* 33, no. 3 (February 1943).

Shively, Donald H. "Sumptuary Regulation and Status in Early Tokugawa Japan." *Harvard Journal of Asiatic Studies* 25 (1964–65): 123–64.

"Shōgeki no sutā ningen bunkai shirīzu: dai 2-dan Gushiken Yōkō." *Shūkan taishū* (11 January 1979): 42–49.

Shuhō Saburō [pseud.]. "Puro no NO. 1 Sawamura tōshu to ichimon ittō." *Yakyūkai* 27, no. 13 (October 1937): 174–75.

Silverberg, Miriam. *Erotic Grotesque Nonsense: The Mass Culture of Japanese Modern Times*. Berkeley, CA: University of California Press, 2006.

———. "The Modern Girl as Militant." In *Recreating Japanese Women, 1600–1945*, ed. Gail Lee Bernstein, 239–55. Berkeley, CA: University of California Press, 1991.

Smart, Barry. *The Sport Star: Modern Sport and the Cultural Economy of Sporting Celebrity*. London: Sage Publications, 2005.

Smith, Henry D. "The Edo-Tokyo Transition: In Search of Common Ground." In *Japan in Transition: From Tokugawa to Meiji*, ed. Marius B. Jansen and Gilbert Rozman, 347–74. Princeton, NJ: Princeton University Press, 1986.

Smits, Gregory. "Making Japanese Through War and Peace, Part Two." In *Making Japanese*.
http://www.east-asian-history.net/textbooks/MJ/ch8.htm

———. *Visions of Ryukyu: Identity and Ideology in Early-Modern Thought and Politics*. Honolulu, HI: University of Hawai'i Press, 1999.

"Sociological Mirrors." *Taiyō* 7, no. 14 (5 December 1901): 5.

Sugiyama Shigeru and Kadokawa intarakutibu media. *Terebi supōtsu 50 nen: Orinpikku to terebi no hatten—Rikidōzan kara Matsui Hideki made*. Tokyo: Kadokawa intarakutibu media, 2003.

Sutaruhin, Natāsha. *Roshia kara kita ēsu: 300-shō tōshu Sutaruhin no mō hitotsu no tatakai*. Tokyo: PHP kenkyūjo, 1986.

Suzuki Hikojirō. "Hitachiyama kesshi no sumō." *Shōnen kurabu* 25, no. 14 (December 1938): 150–62.

———. *Hitachiyama Taniemon*. Ōsaka: Kibunkan, Ōsaka Pakkusha, 1941.

Suzuki Ryūji. "Daitōa sensō to Nihon yakyū no shimei." *Yakyūkai* 32, no. 16 (August 1942): 124–25.

———. "Nihon yakyū no shin dōkō." *Yakyūkai* 32, no. 1 (January 1942): 96–97.

Suzuki Sōtarō. *Fumetsu no daitōshu: Sawamura Eiji*. Shinsōban. Tokyo: Kōbunsha, 1982.

——. "Omoideru mama ni: Sawamura Eiji seiritsu no ki." Parts 7 and 8. *Yakyūkai* 27, no. 14 (November 1937): 238–40; no. 15 (December 1937): 232–35.

——. "Senji Nihon yakyū ron." *Yakyūkai* 32, no. 2 (January 1942): 126–31.

——. "Yakyū shinpō no dankai: kaisoku tōshu o sūjiku toshite no kenkyū." *Sumō to yakyū* 33, no. 2 (January 1943): 108–19.

Tachibana Mayumi. *Nihon no onna: dono yō ni onna tachi wa ikitekita no ka: senzen hen*. Tokyo: Genseirin, 1980.

"Tachiyama wa dore dake tsuyoi ka." *Kokugi* (October 1914): 10.

"Taikaku o aisu." *Kokugi* (June 1914): 2.

"Taitoru bōei no Nihon kiroku o mezasu dōtei chanpion." *Shūkan shōsetsu* (31 January 1977): 122–25.

Takamatsu bangarō shujin [pseud.]. "Manshūkoku yakyūbu o kiku: Manshūkoku Mitsumune senshu to kataru." *Yakyūkai* 24, no. 6 (May 1934): 184–87.

Takasaki Mieko. "Takasaki Mieko no iro iro taidan 10: gesuto Gushiken Yōkō." *Shūkan sankei* (4 August 1977): 58–62.

Tanizaki Jun'ichirō. *Chijin no Ai*. Tokyo: Kaizōsha, 1925.

——. *Naomi*. Translated by Anthony H. Chambers. New York: Vintage International, 1985.

Tanji, Miyume. *Myth, Protest and Struggle in Okinawa*. New York: Routledge, 2006.

Tansman, Alan. "Misora Hibari: The Postwar Myth of Mournful Tears and Sake." In *The Human Tradition in Modern Japan*, ed. Anne Walthall, 213–29. Lanham, MD: SR Books, 2002.

Tanuma Yūichi. *Nichibei yakyū eiga kinemakan*. Tokyo: Hōchi shinbunsha, 1996.

"Tenran-zumō o negai izu." *Sumō sekai*, no. 2 (June 1912): 1.

Teratani Yūji. Sketch. "Gongu no hiroba." *Gongu* 14, no. 5 (May 1981): 155.

Terauchi Daikichi. "Hakairyoku to reisei pēsu zukuri." Foreword to *Okinawa no hoshi: Gushiken Yōkō: wan ya kanmuriwashi*, by Ashizawa Seiichi. Tokyo: Deirī supōtsu jigyōsha, 1977.

Terayama Shūji, dir. *Bokusa*. 94 min. Tōei bideo. 1977. Videocassette.

"Teishu kanpaku!? Achira ga tsuyosugite." *Shūkan myōjō* (7 May 1981): front photo section.

Thelin, John R. *Games Colleges Play: Scandal and Reform in Intercollegiate Athletics*. Baltimore, MD: Johns Hopkins University Press, 1996.

Thompson, Lee. "The Invention of the *Yokozuna* and Championship System, or, Futohaguro's Revenge." In *Mirror of Modernity: Invented Traditions of Modern Japan*, ed. Stephen Vlastos, 174–87. Berkeley, CA: University of California Press, 1998.

Tierney, Roderic Kenji. "Wrestling with Tradition: Sumo, National Identity and Trans/national Popular Culture." Ph.D. diss., University of California Berkeley, 2002.

Tittle, H. *Sumo, der japanische Ringkampf nach japanischen Quellen* (Sumo, the Japanese Wrestling, from Japanese Sources). Trans. by Joseph R. Svinth. *Journal of Combative Sport* (June 2000). http://ejmas.com/jcs/jcsart_svinth1_0600.htm

"Tobe! 'kanmuriwashi nisei' Tokashiki Katsuo." *Shūkan hōseki* (7 November 1981): front photo section.

Toda Jun. *Kinue koi: boku no Hitomi Kinue den*. Tokyo: Self-published, 2001.

Tokugawa bungei ruijū, vol. 12. Tokyo: Kokusho kankōkai, 1914.

Tōkyō rokudaigaku yakyū renmei. *Shichijūnen no ayumi*. Tokyo: Rokudaigaku yakyū renmei, 1997.

Tokyo: Sports Center of the Orient. Tokyo: Tokyo Municipal Government, 1933.

"Tonkatsuya no sara arai kara chanpion e: Gushiken no 'kagirinai miryoku' to wa." *Shūkan shinchō* (20 October 1977): 122–23.

Tsurumi Shunsuke. *A Cultural History of Postwar Japan, 1945–1980*. London: Kegan Paul International, 1987.

Ueda Akinari. *Tandai shōshin roku*. Sumo-related sections reproduced and available electronically at Tsubota Atsuo. "Shiryōko." *Sumō hyōronka no pēji*. 1996. http://www.ep.sci.hokudai.ac.jp/-tsubota/chrono/tandaish.html

Ueda Seiichi. "Joshi kyōgi." In *Meiji Jingū Taiiku Taikai hōkokusho: dai 6–8 kai*, vol. 3, 446–47. Tokyo: Meiji Jingū taiikukai, 1936.

Umehara Hokumei, ed. *Kindai sesō zenshi: Keiō yori Taishō made no shinbun jūyō kiji no shūsei*. Tokyo: Hakuhōsha, 1931.

Uhlan, Edward, and Dana L. Thomas. *Shoriki: Miracle Man of Japan: A Biography*. New York: Exposition Press, 1957.

Van Meter Memories, Inc. dba Bob Feller Museum. *Bob Feller Museum*. 2007. http://www.bobfellermuseum.org/.

Vaporis, Constantine Nomikos. *Breaking Barriers: Travel and the State in Early Modern Japan*. Cambridge, MA: Council on East Asian Studies, Harvard University, 1994.

——. *Tour of Duty: Samurai, Military Service in Edo, and the Culture of Early Modern Japan*. Honolulu, HI: University of Hawai'i Press, 2008.

Vavich, Dee Ann. "The Japanese Woman's Movement: Ichikawa Fusae, A Pioneer in Woman's Suffrage." *Monumenta Nipponica* 22, nos. 3–4 (1967): 401–36.

Vlastos, Stephen, ed. *Mirror of Modernity: Invented Traditions of Modern Japan*. Berkeley, CA: University of California Press, 1998.

"Waido tokushū: eikō no otokotachi no fuan." *Shūkan sankei* (19 June 1980): 24–27.

Wakamori Tarō and Kojima Teiji. *Ōzumō meirikishi hyakusen*. Tokyo: Akita shoten, 1972.

Wārudo bokushingu henshūbu, ed. *Nippon Sports Mook 31: Boxing Classics: Nippon supōtsu mukku: bokushingu 100 nen: mireniamu kinen gō*. Tokyo: Nihon supōtsu shuppansha, 2001.

Weiner, Michael, ed. *Japan's Minorities: The Illusion of Homogeneity*. Sheffield Centre for Japanese Studies/Routledge Series. London: Routledge, 1997.

Welky, David B. "Viking Girls, Mermaids, and Little Brown Men: U.S. Journalism and the 1932 Olympics." *Journal of Sport History* 24, no. 1 (Spring 1997): 24–49.

Whannel, Garry. *Media Sport Stars: Masculinities and Moralities*. London: Routledge, 2002.

——. "Sports Stars, Narrativization, and Masculinities." *Leisure Studies* 18 (1999): 249–65.

Whiting, Robert. *The Chrysanthemum and the Bat: Baseball Samurai Style*. New York: Dodd, Mead, 1977.

—— [Robāto Howaitingu]. *Ichiro kakumei: Nihonjin mejā rīgā to bēsubōru no shin jidai*. Trans. Matsui Midori. Tokyo: Hayakawa shobō, 2004.

——. *The Samurai Way of Baseball: The Impact of Ichiro and the New Wave from Japan*. New York: Warner Books, 2004.

——. *You Gotta Have Wa: When Two Cultures Collide on the Baseball Diamond*. New York: Macmillan Publishing, 1989.

Whitney, Caspar. "Athletic Awakening of the Japanese." *Harper's Weekly* 42 (12 February 1898): 165–66.

Williams, Peter. *The Sports Immortals: Deifying the American Athlete*. Bowling Green, OH: Bowling Green State University Popular Press, 1994.

XYZ [pseud.]. "Naze fujin kōminken'an wa tōranakatta ka." *Fujin saron* (May 1931): 42–44.

Yamakawa Tatenobu. *Yakyū tōsei no hanashi*. Tokyo: Monbushō, 1932.

Yamamoto Giichi. *Jitsuroku kokon meirikishi hyaku reiden*. Tokyo: Hakubunkan, 1940.

Yanagiwara Ryokufū. "Hitachiyama Taniemon." In *Shōnen shōjo kyōiku kōdan zenshū*, ed. Noma Seiji, 343–74. Tokyo: Dai Nihon Yūbenkai Kōdansha, 1931.

Yazaki Hirotsune. "Sūpā sutā kenkyū 2: Gushiken Yōkō." *Hanashi no tokushū*, no. 157 (February 1979): 53–59.

Yokohama shinpōsha. *Tōsei rikishi meimeiden*. Yokohama: Yokohama shinpōsha, 1903.

Yokoyama Kendō. "Hitachiyama Taniemon." In *Kinsei meijin tatsujin daibungō*, ed. Dai Nihon Yūben Kai Kōdansha, 128–54. Tokyo: Dai Nihon Yūbenkai Kōdansha, 1928.

——. *Nihon sumō shi*. Tokyo: Fuzanbo, 1943.

Yomiuri shinbun Ōsaka honsha shakaibu. *Sensō 9: senbotsu yakyū jin*. Tokyo: Yomiuri shinbunsha, 1980.

Yoshida Akinobu. "Ningen no chikara no tsuyosa." In Zaidan hōjin Nihon sumō kyōkai. Newspaper Scrapbook Collection, volume 198.49. 6 May 1922 (Taishō 11) through 13 January 1923 (Taishō 12). Sumō Hakubutsukan. Kokugikan, Tokyo, Japan.

Yoshida, Kensei. *Democracy Betrayed: Okinawa Under U.S. Occupation*. Bellingham, WA: Center for East Asian Studies, Western Washington University, 2001.

Yudate Shōgaku. "Supōtsu jinkokki." *Chūō kōron* 46, no. 5 (May 1931): 224–33.

Zaidan hōjin Nihon sumō kyōkai. Newspaper Scrapbook Collection, volume 11. 12 January 1903 (Meiji 36) through 1904 (Meiji 37). Sumō hakubutsukan. Kokugikan, Tokyo, Japan.

——. Newspaper Scrapbook Collection, volume 12. 1902 (Meiji 35) through 1913 (Taishō 2). Sumō hakubutsukan. Kokugikan, Tokyo, Japan.

——. Newspaper Scrapbook Collection, volume 14. 25 May 1906 (Meiji 39) through 1908 (Meiji 41). Sumō hakubutsukan. Kokugikan, Tokyo, Japan.

——. Newspaper Scrapbook Collection, volume 15. 5 January 1907 (Meiji 40) through 22 January 1908 (Meiji 41). Sumō hakubutsukan. Kokugikan, Tokyo, Japan.

——. Newspaper Scrapbook Collection, volume 16. January through May 1908 (Meiji 41). Sumō hakubutsukan. Kokugikan, Tokyo, Japan.
——. Newspaper Scrapbook Collection, volume 17. 14 May through 2 June 1908 (Meiji 41). Sumō hakubutsukan. Kokugikan, Tokyo, Japan.
——. Newspaper Scrapbook Collection, volume 161.12. 29 May through 30 December 1914 (Taishō 3). Sumō hakubutsukan. Kokugikan, Tokyo, Japan.
——. Newspaper Scrapbook Collection, volume 198.49. 6 May 1922 (Taishō 11) through 13 January 1923 (Taishō 12). Sumō hakubutsukan. Kokugikan, Tokyo, Japan.
Zaidan hōjin yakyū taiiku hakubutsukan. Newspaper Scrapbook Collection. 1934. Toshoshitsu. Yakyū taiiku hakubutsukan. Tōkyō dōmu, Tokyo, Japan.
——. Newspaper Scrapbook Collection. 1937. Toshoshitsu. Yakyū taiiku hakubutsukan. Tokyo dōmu, Tōkyō, Japan.
——. Newspaper Scrapbook Collection. 1940. Manshū rīgusen, 29 April through 15 August 1940 (Shōwa 15). *Manshū Nichinichi shinbun*, vol. 1. Toshoshitsu. Yakyū taiiku hakubutsukan. Tōkyō dōmu, Tokyo, Japan.
——. "Sawamura Eiji." *The Baseball Hall of Fame and Museum*. http://english.baseball-museum.or.jp/baseball_hallo/detail/detail_008.html
"Zen-Beigun Nihon inshō roku." *Yakyūkai* 25, no. 1 (January 1935): 38–43.
Zirin, Dave. "Edge of Sports: Danica's Overexposure." *The Progressive* 72, no. 7 (July 2008): 20.

Index

Harvard East Asian Monographs

(*out-of-print)

*1. Liang Fang-chung, *The Single-Whip Method of Taxation in China*
*2. Harold C. Hinton, *The Grain Tribute System of China, 1845–1911*
3. Ellsworth C. Carlson, *The Kaiping Mines, 1877–1912*
*4. Chao Kuo-chün, *Agrarian Policies of Mainland China: A Documentary Study, 1949–1956*
*5. Edgar Snow, *Random Notes on Red China, 1936–1945*
*6. Edwin George Beal, Jr., *The Origin of Likin, 1835–1864*
7. Chao Kuo-chün, *Economic Planning and Organization in Mainland China: A Documentary Study, 1949–1957*
*8. John K. Fairbank, *Ching Documents: An Introductory Syllabus*
*9. Helen Yin and Yi-chang Yin, *Economic Statistics of Mainland China, 1949–1957*
10. Wolfgang Franke, *The Reform and Abolition of the Traditional Chinese Examination System*
11. Albert Feuerwerker and S. Cheng, *Chinese Communist Studies of Modern Chinese History*
12. C. John Stanley, *Late Ching Finance: Hu Kuang-yung as an Innovator*
13. S. M. Meng, *The Tsungli Yamen: Its Organization and Functions*
*14. Ssu-yü Teng, *Historiography of the Taiping Rebellion*
15. Chun-Jo Liu, *Controversies in Modern Chinese Intellectual History: An Analytic Bibliography of Periodical Articles, Mainly of the May Fourth and Post-May Fourth Era*
*16. Edward J. M. Rhoads, *The Chinese Red Army, 1927–1963: An Annotated Bibliography*
*17. Andrew J. Nathan, *A History of the China International Famine Relief Commission*
*18. Frank H. H. King (ed.) and Prescott Clarke, *A Research Guide to China-Coast Newspapers, 1822–1911*
*19. Ellis Joffe, *Party and Army: Professionalism and Political Control in the Chinese Officer Corps, 1949–1964*
*20. Toshio G. Tsukahira, *Feudal Control in Tokugawa Japan: The Sankin Kōtai System*
*21. Kwang-Ching Liu, ed., *American Missionaries in China: Papers from Harvard Seminars*
*22. George Moseley, *A Sino-Soviet Cultural Frontier: The Ili Kazakh Autonomous Chou*

23. Carl F. Nathan, *Plague Prevention and Politics in Manchuria, 1910–1931*
*24. Adrian Arthur Bennett, *John Fryer: The Introduction of Western Science and Technology into Nineteenth-Century China*
*25. Donald J. Friedman, *The Road from Isolation: The Campaign of the American Committee for Non-Participation in Japanese Aggression, 1938–1941*
*26. Edward LeFevour, *Western Enterprise in Late Ching China: A Selective Survey of Jardine, Matheson and Company's Operations, 1842–1895*
27. Charles Neuhauser, *Third World Politics: China and the Afro-Asian People's Solidarity Organization, 1957–1967*
*28. Kungtu C. Sun, assisted by Ralph W. Huenemann, *The Economic Development of Manchuria in the First Half of the Twentieth Century*
*29. Shahid Javed Burki, *A Study of Chinese Communes, 1965*
30. John Carter Vincent, *The Extraterritorial System in China: Final Phase*
31. Madeleine Chi, *China Diplomacy, 1914–1918*
*32. Clifton Jackson Phillips, *Protestant America and the Pagan World: The First Half Century of the American Board of Commissioners for Foreign Missions, 1810–1860*
*33. James Pusey, *Wu Han: Attacking the Present Through the Past*
*34. Ying-wan Cheng, *Postal Communication in China and Its Modernization, 1860–1896*
35. Tuvia Blumenthal, *Saving in Postwar Japan*
36. Peter Frost, *The Bakumatsu Currency Crisis*
37. Stephen C. Lockwood, *Augustine Heard and Company, 1858–1862*
38. Robert R. Campbell, *James Duncan Campbell: A Memoir by His Son*
39. Jerome Alan Cohen, ed., *The Dynamics of China's Foreign Relations*
40. V. V. Vishnyakova-Akimova, *Two Years in Revolutionary China, 1925–1927*, trans. Steven L. Levine
41. Meron Medzini, *French Policy in Japan During the Closing Years of the Tokugawa Regime*
42. Ezra Vogel, Margie Sargent, Vivienne B. Shue, Thomas Jay Mathews, and Deborah S. Davis, *The Cultural Revolution in the Provinces*
43. Sidney A. Forsythe, *An American Missionary Community in China, 1895–1905*
*44. Benjamin I. Schwartz, ed., *Reflections on the May Fourth Movement.: A Symposium*
*45. Ching Young Choe, *The Rule of the Taewŏngun, 1864–1873: Restoration in Yi Korea*
46. W. P. J. Hall, *A Bibliographical Guide to Japanese Research on the Chinese Economy, 1958–1970*
47. Jack J. Gerson, *Horatio Nelson Lay and Sino-British Relations, 1854–1864*
48. Paul Richard Bohr, *Famine and the Missionary: Timothy Richard as Relief Administrator and Advocate of National Reform*
49. Endymion Wilkinson, *The History of Imperial China: A Research Guide*
50. Britten Dean, *China and Great Britain: The Diplomacy of Commercial Relations, 1860–1864*
51. Ellsworth C. Carlson, *The Foochow Missionaries, 1847–1880*
52. Yeh-chien Wang, *An Estimate of the Land-Tax Collection in China, 1753 and 1908*
53. Richard M. Pfeffer, *Understanding Business Contracts in China, 1949–1963*

- *54. Han-sheng Chuan and Richard Kraus, *Mid-Ching Rice Markets and Trade: An Essay in Price History*
- 55. Ranbir Vohra, *Lao She and the Chinese Revolution*
- 56. Liang-lin Hsiao, *China's Foreign Trade Statistics, 1864–1949*
- *57. Lee-hsia Hsu Ting, *Government Control of the Press in Modern China, 1900–1949*
- *58. Edward W. Wagner, *The Literati Purges: Political Conflict in Early Yi Korea*
- *59. Joungwon A. Kim, *Divided Korea: The Politics of Development, 1945–1972*
- 60. Noriko Kamachi, John K. Fairbank, and Chūzō Ichiko, *Japanese Studies of Modern China Since 1953: A Bibliographical Guide to Historical and Social-Science Research on the Nineteenth and Twentieth Centuries, Supplementary Volume for 1953–1969*
- 61. Donald A. Gibbs and Yun-chen Li, *A Bibliography of Studies and Translations of Modern Chinese Literature, 1918–1942*
- 62. Robert H. Silin, *Leadership and Values: The Organization of Large-Scale Taiwanese Enterprises*
- 63. David Pong, *A Critical Guide to the Kwangtung Provincial Archives Deposited at the Public Record Office of London*
- *64. Fred W. Drake, *China Charts the World: Hsu Chi-yü and His Geography of 1848*
- *65. William A. Brown and Urgrunge Onon, translators and annotators, *History of the Mongolian People's Republic*
- 66. Edward L. Farmer, *Early Ming Government: The Evolution of Dual Capitals*
- *67. Ralph C. Croizier, *Koxinga and Chinese Nationalism: History, Myth, and the Hero*
- *68. William J. Tyler, tr., *The Psychological World of Natsume Sōseki*, by Doi Takeo
- 69. Eric Widmer, *The Russian Ecclesiastical Mission in Peking During the Eighteenth Century*
- *70. Charlton M. Lewis, *Prologue to the Chinese Revolution: The Transformation of Ideas and Institutions in Hunan Province, 1891–1907*
- 71. Preston Torbert, *The Ching Imperial Household Department: A Study of Its Organization and Principal Functions, 1662–1796*
- 72. Paul A. Cohen and John E. Schrecker, eds., *Reform in Nineteenth-Century China*
- 73. Jon Sigurdson, *Rural Industrialism in China*
- 74. Kang Chao, *The Development of Cotton Textile Production in China*
- 75. Valentin Rabe, *The Home Base of American China Missions, 1880–1920*
- *76. Sarasin Viraphol, *Tribute and Profit: Sino-Siamese Trade, 1652–1853*
- 77. Ch'i-ch'ing Hsiao, *The Military Establishment of the Yuan Dynasty*
- 78. Meishi Tsai, *Contemporary Chinese Novels and Short Stories, 1949–1974: An Annotated Bibliography*
- *79. Wellington K. K. Chan, *Merchants, Mandarins and Modern Enterprise in Late Ching China*
- 80. Endymion Wilkinson, *Landlord and Labor in Late Imperial China: Case Studies from Shandong by Jing Su and Luo Lun*
- *81. Barry Keenan, *The Dewey Experiment in China: Educational Reform and Political Power in the Early Republic*
- *82. George A. Hayden, *Crime and Punishment in Medieval Chinese Drama: Three Judge Pao Plays*

- *83. Sang-Chul Suh, *Growth and Structural Changes in the Korean Economy, 1910–1940*
- 84. J. W. Dower, *Empire and Aftermath: Yoshida Shigeru and the Japanese Experience, 1878–1954*
- 85. Martin Collcutt, *Five Mountains: The Rinzai Zen Monastic Institution in Medieval Japan*
- 86. Kwang Suk Kim and Michael Roemer, *Growth and Structural Transformation*
- 87. Anne O. Krueger, *The Developmental Role of the Foreign Sector and Aid*
- *88. Edwin S. Mills and Byung-Nak Song, *Urbanization and Urban Problems*
- 89. Sung Hwan Ban, Pal Yong Moon, and Dwight H. Perkins, *Rural Development*
- *90. Noel F. McGinn, Donald R. Snodgrass, Yung Bong Kim, Shin-Bok Kim, and Quee-Young Kim, *Education and Development in Korea*
- *91. Leroy P. Jones and II SaKong, *Government, Business, and Entrepreneurship in Economic Development: The Korean Case*
- 92. Edward S. Mason, Dwight H. Perkins, Kwang Suk Kim, David C. Cole, Mahn Je Kim et al., *The Economic and Social Modernization of the Republic of Korea*
- 93. Robert Repetto, Tai Hwan Kwon, Son-Ung Kim, Dae Young Kim, John E. Sloboda, and Peter J. Donaldson, *Economic Development, Population Policy, and Demographic Transition in the Republic of Korea*
- 94. Parks M. Coble, Jr., *The Shanghai Capitalists and the Nationalist Government, 1927–1937*
- 95. Noriko Kamachi, *Reform in China: Huang Tsun-hsien and the Japanese Model*
- 96. Richard Wich, *Sino-Soviet Crisis Politics: A Study of Political Change and Communication*
- 97. Lillian M. Li, *China's Silk Trade: Traditional Industry in the Modern World, 1842–1937*
- 98. R. David Arkush, *Fei Xiaotong and Sociology in Revolutionary China*
- *99. Kenneth Alan Grossberg, *Japan's Renaissance: The Politics of the Muromachi Bakufu*
- 100. James Reeve Pusey, *China and Charles Darwin*
- 101. Hoyt Cleveland Tillman, *Utilitarian Confucianism: Chen Liang's Challenge to Chu Hsi*
- 102. Thomas A. Stanley, *Ōsugi Sakae, Anarchist in Taishō Japan: The Creativity of the Ego*
- 103. Jonathan K. Ocko, *Bureaucratic Reform in Provincial China: Ting Jih-ch'ang in Restoration Kiangsu, 1867–1870*
- 104. James Reed, *The Missionary Mind and American East Asia Policy, 1911–1915*
- 105. Neil L. Waters, *Japan's Local Pragmatists: The Transition from Bakumatsu to Meiji in the Kawasaki Region*
- 106. David C. Cole and Yung Chul Park, *Financial Development in Korea, 1945–1978*
- 107. Roy Bahl, Chuk Kyo Kim, and Chong Kee Park, *Public Finances During the Korean Modernization Process*
- 108. William D. Wray, *Mitsubishi and the N.Y.K, 1870–1914: Business Strategy in the Japanese Shipping Industry*
- 109. Ralph William Huenemann, *The Dragon and the Iron Horse: The Economics of Railroads in China, 1876–1937*
- *110. Benjamin A. Elman, *From Philosophy to Philology: Intellectual and Social Aspects of Change in Late Imperial China*
- 111. Jane Kate Leonard, *Wei Yüan and China's Rediscovery of the Maritime World*

112. Luke S. K. Kwong, *A Mosaic of the Hundred Days:. Personalities, Politics, and Ideas of 1898*
*113. John E. Wills, Jr., *Embassies and Illusions: Dutch and Portuguese Envoys to K'ang-hsi, 1666–1687*
114. Joshua A. Fogel, *Politics and Sinology: The Case of Naitō Konan (1866–1934)*
*115. Jeffrey C. Kinkley, ed., *After Mao: Chinese Literature and Society, 1978–1981*
116. C. Andrew Gerstle, *Circles of Fantasy: Convention in the Plays of Chikamatsu*
117. Andrew Gordon, *The Evolution of Labor Relations in Japan: Heavy Industry, 1853–1955*
*118. Daniel K. Gardner, *Chu Hsi and the "Ta Hsueh": Neo-Confucian Reflection on the Confucian Canon*
119. Christine Guth Kanda, *Shinzō: Hachiman Imagery and Its Development*
*120. Robert Borgen, *Sugawara no Michizane and the Early Heian Court*
121. Chang-tai Hung, *Going to the People: Chinese Intellectual and Folk Literature, 1918–1937*
*122. Michael A. Cusumano, *The Japanese Automobile Industry: Technology and Management at Nissan and Toyota*
123. Richard von Glahn, *The Country of Streams and Grottoes: Expansion, Settlement, and the Civilizing of the Sichuan Frontier in Song Times*
124. Steven D. Carter, *The Road to Komatsubara: A Classical Reading of the Renga Hyakuin*
125. Katherine F. Bruner, John K. Fairbank, and Richard T. Smith, *Entering China's Service: Robert Hart's Journals, 1854–1863*
126. Bob Tadashi Wakabayashi, *Anti-Foreignism and Western Learning in Early-Modern Japan: The "New Theses" of 1825*
127. Atsuko Hirai, *Individualism and Socialism: The Life and Thought of Kawai Eijirō (1891–1944)*
128. Ellen Widmer, *The Margins of Utopia: "Shui-hu hou-chuan" and the Literature of Ming Loyalism*
129. R. Kent Guy, *The Emperor's Four Treasuries: Scholars and the State in the Late Chien-lung Era*
130. Peter C. Perdue, *Exhausting the Earth: State and Peasant in Hunan, 1500–1850*
131. Susan Chan Egan, *A Latterday Confucian: Reminiscences of William Hung (1893–1980)*
132. James T. C. Liu, *China Turning Inward: Intellectual-Political Changes in the Early Twelfth Century*
*133. Paul A. Cohen, *Between Tradition and Modernity: Wang T'ao and Reform in Late Ching China*
134. Kate Wildman Nakai, *Shogunal Politics: Arai Hakuseki and the Premises of Tokugawa Rule*
*135. Parks M. Coble, *Facing Japan: Chinese Politics and Japanese Imperialism, 1931–1937*
136. Jon L. Saari, *Legacies of Childhood: Growing Up Chinese in a Time of Crisis, 1890–1920*
137. Susan Downing Videen, *Tales of Heichū*
138. Heinz Morioka and Miyoko Sasaki, *Rakugo: The Popular Narrative Art of Japan*
139. Joshua A. Fogel, *Nakae Ushikichi in China: The Mourning of Spirit*

140. Alexander Barton Woodside, *Vietnam and the Chinese Model: A Comparative Study of Vietnamese and Chinese Government in the First Half of the Nineteenth Century*
*141. George Elison, *Deus Destroyed: The Image of Christianity in Early Modern Japan*
142. William D. Wray, ed., *Managing Industrial Enterprise: Cases from Japan's Prewar Experience*
*143. T'ung-tsu Ch'ü, *Local Government in China Under the Ching*
144. Marie Anchordoguy, *Computers, Inc.: Japan's Challenge to IBM*
145. Barbara Molony, *Technology and Investment: The Prewar Japanese Chemical Industry*
146. Mary Elizabeth Berry, *Hideyoshi*
147. Laura E. Hein, *Fueling Growth: The Energy Revolution and Economic Policy in Postwar Japan*
148. Wen-hsin Yeh, *The Alienated Academy: Culture and Politics in Republican China, 1919–1937*
149. Dru C. Gladney, *Muslim Chinese: Ethnic Nationalism in the People's Republic*
150. Merle Goldman and Paul A. Cohen, eds., *Ideas Across Cultures: Essays on Chinese Thought in Honor of Benjamin L Schwartz*
151. James M. Polachek, *The Inner Opium War*
152. Gail Lee Bernstein, *Japanese Marxist: A Portrait of Kawakami Hajime, 1879–1946*
*153. Lloyd E. Eastman, *The Abortive Revolution: China Under Nationalist Rule, 1927–1937*
154. Mark Mason, *American Multinationals and Japan: The Political Economy of Japanese Capital Controls, 1899–1980*
155. Richard J. Smith, John K. Fairbank, and Katherine F. Bruner, *Robert Hart and China's Early Modernization: His Journals, 1863–1866*
156. George J. Tanabe, Jr., *Myōe the Dreamkeeper: Fantasy and Knowledge in Kamakura Buddhism*
157. William Wayne Farris, *Heavenly Warriors: The Evolution of Japan's Military, 500–1300*
158. Yu-ming Shaw, *An American Missionary in China: John Leighton Stuart and Chinese-American Relations*
159. James B. Palais, *Politics and Policy in Traditional Korea*
*160. Douglas Reynolds, *China, 1898–1912: The Xinzheng Revolution and Japan*
161. Roger R. Thompson, *China's Local Councils in the Age of Constitutional Reform, 1898–1911*
162. William Johnston, *The Modern Epidemic: History of Tuberculosis in Japan*
163. Constantine Nomikos Vaporis, *Breaking Barriers: Travel and the State in Early Modern Japan*
164. Irmela Hijiya-Kirschnereit, *Rituals of Self-Revelation: Shishōsetsu as Literary Genre and Socio-Cultural Phenomenon*
165. James C. Baxter, *The Meiji Unification Through the Lens of Ishikawa Prefecture*
166. Thomas R. H. Havens, *Architects of Affluence: The Tsutsumi Family and the Seibu-Saison Enterprises in Twentieth-Century Japan*
167. Anthony Hood Chambers, *The Secret Window: Ideal Worlds in Tanizaki's Fiction*
168. Steven J. Ericson, *The Sound of the Whistle: Railroads and the State in Meiji Japan*
169. Andrew Edmund Goble, *Kenmu: Go-Daigo's Revolution*

170. Denise Potrzeba Lett, *In Pursuit of Status: The Making of South Korea's "New" Urban Middle Class*
171. Mimi Hall Yiengpruksawan, *Hiraizumi: Buddhist Art and Regional Politics in Twelfth-Century Japan*
172. Charles Shirō Inouye, *The Similitude of Blossoms: A Critical Biography of Izumi Kyōka (1873–1939), Japanese Novelist and Playwright*
173. Aviad E. Raz, *Riding the Black Ship: Japan and Tokyo Disneyland*
174. Deborah J. Milly, *Poverty, Equality, and Growth: The Politics of Economic Need in Postwar Japan*
175. See Heng Teow, *Japan's Cultural Policy Toward China, 1918–1931: A Comparative Perspective*
176. Michael A. Fuller, *An Introduction to Literary Chinese*
177. Frederick R. Dickinson, *War and National Reinvention: Japan in the Great War, 1914–1919*
178. John Solt, *Shredding the Tapestry of Meaning: The Poetry and Poetics of Kitasono Katue (1902–1978)*
179. Edward Pratt, *Japan's Protoindustrial Elite: The Economic Foundations of the Gōnō*
180. Atsuko Sakaki, *Recontextualizing Texts: Narrative Performance in Modern Japanese Fiction*
181. Soon-Won Park, *Colonial Industrialization and Labor in Korea: The Onoda Cement Factory*
182. JaHyun Kim Haboush and Martina Deuchler, *Culture and the State in Late Chosŏn Korea*
183. John W. Chaffee, *Branches of Heaven: A History of the Imperial Clan of Sung China*
184. Gi-Wook Shin and Michael Robinson, eds., *Colonial Modernity in Korea*
185. Nam-lin Hur, *Prayer and Play in Late Tokugawa Japan: Asakusa Sensōji and Edo Society*
186. Kristin Stapleton, *Civilizing Chengdu: Chinese Urban Reform, 1895–1937*
187. Hyung Il Pai, *Constructing "Korean" Origins: A Critical Review of Archaeology, Historiography, and Racial Myth in Korean State-Formation Theories*
188. Brian D. Ruppert, *Jewel in the Ashes: Buddha Relics and Power in Early Medieval Japan*
189. Susan Daruvala, *Zhou Zuoren and an Alternative Chinese Response to Modernity*
*190. James Z. Lee, *The Political Economy of a Frontier: Southwest China, 1250–1850*
191. Kerry Smith, *A Time of Crisis: Japan, the Great Depression, and Rural Revitalization*
192. Michael Lewis, *Becoming Apart: National Power and Local Politics in Toyama, 1868–1945*
193. William C. Kirby, Man-houng Lin, James Chin Shih, and David A. Pietz, eds., *State and Economy in Republican China: A Handbook for Scholars*
194. Timothy S. George, *Minamata: Pollution and the Struggle for Democracy in Postwar Japan*
195. Billy K. L. So, *Prosperity, Region, and Institutions in Maritime China: The South Fukien Pattern, 946–1368*
196. Yoshihisa Tak Matsusaka, *The Making of Japanese Manchuria, 1904–1932*

197. Maram Epstein, *Competing Discourses: Orthodoxy, Authenticity, and Engendered Meanings in Late Imperial Chinese Fiction*
198. Curtis J. Milhaupt, J. Mark Ramseyer, and Michael K. Young, eds. and comps., *Japanese Law in Context: Readings in Society, the Economy, and Politics*
199. Haruo Iguchi, *Unfinished Business: Ayukawa Yoshisuke and U.S.-Japan Relations, 1937–1952*
200. Scott Pearce, Audrey Spiro, and Patricia Ebrey, *Culture and Power in the Reconstitution of the Chinese Realm, 200–600*
201. Terry Kawashima, *Writing Margins: The Textual Construction of Gender in Heian and Kamakura Japan*
202. Martin W. Huang, *Desire and Fictional Narrative in Late Imperial China*
203. Robert S. Ross and Jiang Changbin, eds., *Re-examining the Cold War: U.S.-China Diplomacy, 1954–1973*
204. Guanhua Wang, *In Search of Justice: The 1905–1906 Chinese Anti-American Boycott*
205. David Schaberg, *A Patterned Past: Form and Thought in Early Chinese Historiography*
206. Christine Yano, *Tears of Longing: Nostalgia and the Nation in Japanese Popular Song*
207. Milena Doleželová-Velingerová and Oldřich Král, with Graham Sanders, eds., *The Appropriation of Cultural Capital: China's May Fourth Project*
208. Robert N. Huey, *The Making of 'Shinkokinshū'*
209. Lee Butler, *Emperor and Aristocracy in Japan, 1467–1680: Resilience and Renewal*
210. Suzanne Ogden, *Inklings of Democracy in China*
211. Kenneth J. Ruoff, *The People's Emperor: Democracy and the Japanese Monarchy, 1945–1995*
212. Haun Saussy, *Great Walls of Discourse and Other Adventures in Cultural China*
213. Aviad E. Raz, *Emotions at Work: Normative Control, Organizations, and Culture in Japan and America*
214. Rebecca E. Karl and Peter Zarrow, eds., *Rethinking the 1898 Reform Period: Political and Cultural Change in Late Qing China*
215. Kevin O'Rourke, *The Book of Korean Shijo*
216. Ezra F. Vogel, ed., *The Golden Age of the U.S.-China-Japan Triangle, 1972–1989*
217. Thomas A. Wilson, ed., *On Sacred Grounds: Culture, Society, Politics, and the Formation of the Cult of Confucius*
218. Donald S. Sutton, *Steps of Perfection: Exorcistic Performers and Chinese Religion in Twentieth-Century Taiwan*
219. Daqing Yang, *Technology of Empire: Telecommunications and Japanese Expansionism in Asia, 1883–1945*
220. Qianshen Bai, *Fu Shan's World: The Transformation of Chinese Calligraphy in the Seventeenth Century*
221. Paul Jakov Smith and Richard von Glahn, eds., *The Song-Yuan-Ming Transition in Chinese History*
222. Rania Huntington, *Alien Kind: Foxes and Late Imperial Chinese Narrative*
223. Jordan Sand, *House and Home in Modern Japan: Architecture, Domestic Space, and Bourgeois Culture, 1880–1930*

224. Karl Gerth, *China Made: Consumer Culture and the Creation of the Nation*
225. Xiaoshan Yang, *Metamorphosis of the Private Sphere: Gardens and Objects in Tang-Song Poetry*
226. Barbara Mittler, *A Newspaper for China? Power, Identity, and Change in Shanghai's News Media, 1872–1912*
227. Joyce A. Madancy, *The Troublesome Legacy of Commissioner Lin: The Opium Trade and Opium Suppression in Fujian Province, 1820s to 1920s*
228. John Makeham, *Transmitters and Creators: Chinese Commentators and Commentaries on the Analects*
229. Elisabeth Köll, *From Cotton Mill to Business Empire: The Emergence of Regional Enterprises in Modern China*
230. Emma Teng, *Taiwan's Imagined Geography: Chinese Colonial Travel Writing and Pictures, 1683–1895*
231. Wilt Idema and Beata Grant, *The Red Brush: Writing Women of Imperial China*
232. Eric C. Rath, *The Ethos of Noh: Actors and Their Art*
233. Elizabeth Remick, *Building Local States: China During the Republican and Post-Mao Eras*
234. Lynn Struve, ed., *The Qing Formation in World-Historical Time*
235. D. Max Moerman, *Localizing Paradise: Kumano Pilgrimage and the Religious Landscape of Premodern Japan*
236. Antonia Finnane, *Speaking of Yangzhou: A Chinese City, 1550–1850*
237. Brian Platt, *Burning and Building: Schooling and State Formation in Japan, 1750–1890*
238. Gail Bernstein, Andrew Gordon, and Kate Wildman Nakai, eds., *Public Spheres, Private Lives in Modern Japan, 1600–1950: Essays in Honor of Albert Craig*
239. Wu Hung and Katherine R. Tsiang, *Body and Face in Chinese Visual Culture*
240. Stephen Dodd, *Writing Home: Representations of the Native Place in Modern Japanese Literature*
241. David Anthony Bello, *Opium and the Limits of Empire: Drug Prohibition in the Chinese Interior, 1729–1850*
242. Hosea Hirata, *Discourses of Seduction: History, Evil, Desire, and Modern Japanese Literature*
243. Kyung Moon Hwang, *Beyond Birth: Social Status in the Emergence of Modern Korea*
244. Brian R. Dott, *Identity Reflections: Pilgrimages to Mount Tai in Late Imperial China*
245. Mark McNally, *Proving the Way: Conflict and Practice in the History of Japanese Nativism*
246. Yongping Wu, *A Political Explanation of Economic Growth: State Survival, Bureaucratic Politics, and Private Enterprises in the Making of Taiwan's Economy, 1950–1985*
247. Kyu Hyun Kim, *The Age of Visions and Arguments: Parliamentarianism and the National Public Sphere in Early Meiji Japan*
248. Zvi Ben-Dor Benite, *The Dao of Muhammad: A Cultural History of Muslims in Late Imperial China*
249. David Der-wei Wang and Shang Wei, eds., *Dynastic Crisis and Cultural Innovation: From the Late Ming to the Late Qing and Beyond*

250. Wilt L. Idema, Wai-yee Li, and Ellen Widmer, eds., *Trauma and Transcendence in Early Qing Literature*
251. Barbara Molony and Kathleen Uno, eds., *Gendering Modern Japanese History*
252. Hiroshi Aoyagi, *Islands of Eight Million Smiles: Idol Performance and Symbolic Production in Contemporary Japan*
253. Wai-yee Li, *The Readability of the Past in Early Chinese Historiography*
254. William C. Kirby, Robert S. Ross, and Gong Li, eds., *Normalization of U.S.-China Relations: An International History*
255. Ellen Gardner Nakamura, *Practical Pursuits: Takano Chōei, Takahashi Keisaku, and Western Medicine in Nineteenth-Century Japan*
256. Jonathan W. Best, *A History of the Early Korean Kingdom of Paekche, together with an annotated translation of* The Paekche Annals *of the* Samguk sagi
257. Liang Pan, *The United Nations in Japan's Foreign and Security Policymaking, 1945–1992: National Security, Party Politics, and International Status*
258. Richard Belsky, *Localities at the Center: Native Place, Space, and Power in Late Imperial Beijing*
259. Zwia Lipkin, *"Useless to the State": "Social Problems" and Social Engineering in Nationalist Nanjing, 1927–1937*
260. William O. Gardner, *Advertising Tower: Japanese Modernism and Modernity in the 1920s*
261. Stephen Owen, *The Making of Early Chinese Classical Poetry*
262. Martin J. Powers, *Pattern and Person: Ornament, Society, and Self in Classical China*
263. Anna M. Shields, *Crafting a Collection: The Cultural Contexts and Poetic Practice of the* Huajian ji 花間集 *(Collection from Among the Flowers)*
264. Stephen Owen, *The Late Tang: Chinese Poetry of the Mid-Ninth Century (827–860)*
265. Sara L. Friedman, *Intimate Politics: Marriage, the Market, and State Power in Southeastern China*
266. Patricia Buckley Ebrey and Maggie Bickford, *Emperor Huizong and Late Northern Song China: The Politics of Culture and the Culture of Politics*
267. Sophie Volpp, *Worldly Stage: Theatricality in Seventeenth-Century China*
268. Ellen Widmer, *The Beauty and the Book: Women and Fiction in Nineteenth-Century China*
269. Steven B. Miles, *The Sea of Learning: Mobility and Identity in Nineteenth-Century Guangzhou*
270. Lin Man-houng, *China Upside Down: Currency, Society, and Ideologies, 1808–1856*
271. Ronald Egan, *The Problem of Beauty: Aesthetic Thought and Pursuits in Northern Song Dynasty China*
272. Mark Halperin, *Out of the Cloister: Literati Perspectives on Buddhism in Sung China, 960–1279*
273. Helen Dunstan, *State or Merchant? Political Economy and Political Process in 1740s China*
274. Sabina Knight, *The Heart of Time: Moral Agency in Twentieth-Century Chinese Fiction*
275. Timothy J. Van Compernolle, *The Uses of Memory: The Critique of Modernity in the Fiction of Higuchi Ichiyō*

276. Paul Rouzer, *A New Practical Primer of Literary Chinese*
277. Jonathan Zwicker, *Practices of the Sentimental Imagination: Melodrama, the Novel, and the Social Imaginary in Nineteenth-Century Japan*
278. Franziska Seraphim, *War Memory and Social Politics in Japan, 1945–2005*
279. Adam L. Kern, *Manga from the Floating World: Comicbook Culture and the* Kibyōshi *of Edo Japan*
280. Cynthia J. Brokaw, *Commerce in Culture: The Sibao Book Trade in the Qing and Republican Periods*
281. Eugene Y. Park, *Between Dreams and Reality: The Military Examination in Late Chosŏn Korea, 1600–1894*
282. Nam-lin Hur, *Death and Social Order in Tokugawa Japan: Buddhism, Anti-Christianity, and the* Danka *System*
283. Patricia M. Thornton, *Disciplining the State: Virtue, Violence, and State-Making in Modern China*
284. Vincent Goossaert, *The Taoists of Peking, 1800–1949: A Social History of Urban Clerics*
285. Peter Nickerson, *Taoism, Bureaucracy, and Popular Religion in Early Medieval China*
286. Charo B. D'Etcheverry, *Love After* The Tale of Genji*: Rewriting the World of the Shining Prince*
287. Michael G. Chang, *A Court on Horseback: Imperial Touring & the Construction of Qing Rule, 1680–1785*
288. Carol Richmond Tsang, *War and Faith:* Ikkō Ikki *in Late Muromachi Japan*
289. Hilde De Weerdt, *Competition over Content: Negotiating Standards for the Civil Service Examinations in Imperial China (1127–1279)*
290. Eve Zimmerman, *Out of the Alleyway: Nakagami Kenji and the Poetics of Outcaste Fiction*
291. Robert Culp, *Articulating Citizenship: Civic Education and Student Politics in Southeastern China, 1912–1940*
292. Richard J. Smethurst, *From Foot Soldier to Finance Minister: Takahashi Korekiyo, Japan's Keynes*
293. John E. Herman, *Amid the Clouds and Mist: China's Colonization of Guizhou, 1200–1700*
294. Tomoko Shiroyama, *China During the Great Depression: Market, State, and the World Economy, 1929–1937*
295. Kirk W. Larsen, *Tradition, Treaties and Trade: Qing Imperialism and Chosŏn Korea, 1850–1910*
296. Gregory Golley, *When Our Eyes No Longer See: Realism, Science, and Ecology in Japanese Literary Modernism*
297. Barbara Ambros, *Emplacing a Pilgrimage: The Ōyama Cult and Regional Religion in Early Modern Japan*
298. Rebecca Suter, *The Japanization of Modernity: Murakami Haruki between Japan and the United States*
299. Yuma Totani, *The Tokyo War Crimes Trial: The Pursuit of Justice in the Wake of World War II*

300. Linda Isako Angst, *In a Dark Time: Memory, Community, and Gendered Nationalism in Postwar Okinawa*
301. David M. Robinson, ed., *Culture, Courtiers, and Competition: The Ming Court (1368–1644)*
302. Calvin Chen, *Some Assembly Required: Work, Community, and Politics in China's Rural Enterprises*
303. Sem Vermeersch, *The Power of the Buddhas: The Politics of Buddhism During the Koryŏ Dynasty* (918–1392)
304. Tina Lu, *Accidental Incest, Filial Cannibalism, and Other Peculiar Encounters in Late Imperial Chinese Literature*
305. Chang Woei Ong, *Men of Letters Within the Passes: Guanzhong Literati in Chinese History, 907–1911*
306. Wendy Swartz, *Reading Tao Yuanming: Shifting Paradigms of Historical Reception (427–1900)*
307. Peter K. Bol, *Neo-Confucianism in History*
308. Carlos Rojas, *The Naked Gaze: Reflections on Chinese Modernity*
309. Kelly H. Chong, *Deliverance and Submission: Evangelical Women and the Negotiation of Patriarchy in South Korea*
310. Rachel DiNitto, *Uchida Hyakken: A Critique of Modernity and Militarism in Prewar Japan*
311. Jeffrey Snyder-Reinke, *Dry Spells: State Rainmaking and Local Governance in Late Imperial China*
312. Jay Dautcher, *Down a Narrow Road: Identity and Masculinity in a Uyghur Community in Xinjiang China*
313. Xun Liu, *Daoist Modern: Innovation, Lay Practice, and the Community of Inner Alchemy in Republican Shanghai*
314. Jacob Eyferth, *Eating Rice from Bamboo Roots: The Social History of a Community of Handicraft Papermakers in Rural Sichuan, 1920–2000*
315. David Johnson, *Spectacle and Sacrifice: The Ritual Foundations of Village Life in North China*
316. James Robson, *Power of Place: The Religious Landscape of the Southern Sacred Peak (Nanyue 南嶽) in Medieval China*
317. Lori Watt, *When Empire Comes Home: Repatriation and Reintegration in Postwar Japan*
318. James Dorsey, *Critical Aesthetics: Kobayashi Hideo, Modernity, and Wartime Japan*
319. Christopher Bolton, *Sublime Voices: The Fictional Science and Scientific Fiction of Abe Kōbō*
320. Si-yen Fei, *Negotiating Urban Space: Urbanization and Late Ming Nanjing*
321. Christopher Gerteis, *Gender Struggles: Wage-Earning Women and Male-Dominated Unions in Postwar Japan*
322. Rebecca Nedostup, *Superstitious Regimes: Religion and the Politics of Chinese Modernity*
323. Lucien Bianco, *Wretched Rebels: Rural Disturbances on the Eve of the Chinese Revolution*
324. Cathryn H. Clayton, *Sovereignty at the Edge: Macau and the Question of Chineseness*
325. Micah S. Muscolino, *Fishing Wars and Environmental Change in Late Imperial and Modern China*

326. Robert I. Hellyer, *Defining Engagement: Japan and Global Contexts, 1750–1868*
327. Robert Ashmore, *The Transport of Reading: Text and Understanding in the World of Tao Qian (365–427)*
328. Mark A. Jones, *Children as Treasures: Childhood and the Middle Class in Early Twentieth Century Japan*
329. Miryam Sas, *Experimental Arts in Postwar Japan: Moments of Encounter, Engagement, and Imagined Return*
330. H. Mack Horton, *Traversing the Frontier: The* Man'yōshū *Account of a Japanese Mission to Silla in 736–737*
331. Dennis J. Frost, *Seeing Stars: Sports Celebrity, Identity, and Body Culture in Modern Japan*